ANNUAL EDITIONS

Child Growth and Development

03/04

Tenth Edition

EDITORS

Ellen N. Junn

California State University, Fullerton

Ellen Junn is a professor of child and adolescent studies and associate dean of the College of Human Development and Community Service at California State University, Fullerton. She received her B.S. with distinction in psychology and with high honors from the University of Michigan and her M.A. and Ph.D. in cognitive and developmental psychology from Princeton University. Dr. Junn's areas of research include college teaching effectiveness, educational equity, faculty development, and public policy as it affects children and families.

Chris J. Boyatzis

Bucknell University

Dr. Chris Boyatzis is an associate professor of psychology at Bucknell University. He received a B.A. with distinction in psychology from Boston University and his M.A. and Ph.D. in developmental psychology from Brandeis University. His primary research focus is religion and spiritual development across the lifespan but especially during childhood, adolescence, and the college years. He is on the editorial boards of several psychology journals.

McGraw-Hill/Dushkin

530 Old Whitfield Street, Guilford, Connecticut 06437

Visit us on the Internet
http://www.dushkin.com

Credits

1. **Conception to Birth**
   Unit photo—© 2003 by PhotoDisc, Inc.
2. **Cognition, Language, and Learning**
   Unit photo—© 2003 by Cleo Freelance Photography.
3. **Social and Emotional Development**
   Unit photo—Courtesy of Robin Gallagher.
4. **Parenting and Family Issues**
   Unit photo—Courtesy of McGraw-Hill/Dushkin.
5. **Cultural and Societal Influences**
   Unit photo—© 2003 by Cleo Freelance Photography.

Copyright

Cataloging in Publication Data
Main entry under title: Annual Editions: Child Growth and Development. 2003/2004.
1. Child Growth and Development—Periodicals. I. Junn, Ellen N., *comp.* II Boyatzis, Chris J., *comp.* III. Title: Child Growth and Development.
ISBN 0–07–283853–1   658'.05   ISSN 1075–5217

Tenth Edition

Cover image © 2003 PhotoDisc, Inc.
Printed in the United States of America   1234567890BAHBAH543   Printed on Recycled Paper

Editors/Advisory Board

Members of the Advisory Board are instrumental in the final selection of articles for each edition of ANNUAL EDITIONS. Their review of articles for content, level, currentness, and appropriateness provides critical direction to the editor and staff. We think that you will find their careful consideration well reflected in this volume.

EDITORS

Ellen N. Junn
California State University - Fullerton

Chris J. Boyatzis
Bucknell University

ADVISORY BOARD

Michael S. Becker
York College

Linda S. Behrendt
Concordia College

Mary Belcher
Orange Coast College

Catherine Crain-Thoreson
Cascadia Community College

Patrick M. Drumm
Ohio State University - Lancaster

JoAnn M. Farver
University of Southern California

Kathy E. Fite
Southwest Texas State University

Trisha Folds-Bennett
College of Charleston

Betty K. Hathaway
University of Arkansas

Charles D. Hoffman
California State University—San Bernardino

Dene G. Klinzing
University of Delaware

Marcia Lasswell
California State Polytechnic University

Nancy G. McCarley
Mississippi State University

Joann M. Montepare
Emerson College

Karen L. Peterson
Washington State University

Derek Price
Wheaton College

Lauretta Reeves
Rowan University

Robin L. Rohrer
Seton Hill College

Nadia A. Sangster
Wheelock College

Sally M. Sentner
Clarion University

Daniel D. Shade
University of Delaware

Mary Helen Spear
Prince George's Community College

Connie Steele
University of Tennessee

Harold R. Strang
University of Virginia

Gloria Wellman
Santa Rosa Junior College

Staff

EDITORIAL STAFF

Ian A. Nielsen, Publisher
Roberta Monaco, Senior Developmental Editor
Dorothy Fink, Associate Developmental Editor
Iain Martin, Associate Developmental Editor
Addie Raucci, Senior Administrative Editor
Robin Zarnetske, Permissions Editor
Marie Lazauskas, Permissions Assistant
Diane Barker, Proofreader
Lisa Holmes-Doebrick, Senior Program Coordinator

TECHNOLOGY STAFF

Richard Tietjen, Senior Publishing Technologist
Jonathan Stowe, Executive Director of eContent
Marcuss Oslander, Sponsoring Editor of eContent
Christopher Santos, Senior eContent Developer
Janice Ward, Software Support Analyst
Angela Mule, eContent Developer
Michael McConnell, eContent Developer
Ciro Parente, Editorial Assistant
Joe Offredi, Technology Developmental Editor

PRODUCTION STAFF

Brenda S. Filley, Director of Production
Charles Vitelli, Designer
Mike Campell, Production Coordinator
Laura Levine, Graphics
Tom Goddard, Graphics
Eldis Lima, Graphics
Nancy Norton, Graphics
Juliana Arbo, Typesetting Supervisor
Karen Roberts, Typesetter
Jocelyn Proto, Typesetter
Cynthia Powers, Typesetter
Cathy Kuziel, Typesetter
Larry Killian, Copier Coordinator

To the Reader

In publishing ANNUAL EDITIONS we recognize the enormous role played by the magazines, newspapers, and journals of the public press in providing current, first-rate educational information in a broad spectrum of interest areas. Many of these articles are appropriate for students, researchers, and professionals seeking accurate, current material to help bridge the gap between principles and theories and the real world. These articles, however, become more useful for study when those of lasting value are carefully collected, organized, indexed, and reproduced in a low-cost format, which provides easy and permanent access when the material is needed. That is the role played by ANNUAL EDITIONS.

We are delighted to welcome you to this tenth volume of *Annual Editions: Child Growth and Development 03/04*. The amazing sequence of events of prenatal development that lead to the birth of a baby is an awe-inspiring process. Perhaps more intriguing is the question of what the future may hold for this newly arrived baby—for instance, will this child become a doctor, a lawyer, an artist, a beggar, or a thief? Although philosophers and prominent thinkers such as Charles Darwin and Sigmund Freud have long speculated about the importance of infancy on subsequent development, not until the 1960s did the scientific study of infants and young children flourish. Since then, research and theory in infancy and childhood have exploded, resulting in a wealth of new knowledge about child development.

Past accounts of infants and young children as passive, homogeneous organisms have been replaced with investigations aimed at studying infants and young children at a "microlevel" as active individuals with many inborn competencies, who are capable of shaping their own environment, as well as at a "macrolevel" by considering the larger context surrounding the child. In short, children are not "blank slates," and development does not take place in a vacuum; children arrive with many skills and grow up in a complex web of social, historical, political, economic, and cultural spheres.

As was the case for previous editions, we hope to achieve at least four major goals with this volume. First, we hope to present you with the latest research and thinking to help you better appreciate the complex interactions that characterize human development in infancy and childhood. Second, in light of the feedback we received on previous editions, we have placed greater emphasis on important contemporary issues and challenges, exploring topics such as understanding development in the context of current societal and cultural influences. Third, attention is given to articles that also discuss effective, practical applications. Finally, we hope that this anthology will serve as a catalyst to help students become more effective future professionals and parents.

To achieve these objectives, we carefully selected articles from a variety of sources, including scholarly research journals and texts as well as semiprofessional journals and popular publications. Every selection was scrutinized for readability, interest level, relevance, and currency. In addition, we listened to the valuable input and advice from members of our advisory board, consisting of faculty from a range of institutions of higher education, including community and liberal arts colleges as well as research and teaching universities. We are most grateful to the advisory board as well as to the excellent editorial staff of McGraw-Hill/Dushkin.

Annual Editions: Child Growth and Development 03/04 is organized into five major units. Unit 1 focuses on conception, prenatal development, and childbirth. Unit 2 presents information regarding developments in cognition, language, learning, and school. Unit 3 focuses on social and emotional development, while unit 4 is devoted to parenting and family issues such as child care issues, fathering, moral development, and discipline. Finally, unit 5 focuses on larger cultural and societal influences (such as after-school care and violence among youth) and on special challenges (such as poverty, childhood victimization and abuse, resilience, and children with autism).

Instructors for large lecture courses may wish to adopt this anthology as a supplement to a basic text, whereas instructors for smaller sections might also find the readings effective for promoting student presentations or for stimulating discussions and applications. Whatever format is utilized, it is our hope that the instructor and the students will find the readings interesting, illuminating, and provocative.

As the title indicates, *Annual Editions: Child Growth and Development* is by definition a volume that undergoes continual review and revision. Thus, we welcome and encourage your comments and suggestions for future editions of this volume. Simply fill out and return the *article rating form* found at the end of this book. Best wishes, and we look forward to hearing from you!

Ellen N. Junn
Editor

Chris J. Boyatzis
Editor

Contents

UNIT 1
Conception to Birth

Three articles discuss the development of the child from the prenatal state to birth.

UNIT 2
Cognition, Language, and Learning

Nine selections consider the growth of children's cognitive and language abilities and their experiences in the learning process in school.

The concepts in bold italics are developed in the article. For further expansion, please refer to the Topic Guide and the Index.

The concepts in bold italics are developed in the article. For further expansion, please refer to the Topic Guide and the Index.

UNIT 3
Social and Emotional Development

Five articles follow a child's emotional development into the larger social world.

UNIT 4
Parenting and Family Issues

Six articles assess the latest implications of child development with regard to attachment, marital transitions, day care, and the moral development of children.

The concepts in bold italics are developed in the article. For further expansion, please refer to the Topic Guide and the Index.

UNIT 5
Cultural and Societal Influences

Eight selections examine the impact that society and culture have on the development of the child as well as special challenges such as child abuse, poverty, and autism.

The concepts in bold italics are developed in the article. For further expansion, please refer to the Topic Guide and the Index.

The concepts in bold italics are developed in the article. For further expansion, please refer to the Topic Guide and the Index.

Topic Guide

This topic guide suggests how the selections in this book relate to the subjects covered in your course. You may want to use the topics listed on these pages to search the Web more easily.

On the following pages a number of Web sites have been gathered specifically for this book. They are arranged to reflect the units of this *Annual Edition.* You can link to these sites by going to the DUSHKIN ONLINE support site at *http://www.dushkin.com/online/.*

ALL THE ARTICLES THAT RELATE TO EACH TOPIC ARE LISTED BELOW THE BOLD-FACED TERM.

Adoption
19. What Matters? What Does Not? Five Perspectives on the Association Between Marital Transitions and Children's Adjustment

Aggression
6. Evolution and Developmental Sex Differences
17. Bullying Among Children
28. The Effects of Poverty on Children
31. Voices of the Children: We Beat and Killed People

Aging
2. Making Time for a Baby

Alcohol
25. Getting Stupid

Attachment
18. Contemporary Research on Parenting: The Case for Nature *and* Nurture
19. What Matters? What Does Not? Five Perspectives on the Association Between Marital Transitions and Children's Adjustment
21. American Child Care Today

Birth and birth defects
2. Making Time for a Baby
3. The Mystery of Fetal Life: Secrets of the Womb

Brain development
3. The Mystery of Fetal Life: Secrets of the Womb
5. Long-Term Recall Memory: Behavioral and Neuro-Developmental Changes in the First 2 Years of Life
25. Getting Stupid
29. Scars That Won't Heal: The Neurobiology of Child Abuse
30. The Early Origins of Autism

Child abuse
29. Scars That Won't Heal: The Neurobiology of Child Abuse
31. Voices of the Children: We Beat and Killed People

Children
2. Making Time for a Baby
12. Where the Boys Are
14. What Ever Happened to Play?
17. Bullying Among Children
22. Do Working Parents Make the Grade?

Classroom management
17. Bullying Among Children

Cognition
3. The Mystery of Fetal Life: Secrets of the Womb
10. The First Seven … and the Eighth: A Conversation With Howard Gardner
28. The Effects of Poverty on Children

Cognitive development
3. The Mystery of Fetal Life: Secrets of the Womb
4. The Quest for a Super Kid
7. Categories in Young Children's Thinking
8. Do Young Children Understand What Others Feel, Want, and Know?
9. Giftedness: Current Theory and Research
10. The First Seven … and the Eighth: A Conversation With Howard Gardner
11. How Should Reading Be Taught?
12. Where the Boys Are
25. Getting Stupid

Cross-cultural issues
1. The End of Nature Versus Nurture
6. Evolution and Developmental Sex Differences
26. How U.S. Children and Adolescents Spend Time: What It Does (and Doesn't) Tell Us About Their Development
31. Voices of the Children: We Beat and Killed People

Culture
24. Tomorrow's Child
28. The Effects of Poverty on Children

Development, human
14. What Ever Happened to Play?

Development, moral
23. The Moral Development of Children

Developmental disabilities
29. Scars That Won't Heal: The Neurobiology of Child Abuse

Diet
24. Tomorrow's Child
28. The Effects of Poverty on Children

Discipline
17. Bullying Among Children
20. Who's in Charge Here?
23. The Moral Development of Children

Divorce
19. What Matters? What Does Not? Five Perspectives on the Association Between Marital Transitions and Children's Adjustment

Drug abuse
1. The End of Nature Versus Nurture
3. The Mystery of Fetal Life: Secrets of the Womb

Drug use
25. Getting Stupid

Economic issues
21. American Child Care Today

World Wide Web Sites

The following World Wide Web sites have been carefully researched and selected to support the articles found in this reader. The easiest way to access these selected sites is to go to our DUSHKIN ONLINE support site at *http://www.dushkin.com/online/*.

AE: Child Growth and Development 03/04

The following sites were available at the time of publication. Visit our Web site—we update DUSHKIN ONLINE regularly to reflect any changes.

General Sources

American Academy of Pediatrics
http://www.aap.org

This organization provides data for optimal physical, mental, and social health for all children.

CYFERNet
http://www.cyfernet.mes.umn.edu

The Children, Youth, and Families Education Research Network is sponsored by the Cooperative Extension Service and USDA's Cooperative State Research Education and Extension Service. This site provides practical research-based information in areas including health, child care, family strengths, science, and technology.

KidsHealth
http://kidshealth.org

This site was developed to help parents find reliable children's health information. Click on the topic bars: Baby's Development, Nutrition, Pediatric News, Safety and Accident Prevention, and Childhood Infections.

National Institute of Child Health and Human Development
http://www.nichd.nih.gov

The NICHD conducts and supports research on the reproductive, neurobiological, developmental, and behavioral processes that determine and maintain the health of children, adults, families, and populations.

UNIT 1: Conception to Birth

Babyworld
http://www.babyworld.com

Extensive information on caring for infants can be found at this site. There are also links to numerous other related sites.

Children's Nutrition Research Center (CNRC)
http://www.bcm.tmc.edu/cnrc/

CNRC, one of six USDA/ARS (Agricultural Research Service) facilities, is dedicated to defining the nutrient needs of healthy children, from conception through adolescence, and pregnant and nursing mothers. The *Nutrition and Your Child* newsletter is of general interest and can be accessed from this site.

Zero to Three: National Center for Infants, Toddlers, and Families
http://www.zerotothree.org

This national organization is dedicated solely to infants, toddlers, and their families. It is headed by recognized experts in the field and provides technical assistance to communities, states, and the federal government. The site provides information that the organization gathers and disseminates through its publications.

UNIT 2: Cognition, Language, and Learning

Educational Resources Information Center (ERIC)
http://www.ed.gov/pubs/pubdb.html

This Web site is sponsored by the U.S. Department of Education and will lead to numerous documents related to elementary and early childhood education, as well as other curriculum topics and issues.

I Am Your Child
http://iamyourchild.org

Information regarding early childhood development is provided on this site. Resources for parents and caregivers are available.

National Association for the Education of Young Children (NAEYC)
http://www.naeyc.org

The National Association for the Education of Young Children provides a useful link from its home page to a "parent information" site.

Results of NICHD Study of Early Child Care
http://156.40.88.3/publications/pubs/early_child_care.htm

This study indicates that the quality of child care for very young children does matter for their cognitive development and their use of language. Quality child care also leads to better mother-child interaction, the study finds.

Vandergrift's Children's Literature Page
http://www.scils.rutgers.edu/special/kay/sharelit.html

This site provides information about children's literature and links to a variety of resources related to literacy for children.

Project Zero
http://pzweb.harvard.edu

Harvard Project Zero, a research group at the Harvard Graduate School of Education, has investigated the development of learning processes in children and adults for 30 years. Today, Project Zero is building on this research to help create communities of reflective, independent learners, to enhance deep understanding within disciplines, and to promote critical and creative thinking. Project Zero's mission is to understand and enhance learning, thinking, and creativity in the arts and other disciplines for individuals and institutions.

UNIT 3: Social and Emotional Development

Max Planck Institute for Psychological Research
http://www.mpipf-muenchen.mpg.de/BCD/bcd_e.htm

Several behavioral and cognitive development research projects are available on this site.

National Child Care Information Center (NCCIC)
http://www.nccic.org

Information about a variety of topics related to child care and development is available on this site. Links to the *Child Care Bulletin,* which can be read online, and to the ERIC database of online and library-based resources are available.

www.dushkin.com/online/

Serendip

http://serendip.brynmawr.edu/serendip/

Organized into five subject areas (brain and behavior, complex systems, genes and behavior, science and culture, and science education), Serendip contains interactive exhibits, articles, links to other resources, and a forum area for comments and discussion.

UNIT 4: Parenting and Family Issues

Facts for Families

http://www.aacap.org/publications/factsfam/index.htm

The American Academy of Child and Adolescent Psychiatry here provides concise, up-to-date information on issues that affect teenagers and their families. Fifty-six fact sheets include issues concerning teenagers, such as coping with life, sad feelings, inability to sleep, getting involved with drugs, or not getting along with family and friends.

Families and Work Institute

http://www.familiesandworkinst.org

Resources from the Families and Work Institute, which conducts policy research on issues related to the changing workforce and operates a national clearinghouse on work and family life, are provided.

The National Academy for Child Development

http://www.nacd.org

This international organization is dedicated to helping children and adults reach their full potential. Its home page presents links to various programs, research, and resources in topics related to the family and society.

National Council on Family Relations

http://www.ncfr.com

This NCFR home page will lead you to articles, research, and a lot of other resources on important issues in family relations, such as stepfamilies, couples, and divorce.

The National Parent Information Network (NPIN)

http://ericps.ed.uiuc.edu/npin/

The National Parent Information Network contains resources related to many of the controversial issues faced by parents raising children in contemporary society. In addition to articles and resources, discussion groups are also available.

Parenting and Families

http://www.cyfc.umn.edu

The University of Minnesota's Children, Youth, and Family Consortium site will lead you to many organizations and other resources related to divorce, single parenting, and step-families, as well as information about other topics of interest in the study of children's development and the family.

Parentsplace.com: Single Parenting

http://www.parentsplace.com/family/archive/0,10693,239458,00.html

This resource focuses on issues concerning single parents and their children. Although the articles range from parenting children from infancy through adolescence, most of the articles deal with middle childhood.

Stepfamily Association of America

http://www.stepfam.org

This Web site is dedicated to educating and supporting stepfamilies and to creating a positive family image.

UNIT 5: Cultural and Societal Influences

Ask NOAH About: Mental Health

http://www.noah-health.org/english/illness/mentalhealth/mental.html

This enormous resource contains information about child and adolescent family problems, mental conditions and disorders, suicide prevention, and much more, all organized in a "clickable" outline form.

Association to Benefit Children (ABC)

http://www.a-b-c.org

ABC presents a network of programs that includes child advocacy, education for disabled children, care for HIV-positive children, employment, housing, foster care, and day care.

Children Now

http://www.childrennow.org

Children Now focuses on improving conditions for children who are poor or at risk. Articles include information on education, influence of media, health, and security.

Council for Exceptional Children

http://www.cec.sped.org

This is the home page for the Council for Exceptional Children, a large professional organization that is dedicated to improving education for children with exceptionalities, students with disabilities, and/or the gifted child. It leads to the ERIC Clearinghouse on disabilities and gifted education and the National Clearinghouse for Professions in Special Education.

National Black Child Development Institute

http://www.nbcdi.org

Resources for improving the quality of life for African American children through public education programs are provided at this site.

Prevent Child Abuse America

http://www.preventchildabuse.org

Dedicated to their child abuse prevention efforts, PCAA's site provides fact sheets and reports that include statistics, a public opinion poll, a 50-state survey, and other resources materials.

We highly recommend that you review our Web site for expanded information and our other product lines. We are continually updating and adding links to our Web site in order to offer you the most usable and useful information that will support and expand the value of your Annual Editions. You can reach us at: *http://www.dushkin.com/annualeditions/*.

UNIT 1
Conception to Birth

Unit Selections

1. **The End of Nature Versus Nurture**, Frans B. M. de Waal
2. **Making Time for a Baby**, Nancy Gibbs
3. **The Mystery of Fetal Life: Secrets of the Womb**, John Pekkanen

Key Points to Consider

- Where do you stand on the nature/nurture issue? Does it comfort you—or unsettle you—to know that the genes you inherited influence your mental health or sexual orientation, and so on? Given the information in the article "The End of Nature Versus Nurture," how would you respond to someone who claimed that a person's mental health or sexual orientation is "determined" by their genes?

- Although not altogether commonplace, there have always been reports of men over the age of 50–70 years fathering children with younger women. Recently medical and technological advances have now made it possible for women in their 50s and sometimes 60s to bear healthy children. Do you feel that the heightened level of media attention, and sometimes disapproval, directed toward women as opposed to men, is fair or warranted? Do you think it is wrong or problematic for older women to want to bear and raise babies? Why or why not? What about a child born into a family where both parents are in their 50s or early 60s? Do you think there should be some limit to the age at which people are told they cannot or should not be able to have or raise children? Defend your answer.

- Interview your mother about what she did or did not do differently in taking care of her health while she was pregnant. Given the host of potential prenatal teratogens that may put a fetus at risk, if you were having a baby, what precautions would you take, if any? Since there are so many potential threats, do you think taking these extra precautions, such as refraining from eating canned tuna to having a glass of wine with dinner while pregnant, is excessive or warranted?

 **Links: www.dushkin.com/online/**
These sites are annotated in the World Wide Web pages.

Babyworld
   http://www.babyworld.com
Children's Nutrition Research Center (CNRC)
   http://www.bcm.tmc.edu/cnrc/
Zero to Three: National Center for Infants, Toddlers, and Families
   http://www.zerotothree.org

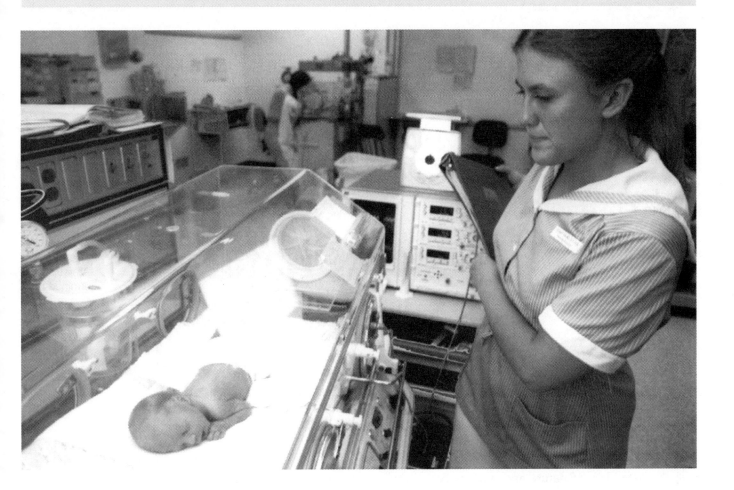

Our understanding of conception and prenatal development is not what it used to be. We are now witness to dramatic changes in reproductive technology. Advances in this new "prenatal science" include fertility treatments for couples who have difficulty conceiving and a host of prenatal diagnostic tests, such as amniocentesis and alpha-fetoprotein testing, which assess the well-being of the fetus as well as detect genetic or chromosomal problems.

Perhaps the oldest debate in the study of human development is the "nature versus nurture" question. Scientists have moved beyond thinking of development as due to either genetics or environment, now recognizing that nature and nurture interact to shape us. Each human is a biological organism, and each is surrounded, from the moment of conception, by environmental forces. According to "The End of Nature Versus Nurture," author Frans de Waal argues for breaking down the dichotomy and instead building research programs that integrate developmental,

genetic, evolutionary, and cultural approaches and theories to better understand human behavior.

Amazing new fertility techniques now make it possible for women and couples who have postponed childbearing to have the chance to have children in their 40s, 50s, and even into their 60s. While these technological advances have done much to permit women and older professional couples with the opportunity to bear children, author Nancy Gibbs discusses the significant personal, ethical, and medical risks and gains that medical advances now afford in "Making Time for a Baby."

Recent research on prenatal development continues to yield new and startling data. For example, "The Mysteries of Fetal Life: Secrets of the Womb" describes the many potential teratogens or potentially harmful threats to a fetus ranging from alcohol, over-the-counter drugs, caffeine, PCBs, and more and reviews some of the data on fetal memory.

The End of Nature versus Nurture

Is human behavior determined by genetics or by environment? It may be time to abandon the dichotomy

by Frans B. M. de Waal

The defenders of nature and nurture have been at each other's throats for as long as I can remember. Whereas biologists have always believed that genes have something to do with human behavior, social scientists have flocked en masse to the opposite position: that we are fully and entirely our own creation, free from the chains of biology.

I felt the heat of this debate in the 1970s whenever, in lectures for general audiences, I mentioned sex differences in chimpanzees, such as that males are more aggressive and more ambitious than females. There would be howls of protest. Wasn't I projecting my own values onto these poor animals? Why did I even bother to compare the sexes? Did I perhaps have a hidden agenda?

Nowadays the same sort of information makes people yawn! Even direct comparisons between human and ape behavior, something that used to be taboo, fail to get anyone excited. Everyone has heard that men are from Mars and women from Venus. Everyone has seen, in *Time* and *Newsweek*, PET scans of the human brain engaged in various tasks, with different areas lighting up in male and female brains.

This time, however, it is my turn to be troubled. Instead of celebrating the victory of the biological approach, I regard some of the contemporary dichotomies between men and women as gross simplifications rendered politi-

cally correct by a fashionable amount of male-bashing (for example, when normal hormonal effects are referred to as "testosterone poisoning"). We remain as far removed as ever from a sophisticated understanding of the interplay between genes and environment. Society has let the pendulum swing wildly back from nurture to nature, leaving behind a number of bewildered social scientists. Yet we still love to phrase everything in terms of one influence or the other, rather than both.

It is impossible to explore where we may be heading 50 years from now without looking back an equal number of years at the charged history of the nature/nurture controversy. The debate is so emotional because any stance one takes comes with serious political implications. Positions have ranged from an unfounded faith in human flexibility by reformists to an obsession with blood and race by conservatives. Each in their own way, these positions have caused incalculable human suffering in the past century.

Learning and Instinct

Fifty years ago the two dominant schools of thought about animal and human behavior had opposite outlooks. Teaching animals arbitrary actions such as lever-pressing, American behaviorists came to view all behavior as the product of trial-and-error learning. This process was considered so universal that differences among species were irrelevant: learning applied to all animals, including humans. As B. F. Skinner, the founder of behaviorism, bluntly put it: "Pigeon, rat, monkey, which is which? It doesn't matter."

In contrast, the ethological school in Europe focused on naturalistic behavior. Each animal species is born with a number of so-called fixed-action patterns that undergo little modification by the environment. These and other species-specific behaviors represent evolutionary adaptations. Thus, no one needs to teach humans how to laugh or cry; these are innate signals, universally used and understood. Similarly, the spider does not need to learn how to construct a web. She is born with a battery of spinnerets (spinning tubes connected to silk glands) as well as a behavioral program that "instructs" her how to weave threads together.

Because of their simplicity, both views of behavior had enormous appeal. And although both paid homage to evolution, they sometimes did so in a superficial, arm-waving sort of way. Behaviorists stressed the continuities between humans and other animals, attributing them to evolution. But because for them behavior was learned rather than inborn, they ignored the genetic side, which is really what evolution is all about. While it is true that evolution implies continuity, it also implies diversity: each animal is adapted to a specific way of life in a specific environment. As is evident from Skinner's statement, this point was blithely ignored.

Similarly, some ethologists had rather vague evolutionary notions, emphasizing phylogenetic descent rather than the processes of natural selection. They saw behavioral traits, such as the inhibition of aggression, as good for the species. The argument was that if animals were to kill one another in fights, the species would not survive. This may be true, but animals have perfectly selfish reasons to avoid the escalation of fights that may harm themselves and their relationships. Hence, these ideas have now been replaced by theories about how traits benefit the actor and its kin; effects on the species as a whole are considered a mere by-product.

Behaviorism started losing its grip with the discovery that learning is not the same for all situations and species. For example, a rat normally links actions with effects only if the two immediately follow each other. So it would be very slow to learn to press a bar if a reward followed minutes later. When it comes to food that makes it sick, however, a delay of hours between consumption and the negative sensation still induces food aversion. Apparently, animals are specialized learners, being best at those contingencies that are most important for survival.

At the same time that behaviorists were forced to adopt the premises of evolutionary biology and to consider the world outside the laboratory, ethologists and ecologists were laying the groundwork for the neo-Darwinian revolution of the 1970s. The pioneer here was

Dutch ethologist Nikolaas Tinbergen, who conducted ingenious field experiments on the survival value of animal behavior. He understood, for instance, why many birds remove eggshells from the nest after the chicks have hatched. Because the outside of a shell is colored for camouflage but the inside is not, predators such as crows easily locate eggs if broken shells are placed next to them. Throwing out the pieces is an automatic response favored by natural selection because the birds that practice this behavior have more surviving offspring.

Others developed theories to explain behavior that at first sight does not seem to help the actor but someone else. Such "altruism" can be seen in ant soldiers giving their lives in defense of their colony or dolphins lifting a drowning companion to the surface. Biologists assumed that natural selection will allow for assistance among relatives as a means of promoting the same genes. Or, if two animals are unrelated, the favor granted by one must be returned at some future time.

The scientists felt so confident about their explanations of cooperative animal societies that they could not resist extending these ideas to our own species. They saw the hugely cooperative enterprise of human society as based on the same premise of family values and economic tit-for-tat.

It fell to an American expert on ants, Edward O. Wilson, to deliver the news in 1975 that a great deal of human behavior was ripe for the Darwinian perspective and that the social sciences should prepare themselves to work together with biologists on this endeavor. Thus far the two disciplines had led separate lives, but from the perspective of a biologist social science is not much more than the study of animal behavior focused on a single species: ours. Because this is not how social scientists see their work, proposals for a united framework were not kindly received. One of Wilson's outraged opponents even poured cold water over Wilson's head after he gave a lecture. For reasons explained below, his new synthesis, dubbed "sociobiology," was equated with the race policies of the past and ultimately with the Holocaust.

Although the criticism was patently unfair—Wilson was offering evolutionary explanations, not policy suggestions—we shouldn't be surprised that the topic of human biology arouses strong emotions.

Burdens of the Past

It is generally believed that some human behavior can easily be changed because it is learned, whereas other behavior resists modification because it is part of our biological heritage.

Ideologues of all colors have grasped this division to argue for the innate nature of certain human characteristics (for example, purported race differences in intelligence) and the plasticity of others (such as the ability to overcome gender stereotypes). Thus, Communism was founded on great confidence in human malleability. Because people, unlike social insects, resist submerging individuality for the greater good, some regimes accompanied their revolutions with massive indoctrination efforts. All of this proved in vain, however. Communism went under because of an economic incentive structure that was out of touch with human nature. Unfortunately, it did so only after having caused great misery and death.

Even more disastrous was the embrace of biology by Nazi Germany. Here, too, the collective (*das Volk*) was placed above the individual, but instead of relying on social engineering the method of choice was genetic manipulation. People were classified into "superior" and "inferior" types, the first of which needed to be protected against contamination by the second. In the horrible medical language of the Nazis, a healthy *Volk* required the cutting out of all "cancerous" elements. This idea was followed to its extreme in a manner that Western civilization has vowed never to forget.

Don't think that the underlying selectionist ideology was restricted to this particular time and place, however. In the early part of the 20th century, the eugenics movement—which sought to improve humanity by "breeding from the fitter stocks"—enjoyed widespread appeal among intellectuals in both the U.S. and Great Britain. Based on ideas going back to Plato's *Republic*, sterilization of the mentally handicapped and of criminals was considered perfectly acceptable. And social Darwinism—the idea that in a laissez-faire capitalist economy the strong will outcompete the weak, resulting in general improvement of the population—still inspires political agendas today. In this view, the poor should not be aided in their struggle for existence so as not to upset the natural order.

Given these ideologies, it is understandable why suppressed categories of people, such as minorities and women, fail to see biology as a friend. I would argue, however, that the danger comes from both directions, from biological determinism as well as its opposite, the denial of basic human needs and the belief that we can be everything we want to be. The hippie communes of the 1960s, the Israeli kibbutzim and the feminist revolution all sought to redefine humans. But denial of sexual jealousy, the parent-child bond or gender differences can be carried only so far before a counter-movement will seek to balance cultural trends with evolved human inclinations.

What makes the present era different is that the genocide of World War II is fading into memory while at the same time the evidence for a connection between genes and behavior is mounting. Studies of twins reared apart have reached the status of common knowledge, and almost every week newspapers report a new human gene. There is evidence for genes involved in schizophrenia, epilepsy and Alzheimer's and even in common behavioral traits such as thrill-seeking. We are also learning more about genetic and neurological differences between men and women, as well as between gay and straight men. For example, a small region of the brain in transsexual men (who dress and behave like women) resembles the same region in women's brains.

The list of such scientific advances is getting longer by the day, resulting in a critical mass of evidence that is impossible to ignore. Understandably, academics who have spent their life condemning the idea that biology influences human behavior are reluctant to change course. But they are being overtaken by the general public, which seems to have accepted that genes are involved in just about everything we do and are. Concurrently resistance to comparisons with other animals has dissipated because of a stream of television nature programs that has brought exotic wildlife into our homes while showing animals to be quite a bit smarter and more interesting than people used to believe.

Studies of chimpanzees and bonobos, such as those by Jane Goodall and myself, show that countless human practices and potentials, from politics and child-rearing to violence and even morality, have parallels in the lives of our closest animal relatives. How can we maintain the dualisms of the past—between humans and animals and between body and mind—in the face of all this evidence to the contrary? Current knowledge about our biological background simply doesn't permit a return to the tabula rasa views of the past.

This doesn't solve the problem of ideological abuse, however. If anything, it makes things worse. So long as people have political agendas, they will depict human nature one way or another for their own purposes. Conservatives like to point out that people are naturally selfish, whereas liberals argue that we have evolved to be social and cooperative. The obvious correctness of both influences goes to show what is wrong with simple-minded genetic determinism.

The Best of Both Worlds

Because genetic language ("a gene for x") plays into our sound-bite culture, there is all the more reason to educate the public that genes, by themselves, are like seeds dropped onto the pavement: powerless to produce anything. When scientists say that a trait is inherited, all they mean is that part of its variability is explained by genetic factors. That the environment usually explains at least as much tends to be forgotten.

As Hans Kummer, a Swiss primatologist, remarked years ago, to try to determine how much of a trait is produced by genes and how much by the environment is as useless as asking whether the drumming that we hear in the distance is made by the percussionist or his instrument. On the other hand, if we pick up distinct sounds on different occasions, we can legitimately ask whether the variation is caused by different drummers or by different drums. This is the only sort of question science addresses when it looks into genetic versus environmental effects.

I foresee a continued mapping of the links between genes and behavior, a much more precise knowledge of how the brain works and a gradual adoption of the evolutionary paradigm in the social sciences. Charles Darwin's portrait will finally decorate the walls of departments of psychology and sociology! But one would hope that all of this will be accompanied by continued assessment of the ethical and political implications of behavioral science.

Traditionally, scientists have acted as if it is none of their business how the information they produce is being used. During some periods they have even actively assisted in political abuse. One notable exception was, of course, Albert Einstein, who may serve as a model of the kind of moral awareness needed in the behavioral and social sciences. If history teaches us anything, it is that it is critical that we remain on the alert against misinterpretations and simplifications. No one is in a better position than the scientists themselves to warn against distortions and to explain the complexities.

In which direction the thinking may develop can perhaps be illustrated with an example from the crossroads between cultural and evolutionary anthropology. Sigmund Freud and many traditional anthropologists, such as Claude Lévi-Strauss, have assumed that the human incest taboo serves to suppress sexual urges between family members. Freud believed that "the earliest sexual excitations of youthful human beings are invariably of an incestuous character." Hence, the incest taboo was seen as the ultimate victory of culture over nature.

In contrast, Edward Westermarck, a Finnish sociologist who lived at about the same time as Freud, hypothesized that early familiarity (such as between mother and child and between siblings) kills sexual desire. Little or no sexual attraction is found, he argued, between individuals who have grown up together. A fervent Darwinian, Westermarck proposed this as an evolved mechanism designed to prevent the deleterious consequences of inbreeding.

In the largest-scale study on this issue to date, Arthur P. Wolf, an anthropologist at Stanford University, examined the marital histories of 14,400 women in a "natural experiment" carried out in Taiwan. Families in this region used to adopt and raise future daughters-in-law, which meant that intended marriage partners grew up together from early childhood. Wolf compared these marriages with those arranged between men and women who did not meet until the wedding day. Using divorce and fertility rates as gauges of marital happiness and sexual activity, respectively, the data strongly supported the Westermarck effect: association in the first years of life appeared to compromise adult marital compatibility. Nonhuman primates are subject to the same mechanism. Many primates prevent inbreeding through migration of one sex or the other at puberty. The migratory sex meets

new, unrelated mates, whereas the resident sex gains genetic diversity from the outside. But close kin who stay together also generally avoid sexual intercourse.

Kisaburo Tokuda first observed this in a group of Japanese macaques at the Kyoto zoo in the 1950s. A young adult male that had risen to the top rank made full use of his sexual privileges, mating frequently with all the females except for one: his mother. This was not an isolated case: mother-son matings are strongly suppressed in all primates. Even in bonobos—probably the most sexually active primates on the earth—this is the one partner combination in which sex is extremely rare or absent. Incest avoidance has now been convincingly demonstrated in a host of primates, and the mediating mechanism is thought to be early familiarity.

The Westermarck effect serves as a showcase for Darwinian approaches to human behavior because it so clearly rests on a combination of nature and nurture. The framework includes a developmental component (learned sexual aversion), an innate component (the effect of early familiarity), a cultural component (some cultures raise unrelated children together, others raise siblings of the opposite sex apart, but most have family arrangements that automatically lead to sexual inhibitions among relatives), a sound evolutionary reason (suppression of inbreeding) and direct parallels with animal behavior. On top of this comes the cultural taboo, which is unique to our species. An intriguing question is whether the incest taboo merely serves to formalize and strengthen the Westermarck effect or whether it adds a substantially new dimension.

The unexpected richness of a research program that integrates developmental, genetic, evolutionary and cultural approaches to a well-circumscribed phenomenon demonstrates the power of breaking down old barriers between disciplines. Most likely what will happen in the next millenium is that evolutionary approaches to human behavior will become more and more sophisticated by explicitly taking cultural flexibility into account. Hence, the traditional either/or approach to learning and instinct will be replaced by a more integrated perspective. In the meantime, students of animal behavior will become more interested in environmental effects on behavior and especially—in animals such as primates and marine mammals—the possibility of cultural transmission of information and habits. For example, some chimpanzee communities use stones to crack nuts in the forest, whereas other communities have the same nuts and stones available but don't do anything with them. Such differences are unexplained by genetic variation.

These two developments together will weaken the dichotomies popular today to the point of eliminating them. Rather than looking at culture as the antithesis of nature, we will be gaining a much more profound understanding of human behavior by silently carrying the old nature/nurture debate to its grave.

FURTHER INFORMATION

SOCIOBIOLOGY: THE NEW SYNTHESIS. Edward O. Wilson. Belknap Press (Harvard University Press), 1975. 25th anniversary edition (in press).

SEXUAL ATTRACTION AND CHILDHOOD ASSOCIATION: A CHINESE BRIEF FOR EDWARD WESTERMARCK. Arthur P. Wolf. Stanford University Press, 1995.

THE MISMEASURE OF MAN. Revised edition. Stephen Jay Gould. W. W. Norton, 1996.

GOOD NATURED: THE ORIGINS OF RIGHT AND WRONG IN HUMANS AND OTHER ANIMALS. Frans de Waal. Harvard University Press, 1997.

FRANS B. M. DE WAAL was trained as a zoologist and ethologist in the European tradition in his native country, the Netherlands. He has been in the U.S. since 1981 and is currently director of the Living Links Center at the Yerkes Regional Primate Research Center in Atlanta and is also C. H. Candler Professor of Primate Behavior in the psychology department at Emory University. His research includes social interactions in primates as well as the origins of morality and justice in human society.

MAKING TIME FOR A BABY

For years, women have been told they could wait until 40 or later to have babies. But a new book argues that's way too late

By NANCY GIBBS

LISTEN TO A SUCCESSFUL WOMAN DISCUSS HER FAILURE TO bear a child, and the grief comes in layers of bitterness and regret. This was supposed to be the easy part, right? Not like getting into Harvard. Not like making partner. The baby was to be Mother Nature's gift. Anyone can do it; high school dropouts stroll through the mall with their babies in a Snugli. What can be so hard, especially for a Mistress of the Universe, with modern medical science devoted to resetting the biological clock? "I remember sitting in the clinic waiting room," recalls a woman who ran the infertility marathon, "and a woman—she was in her mid-40s and had tried everything to get pregnant—told me that one of the doctors had glanced at her chart and said, 'What are you doing here? You are wasting your time.' It was so cruel. She was holding out for that one last glimpse of hope. How horrible was it to shoot that hope down?"

The manner was cold, but the message was clear—and devastating. "Those women who are at the top of their game could have had it all, children and career, if they wanted it," suggests Pamela Madsen, executive director of the American Infertility Association (A.I.A.). "The problem was, nobody told them the truth about their bodies." And the truth is that even the very best fertility experts have found that the hands of the clock will not be moved. Baby specialists can do a lot to help a 29-year-old whose tubes are blocked or a 32-year-old whose husband has a low sperm count. But for all the headlines about 45-year-old actresses giving birth, the fact is that "there's no promising therapy for age-related infertility," says Dr. Michael Soules, a professor at the University of Washington School of Medicine and past president of the Ameri-

can Society for Reproductive Medicine (ASRM). "There's certainly nothing on the horizon."

This means, argues economist Sylvia Ann Hewlett in her new book, *Creating a Life: Professional Women and the Quest for Children* (Talk Miramax Books), that many ambitious young women who also hope to have kids are heading down a bad piece of road if they think they can spend a decade establishing their careers and wait until 35 or beyond to establish their families. Even as more couples than ever seek infertility treatment—the number of procedures performed jumped 27% between 1996 and 1998—doctors are learning that the most effective treatment may be prevention, which in this case means knowledge. "But the fact that the biological clock is real is unwelcome news to my 24-year-old daughter," Hewlett observes, "and she's pretty typical."

27 IS THE AGE AT WHICH A WOMAN'S CHANCE OF GETTING PREGNANT BEGINS TO DECLINE

At 20, the risk of miscarriage is about 9%; it doubles by 35, then doubles again by the time a woman reaches her early 40s

At 42, 90% of a woman's eggs are abnormal; she has only a 7.8% chance of having a baby without using donor eggs

The Limits Of Science

ASSISTED REPRODUCTIVE TECHNOLOGY IS ONE OF THE great medical success stories of the late 20th century. Thanks to fertility drugs, in-vitro fertilization (IVF) and a growing list of even more sophisticated techniques, tens of thousands of healthy babies are born each year that otherwise might never have been conceived. But the process is neither foolproof nor risk free. There are limits to what science can do for infertile couples, and the more doctors have to intervene with drugs, needles and surgery to get sperm to meet egg, the greater the chance that something will go wrong. Among the pitfalls:

OVARIAN HYPERSTIMULATION The first step in most assisted-fertilization techniques is to trick the ovaries into producing a lot of eggs at once. But the hormones doctors use to do this are powerful drugs and in rare cases can cause serious complications, including blood clots and kidney damage.

MULTIPLE GESTATION Not being able to have a baby can be heartbreaking. But having too many at once can be even worse. About 20% to 35% of IVF pregnancies produce multiple fetuses, usually twins. Having more than two or three babies at once is often a medical disaster. Babies that develop in a crowded uterus or are born too early are at risk for a lifetime of developmental problems, including mental retardation, paralysis and blindness. Trying to reduce the number of fetuses through selective abortion has its own problems, not the least of which is an increased chance of miscarriage.

LOW BIRTH WEIGHT Twins and triplets (not to mention septuplets) often weigh less than normal at birth. But a recent study from the U.S. Centers for Disease Control suggests that even single babies conceived through IVF are more likely to be born underweight. Whether that also puts them at greater risk of developmental problems is uncertain.

BIRTH DEFECTS An Australian study published in March reported that IVF children are twice as likely to suffer birth defects—such as cleft palate, a hole in the heart or kidney problems—as children conceived the usual way. Several earlier studies have shown no difference between the two kinds of babies, so further research is needed. Even if the apparent increase is real, it might not be clear whether the birth defects are caused by the artificial reproductive technology or by whatever underlying problem caused the infertility in the first place.

Even the most powerful techniques can turn back a woman's biological clock only so far. Women in their early 30s who want to use their own eggs have a better than 30% chance of delivering a live baby by artificial means. After age 43, the success rate drops to a forbidding 3%.

—*By Christine Gorman*

THE DANGERS OF WAITING

Older women have a harder time getting pregnant and face greater risks when they do

Pregnancy *Odds each month*

Normal cycle or artificial insemination, based on data from Reproductive Medicine Associates of New Jersey

Miscarriage

Risk by age

Ectopic pregnancy

Risk by age

Chromosomal abnormality

Fetal risk by maternal age

Sources: American Society for Reproductive Medicine; National Center for Health. Statistics; CDC; *British Medical Journal*; Mayo Clinic. TIME Graphic by Lon Tweeten and Ed Gabel; text by Laura Bradford

8

THREE WAYS TO GIVE NATURE A HELPING HAND

Sometimes hormone therapy does the trick, but many infertile couples require more sophisticated manipulation of sperm and eggs. Among the techniques that offer the greatest hope for success:

In vitro fertilization

HOW THEY DO IT A woman's eggs are extracted and mixed with her partner's sperm in a Petri dish. The resulting embryo is transferred to her uterus through the cervix
POPULARITY At least 60,000 IVF procedures are performed in the U.S. annually, with an average birthrate of 25%

ICSI (intracytoplasmic sperm injection)

HOW THEY DO IT To counteract problems with sperm count, quality or mobility, doctors inject a single sperm directly into a mature egg to increase the chance of fertilization
POPULARITY ICSI accounts for approximately 24,000 IVF procedures annually. Average birthrate: 30%

Egg donation

HOW THEY DO IT When the problem is aging eggs, a young woman may donate her eggs to the couple. Fertilized with the man's sperm, the resulting embryo is implanted in the older woman's womb
POPULARITY More than 5,000 eggs are donated yearly. After the eggs are fertilized, the birthrate is approximately 40%

Sources: American Society for Reproductive Medicine; National Center for Health Statistics; CDC; *British Medical Journal*; Mayo Clinic; text by Laura Bradford.

Women have been debating for a generation how best to balance work and home life, but somehow each new chapter starts a new fight, and Hewlett's book is no exception. Back in 1989, when Felice Schwartz discussed in the *Harvard Business Review* how to create more flexibility for career women with children (she never used the phrase Mommy Track herself), her proposals were called "dangerous" and "retrofeminist" because they could give corporations an excuse to derail women's careers. Slow down to start a family, the skeptics warned, and you run the risk that you will never catch up.

And so, argues Hewlett, many women embraced a "male model" of single-minded career focus, and the result is "an epidemic of childlessness" among professional women. She conducted a national survey of 1,647 "high-achieving women," including 1,168 who earn in the top 10% of income of their age group or hold degrees in law or medicine, and another 479 who are highly educated but are no longer in the work force. What she learned shocked her: she found that 42% of high-achieving women in corporate America (defined as companies with 5,000 or more employees) were still childless after age 40. That figure rose to 49% for women who earn $100,000 or more. Many other women were able to have only one child because they started their families too late. "They've been making a lot of money," says Dr. David Adamson, a leading fertility specialist at Stanford University, "but it won't buy back the time."

Recent Census data support Hewlett's research: childlessness has doubled in the past 20 years, so that 1 in 5 women between ages 40 and 44 is childless. For women that age and younger with graduate and professional degrees, the figure is 47%. This group certainly includes women for whom having children was never a priority: for them, the opening of the work force offered many new opportunities, including the chance to define success in realms other than motherhood. But Hewlett argues that many other women did not actually choose to be childless. When she asked women to recall their intentions at the time they were finishing college, Hewlett found that only 14% said that they definitely did not want to have children.

For most women Hewlett interviewed, childlessness was more like what one called a "creeping nonchoice." Time passes, work is relentless. The travel, the hours—relationships are hard to sustain. By the time a woman is married and settled enough in her career to think of starting a family, it is all too often too late. "They go to a doctor, take a blood test and are told the game is over before it even begins," says A.I.A.'s Madsen. "They are shocked, devastated and angry." Women generally know their fertility declines with age; they just don't realize how much and how fast. According to the Centers for Disease Control, once a woman celebrates her 42nd birthday, the chances of her having a baby using her own eggs, even with advanced medical help, are less than 10%. At age 40, half of her eggs are chromosomally abnormal; by 42, that figure is 90%. "I go through Kleenex in my office like it's going out of style," says reproductive endocrinologist Michael Slowey in Englewood, N.J.

Hewlett and her allies say they are just trying to correct the record in the face of widespread false optimism. Her survey found that nearly 9 out of 10 young women were confident of their ability to get pregnant into their 40s.

Last fall the A.I.A. conducted a fertility-awareness survey on the women's website iVillage.com. Out of the 12,524 respondents, only one answered all 15 questions correctly. Asked when fertility begins to decline, only 13% got it right (age 27); 39% thought it began to drop at 40. Asked how long couples should try to conceive on their own before seeking help, fully 42% answered 30 months. That is a dangerous combination: a couple that imagines fertility is no problem until age 40 and tries to get pregnant for 30 months before seeing a doctor is facing very long odds of ever becoming parents.

In one sense, the confusion is understandable: it is only in the past 10 years that doctors themselves have discovered the limitations. "I remember being told by a number of doctors, 'Oh, you have plenty of time,' even when I was 38," says Claudia Morehead, 47, a California insurance lawyer who is finally pregnant, using donor eggs. Even among fertility specialists, "it was shocking to us that IVF didn't work so well after age 42," admits Dr. Sarah Berga, a reproductive endocrinologist at the University of Pittsburgh School of Medicine. "The early '90s, to my mind, was all about how shocked we were that we couldn't get past this barrier." But even as doctors began to try to get the word out, they ran into resistance of all kinds.

One is simply how information is shared. Childlessness is a private sorrow; the miracle baby is an inevitable headline. "When you see these media stories hyping women in their late 40s having babies, it's with donor eggs," insists Stanford's Adamson, "but that is conveniently left out of the stories." The more aggressive infertility clinics have a financial incentive to hype the good news and bury the facts: a 45-year-old woman who has gone through seven cycles of IVF can easily spend $100,000 on treatment. But even at the best fertility clinics in the country, her chance of taking a baby home is in the single digits.

In hopes of raising women's awareness, ASRM launched a modest $60,000 ad campaign last fall, with posters and brochures warning that factors like smoking, weight problems and sexually transmitted infections can all harm fertility. But the furor came with the fourth warning, a picture of a baby bottle shaped like an hourglass: "Advancing age decreases your ability to have children." The physicians viewed this as a public service, given the evidence of widespread confusion about the facts, but the group has come under fire for scaring women with an oversimplified message on a complex subject.

"The implication is, 'I have to hurry up and have kids now or give up on ever having them,'" says Kim Gandy, president of the National Organization for Women. "And that is not true for the vast majority of women." Gandy, 48, had her first child at 39. "It was a choice on my part, but in most ways it really wasn't. It's not like you can create out of whole cloth a partner you want to have a family with and the economic and emotional circumstances that allow you to be a good parent. So to put pressure on

young women to hurry up and have kids when they don't have those other factors in place really does a disservice to them and to their kids."

To emphasize a woman's age above all other factors can be just one more piece of misleading information, Gandy suggests. "There are two people involved [in babymaking], and yet we're putting all the responsibility on women and implying that women are being selfish if they don't choose to have children early." She shares the concern that women will hear the research and see the ads and end up feeling it is so hard to strike a balance that it's futile to even try. "There is an antifeminist agenda that says we should go back to the 1950s," says Caryl Rivers, a journalism professor at Boston University. "The subliminal message is, 'Don't get too educated; don't get too successful or too ambitious.'"

Allison Rosen, a clinical psychologist in New York City who has made it her mission to make sure her female patients know the fertility odds, disagrees. "This is not a case of male doctors' wanting to keep women barefoot and pregnant," she says. "You lay out the facts, and any particular individual woman can then make her choices." Madsen of A.I.A. argues that the biological imperative is there whether women know it or not. "I cringe when feminists say giving women reproductive knowledge is pressuring them to have a child," she says. "That's simply not true. Reproductive freedom is not just the ability not to have a child through birth control. It's the ability to have one if and when you want one."

YOU CAN TRACE THE STRUGGLE BETWEEN HOPE AND BIOLOGY back to *Genesis*, when Abraham and Sarah gave thanks for the miracle that brought them their son in old age. "She was the first infertile woman," notes Zev Rosenwaks, the director of New York Presbyterian Hospital's infertility program. "It was so improbable that an allegedly menopausal woman could have a baby that her firstborn was named Isaac, which means 'to laugh.'" The miracle stories have fed the hope ever since, but so does wishful thinking. "It's tremendously comforting for a 34- or 36-year-old professional woman to imagine that she has time on her side," says Hewlett, which can make for resistance to hearing the truth.

"In just 30 years we've gone from fearing our fertility to squandering it— and very unwittingly."

This is the heart of Hewlett's crusade: that it is essential for women to plan where they want to be at 45 and work backward, armed with the knowledge that the window for having children is narrower than they have been led to believe and that once it begins to swing shut, science can do little to pry it open. And Hewlett argues as well that employers and policymakers need to do more to help families make the balancing act work. "The greatest choice facing modern women is to freely choose to have both, a job and a family, and be supported and admired for it, not be seen as some overweening yuppie."

As it happens, Hewlett knows from personal experience. She says she didn't set out to write about how hard it is for professional women to be moms. She planned to do a book celebrating women turning 50 at the millennium and to look at what forces had shaped their lives. Then she discovered, in interview after interview with college deans and opera divas, a cross section of successful women in various fields, that none of them had children—and few of them had chosen to be childless. Many blamed themselves for working too hard and waiting too long—and waking up to the truth too late. "When I talked to these women," she recalls, "their sense of loss was palpable."

Hewlett had spent most of her professional life writing and lecturing on the need for business and government to develop more family-friendly workplaces; she has a Ph.D. in economics from Harvard. And she has had children and lost them and fought to have more. As a young Barnard professor with a toddler at home, she lost twins six months into her pregnancy: If only, she thought, I had taken time off from work, taken it easier. A year and a half later, she writes, she was turned down for tenure by an appointments committee that believed, in the words of one member, that she had "allowed childbearing to dilute my focus." Hewlett was lucky: she went on to have three more children, including Emma, to whom she gave birth at 51 using her own egg and infertility treatments. Hewlett says she understands "baby hunger."

At least she understands it for women. Men, she argues, have an unfair advantage. "Nowadays," she says, "the rule of thumb seems to be that the more successful the woman, the less likely it is she will find a husband or bear a child. For men, the reverse is true. I found that only one-quarter of high-achieving men end up without kids. Men generally find that if they are successful, everything else follows naturally." But that view of men doesn't quite do justice to the challenges they face as well. Men too are working harder than ever; at the very moment that society sends the message to be more involved as fathers, the economy makes it harder—and Hewlett's prescription that women need to think about having their children younger leaves more men as primary breadwinners. They would be fathers as far as biology goes, but they wouldn't get much chance to be parents. "A lot of my friends who are men and have had families are now divorced," Stanford's Adamson admits. "When you ask them what happened, the vast majority will say, 'Well, I was never home. I was working all the time. I didn't pay enough attention to my family. I wish I had, but it's too late now.'"

Hewlett still insists that men don't face the same "cruel choices" that women confront. "Men who find that they

have no relationship with their adult kids at least have a second chance as grandfathers," she argues. "For women, childlessness represents a rolling loss into the future. It means having no children and no grandchildren." While her earlier books are full of policy prescriptions, this one is more personal. She salts the book with cautionary tales: women who were too threatening to the men they dated, too successful and preoccupied, too "predatory" to suit men who were looking for "nurturers." The voices are authentic but selective; taken together, it is easy to read certain passages and think she is calling for a retreat to home and hearth, where motherhood comes before every other role.

Hewlett replies that she is simply trying to help women make wise choices based on good information. She is not proposing a return to the '50s, she says, or suggesting that women should head off to college to get their MRS. and then try to have children soon after graduation. "Late 20s is probably more realistic, because men are not ready to commit earlier than that. And the 20s still needs to be a decade of great personal growth." She recommends that women get their degrees, work hard at their first jobs—but then be prepared to plateau for a while and redirect their energy into their personal lives, with the intention of catching up professionally later. "You will make some compromises in your career. But you will catch up, reinvent yourself, when the time is right."

100% RISE IN PAST 20 YEARS OF CHILDLESS WOMEN AGES 40 TO 44

Only 0.1% of babies in the U.S. are born to women age 45 or older

The problem is that Hewlett's own research argues otherwise: in her book all of the examples of successful women who also have families gave birth in their 20s. These women may escape the fate of would-be mothers who waited too long, but they encounter a whole different set of obstacles when it comes to balancing work and family. Biology may be unforgiving, but so is corporate culture: those who voluntarily leave their career to raise children often find that the way back in is extremely difficult. Many in her survey said they felt forced out by inflexible bosses; two-thirds say they wish they could return to the work force.

Much would have to change in the typical workplace for parents to be able to downshift temporarily and then resume their pace as their children grew older. Hewlett hopes that the war for talent will inspire corporations to adopt more family-friendly policies in order to attract and maintain the most talented parents, whether male or female. Many of her policy recommendations, however, are unlikely to be enacted anytime soon: mandatory paid parental leave; official "career breaks" like the generous policy at IBM that grants workers up to three years' leave with the guarantee of return to the same or a similar job; a new Fair Labor Standards Act that would discourage 80-hour workweeks by making all but the very top executives eligible for overtime pay.

Hewlett calls herself a feminist, but she has often crossed swords with feminists who, she charges, are so concerned with reproductive choice that they neglect the needs of women who choose to be mothers. In the history of the family, she notes, it is a very recent development for women to have control over childbearing, thanks to better health care and birth control. But there's an ironic twist now. "In just 30 years, we've gone from fearing our fertility to squandering it—and very unwittingly." The decision of whether to have a child will always be one of the most important anyone makes; the challenge is not allowing time and biology to make it for them.

—Reported by Janice M. Horowitz,
Julie Rawe and Sora Song/New York

THE MYSTERY OF FETAL LIFE:
SECRETS OF THE WOMB

JOHN PEKKANEN

In the dim light of an ultrasound room, a wand slides over the abdomen of a young woman. As it emits sound waves, it allows us to see into her womb. The video screen brightens with a grainy image of a 20-week-old fetus. It floats in its amniotic sac, like an astronaut free of gravity.

The fetal face stares upward, then turns toward us, as if to mug for the camera. The sound waves strike different tissues with different densities, and their echoes form different images. These images are computer-enhanced, so although the fetus weights only 14 ounces and is no longer than my hand, we can see its elfin features.

Close up, we peek into the fetal brain. In the seconds we observe, a quarter million new brain cells are born. This happens constantly. By the end of the nine months, the baby's brain will hold 100 billion brain cells.

The sound waves focus on the chest, rendering images of a vibrating four-chambered heart no bigger than the tip of my little finger. The monitor tells us it is moving at 163 beats a minute. It sounds like a frightened bird fluttering in its cage.

We watch the rib cage move. Although the fetus lives in an airless environment, it "breathes" intermittently inside the womb by swallowing amniotic fluid. Some researchers speculate that the fetus is exercising its chest and diaphragm as its way of preparing for life outside the womb.

The clarity of ultrasound pictures is now so good that subtle abnormalities can be detected. The shape of the skull, brain, and spinal cord, along with the heart and other vital organs, can be seen in breathtaking detail.

In this ultrasound exam, there are no hints to suggest that anything is abnormal. The husband squeezes his wife's hand. They both smile.

The fetus we have just watched is at the midpoint of its 40-week gestation. At conception 20 weeks earlier, it began as a single cell that carried in its nucleus the genetic code for the human it will become.

After dividing and redividing for a week, it grew to 32 cells. Like the initial cell, these offspring cells carry 40,000 or so genes, located on 23 pairs of chromosomes inherited from the mother and father. Smaller than the head of a pin, this clump of cells began a slow journey down the fallopian tube and attached itself to the spongy wall of the uterus.

Once settled, some embryonic cells began to form a placenta to supply the embryo with food, water, and nutrients from the mother's bloodstream. The placenta also filtered out harmful substances in the mother's bloodstream. The embryo and mother exchange chemical information to ensure that they work together toward their common goal.

Instructed by their genes, the cells continued to divide but didn't always produce exact replicas. In a process still not well understood, the cells began to differentiate to seek out their own destinies. Some helped build internal organs, others bones, muscles, and brain.

At 19 days postconception, the earliest brain tissues began to form. They developed at the top end of the neural tube, a sheath of cells that ran nearly the entire length of the embryo.

The human brain requires virtually the entire pregnancy to emerge fully, longer than the other organ systems. Even in the earliest stage of development, the fetus knows to protect its brain. The brain gets the most highly oxygenated blood, and should there be any shortage, the fetus will send the available blood to the brain.

Extending downward from the brain, the neural tube began to form the spinal cord. At four weeks, a rudimentary heart started to beat, and four limbs began sprouting. By eight weeks, the two-inch-long embryo took human form and was more properly called a fetus. At 10 to 12 weeks, it began moving its arms and legs, opened its jaws, swallowed, and yawned, Mostly it slept.

"We are never more clever than we are as a fetus," says Dr. Peter Nathanielsz, a fetal researcher, obstetrician, and professor of reproductive medicine at Cornell University. "We pass far more biological milestones before we are born than we'll ever pass after we're born."

Not long ago, the process of fetal development was shrouded in mystery. But through the power of scanning techniques, biotechnology, and fetal and animal studies, much of the mystery of fetal life has been unveiled.

We now know that as the fetus matures it experiences a broad range of sensory stimulation. It hears, sees, tastes, smells, feels, and has rapid eye movement (REM) sleep, the sleep stage we associate with dreaming. From observation of its sleep and wake cycles, the fetus appears to know night from day. It learns and remembers, and it may cry. It seems to do everything in utero that it will do after it is born. In the words of one researcher, "Fetal life is us."

Studies now show that it's the fetus, not the mother, who sends the hormonal signals that determine when a baby will be born. And we've found out that its health in the womb depends in part on its mother's health when she was in the womb.

Finally, we've discovered that the prenatal environment is not as benign, or as neutral, as once thought. It is sensitive to the mother's health, emotions, and behavior.

The fetus is strongly affected by the mother's eating habits. If the mother exercises more than usual, the fetus may become temporarily short of oxygen. If she takes a hot bath, the fetus feels the heat. If she smokes, so does the fetus. One study has found that pregnant women exposed to more sunlight had more-outgoing children.

We now know that our genes do not encode a complete design for us, that our "genetic destiny" is not hard-wired at the time of conception. Instead, our development involves an interplay between genes and the environment, including that of the uterus. Because genes take "cues" from their environment, an expectant mother's physical and psychological health influences her unborn child's genetic well-being.

Factors such as low prenatal oxygen levels, stress, infections, and poor maternal nutrition may determine whether certain genes are switched on or off. Some researchers believe that our time in the womb is the single most important period of our life.

"Because of genetics, we once thought that we would unfold in the womb like a blueprint, but now we know it's not that simple," says Janet DiPietro, an associate professor of maternal and child health at the Johns Hopkins School of Public Health and one of a handful of fetal-behavior specialists. "The mother and the uterine environment she creates have a major impact on many aspects of fetal development, and a number of things laid down during that time remain with you throughout your life."

The impact of the womb on our intelligence, personality, and emotional and physical health is beginning to be understood. There's also an emerging understanding of something called fetal programming, which says that the effects of our life in the womb may be not felt until decades after we're born, and in ways that are more powerful than previously imagined.

Says Dr. Nathanielsz, whose book *Life in the Womb* details the emerging science of fetal development: "It's an area of great scientific importance that until recently remained largely unknown."

"I'm pregnant. Is it okay to have a glass of wine? Can I take my Prozac? What about a Diet Coke?"

Years ago, before she knew she was pregnant, a friend of mine had a glass of wine with dinner. When she discovered she was pregnant, she worried all through her pregnancy and beyond. She feels some guilt to this day, even though the son she bore turned out very well.

Many mothers have experienced the same tangled emotions. "There's no evidence that a glass of wine a day during pregnancy has a negative impact on the developing fetus," says Dr. John Larsen, professor and chair of obstetrics and gynecology at George Washington University. Larsen says that at one time doctors gave alcohol by IV to pregnant women who were experiencing preterm labor; it relaxed the muscles and quelled contractions.

Larsen now sometimes recommends a little wine to women who experience mild contractions after a puncture from an amniocentesis needle, and some studies suggest that moderate alcohol intake in pregnancy may prevent preterm delivery in some women.

Even though most experts agree with Larsen, the alcohol message that most women hear calls for total abstinence. Experts worry that declaring moderate alcohol intake to be safe in pregnancy may encourage some pregnant women to drink immoderately. They say that pregnant women who have an occasional drink should not think they've placed their baby at risk.

What is safe? Some studies show children born to mothers who consumed three drinks a day in pregnancy averaged seven points lower on IQ tests than unexposed children. There is evidence that six drinks a day during pregnancy puts babies at risk of fetal alcohol syndrome (FAS), a constellation of serious birth defects that includes mental retardation. The higher the alcohol intake, the higher the FAS risk.

Are there drugs and drug combinations that women should avoid or take with caution during pregnancy? Accutane (isotretinoin), a prescription drug for acne and psoriasis, is known to cause birth defects. So too are some anticonvulsant drugs, including Epitol, Tegretol, and Valproate. Tetracycline, a widely prescribed antibiotic, can cause bone-growth delays and permanent teeth problems for a baby if a mother takes it during pregnancy.

Most over-the-counter drugs are considered safe in pregnancy, but some of them carry risks. Heavy doses of aspirin and other nonsteroidal anti-inflammatory drugs such as ibuprofen can delay the start of labor. They are also linked to a life-threatening disorder of newborns called persistent pulmonary hypertension (PPHN), which diverts airflow away from the baby's lungs, causing oxygen depletion. The March issue of the journal

Pediatrics published a study linking these nonprescription pain-killers to PPHN, which results in the death of 15 percent of the infants who have it.

OTC DRUGS

In 1998, researchers at the University of Nebraska Medical Center reported dextromethorphan, a cough suppressant found in 40 or more OTC drugs including Nyquil, Tylenol Cold, Dayquil, Robitussin Maximum Strength, and Dimetapp DM, caused congenital malformations in chick embryos. The research was published in *Pediatric Research* and supported by the National Institutes of Health.

Although no connection between dextromethorphan and human birth defects has been shown, the Nebraska researchers noted that similar genes regulate early development in virtually all species. For this reason, the researchers predicted that dextromethorphan, which acts on the brain to suppress coughing, would have the same harmful effect on a human fetus.

Many women worry about antidepressants. Some need them during pregnancy or took them before they knew they were pregnant. A study published in the *New England Journal of Medicine* found no association between fetal exposure to antidepressants and brain damage. The study compared the IQ, temperament, activity level, and distractibility of more than 125 children whose mothers took antidepressants in pregnancy with 84 children whose mothers took no drugs known to harm the fetus.

The two groups of children, between 16 months and eight years old when tested, were comparable in every way. The antidepressants taken by the mothers included both tricyclates such as Elavil and Tofranil and selective serotonin reuptake inhibitors such as Prozac.

Not all mood-altering drugs may be safe. There is some evidence that minor tranquilizers taken for anxiety may cause developmental problems if taken in the first trimester, but there is no hard proof of this. Evidence of fetal damage caused by illegal drugs such as cocaine is widely accepted, as is the case against cigarette smoking. A 1998 survey found that 13 percent of all mothers who gave birth smoked. Evidence is striking that cigarette smoking in pregnancy lowers birth weight and increases the risks of premature birth, attention deficit hyperactive disorder, and diminished IQ.

A long-running study based on information from the National Collaborative Perinatal Project found that years after they were born, children were more apt to become addicted to certain drugs if their mother took them during delivery.

"We found drug-dependent individuals were five times more likely to have exposure to high doses of painkillers and anesthesia during their delivery than their nonaddicted siblings," says Stephen Buka of the Harvard School of Public Health. Buka suspects this is caused by a modification in the infant's brain receptors as the drugs pass from mother to child during an especially sensitive time.

CAFFEINE

Coffee consumption has worried mothers because there have been hints that caffeine may be harmful to the fetus. Like most things in life, moderation is the key. There's no evidence that 300 milligrams of caffeine a day (about three cups of coffee, or four or five cups of most regular teas, or five to six cola drinks) harms a developing baby. Higher caffeine consumption has been weakly linked to miscarriage and difficulty in conceiving.

Expectant mothers concerned about weight gain should be careful of how much of the artificial sweetener aspartame they consume. Marketed under brand names such as NutraSweet and Equal, it's found in diet soft drinks and foods.

The concern is this: In the body, aspartame converts into phenylalanine, a naturally occurring amino acid we ingest when we eat protein. At high levels, phenylalanine can be toxic to brain cells.

When we consume phenylalanine in protein, we also consume a number of other amino acids that neutralize any ill effects. When we consume it in aspartame, we get none of the neutralizing amino acids to dampen phenylalanine's impact. And as it crosses the placenta, phenylalanine's concentrations are magnified in the fetal brain.

If a fetal brain is exposed to high levels of phenylalanine because its mother consumes a lot of aspartame, will it be harmed? One study found average IQ declines of ten points in children born to mothers with a fivefold increase of phenylalanine blood levels in pregnancy. That's a lot of aspartame, and it doesn't mean an expectant mother who drinks moderate amounts of diet soda need worry.

Researchers say consuming up to three servings of aspartame a day—in either diet soda or low-calorie foods—appears to be safe for the fetus. However, a pregnant woman of average weight who eats ten or more servings a day may put her unborn baby at risk. In testimony before Congress, Dr. William Pardridge, a neuroscience researcher at UCLA, said it's likely that the effect of high phenylalanine levels in the fetal brain "will be very subtle" and many not manifest until years later.

One wild card concerns the 10 to 20 million Americans who unknowingly carry a gene linked to a genetic disease called phenylketonuria (PKU), which can lead to severe mental retardation. Most carriers don't know it, because PKU is a recessive genetic disorder, and both mother and father must carry the defective gene to pass PKU on to their child. A carrier feels no ill effects. According to researchers, a pregnant woman who unknowingly carries the PKU gene might place her unborn child at risk if she consumes even relatively moderate amounts of aspartame. There is no hard evidence that this will happen, but it remains a serious concern. PKU can be detected in the fetus by amniocentesis; a restrictive diet can prevent the worst effects of PKU on the child.

How does a mother's getting an infection affect her unborn baby? And should she be careful of cats?

Many experts think pregnant women should be more concerned about infections and household pets than a glass of wine or can of diet drink. There's overwhelming evidence of the potential harm of infections during pregnancy. We've known for a long time that rubella (German measles), a viral infection, can cause devastating birth defects.

More worrisome are recent studies showing that exposure to one of the most common of winter's ills—influenza—may put an unborn child at risk of cognitive and emotional problems. If flu strikes in the second trimester, it may increase the unborn baby's risk of developing schizophrenia later in life. While the flu may be a trigger, it's likely that a genetic susceptibility is also needed for schizophrenia to develop.

Some evidence exists that maternal flu may also lead to dyslexia, and suspicions persist that a first-trimester flu may cause fetal neural-tube defects resulting in spina bifida. The common cold, sometimes confused with the flu, has not been linked to any adverse outcomes for the baby.

"Infections are probably the most important thing for a pregnant woman to protect herself against," says Lise Eliot, a developmental neurobiologist at the Chicago Medical School. "She should always practice good hygiene, like washing her hands frequently, avoiding crowds, and never drinking from someone else's cup." She adds that the flu vaccine has been approved for use during pregnancy.

Some researchers recommend that pregnant women avoid close contact with cats. Toxoplasmosis, a parasitic infection, can travel from a cat to a woman to her unborn child.

Most humans become infected through cat litter boxes. An infected woman might experience only mild symptoms, if any, so the illness usually goes undetected. If she is diagnosed with the infection, antiparasitic drugs are helpful, but they don't completely eliminate the disease. The infection is relatively rare, and the odds of passing it from mother to child are only one in five during the first two trimesters, when the fetal harm is most serious. The bad news is that a fetus infected by toxoplasmosis can suffer severe brain damage, including mental retardation and epilepsy. Some researchers also suspect it may be a latent trigger for serious mental illness as the child grows older.

CEREBRAL PALSY

An expectant mother may not realize she has potentially harmful infections. The prime suspects are infections in the reproductive tract. Researchers suspect most cerebral-palsy cases are not caused by delivery problems, as has been widely assumed. There's strong evidence that some cases of cerebral-palsy may be linked to placental infections that occur during uterine life. Other cerebral-palsy cases may be triggered by oxygen deprivation in early development, but very few appear to be caused by oxygen deprivation during delivery. It's now estimated that only 10 percent of cerebral-palsy cases are related to delivery problems.

Maternal urinary-tract infections have been linked to lower IQs in children. Another infection, cytomegalovirus (CMV), has been linked to congenital deafness. Sexually transmitted diseases such as chlamydia are suspected to be a trigger for preterm birth. Despite the serious threat posed to developing babies, infections during pregnancy remain poorly understood.

"We just don't know right now when or how the uterine infections that really make a difference to the fetus are transmitted

in pregnancy," says Dr. Karin Nelson, a child neurologist and acting chief of the neuro-epidemiology branch of the National Institute of Neurologic Disorders and Stroke at NIH. "Nor do we know all the potential problems they may cause."

Because of this, researchers offer little in the way of recommendations other than clean living and careful sex. They recommend that any woman contemplating pregnancy get in her best physical condition, because a number of studies have found that a woman's general health before she becomes pregnant is vital to fetal health. They also recommend a thorough gynecological exam because it may detect a treatable infection that could harm the fetus.

Rachel Carson was right about pesticides. So if you're pregnant, how careful should you be about what you eat?

In her book *Silent Spring,* author Rachel Carson noted that when pregnant mammals were exposed to synthetic pesticides, including DDT and methoxychlor, the pesticides caused developmental abnormalities in offspring. Carson, a scientist, noted that some pesticides mimicked the female hormone estrogen and caused the male offspring to be feminized.

About the time of Carson's 1962 book, another story was emerging about diethylstilbestrol (DES), a man-made female hormone administered in the 1940s and '50s to prevent miscarriages. In the 1960s it became clear that many young daughters of DES mothers were turning up reproductive malformations and vaginal cancers. Sons born to DES mothers suffered reproductive problems, including undescended testicles and abnormal sperm counts.

ENDOCRINE DISRUPTERS

Over the years, suspicion grew from both animal and human studies that something in the environment was disrupting fetal development. In the 1990s it was given a name—endocrine disruption. The theory was that DES and the pesticides cited by Carson caused defects in offspring because they disrupted the normal endocrine process. They did this by mimicking hormones inside the human body.

It's now clear that DDT and DES are the tip of the iceberg. Today more than 90,000 synthetic chemicals are used, most made after World War II. New chemicals are produced every week. They are used in everything from pesticides to plastics.

How many of these man-made chemicals might act as endocrine disrupters? More than 50 have been identified, and hundreds more are suspects.

To understand the threat from endocrine disrupters, it helps to understand what human hormones do. Secreted by endocrine glands, these tiny molecules circulate through the bloodstream to the organs. They include estrogen, adrenalin, thyroid, melatonin, and testosterone. Each is designed to fit only into a specific receptor on a cell, like a key that fits only one lock. When a hormone connects with the cell receptor, it enters the cell's nucleus. Once there, the hormone acts as a signaling agent to direct the cell's DNA to produce specific proteins.

During fetal life, the right type and concentration of hormones must be available at the right time for normal fetal development to occur. Produced by both mother and fetus, hormones are involved in cell division and differentiation, the development of the brain and reproductive organs, and virtually everything else needed to produce a baby.

"We know from animal experiments and wildlife observations that periods in development are very sensitive to alterations in the hormone levels," says Robert Kavlock, director of reproductive toxicology for the Environmental Protection Agency.

The damage is done when chemical mimickers get into cells at the wrong time, or at the wrong strength, or both. When this happens, something in the fetus will not develop as it should.

After years of witnessing the harmful impact on wildlife, we now know that humans are not immune to endocrine disrupters. More troubling, because of the pervasiveness of these chemicals, is that we can't escape them. We get them in the food we eat, the water we drink, the products we buy.

One of the most dramatic examples came to light in the 1970s when researchers wanted to find out why so many babies born in the Great Lakes region suffered serious neurological defects. They found the answer in polychlorinated biphenyls (PCBs), organic chemicals once used in electrical insulation and adhesives. Heavy PCB contamination of Great Lakes fish eaten by the mothers turned out to be the cause.

It is not clear how PCBs cause fetal brain damage, but it's believed to happen when they disrupt thyroid hormones. Severe thyroid deficiency in pregnancy is known to cause mental retardation. Another study found reduced penis size in boys born to mothers exposed to high levels of PCBs.

The U.S. manufacture of PCBs ended in 1977. PCB levels found in the mothers and the fish they ate suggested at the time that only very high exposure caused a problem for developing babies. Now we know this isn't true.

Because PCBs don't break down, they've remained a toxin that continues to enter our bodies through the food we eat. They have leached into soil and water and are found in shellfish and freshwater fish and to a smaller degree in ocean fish. Bottom-feeding freshwater fish, such as catfish and carp, have the highest PCB concentrations.

PCBs store in fat tissue and are found in dairy products and meats. Fatty meats, especially processed meats like cold cuts, sausages, and hot dogs, are usually heaviest in PCBs. They get into these products because farm animals graze on PCB-contaminated land. However, eating fish from PCB-contaminated water remains the primary way we get these chemicals into our systems. In pregnant women, PCBs easily cross the placenta and circulate in the fetus.

PCBs are ubiquitous. They've been detected in the Antarctic snow. If you had detection equipment sensitive enough, you'd find them in the milk at the supermarket.

What concerns experts are findings from studies in the Netherlands and upstate New York that found even low maternal PCB exposures pose risk to a fetus.

The Dutch study followed 418 children from birth into early childhood. In the final month of pregnancy, researchers measured the maternal PCB blood levels, and at birth they measured PCB levels in the umbilical cord. None of the mothers was a heavy fish eater or had any history of high PCB exposure, and none of their PCB levels was considered high by safety standards.

At 3 1/2 years of age, the children's cognitive abilities were assessed with tests. After adjusting for other variables, the researchers found that maternal and cord blood PCB levels correlated with the children's cognitive abilities. As the PCB blood levels went up, the children suffered more attention problems and their cognitive abilities went down. It should be noted that the brain damage in these Dutch children was not devastating. They were not retarded or autistic. But on a relative scale, they had suffered measurable harm.

The Dutch researchers concluded that the in utero PCB exposure, and not any postnatal exposure, caused the children's brain damage. The study also revealed that these children had depressed immune function.

"All we can say now," says Deborah Rice, a toxicologist at the EPA's National Center for Environmental Assessment in Washington, "is we have strong evidence that PCB levels commonly found among women living in industrialized society can cause subtle neurological damage in their offspring." But one of the difficulties, according to Rice, is that we really don't yet know what an unsafe maternal PCB level might be.

"I think the bottom line is that women should be aware of PCBs and aware of what they're putting in their mouth," adds Rice.

The Dutch study is a warning not only about the potential impact of low levels of PCBs but about the potential harm from low levels of other endocrine disrupters.

More news arrived in March when the results from the federal government's on-going Fourth National Health and Nutrition Examination Survey (NHANES) became public. The survey of 38,000 people revealed that most of us have at least trace levels of pesticides, heavy metals, and plastics in our body tissues. In all, NHANES tested for 27 elements.

The survey found widespread exposure to phthalates, synthetic chemicals used as softeners in plastics and other products. Phthalates are one of the most heavily produced chemicals and have been linked in animal studies to endocrine disruption and birth defects. The likely sources of human exposure are foods and personal-care products such as shampoos, lotions, soaps, and perfumes; phthalates are absorbed through the skin.

Dr. Ted Schettler, a member of the Greater Boston Physicians for Social Responsibility, suspects endocrine disrupters may be linked to increases in the three hormone-driven cancers—breast, prostate, and testicular. The rate of testicular cancer among young men has nearly doubled in recent years, and the rates of learning disabilities and infertility also have increased.

"We can't blame all that is happening on toxic chemicals," says Schettler, who coauthored *In Harm's Way,* a report on how chemical contaminants affect human health. "But we need to ask ourselves if we're seeing patterns that suggest these chemicals are having a major impact on fetal development and human populations. We also need to ask what level of evidence we're going to need before we take public-health measures. That's a political question."

The EPA's Kavlock says, "We don't know the safe or unsafe levels for many of these chemicals." Nor do we know how many of the thousands of man-made chemicals in the environment will turn out to be endocrine disrupters or cause human harm. The EPA received a mandate from Congress in 1996 to find the answers, but it will be a long wait.

"If we devoted all the toxicology testing capacity in the entire world to look for endocrine-disrupting chemicals, we couldn't do all the chemicals. There's just not enough capacity," Kavlock says. "So we are focusing on 500 to 1,000 chemicals that are the major suspects. It will take many years and a lot of money just to understand how they interact with hormonal-system and fetal development."

What is all this bad stuff we can get from eating fish or from microwaving food in plastics? Do vitamins help?

Methylmercury is a heavy metal that can cause fetal brain damage. NHANES revealed that 10 percent of American women of child-bearing age—a representative sample of all American women—had methylmercury blood and hair levels close to "potentially hazardous levels." The EPA and some nongovernment experts consider these existing methylmercury levels already above what is safe.

Dr. Jill Stein, an adolescent-medicine specialist and instructor at Harvard Medical School, has studied methylmercury's toxicity. She says the acceptable levels of methylmercury in the NHANES report were too high and that many more women are in the danger zone. "The NHANES data tells me that more than 10 percent of American women today are carrying around enough mercury to put their future children at risk for learning and behavior problems," she says.

Like PCBs and other toxic chemicals, mercury is hard to avoid because it is abundant in our environment. It comes from natural and man-made sources, chiefly coal-fired power plants and municipal waste treatment. Each year an estimated 160 tons of mercury is released into the nation's environment. In water, mercury combines with natural bacteria to form methylmercury, a toxic form of the metal. It is easily absorbed by fish. When a pregnant woman consumes the contaminated fish, methylmercury crosses the placenta and the fetal blood-brain barrier.

The world became aware of methylmercury's potential for harm more than 40 years ago in the fishing village of Minamata in Japan. People there were exposed to high levels of the heavy metal from industrial dumping of mercury compounds into Minamata Bay. The villagers, who ate a diet heavy in fish caught in the bay, experienced devastating effects. The hardest hit were the unborn. Women gave birth to babies with cerebral-palsy-like symptoms. Many were retarded.

MERCURY

Fish are the major source of mercury for humans. The Food and Drug Administration recommends that pregnant women not eat swordfish, king mackerel, shark, and tilefish. These fish are singled out because large oceangoing fish contain more methylmercury. Smaller ocean fish, especially cod, haddock, and pollock, generally have low methylmercury levels. A whitefish found off the coast of Alaska, pollock is commonly found in fish sticks and fast-food fish. Salmon have low methylmercury levels, but they are a fatty fish and apt to carry higher levels of PCBs.

Like the Dutch PCB studies, recent studies of maternal methylmercury exposure have turned up trouble. They've shown that the so-called "safe" maternal levels of the metal can cause brain damage during fetal development.

One study was carried out in the 1990s by a Danish research team that studied 917 children in the Faroe Islands, where seafood is a big part of the diet. Children were grouped into categories depending on their level of maternal methylmercury exposure; they were assessed up to age seven by neurological tests. None of the children's methylmercury exposure levels was considered high, yet many of the children had evidence of brain damage, including memory, attention, and learning problems.

"Subtle effects on brain function therefore seem to be detectable at prenatal methylmercury exposure levels currently considered safe," the study concluded. In a follow-up report published in a 1999 issue of the *Journal of the American Medical Association,* the authors said the blood concentrations of methylmercury found in the umbilical cord corresponded with the severity of the neurological damage suffered by the children.

In a study of 237 children, New Zealand researchers found similar neurological harm, including IQ impairment and attention problems, in children whose mothers' exposure to methylmercury came from fish they ate during pregnancy.

"The children in these studies were not bathed in methylmercury," notes Rita Schoeny, a toxicologist in the EPA's Office of Water. "Can people in the U.S. be exposed to the same levels of mercury in the course of their dietary practice? We think so."

Jill Stein and other experts worry that the more scientific studies we do, the more we'll realize that in fetal development there may be no such thing as a "safe" maternal level for methylmercury, PCBs, and scores of other synthetic chemicals.

"We keep learning from studies that these chemicals are harmful to fetal development at lower and lower doses," Stein says. "It's what we call the declining threshold of harm."

What about canned tuna? It has been assumed to contain low methylmercury levels because most of it comes from smaller fish. The FDA offers no advisories about it. But according to EPA researchers, a recent State of Florida survey of more than 100 samples of canned tuna found high levels of methylmercury. The more-expensive canned tuna, such as albacore and solid white tuna, usually carried higher methylmercury levels, according to the survey. This apparently is because more expensive canned tuna comes from larger tuna. In some of the canned tuna, the methylmercury levels were high enough to prevent their export to several countries, including Canada.

Some of the methylmercury levels were "worrisomely high," according to Kathryn Mahaffey, a toxicologist and director of the division of exposure assessment at the EPA. They were high enough to cause concern for pregnant women.

"A big problem is the tremendous variability out there in the tuna supply," adds Stein. "You have no idea when you're eating a can of tuna how much methylmercury you're getting."

"Even if you ate just a small serving of some of these canned tunas each day," says Mahaffey, "you'd be substantially above a level we would consider safe."

Mahaffey and Stein agree that an expectant mother who ate even a few servings a week with methylmercury levels found in some of the canned tuna would put her developing baby at risk of brain and other neurological damage.

Now that we know a developing fetus is sensitive to even low levels of toxic chemicals, women can exercise some basic precautions to help protect their developing babies.

Don't microwave food that is wrapped in plastic or is still in plastic containers. "There are endocrine-disrupting chemicals in these plastics," Schettler says, "that leach right into the food when it's microwaved. This has been well documented and measured." Studies suggest that even at very low levels these chemicals can have an adverse effect on the fetus's hormonal system.

The EPA's Kavlock considers the fruits and vegetables you buy at the supermarket to be safe in pregnancy, but Schettler says you should try to eat organic foods to avoid even trace amounts of pesticides. Wash fruits and vegetables before eating them. Avoid pesticides or insecticide use around the house during pregnancy as well as the use of chemical solvents for painting or remodeling.

Herbicides and pesticides have leached into reservoirs that supply home drinking water, and filtration plants can't remove them all. Some are known to be endocrine disrupters. Home water filters can reduce contaminants; the best ones use active charcoal as a filtering agent.

Experts agree that a pregnant woman, or a woman who may get pregnant, can eat fish but should be careful about the kind she eats and how much of it. EPA's Rice cautions any woman who is pregnant or thinking of becoming pregnant to avoid eating any sport fish caught in a lake or river.

VEGETABLE FATS

Rice adds that the PCB risk with fish can be reduced. "Trim the fish of fat and skin, and broil or grill it," see says. "That way you cook off fat and minimize your PCB exposure." There is not much you can do to reduce the methylmercury levels in fish because it binds to protein.

"Fat is important for a baby's neurological development before and after birth, so pregnant women should consider vegetable fats like olive oil and flaxseed oil as a source," Rice adds. She says low fat dairy and meat products carry fewer PCBs than higher-fat ones.

The EPA has issued a PCB advisory for the Potomac River in the District, Virginia, and Maryland, citing in particular catfish and carp. You can go to *www.epa.gov/ost/fish/epafish.pdf* for EPA advisories on PCB and methylmercury environmental contamination. From there you can connect to state Web sites for advisories on local waters and specific fish.

Women can help prevent neurological and other birth defects by taking vitamin supplements before pregnancy. A daily dose of 400 micrograms of folic acid can reduce the risk of such problems as spina bifida by more than 70 percent as well as prevent brain defects and cleft lip and palate. Indirect evidence from a study published last year in the *New England Journal of Medicine* suggests that folic acid may also help prevent congenital heart defects.

To be effective, folic acid should be taken before pregnancy to prevent developmental defects. Folic acid comes in multivitamins and prenatal vitamins and is found naturally in legumes, whole-wheat bread, citrus fruits, fortified breakfast cereal, and leafy green vegetables. Despite the proven value of folic acid, a recent March of Dimes survey found that only 32 percent of American women of childbearing age—including pregnant women—took folic-acid supplements.

What can a fetus learn in the womb? And does playing Mozart make a baby lots smarter?

Developmental psychologist Anthony DeCasper wanted to answer two questions: What does a fetus know, and when does it know it?

DeCasper's aim was to find out if a fetus could learn in utero and remember what it learned after it was born. He enlisted the help of 33 healthy expectant mothers and asked each to tape-record herself reading passages from Dr. Seuss's *The Cat in the Hat* or from another children's book, *The King, the Mice, and the Cheese*. The mothers were randomly assigned to play one of these readings, each of which lasted two or three minutes, to their unborn children three times a day during the final three weeks of their pregnancies.

DeCasper, a professor of developmental psychology at the University of North Carolina at Greensboro, could do the experiment because it was known that fetuses could hear by the third trimester and probably earlier. DeCasper had shown earlier that at birth, babies preferred their mother's voice to all other voices. Studies in the early 1990s found that fetuses could be soothed by lullabies and sometimes moved in rhythm to their mother's voice. Fetuses hear their mother's voice from the outside, just as they can hear any other voice, but they hear the mother's voice clearer and stronger through bone conduction as it resonates inside her.

A little more than two days after birth, each of the newborns in DeCasper's study was given a specially devised nipple. The device worked by utilizing the baby's sucking reflex. When the baby sucked on the nipple, it would hear its mother's voice. But if it paused for too long a time between sucks, it would hear another woman's voice. This gave the baby control over whose voice it would hear by controlling the length of its pause between sucks.

DeCasper also placed small earphones over the infant's ears through which it could hear its mother's voice read from the books.

"Now two days or so after it was born, the baby gets to choose between two stories read by its own mother," DeCasper said. "One was the story she'd recited three times a day for the last three weeks of pregnancy, and the other is one the baby's never heard before, except for the one day his mother recorded it. So the big question was: Would the babies prefer the story they'd heard in the womb, or wouldn't they? The answer was a clear yes—the babies preferred to hear the familiar story."

DeCasper did a second experiment by having women who were not the baby's mothers recite the same two stories. The babies again showed a strong preference for the story they'd heard in the womb.

"These studies not only tell us something about the fidelity with which the fetal ear can hear," DeCasper says, "but they also show that during those two or three weeks in the womb, fetal learning and memory are occurring."

British researchers observed expectant mothers who watched a TV soap opera. The researchers placed monitors on the mother's abdomens to listen in on fetal movements when the program aired. By the 37th week of pregnancy, the babies responded to the show's theme music by increasing their movements, an indication they remembered it.

Soon after the babies were born, the researchers replayed the theme music to them. This time, instead of moving more, the babies appeared to calm down and pay attention to the music. The researchers considered this a response to familiar music.

FETAL MEMORY

"The fact that we find evidence of fetal memory doesn't mean fetuses carry conscious memories, like we remember what we ate for breakfast," explains Lise Eliot, author of *What's Going On in There?*, a book on early brain development. "But we now know there is a tremendous continuity from prenatal to postnatal life, and the prenatal experience begins to shape a child's interaction with the world it will confront after birth. Babies go through the same activity patterns and behavioral states before and after birth. Well before it is born, the baby is primed to gravitate to its mother and its mother's voice."

Some researchers speculate a baby's ability to remember in the womb may be a way of easing its transition from prenatal life to postnatal life. A baby already accustomed to and comforted by its mother's voice may be reassured as it enters a new world of bright lights, needle pricks, curious faces, and loud noises.

The question arises: Can the uterine environment affect a baby's intelligence? Twins studies have shown that genes exert an all-powerful influence on IQ. The role of environment in IQ has traditionally meant the nurturance and stimulation the baby receives after birth.

Bernie Devlin, a biostatistician and assistant professor of psychiatry at the University of Pittsburgh, did an analysis of 212 twins studies on intelligence. In a paper published in *Nature,* he concluded that the accepted figure of 60 to 80 percent for IQ heritability is too high. It should be closer to 50 percent, he says, which leaves more room for environmental factors. Devlin says the one environmental factor that's been missing in understanding human intelligence is time in the womb.

"I'm surprised that the impact of fetal life on a child's intelligence had not been accounted for in these IQ studies," Devlin says. "I know it's very complicated, but it's surprising that people who study the heritability of intelligence really haven't considered this factor."

What is the impact of life in the womb on intelligence? Devlin thinks it's equal to if not greater than the impact of a child's upbringing. In other words, it's possible a mother may have more influence over her child's intelligence before birth than after.

As the brain develops in utero, we know it undergoes changes that affect its ultimate capacity. Nutritional and hormonal influences from the mother have a big impact. And twins studies show that the heavier twin at birth most often has the higher IQ.

A number of studies from the United States and Latin America also found that a range of vitamins, as well as sufficient protein in the mother's prenatal diet, had an impact on the child's intelligence.

Links between specific vitamins and intelligence have been borne out in two studies. An animal study conducted at the University of North Carolina and published in the March issue of *Developmental Brain Research* found that rats with a choline deficiency during pregnancy gave birth to offspring with severe brain impairments. Choline, a B-complex vitamin involved in nerve transmission, is found in eggs, meat, peanuts, and dietary supplements.

The August 1999 issue of the *New England Journal of Medicine* reported that expectant mothers with low thyroid function gave birth to children with markedly diminished IQs as well as motor and attention deficits. The study said one cause of hypothyroidism—present in 2 to 3 percent of American women—is a lack of iodine in the American diet. Women whose hypothyroidism was detected and treated before pregnancy had children with normal test scores. Hypothyroidism can be detected with a blood test, but expectant mothers who receive little or late prenatal care often go undiagnosed or are diagnosed too late to help their child.

Although most American women get the nutrition they need through diet and prenatal vitamins, not all do. According to a National Center for Health Statistics survey, more than one in four expectant mothers in the U.S. received inadequate prenatal care.

Devlin's *Nature* article took a parting shot at the conclusions reached in the 1994 book *The Bell Curve,* in which Richard J. Herrnstein and Charles Murray argued that different social classes are a result of genetically determined, and therefore unalterable, IQ levels. The lower the IQ, the argument goes, the lower the social class.

Not only does the data show IQ to be far less heritable than that book alleges, Devlin says, but he suspects improvements in the health status of mostly poor expectant mothers would see measurable increases in the IQs of their offspring.

Devlin's argument is supported by Randy Thornhill, a biologist at the University of New Mexico. Thornhill's research suggests that IQ differences are due in part to what he calls "heritable vulnerabilities to environmental sources of developmental stress." In other words, vulnerable genes interact with environmental insults in utero resulting in gene mutations that affect fetal development. Thornhill says environmental insults may include viruses, maternal drug abuse, or poor nutrition.

"The developmental instability that results," Thornhill says, "is most readily seen in the body's asymmetry when one side of the body differs from the other. For example, on average an individual's index fingers will differ in length by about two millimeters. Some people have much more asymmetries than others."

But the asymmetries we see on the outside also occur in the nervous system. When this happens, neurons are harmed and memory and intelligence are impaired. Thornhill says the more physical asymmetries you have, the more neurological impairment you have. He calculates that these factors can account for as much as 50 percent of the differences we find in IQ.

Thornhill adds that a fetus that carries these genetic vulnerabilities, but develops in an ideal uterine environment, will not experience any serious problems because the worrisome mutations will not occur.

"The practical implications for this are tremendous," Thornhill says. "If we can understand what environmental factors most disrupt fetal development of the nervous system, then we'll be in a position to remove them and have many more intelligent people born."

Studies on fetal IQ development suggest that the current emphasis on nurturance and stimulation for young children be rethought. The philosophy behind initiatives such as Zero to Three and Early Head Start makes sense. The programs are based on evidence that the first three years are very important for brain development and that early stimulation can effect positive changes in a child's life. But Devlin and Thornhill's research suggests a stronger public-health emphasis on a baby's prenatal life if we are to equalize the opportunities for children.

Does that mean unborn babies need to hear more Mozart? Companies are offering kits so expectant mothers can play music or different sounds to their developing babies—the prenatal "Mozart effect." One kit promises this stimulation will lead to "longer new-born attention span, better sleep patterns, accelerated development, expanded cognitive powers, enhanced social awareness and extraordinary language abilities." Will acceptance to Harvard come next?

"The number of bogus and dangerous devices available to expectant parents to make their babies smarter constantly shocks me," says DiPietro. "All these claims are made without a shred of evidence to support them."

Adds DeCasper: "I think it is dangerous to stimulate the baby in the womb. If you play Mozart and it remembers Mozart, is it going to be a smarter baby? I haven't got a clue. Could it hurt the baby? Yes, I think it could. If you started this stimulation too early and played it too loud, there is evidence from animal studies that you can destroy the ear's ability to hear sounds in a particular range. That's an established fact. Would I take a risk with my fetus? No!"

DeCasper and other researches emphasize that no devices or tricks can enhance the brainpower of a developing baby. Their advice to the expectant mother: Take the best possible care of yourself.

"The womb is a quiet, protective place for a reason," DiPietro concludes. "Nature didn't design megaphones to be placed on the abdomen. The fetus gets all the stimulation it needs for its brain to develop."

Mr. Pekkanen is a contributing editor to The Washingtonian. *From "Secrets of the Womb," by John Pekkanen,* The Washingtonian, *August 2001, pages 44–51, 126–135.*

From *Current*, September 2001, pp. 20-29. © 2001 by Current.

UNIT 2
Cognition, Language, and Learning

Unit Selections

Key Points to Consider

- If sex differences between boys and girls are based on evolutionary principles, should we still teach boys to be less aggressive or girls to be more independent? Explain why or why not.

- Do you think boys are at a serious academic disadvantage in schools? Why or why not? If boys are at a disadvantage, what steps should schools and parents take to correct this imbalance? Explain.

- According to Howard Gardner, there are eight intelligences. Do you think there are more? Explain.

- When you were learning to read in school, were you taught using the phonics or the whole-language approach? Did you think the method of teaching had any long-term consequences on your ability or liking of reading and spelling?

- In "Where the Boys Are," the article suggests that boys are being shortchanged by our schools. How do you reconcile this trend, given the research in recent years implicating greater discrimination and negative effects for girls rather than boys?

 **Links: www.dushkin.com/online/**
These sites are annotated in the World Wide Web pages.

Educational Resources Information Center (ERIC)
http://www.ed.gov/pubs/pubdb.html
I Am Your Child
http://iamyourchild.org
National Association for the Education of Young Children (NAEYC)
http://www.naeyc.org
Results of NICHD Study of Early Child Care
http://156.40.88.3/publications/pubs/early_child_care.htm
Vandergrift's Children's Literature Page
http://www.scils.rutgers.edu/special/kay/sharelit.html
Project Zero
http://pzweb.harvard.edu

We have come a long way from the days when the characterization of cognition of infants and young children included phrases like "tabula rasa" and "booming, buzzing confusion." Infants and young children are no longer viewed by researchers as blank slates, passively waiting to be filled up with knowledge. Today, experts in child development are calling for a reformulation of assumptions about children's cognitive abilities, as well as calling for reforms in the ways we teach children in our schools. Hence, the articles in the first subsection highlight some of the new knowledge of the cognitive abilities of infants and young children.

Recent brain development research indicates that newborns possess a number of impressive abilities. The essay "Categories in Young Children's Thinking" describes how scientists are discovering, by employing ingenious experimental techniques, that infants possess many heretofore unrealized skills that are heavily influenced by both nature and early experiences.

Parents today seem increasingly concerned with raising the "perfect" child. As a result, more parents have begun to question whether or not their infant or toddler is learning to crawl or walk on time. Increasingly it seems that some parents pressure their toddlers and children into becoming "geniuses. "The Quest for a Super Kid" helps to debunk some of these potentially harmful myths and provide parents with healthier perspectives and alternatives.

Researcher Patricia Bauer in "Long-term Recall Memory: Behavioral and Neuro-Developmental Changes in the First 2 Years of Life" presents data showing that even very young children under the age of 2 years possess rudimentary long-term memory abilities. The author goes on to link these developments in memory capacity to brain development.

What accounts for sex differences between boys and girls? Are boys and girls programmed by their genes to behave in certain ways or are these behavioral differences the result of socialization and culture? David Geary, in "Evolution and Developmental Sex Differences," argues that an evolutionary perspective along with cultural factors may help to explain some of these differences.

Learning to understand the thoughts and feelings of others is an important developmental milestone for children. The authors of "Do Young Children Understand What Others Feel, Want, and Know?" describe research showing how children often initially begin with intuitive or folk understandings and how parents and their culture can influence this progression.

How do you know if your child is gifted or not? Harvard psychologist Dr. Ellen Winner summarizes some of the research findings about the qualities and characteristics of gifted children and raises important future questions about the respective contributions of genetics and environment in creating and supporting gifted children.

Famed educator and author Howard Gardner in "The First Seven… and the Eighth" explains his theory of multiple intelligences—and how these abilities are influenced by teaching and learning.

Learning to read is an important hallmark achievement of children in school. The debate on the best method to teach children to read continues to generate heat. In "How Should Reading Be Taught?" the authors make the case that the "phonics" approach is more effective than the "whole-language" approach in helping young children learn to read and spell.

Recent controversy abounds on the topic of whether girls or boys are being shortchanged by our schools. Cathy Young in "Where the Boys Are" reviews the various camps on whether boys or girls are at more educational risk in elementary, secondary, and college settings and makes the case for balancing the record and rhetoric on this hot issue.

The Quest For A

SUPERKID

Geniuses are made, not born—or so parents are told.
But can we really train baby brains, and should we try?

By JEFFREY KLUGER with ALICE PARK

T OM MARTON AND DANIT BEN-ARI OF Brookline, Mass., have a cunning strategy for successful child rearing. Like most other parents, they wouldn't mind if their two daughters turned out to be among the next Mozarts or Martha Grahams or Mia Hamms. But essentially, they just want to help the girls get the most out of their lives. The key, they've decided, is the weekends, when they see to it that their daughters do… pretty much nothing at all.

Actually, "nothing at all" isn't quite accurate. If the girls, ages 4 and 7, want to sleep late, they do—as do Mom and Dad. After that, there's time for a family breakfast and a lazy morning and an afternoon of outside play or a museum trip or whatever else strikes the family's fancy. Monday, they all know, will come soon enough, and the girls will be going back to the high-stakes race of schoolwork and homework and ballet or chess or soccer practice. But until then, they are going to have a chance to breathe. "My children," Ben-Ari insists, "will have all the time they need simply to hang out and be children."

There was a time when kids being kids wasn't a radical notion. For generations,

childhood may have been life's one, true sweetheart deal: go to school six hours a day, take up hobbies or sports to keep your mind and body active, and the rest of the time you play. If along the way you turned out to have some remarkable talent or unexpected gift, fine. But that wasn't one of the job requirements.

In the past few years, however, all that has changed. At the dawn of the 21st century, a curious—and unsettling—transformation has come over American kids. The marvelously anarchic institution of childhood has been slowly turning into little more than an apprentice adulthood. Toddlers who once would have been years away from starting their formal education are being hothoused in nursery schools. Preschoolers who would have spent their time learning simply to play and share are being bombarded with flash cards, educational CD-ROMs and other gadgets designed to teach reading, writing and even second languages. Grade-schoolers are spending longer hours at school, still longer ones sweating over homework and filling what time they have left with a buffet line of outside activities that may or may not build

character but definitely build résumés. Kids who once had childhoods now have curriculums; kids who ought to move with the lunatic energy of youth now move with the high purpose of the worker bee.

The Myth

A MORE STIMULATED BRAIN IS A SMARTER ONE

Not true. Neurons grow explosively before age 5, but many may shut down after that. Stimulation can help babies learn skills, but overall aptitude is unchanged

The engine behind this early striving is, often, the parents, who are increasingly consumed by the idea that if they can't perfect their children, they must at least get them as close to that ideal as possible. And who can blame them? Birth rates, while short of baby-boom levels, are nonetheless robust, tightening the competition for spots in the best schools. At the same time, almost all those schools have democratized their admissions policies, meaning it's no longer just the élite who can attend. With competition getting ever keener, kids have to do ever more to distinguish themselves.

Parents are also driven by something a lot more primal: old-fashioned guilt. Even as men take on more responsibility for rearing children, the lion's share of baby care is still handled by mothers. But in an era in which it often takes two incomes to meet the monthly nut, increasing numbers of moms can't spend nearly as much time with their kids as they'd like. In 1999, 62% of mothers worked outside the home. That figure was 54% in 1985 and just 44% in 1975. "Parents feel tremendous guilt because they feel they're spreading themselves too thin," says Dr. Joshua Sparrow of Children's Hospital in Boston. "When parents have time, they can wait for things to happen," adds Rachelle Tyler, an M.D. and professor of pediatrics at UCLA. "But when they're pressured, they feel they've got to see their children respond now."

Into this anxious mix have stepped hucksters and marketers who see worried parents as the most promising pigeons. Store shelves groan with new products purported to stimulate babies' brains in ways harried parents don't have time for. There are baby Mozart tapes said to enhance spatial reasoning and perhaps musical and artistic abilities too. There are black, white and red picture books, said to sharpen visual acuity. There are bilingual products said to train baby brains so they will be more receptive to multiple languages. The hard sell even follows kids to the one place you'd think they'd be allowed some peace—the womb—with hand-held tummy speakers designed to pipe music and voices to the unborn baby, the better to stimulate the growing brain and get it ready for the work it will eventually have to do. Parents who don't avail themselves of these products do so at their children's peril: the brain, they are told, has very limited windows for learning certain skills. Let them close, and kids may be set back forever.

But is any of this true? Is it possible to turn an ordinary kid into an exceptional kid? Even if it is, is it worth it to try? Is it better to steer children gently through childhood, letting them make some mistakes and take some scrapes and accept the fact that some of them may not be marked for excellence? Or is it better to strive for a family of superkids, knowing that they are getting the most out of their potential if not out of their youth? Clearly, many parents are caught up in that quest, even if they quietly harbor doubts about its merits. "Parents

have, to a large extent, lost confidence in themselves and in their own good judgment," says Peter Gorski, a committee chair of the American Academy of Pediatrics.

The Myth

LISTENING TO MUSIC CAN BOOST CREATIVITY

Nope. The so-called Mozart effect doesn't enhance artistic skills but may improve spatial skills. The effect is just temporary, though, and seen only in adults.

The phenomenon of the driven child has been coming for a while, but it was in 1994 that the new breed was truly born. That was the year the Carnegie Corp. published a 134-page report describing a "quiet crisis" among U.S. children, who it argued were being ill served by their twin-career parents and their often failing school systems. The report's findings were worrisome enough, but buried in its pages were two disturbing paragraphs warning that schoolkids might not be the only ones suffering; babies could be too. Young brains are extremely sensitive to early influences, the report cautioned, and the right—or wrong—stimuli could have a significant impact on later development.

Those paragraphs went off like a grenade in the otherwise unremarkable study. The press ran alarming stories about blameless children being left behind. The White House called a conference on childhood development. Parents snapped up news of both, hoping it wasn't too late to undo whatever damage they had unwittingly done to their kids. "Every parent began to worry," says John Bruer, president of the McDonnell Foundation and author of the book *The Myth of the First Three Years*. "They thought, 'If I don't have the latest Mozart CD, my child is going to jail rather than Yale?'"

In order to make up for their feared lapses, parents indeed started buying the approved kinds of music—and a whole lot more. A study conducted by Zero to Three, a nonprofit research group, found that almost 80% of parents with a high school education or less were assiduously using flash cards, television and computer games to try to keep their babies' minds engaged.

Child-development experts, however, consider these sterile tools inferior to more

social and emotional activities such as talking with or reading to children. These specialists agree that the only thing shown to optimize children's intellectual potential is a secure, trusting relationship with their parents. Time spent cuddling, gazing and playing establishes a bond of security, trust and respect on which the entire child-development pyramid is based. "We have given social and emotional development a back seat," says UCLA's Tyler, "and that's doing a great disservice to kids and to our society."

Trying to pump up children's IQs in artificial ways may also lead to increased stress on the kids, as the parents' anxiety starts to rub off. By four or five years old, the brains of stressed kids can start to look an awful lot like the brains of stressed adults, with increased levels of adrenaline and cortisol, the twitchy chemicals that fuel the body's fight-or-flight response. Keep the brain on edge long enough, and the changes become long-lasting, making learning harder as kids get older.

But the fact is, the kids don't have to feel so pressured—and neither do their parents. It is true, as the marketers say, that a baby's brain is a fast-changing thing. Far from passively sponging up information, it is busy from birth laying complex webs of neurons that help it grow more sophisticated each day. It takes anywhere from a year to five years, depending on the part of the brain, for this initial explosion of connections to be made, after which many of them shut down and wither away, as the brain decides which it will keep, which new ones it will need and which it can do without. During this period, it's important that babies get the right kinds of stimulation so their brains can make the right decisions. The right kinds of stimulation, however, may not be the ones people think they are.

Asked in a recent study what skills children need in order to be prepared for school, parents of kindergartners routinely cited definable achievements such as knowing numbers, letters, colors and shapes. Teachers, however, disagree. Far more important, they say, are social skills, such as sharing, interacting with others and following instructions. Kids who come to school with a mastery of these less showy abilities stand a better chance of knocking off not only reading and writing when they are eventually presented but everything else that comes along as well. "Intelligence is based on emotional adequacy," says child-development expert T. Berry Brazelton. "The concept of emotional intelligence is at the base of all this."

A SMART TOY GUIDE (Parents Not Included)

Marketers are offering an explosion of new products to parents who think they can make their kids smarter by simply pressing PLAY. That's a myth, but some toys are better than others.

	Birth to 1 Year	1 to 3 Years	3 to 5 Years	6 to 8 Years
	Babies are developing an attention span and motor control	*Toddlers are improving hand-eye coordination, developing the ability to count and to think symbolically*	*Preschoolers are acting out fantasies and may become interested in playing an instrument*	*Grade schoolers are learning to channel emotions, developing competitiveness*
GOOD	Fisher-Price **Kick & Play Piano** ($25) attaches to the crib. Babies learning to kick and grasp are rewarded with songs, sounds and trinkling lights. Once babies learn to sit, at around seven months, the toy can be played on the floor like a piano.	**Duplos,** the junior version of Legos, and other **building blocks** help strengthen sorting and fine-motor skills.	**Crayons** help kids express themselves and use their imagination. **Dress-up clothes** encourage role playing.	**Action figures** help kids express their feelings through a surrogate. **Monoploy** ($11) helps build strategic thinking.
FAIR	**Black-white-and-red toys** attract babies' attention, but researchers say kids learn to track moving objects at their own pace with or without these bold patterns.	LeapFrog's **Fun & Learn Phonics Bus** ($25) helps toddlers learn the alphabet, but teachers say that's what school is for. Best way to prepare kids for preschool: teach them how to share and follow directions.	**LeapPad Pro** talking books ($65) "read" to preschoolers, who can interrupt the story by pointing a "magic pen" at a word to hear it pronounced or at a picture to hear a sound effect. It's better—and cheaper—for parents to do the tutoring.	**Backyard Baseball CD-ROM** ($20) lets kids take a swing at managing a team. Of course, they also would benefit from actually playing ball.
HMMM...	**The Babbler** (%50) and foreign-language videos may introduce infants to a few sounds and words, but a language has to be spoken in the home for kids to become bilingual.	The **Baby Genius** product line and other music videos and CDs may soothe and entertain but won't make your kid any smarter.	Golden Books' *The Poky Little Puppy* **CD-ROM** ($15) and other interactive stories don't improve much on the paper versions—and they keep kids tied to a computer.	**Poo-Chi** ($20) outsold every toy last year except Hot Wheels cars. But the interactive dog restricts a child's imagination by programming play.

Compiled by Julie Rawe

Milestones in the Smart-Baby Industry

1984	1987	1995	1998	1999	2001
Wimmer-Ferguson's **Stim-Mobile** hits stores, launching a trend of black-white-and-red baby gear.	A study shows that preemies exposed to **music, massage and pictures** are more likely to develop normally.	First video targeting infant audiences, **Babymugs!**, which consists of babies making faces, debuts. It launches a whole new video industry. A study published on the **"Mozart effect"** leads to the belief that classical music makes kids smarter. Sales of pregaphones, which are headphones worn on an expectant mother's belly, boom.	Georgia Governor **Zell Miller** allocates $105,000 in his budget proposal to give every newborn a classical CD or cassette; mompreneur Julie Aigner-Clark sells $1 million worth of her *Baby Mozart* and *Baby Einstein* videos.	"Mozart effect" co-author reports that test scores improve when kids make music rather than just listen to it: companies begin cranking out **instruments** for infants and toddlers.	American Academy of Pediatrics advises against letting kids under 2 watch **TV.** The group initiates the first studies on the effect of **computers** on young children. The findings won't be ready until next year.

It may not even be possible to prod children's intellectual growth. As babies' brains weave their neuronal connections, parents may be able to stimulate, say, the visual or musical ones by exposing kids to picture books or CDs, but it is doubtful that these fortify the brain in any meaningful way. "It's a myth that we can accelerate a child's developmental milestones," says Alan Woolf, a pediatrician at Children's Hospital. "Children are kind of preprogrammed to reach those points." Bruer puts it more bluntly: "The idea that you can provide more synapses by stimulating the child more has no basis in science."

One of the greatest sources of misunderstanding surrounds the so-called Mozart effect. For years researchers have found that playing background music can improve the spatial skills of listeners, causing many laymen to conclude that creative skills can be boosted too. Last year Harvard University released a study called Project Zero that analyzed 50 years of research on this idea. The studies showed that college students who had listened to music performed better on paper-and-pencil spatial tests, but the effect lasted no more than 15 minutes and then faded away. There was no evidence that the listening improved brain power or artistic skills, and certainly none that suggested babies could realize any benefit at all.

Many other misconceptions about brain potential can probably be traced to a series of studies in the 1970s showing that young rats raised with access to mazes and toys had more neural connections than those kept in barren cages. Similarly, studies indicate that children raised without sufficient nurturing often suffer from cognitive deficiencies. However, no evidence indicates that a lot of attention, in the form of early and constant stimulation, enhances a child's intellectual growth. According to the current scientific literature, the type and amount of stimulation needed for proper childhood development is already built into the normal life of an average baby. No whizbang tricks are necessary.

Parents might find it easier to believe all this if it weren't for the increasingly fashionable theory of windows of opportunity for learning—the idea that there are comparatively narrow periods when various parts of the brain can be taught various types of skills. What gives the theory special weight is that there is, in fact, a little truth to it—but only very little. When it comes to language—perhaps the most nuanced skill a person can master—the brain does appear to have fertile and less fertile periods. At birth, babies have the potential to learn any language with equal ease, but by six months, they have begun to focus on the one tongue they hear spoken most frequently. Parents can take advantage of this brain plasticity by introducing a second or even third language, but only if they intend to speak them all with equal frequency until the child is fluent. Merely buying the occasional bilingual toy or videotape will teach kids little, and it certainly will not make it easier for children to learn for real when they get to school.

When it comes to other skills, such as math or music, there is virtually no evidence for learning windows at all. Children grasp things at different rates, and parents whose child can read by age 3 may thus conclude that they somehow threaded the teaching needle perfectly, introducing letters and words at just the right time. But the reality is often that they simply got lucky and had a kid who took a shine early on to a particular skill. "People took the notion of a critical period and misunderstood it to apply to all learning," says Dr. Sparrow of Children's Hospital.

So if parents should be putting down the brain toys, what should they be picking up? For one thing, the kids themselves. If interpersonal skills are the true predictors of how well a child will do in school, parents are the best tutors. Experiments reveal that by the time babies are two months old, they are already fluent in the complex language of their parents' faces, and count on them for their sense of well-being. "Think about the human face," says Sparrow, "the wrinkles, the expressions in the eyes—and think about the infant brain being stimulated by that." To believe that even the best video game or toy could replace this kind of learning, Sparrow thinks, misses the point of just what it is babies are truly hungering to know.

Does this mean educational toys are useless? No. Babies are as engaged by pictures as adults are, and exposing them to books or flash cards early—especially black, white and red ones, which are indeed easier for them to perceive—helps them develop their ability to focus and follow, undeniably a form of learning. Babies are as soothed by music as their parents are, and a little Mozart may indeed hold their attention better than something less rich. Beyond that, however, there's a limit to what the products can do—and parents who follow their children's cues quickly learn that. "When our son was little, all he wanted to do was play with us," says Sharon Chantiles, a casting director and the mother of a four-year-old. "I decided to walk away from the fancy toys and invest in him as a child."

What's at stake for parents is far more than simply a child's school transcript or college options; it's a child's spirit. Recently, author David Brooks spent time on the campus of Princeton University getting to know the students, and he published what he learned in a searching article in the *Atlantic* magazine. The students were thoroughbred products of the American educational system—gifted, disciplined, driven to succeed, with a calm but consuming focus. And, Brooks found, they were curiously flattened too. There was no evidence of the wildfire energy of the college student, no evidence of much moral passion. More troublingly, there was no sign at all of the sweet and fleeting belief that they could try things and fail at them and try other things and discard them until they found something that truly touched and transformed them—and that they could do for the rest of their lives.

It's a high-stakes game letting kids roll the dice with their futures this way, and the risk—indeed the certainty—exists that at least a few of them will fail. But with their parents standing watchfully by, they need to be allowed to try. The more chances kids take, the greater the odds they will come up winners—and the chips they collect if they do can be priceless.

From *Time*, April 30, 2001, pp. 50-55. © 2001 by Time Inc. Reprinted by permission.

Long-Term Recall Memory: Behavioral and Neuro-Developmental Changes in the First 2 Years of Life

Patricia J. Bauer[1]
Institute of Child Development, University of Minnesota, Minneapolis, Minnesota

Abstract
Until not long ago, psychologists conceptually and methodologically linked the capacity for recall of the past to developments in language. With the advent of a nonverbal measure of recall, this association has been challenged. It now is apparent that the capacity for long-term recall emerges well before the verbal ability to describe past experiences. Long-term recall is newly (or recently) emergent late in the 1st year of life; over the 2nd year, it consolidates and becomes reliable. The course of age-related changes in mnemonic behavior is consistent with current understanding of developments in the neural substrate implicated in recall memory.

Keywords
    development; memory; recall; developmental neuroscience

The late 20th century was witness to a pronounced change in perspective on the mnemonic abilities of infants and young children. For much of the century, children younger than 18 to 24 months were thought unable to represent information not available to the senses (i.e., to *re-present* it; Piaget, 1952), and, as a consequence, to live in a "here and now" world. That is not to say that infants were considered to lack all forms of memory. On the contrary, there was ample evidence that they could be conditioned and could recognize some types of stimuli (e.g., faces) even after a delay (see Bauer, in press, for a review). Conspicuously absent from the literature, however, was compelling evidence of recall and, in particular, long-term recall. In contrast to recognition, recall involves accessing a cognitive structure based in past experience in the absence of ongoing perceptual support. We engage in recall when we think about what we had for dinner last evening or about the beautiful hotel in which we stayed on our first trip to Italy. Both conceptually and methodologically, the capacity for recall has been linked with the ability to provide a verbal report. Because infants are without language, they were thought to lack this fundamental competence.

The assumption that infants were without an ability that most adults take for granted seemingly was supported by research on adults' memories of childhood: The average age of earliest verbalizable memory is 3 1/2 years, and adults report fewer memories from ages 3 1/2 to 7 than expected based on forgetting alone (e.g., West & Bauer, 1999). This phenomenon of *infantile amnesia*, described by Freud (1916/1966) as "the amnesia that veils our earliest youth from us and makes us strangers to it" (p. 326), is one of the great curiosities in the field. As recently as the middle 1980s, investigators were stymied in their attempts to examine one possible explanation for the paucity of early memories, namely, that infants simply are unable to form them. A major impediment was how to assess recall in an organism not adept at language. Even in the 3rd year, when children readily talk about the present, they do not easily talk about the past. This reality, and the fact that the average age of adults' first memories is 3 1/2, reinforced the notion that age 3 years marked the onset of the ability to recall.

TESTING RECALL NONVERBALLY

The opportunity to test the assumption that preverbal children lack the capacity for recall was afforded by development of a nonverbal analogue to verbal report: elicited imitation. Elicited imitation involves using objects to produce an action or action sequence, and then allowing the infant or child to imitate. For example, to *make a gong*, children are given a base resembling the support for a swing set, a bar sized to span the distance between the posts of the base, a metal plate with a lip, and a mallet. The experimenter models (a) putting the bar across the posts (to form a crosspiece), (b) hanging the plate from the bar, and (c) "ringing" the gong by hitting the plate with the mallet (see Bauer, in press, for other examples and procedural detail).

There are excellent reasons to believe that elicited imitation is a nonverbal analogue to verbal report. First, Piaget (1952) himself viewed imitation after exposure to a model as one of the hallmarks of representational capacity. Second, once children have the linguistic capacity to do so, they talk about events experienced in the context of imitation (see Bauer, in press, for a review). This is strong evidence that the representational format in which the memories are encoded is compatible with language, if not itself symbolic. Third, the paradigm passes the "amnesia test." That is, adults suffering from temporal lobe amnesia (a condition that impairs the ability to form new memories that can be brought to awareness) are unable to perform an age-appropriate version of the task (McDonough, Mandler, McKee, &

Squire, 1995). This suggests that the imitation procedure taps the type of memory that gives rise to recall (see Bauer, in press, for development of this argument). Multistep sequences are especially well suited to evaluation of recall because ordered reproduction of them cannot be accomplished through recognition. Once demonstration of a sequence is complete, information about the order of actions is not perceptually available. To reproduce a sequence in order, a person must retrieve temporal information from a representation of the event, in the absence of ongoing perceptual support. In this requirement, the task is analogous to verbal report.

LONG-TERM RECALL IN THE FIRST 2 YEARS

Using imitation, researchers have found evidence of long-term recall in children well under 3 years of age. Indeed, it appears that long-term recall processes are emergent by 9 months, and that they become reliable over the 2nd year.

Change in the Reliability of Long-Term Recall

In one study, Carver and I tested 9-month-olds' recall of two-step sequences after a 1-month delay (Carver & Bauer, 1999). As a group, the 9-month-olds recalled the individual actions of the events. That is, after 1 month, the infants produced more actions from the events to which they had been exposed than from new, control events. However, only 45% of the infants evidenced ordered recall (i.e., performed the actions in the order in which they had been modeled). This same pattern was apparent in a second study (Bauer, Wiebe, Waters, & Bangston, 2001), in which 43% of 9-month-olds evidenced ordered recall. Thus, there are substantial individual differences in long-term ordered recall at 9 months. Nevertheless, the behavior of 9-month-olds differs from

that of 6-month-olds, only a small proportion (25%) of whom evidence ordered recall after as few as 24 hr (Barr, Dowden, & Hayne, 1996).

During the 2nd year of life, long-term recall becomes increasingly reliable. In another study (Bauer, Wenner, Dropik, & Wewerka, 2000), children were enrolled at 13, 16, or 20 months of age and tested for recall of multistep sequences after delays of 1, 3, 6, 9, or 12 months. Figure 1 shows the results for ordered recall. In contrast to 9-month-olds, only roughly half of whom demonstrate ordered recall after 1 month (e.g., Bauer et al., 2001), between 78 and 100% of 13-, 16-, and 20-month-olds evidenced ordered recall at this delay. As delay increased, fewer children maintained order information; also, the younger the children were at the time they experienced the events, the faster they "dropped out." These data thus indicate age-related increases in the reliability of long-term ordered recall.

Changes in the Robustness of Long-Term Recall

At 9 months, when the capacity for long-term recall is newly or recently emergent, the ability is fragile: It depends on multiple experiences of events. If infants receive fewer than three exposures to events before the delay, at most only 21% of them demonstrate ordered recall after 1 month (Bauer et al., 2001). In contrast, by 13 months, a single experience supports ordered recall (see Bauer, in press, for a review). Nevertheless, over the 2nd year, there are changes in the robustness of memory. For example, my colleagues and I have found reliable age differences in the amount of information retained across delay intervals of 1 to 12 months: Older children recall more than younger children (Bauer et all, 2000). Age effects are especially apparent in recall of temporal order (as opposed to individual actions), and when greater cognitive demands are imposed (e.g., when

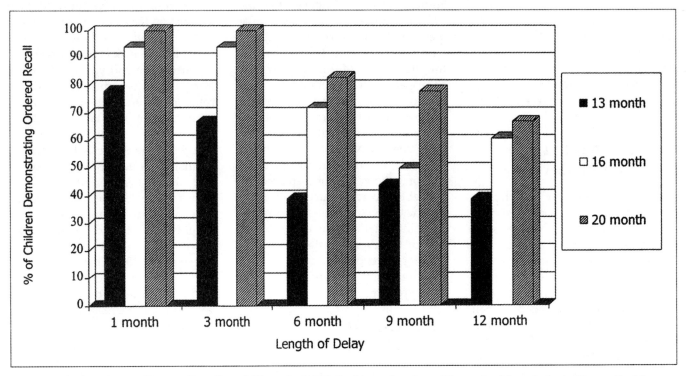

Fig. 1. Results from Bauer, Wenner, Dropik, and Wewerka (2000). In this study, ninety 13-month-olds and ninety 16-month-olds were tested on three-step sequences; ninety 20-month-olds and ninety 16-month-olds were tested on four-step sequences. Differences in sequence length accommodated age-related changes in the lengths of sequences that children can accurately imitate (see Bauer, in press, for a review). At each of three sessions, spaced 1 week apart, the children were exposed to the same six sequences, three of which they never were permitted to imitate, and three of which they were permitted to imitate one time, at the end of the third exposure session. After intervals of 1, 3, 6, 9, or 12 months, the children were tested for recall of the six sequences to which they previously had been exposed, as well as on three new sequences, as a within-subjects control. Because performance did not differ as a function of whether imitation was permitted, the data are collapsed across this manipulation. The values indicate the percentage of children of each age who performed at higher levels on previously experienced relative to control sequences, thereby indicating recall. The values shown for 16-month-olds are for those tested with four-step sequences; the same pattern applies to the 16-month-olds tested on three-step sequences (see Bauer et al., 2000, for details).

delays are increased). In addition, age effects are greatest when children's recall is supported by event-related props alone. When verbal reminders of the sequences are provided, age differences diminish.

Together, changes in the reliability and robustness of long-term recall late in the 1st year and throughout the 2nd year of life are suggestive of consolidation of mnemonic function in this time frame. Whereas at 9 months of age, individual differences in recall after a 1-month delay are the rule, by 13 months, they are the exception. Over the 2nd year, children gain the capacity to recall over longer delays, and by 20 months, almost 70% of children show temporally ordered recall after as many as 12 months have passed.

DEVELOPMENTS IN THE NEURAL SUBSTRATE OF LONG-TERM MEMORY

Available data on age-related changes in the reliability and robustness of long-term recall during the first 2 years of life are consistent with what is known about development of the neural substrate that subserves recall memory. In adult humans, the formation, maintenance, and retrieval of memories over the long term is thought to depend on a multicomponent neural network involving temporal and cortical structures (e.g., Markowitsch, 2000). Briefly, upon experience of an event, sensory and motor inputs from multiple brain regions distributed throughout the cortex are thought to converge on parahippocampal struc-

tures within the temporal lobes (e.g., entorhinal cortex). The work of binding the elements together to create a durable, integrated memory trace is carried out by another temporal lobe structure, the hippocampus. Prefrontal structures in the front of the brain are implicated in retrieval of memories after a delay. Thus, long-term recall requires multiple corital regions, including prefrontal cortex; temporal structures; and intact connections between them.

Given that long-term recall memory depends on a multicomponent neural network, it is logical to expect that it will emerge as the structures and their interconnections reach a minimum level of functional maturity. In primates, most of the hippocampus matures early. Indeed, some of the earliest apparent forms of memory, such as conditioning, likely depend on the hippocampus for maintenance, retrieval, or both (C. A. Nelson, 1997). Evidence of young infants' recall of single actions over brief delays (Barr et all, 1996) also is consistent with early maturity of portions of the hippocampal formation. In contrast, the dentate gyrus of the hippocampus (a critical link through which outputs from parahippocampal structures project to the hippocampal formation), the prefrontal cortex (implicated in retrieval from long-term stores), and temporal-cortical connections are later to develop. The full network begins to coalesce in the second half of the 1st year of life; it continues to develop for months thereafter (see, e.g., C. A. Nelson, 1997, for a review). This time frame is consistent with the behavioral observations of emergence of long-term ordered recall at 9 months of age (e.g., Bauer et al., 2001), and developments in its reliability and robustness over the course of the 2nd year (e.g., Bauer et al., 2000).

NEXT STEPS IN THE STUDY OF EARLY RECALL MEMORY

In a relatively short time, psychologists' understanding of the development of long-term recall ability has changed substantially and significantly. Although there are a number of unresolved questions that deserve attention, three areas for future research seem especially compelling. First, we need to know more about early neurocognitive developments. The current state of the art links changes in the developing brain to changes in behavior only loosely. Needed are more detailed models of how developmental changes in the underlying substrate for memory relate to changes in the reliability and robustness of recall. One likely candidate for developmental change is the efficiency with which memories are consolidated for long-term storage and subsequent retrieval. This possibility is consistent with research showing that individual differences in long-term recall correlate with electrophysiological indices of the integrity of the memory trace (Carver, Bauer, & Nelson, 2000).

Second, thus far we have made excellent progress in characterizing mean changes in long-term recall across age groups. We also have identified a number of factors that affect memory performance, such as the nature of the temporal connections in events, the number of exposures to the events, whether the infant or child actively participates by imitating the events, and the availability of reminders during recall (see Bauer et al., 2000, for a review). But these factors only influence memory; they do not determine it. Even once long-term recall becomes reliable and robust, there are individual differences in performance. What remains to be explained, then, is why some infants and children encode, store, and retrieve more information than their same-age peers. My colleagues and I have begun to examine how infants' and children's temperament characteristics relate to their long-term recall abilities. We have found that as the capacity for long-term recall is emerging and becoming reliable (i.e., at 9 to 13 months), the temperament characteristic of positive affect is positively related to memory performance. By 20 months of age, though, recall no longer is predicted by positive affect, but instead is predicted by the ability to sustain and focus attention (Bauer, Burch, & Kleinknecht, in press). In contrast to temperament, children's gender and vocabulary are not related to long-term recall performance.

A third avenue for future research is to determine how the early memory abilities tapped by paradigms such as elicited imitation develop into the deliberate memory skills tested in educational settings and the autobiographical or personal memory skills that are so essential and prominent in social settings. Reliable and robust encoding, storage, and retrieval of memories is necessary, but not sufficient, for these later-developing capacities. Preliminary findings from ongoing studies in my own and other laboratories (Catherine Haden at Loyola University and Peter Ornstein at the University of North Carolina, Chapel Hill) suggest continuity between early-developing recall memory skills and later strategic remembering. There already is strongly suggestive evidence that through conversations with more accomplished partners (e.g., parents), basic memory abilities are molded into narrative capacities that form the basis for autobiography (K. Nelson & Fivush, 2000). Investigations of how neurological developments relate to changes in the reliability and robustness of recall; why some infants and children encode, store, and retrieve more information than others; and how different aspects of mnemonic competence relate across development are important new directions that will ensure continued progress in the field of memory development.

Recommended Reading

Bauer, P. J. (in press). Building toward a past: Construction of a reliable long-term recall memory system. In N. L. Stein, P. J. Bauer, & M. Rabinowitz (Eds.), *Representation, memory, and development: Essays in honor of Jean M. Mandler.* Mahwah, NJ: Erlbaum.

Hudson, J. A., Fivush, R., & Kuebli, J. (1992). Scripts and episodes: The development of event memory. *Applied Cognitive Psychology, 6,* 483–505.

Moscovitch, M. (2000). Theories of memory and consciousness. In E. Tulving & F. I. M. Craik (Eds.), *The Oxford handbook of memory* (pp. 609–625). New York: Oxford University Press.

Mullen, M. K. (1994). Earliest recollections of childhood: A demographic analysis. *Cognition, 52,* 55–79.

Pillemer, D. (1998). What is remembered about early childhood events? *Clinical Psychology Review, 18,* 895–913.

Acknowledgments—Support for data collection was provided by the National Institute of Child Health and Human Development (HD-28425). I thank my many collaborators on the research described in this report, as well as the families and children who have so generously given of their time to make this work possible.

Note

1. Address correspondence to Patricia J. Bauer, Institute of Child Development, 51 East River Rd., University of Minnesota, Minneapolis, MN 55455-0345; e-mail: pbauer@umn.edu.

References

Barr, R., Dowden, A., & Hayne, H. (1996). Developmental changes in deferred imitation by 6- to 24-month-old infants. *Infant Behavior and Development, 19,* 159–170.

Bauer, P. J. (in press). New developments in the study of infant memory. In D. M. Teti (Ed.), *Handbook of research methods in developmental psychology.* Oxford, England: Blackwell.

Bauer, P. J., Burch, M. M., & Kleinknecht, E. E. (in press). Developments in early recall memory: Normative trends and individual differences. In R. Kail (Ed.), *Advances in child development and behavior.* San Diego, CA: Academic Press.

Bauer, P. J., Wenner, J. A., Dropik, P. L., & Wewerka, S. S. (2000). Parameters of remembering and forgetting in the transition from infancy to early childhood. *Monographs of the Society for Research in Child Development, 65*(4, Serial No. 263).

Bauer, P. J., Wiebe, S. A., Waters, J. M., & Bangston, S. K. (2001). Reexposure breeds recall: Effects of experience on 9-month-olds' ordered recall. *Journal of Experimental Child Psychology, 80,* 174–200.

Carver, L. J., & Bauer, P. J. (1999). When the event is more than the sum of its parts: Nine-month-olds' long-term ordered recall. *Memory, 7,* 147–174.

Carver, L. J., Bauer, P. J., & Nelson, C. A. (2000). Associations between infant brain activity and recall memory. *Developmental Science, 3,* 234–246.

Freud, S. (1966). The archaic features and infantilism of dreams. In J. Strachey (Ed. & Trans.), *Introductory lectures on psychoanalysis* (pp. 199–212). New York: Norton. (Original work published 1916).

Markowitsch, H. J. (2000). Neuroanatomy of memory. In E. Tulving & F. I. M. Craik (Eds.), *The Oxford handbook of memory* (pp. 465–484). New York: Oxford University Press.

McDonough, L., Mandler, J. M., McKee, R. D., & Squire, L. R. (1995). The deferred imitation task as a nonverbal measure of declarative memory. *Proceedings of the National Academy of Sciences, USA, 92,* 7580–7584.

Nelson, C. A. (1997). The neurobiological basis of early memory development. In N. Cowan (Ed.), *The development of memory in childhood* (pp. 41–82). Hove, England: Psychology Press.

Nelson, K., & Fivush, R. (2000). Socialization of memory. In E. Tulving & F. I. M. Craik (Eds.), *The Oxford handbook of memory* (pp. 283–295). New York: Oxford University Press.

Piaget, J. (1952). *The origins of intelligence in children.* New York: International Universities Press.

West, T. A., & Bauer, P. J. (1999). Assumptions of infantile amnesia: Are there differences between early and later memories? *Memory, 7,* 257–278.

Evolution and Developmental Sex Differences

David C. Geary[1] Department of Psychology, University of Missouri at Columbia, Columbia, Missouri

Abstract

From an evolutionary perspective, childhood is the portion of the life span during which individuals practice and refine those competencies that facilitate survival and reproduction in adulthood. Although the skeletal structure of these competencies appears to be inherent, social interaction and play flesh them out during childhood so that they are adapted to local conditions. Darwin's principles of sexual selection, including male-male competition over mates and female choice of mating partners, successfully explain the acquisition and expression of reproduction competencies in hundreds of species. When this perspective is applied to humans, it predicts sex differences that are, in fact, found in the childhood activities of boys and girls and that reflect sex differences in reproductive strategies in adulthood. A few of these differences are described, along with cultural factors that modify their expression. The article closes with a brief discussion of the social and scientific implications.

Keywords

sex differences; sexual selection; development; childhood; culture

Sex differences are inherently interesting to the scientist and layperson alike. They always have been and always will be. Although the existence of such differences has been debated in the past, the scientific issue today concerns the source of these differences. The prevailing view in psychology is that most sex differences result from children's adoption of gender roles, roles that reflect society-wide differences in daily activities of men and women (Eagly, 1987). The goal here is not to provide a review or appraisal of this position, but rather to offer an alternative view of developmental sex differences, a view based on the principles of evolution (Darwin, 1871).

From an evolutionary perspective, cultural and ecological factors are expected to influence the expression of developmental sex differences, and a few of these influences are described in the final section. Before they are discussed, though, a basic evolutionary framework for understanding sex differences in general and developmental sex differences in particular is provided in the first section, and the second provides a few examples of the usefulness of this approach for understanding human developmental sex differences.

EVOLUTION AND DEVELOPMENT

Sexual Selection

One of Darwin's (1871) seminal contributions was the observation that evolutionary pressures often differ for males and females and that many of these differences center around the dynamics of reproduction. These pressures are termed sexual selection and typically result from males competing with one another for social status, resources, or territory—whatever is needed to attract mates—and from females' choice of mating partners (Andersson, 1994). Although the dynamics of male-male competition can vary across species and social and ecological conditions, one common result is the evolution of physical (see Fig. 1), cognitive, and behavioral sex differences. Females' choice of mates has been studied most extensively in birds, although it is also evident in insects, fish, reptiles, and mammals, including humans (Andersson, 1994; Buss, 1994). Females typically choose mates on the basis of indicators of physical, genetic, or behavioral fitness, that is, on the basis of traits that signal a benefit to them (e.g., provisioning) or their offspring (e.g., good genes). One example of the evo-

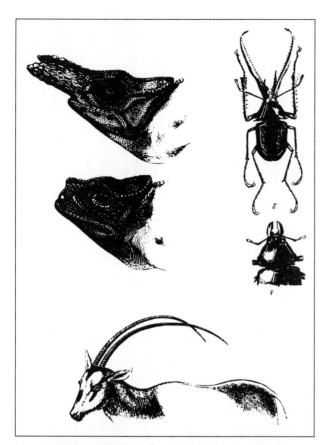

Fig. 1. Examples of sexually selected characteristics used in physical male-male competition. The pair in the upper left are the male (top) and female (bottom) of the *Chamaeleon bifurcus*; the pair in the upper right are the male and female of the beetle *Chiasognathus grantii*; at the bottom is a male *Oryx leucoryx*, a species of antelope (females do not have horns). From Darwin (1871, Vol. II, p. 35; Vol. I, p. 377; and Vol. II, p. 251, respectively). These exaggerated male characteristics are used in male-on-male aggression. For instance, two male *Oryx leucoryx* will compete by kneeling in front of each other, each then trying to maneuver the points of his horns under the body of his competitor. "If one succeeds in doing this, he suddenly springs up, throwing up his head at the same time, and can thus wound or perhaps even transfix his antagonist" (Darwin, 1871, Vol. II, pp. 251-252).

lutionary result of female choice is shown in Figure 2; the long and symmetric tail feathers of the male hummingbird are an indicator of his physical and genetic health.

Male-male competition and female choice are most evident in species in which males devote most of their reproductive energies to attracting mates, and females provide most or all of the parental care (Trivers, 1972), a pattern found in nearly 97% of mammalian species (Clutton-Brock, 1991). As is the case with other mammals, women throughout the world invest more time and resources in the well-being of their children than men do (Geary, 1998). Nonetheless, many men do provide some investment in the well-being of their children, unlike most other mammalian males. Paternal care, in turn, results in female-female competition and male choice of mates, along with male-male competition and female choice of mates.

The sex difference in the level of parental investment, along with other features (see Geary, 1998), results in dif-

ferences in the nature of male-male versus female-female competition, and in the criteria used in mate choice (Geary, 1998). Throughout the world, men compete with one another for the control of culturally prized resources (e.g., status, money, or cows), and they often do so through physical contests (Keeley, 1996). Women compete with one another by means of relational aggression. They gossip, shun, and backbite their competitors (Crick, Casas, & Mosher, 1997). Both men and women want intelligent and cooperative spouses, but women more than men focus on the cultural success (e.g., control of money or cows) of suitors and men more than women focus on physical attractiveness (indicators of fertility; Buss, 1994).

Development

Biologists study development by documenting species' life history and by discerning the function of childhood. Life history refers to the typical ages associated with developmental milestones, such as age of weaning and length of childhood. The function of childhood is to refine the competencies that will be needed to survive and reproduce in adulthood (Mayr, 1974). It appears that many cognitive and behavioral systems are initially skeletal in structure—the basic framework is inborn—but are fleshed out as juveniles play, explore the environment, and interact socially (Gelman, 1990). Fleshing out these competencies results in the refinement of those skills needed to survive and reproduce in the local ecology and social group.

Developmental sex differences are expected to the degree that reproductive demands differ for male and females in adulthood. In species in which male-male competition is more intense than female-female competition, the juvenile period is longer for males than for females. Male satin bowerbirds *(Ptilonorhynchus violaceus)*, for instance, mature many years after females have matured. Although there is some physical competition, males largely compete behaviorally, through the construction of complex stick structures called bowers. (Females make their mate choices, in part, on the basis of the complexity of these bowers.) During development, "young males spend a great deal of time observing older males at their bower, and practice bower building and display behaviors when the owner is absent from the bower site" (Collis & Borgia, 1992, p. 422). Young males also engage in play fighting, which provides the experience needed for dominance-related encounters in adulthood. Thus, delayed maturation and associated play allow for the refinement of those physical, cognitive, and behavioral skills associated with reproductive demands in adulthood.

HUMAN DEVELOPMENTAL SEX DIFFERENCES

Play Patterns

Play, in one form or another, is found in most mammalian species. "The consensus that emerges from the scores of definitions is that play incorporates many physical components of adult behavior patterns, such as those used in aggression, but without their immediate functional consequences" (Walters, 1987, p. 360). Play provides delayed benefits because the individual practices those behaviors that are important for survival and reproduction in adulthood, as described earlier. Sex differences in play patterns are found in many species and mirror sex differences found in adulthood.

Like juveniles of other mammalian species, boys and girls exhibit sex differences in their play patterns, and these differences in play are a reflection of sex differences found in adulthood (Geary, 1998). One of the most consistently found differences is in the frequency and nature of rough-and-tumble play. Beginning at about 3 years of age, groups of boys engage in various forms of play fighting, such as wrestling, three to six times more frequently than groups of girls do. Boys also engage in group-level competitive play (e.g., football) more frequently than girls do. These patterns are found in every culture in which play has been studied, are related to prenatal exposure to male hormones, and mirror the activities associated with primitive warfare (Keeley, 1996). The one-on-one and group-level play fighting of boys can be viewed as an evolved tendency to practice the competencies that were associated with male-male competition during human evolution (Geary, 1998).

Another sex difference, this one favoring girls, is in the frequency of play parenting (e.g., doll play): Play parenting is the norm in female primates and has been shown to significantly reduce the mortality rates of their first-born offspring. Again, this sex difference is found in all cultures in which play has been studied, is related to prenatal exposure to sex hormones, and mirrors the adult sex difference in investment in children. Play parenting can thus be understood as an evolved tendency to seek out activities that will enhance later parenting skills.

Social Development

Beginning in the preschool years and extending throughout the life span, girls and boys and women and men tend to segregate themselves into same-sex groups. One result is that boys and girls grow up in different social cultures. The tendency of boys to play fight and to organize themselves into competing groups is manifested in the context of the boys' culture. Social relationships among girls, in contrast, are more consistently communal: They manifest greater empathy; more concern for the well-being of other girls; and more nurturing, intimacy, and social and emotional support. In short, the social behavior of boys is focused on achieving status and dominance and developing coalitions for competing against groups of other boys. The social behavior of girls is focused on developing and maintaining a network of personal relationships and social support. Similar sex differences have been found in our closest relative,

Fig. 2. Female (left) and male (right) hummingbirds (*Spathura underwoodi*). From Darwin (1871, Vol. II, p. 77). The long and symmetric tail feathers of the male appear to signal to the female that he has immune-system genes that can confer resistance to local parasites (e.g., worms). If she mates with this male, then her offspring will also be resistant to local parasites.

the chimpanzee, suggesting that these are indeed evolved tendencies in humans (de Waal, 1993).

Nonetheless, girls and women can be quite competitive with one another. As noted earlier, this competition takes the form of relational aggression—attempting to disrupt the personal networks that are important to girls and women—and in adulthood, it is often associated with competition over resources (e.g., job promotion) and mates. As is the case with play fighting in boys, relational aggression emerges in the preschool years for girls and appears to be especially intense during early adolescence. It is likely, although not certain, that relational aggression has been shaped by sexual selection and in childhood is practice for later female-female competition.

CULTURAL AND ECOLOGICAL INFLUENCES

If the function of childhood is to adapt inherent skeletal competencies to local conditions, then cultural and ecological factors should influence the expression of developmental sex differences (Gelman, 1990; Mayr, 1974). Although research conducted within Western countries suggests that parents do not influence children's development as strongly as many people assume, cross-cultural studies suggest that there are important socialization influences on the expression (not creation) of developmental sex differences.

Although boys throughout the world engage in one-on-one and group-level competitive play, the nature and intensity of this play varies across cultures. The play fighting of boys tends to be rougher in societies where male-on-male physical aggression is common in adulthood than in other societies. For instance, intergroup aggression occurs frequently among the Yanomamö Indians of South America, and young Yanomamö boys often play fight with clubs or bows and arrows, practices that are typically discouraged in suburban America. In such societies, boys' play fighting often involves inflicting physical pain and sometimes injury, and there are often social rules that discourage boys from expressing this pain. In other words, boys' play fighting is encouraged and channeled to increase the aggressiveness and physical endurance of boys, and decrease their sensitivity to the distress of other people. These practices prepare boys for the life-and-death male-male competition that they will experience as adults. In other societies, such as our own, boys also play fight, but this behavior is relatively subdued and symbolic, as in competitive sports.

In a study of 93 cultures, Low (1989) found that the socialization of girls and boys was systematically related to the cultures' social structures (e.g., stratified vs. nonstratified societies) and marriage systems (i.e., polygynous vs. monogamous). In nonstratified polygynous societies—where men could improve their social status and thus increase the number of women they could marry—the socialization of boys focused on fortitude, aggression, and industriousness, traits that would influence their cultural and reproductive success in adulthood. For these societies, there was a strong linear relation between the socialization of competitiveness in boys and the maximum harem size allowed within the society. The larger the maximum harem size, the more the competitiveness of boys was emphasized in parental socialization.

For girls, there was a relation between the amount of economic and political power held by women in the society and socialization practices. In societies where women could inherit property and hold political office, girls were socialized to be less obedient, more aggressive, and more achievement oriented than were girls who lived in societies in which men had control over economic and political resources. On the basis of these and other patterns, Low (1989) concluded that "there is thus some evidence that patterns of child training across cultures vary in ways predictable from evolutionary theory, differing in specifiable ways between the sexes, and varying with group size, marriage system, and stratification" (p. 318).

CONCLUSION

From an evolutionary perspective, early biases in the ways in which boys and girls orient themselves to other people, in their play patterns, and in how they interact with and explore the wider ecology are expected, and, in fact, such biases are found (Geary, 1998). They lead girls and boys to create different cultures for themselves, and within these cultures to engage in activities that prepare them for the adult life of our ancestors. At the same time, a long childhood and the associated sensitivity to environmental influences ensure that the differences between boys and girls and men and women are not fixed, but rather are responsive to changing social and ecological conditions.

The combination of biological biases and sensitivity to early environmental conditions has important scientific and social implications. For instance, although boys and men are biologically destined to compete, this competition need not be deadly nor even physical, even if the evolutionary history of male-male competition was both physical and deadly (Keeley, 1996). One goal of psychological research, then, is to understand the social and ecological conditions that can push boys and men into deadly physical competition or to compete in ways that are socially beneficial (e.g., that lead to economic development). An evolutionary perspective on development highlights the importance of social and ecological factors in the expression of developmental sex differences and will provide an important theoretical framework for the study of the social and psychological aspects of these differences.

Recommended Reading

Buss, D.M. (1994). (See References)

Darwin, C. (1871). (See References)

Geary, D.C. (1998). (See References)

Morbeck, M.E., Galloway, A., & Zihlman, A.L. (Eds.). (1997). *The evolving female: A life-history perspective.* Princeton, NJ: Princeton University Press.

Note

1. Address correspondence to David C. Geary, Department of Psychology, 210 McAlester Hall, University of Missouri, Columbia, MO 65211-2500; e-mail: gearyd@missouri.edu.

References

Andersson, M. (1994). *Sexual selection.* Princeton, NJ: Princeton University Press.
Buss, D.M. (1994). *The evolution of desire: Strategies of human mating.* New York: Basic Books.
Clutton-Brock, T.H. (1991). *The evolution of parental care.* Princeton, NJ: Princeton University Press.
Collis, K., & Borgia, G. (1992). Age-related effects of testosterone, plumage, and experience on aggression and social dominance in juvenile male satin bowerbirds (*Ptilonorhynchus violaceus*). *Auk, 109,* 422–434.
Crick, N.R., Casas, J.F., & Mosher, M. (1997). Relational and overt aggression in preschool. *Developmental Psychology, 33,* 579–588.
Darwin, C. (1871). *The descent of man and selection in relation to sex* (2 vols.). London: J. Murray.

de Waal, F.B.M. (1993). Sex differences in chimpanzee (and human) behavior: A matter of social values? In M. Hechter, L. Nadel, & R.E. Michod (Eds.), *The origin of values* (pp. 285–303). New York: Aldine de Gruyter.

Eagly, A.H. (1987). *Sex differences in social behavior: A social-role interpretation*. Hillsdale, NJ: Erlbaum.

Geary, D.C. (1998). *Male, female: The evolution of human sex differences*. Washington, DC: American Psychological Association.

Gelman, R. (1990). First principles organize attention to and learning about relevant data: Number and animate-inanimate distinction as examples. *Cognitive Science, 14,* 79–106.

Keeley, L.H. (1996). *War before civilization: The myth of the peaceful savage*. New York: Oxford University Press.

Low, B.S. (1989). Cross-cultural patterns in the training of children: An evolutionary perspective. *Journal of Comparative Psychology, 103,* 311–319.

Mayr, E. (1974). Behavior programs and evolutionary strategies. *American Scientist, 62,* 650–659.

Trivers, R.L. (1972). Parental investment and sexual selection. In B. Campbell (Ed.), *Sexual selection and the descent of man 1871–1971* (pp. 136–179). Chicago: Aldine Publishing.

Walters, J.R. (1987). Transition to adulthood. In B.B. Smuts, D.L. Cheney, R.M. Seyfarth, R.W. Wrangham, & T.T. Struhsaker (Eds.), *Primate societies* (pp. 358–369). Chicago: University of Chicago Press.

From *Current Directions in Psychological Science,* August 1999, pp. 115–120. © 1999 by the American Psychological Society. Reprinted by permission of Blackwell Publishers, Ltd.

Categories in Young Children's Thinking

Susan A. Gelman

The world is potentially a bewildering place for young children. Every day a child's senses are bombarded by countless different sights, sounds, tastes, and smells. Furthermore, all this variety is constantly changing, since the world is not a static place: people move, voices come and go, TV images flit across the screen, and new smells waft in as meals are served. In the nineteenth century William James (1890) suggested that infants and young children are overwhelmed by all this diversity, and they experience the world as a "blooming, buzzing confusion." Over the past few decades, however, researchers have discovered that even young children are able to make sense of the world by forming categories. A *category* is any grouping of things that are different in some way. Every time children use a word, put away a toy in the toy box, recognize a person's gender, or decide that a particular food is "yucky," they are using categories to organize their experience. Simple words like "doggie," "milk," or "ball" are among children's earliest categories of the world around them.

Researchers have consistently found that even newborns form sensible categories of simple sights, sounds, tastes, and smells. In some ways babies seem to be born knowing how to carve up the world into categories.

This article will review some of the research on children's early categories. One of the most important findings from recent studies is that children can be quite sophisticated in how they group objects and think about those groupings. Children certainly do view the world somewhat differently from adults. However, the picture that emerges from recent research is that young children's categories are extremely important for guiding how they think about the world at large.

Early errors

Many past studies have shown that preschool children's categories differ from those of older children or adults. One primary difference is that the preschooler is more focused on superficial properties: how things look or where they can be found. We can see this with children's earliest words. Children younger than about age two-and-a-half typically "overextend" their words by applying them in overly broad ways, such as calling any round object a ball or any four-legged animal a dog (Clark 1973). These overextension errors have been documented in children learning a variety of languages across many different cultures.

Piaget's own observations suggest that throughout early childhood children form categories that seem immature from the standpoint of an adult (Inhelder & Piaget 1964). For example, if a five-year-old is asked to sort a set of plastic shapes, he might arrange them into a picture (such as putting a triangle on top of a square to form a house) rather than place together those of the same shape (such as separating all the triangles from all the squares). Likewise, preschool children often tend to put together items that go together in a scene rather than items that are alike in more fundamental ways. For instance, if a four-year-old is given pictures of a spider, a grasshopper, and a web and is asked to "put together the ones that go together," she typically will place the spider with the web (a *thematic* grouping) rather than with the grasshopper (a *taxonomic* grouping) (Smiley & Brown 1979). At this age, children also typically find it difficult to group together things in two different ways at the same time, such as realizing that someone can be *both* a boy *and* a brother (Piaget 1928; Markman 1989).

These kinds of difficulties are typical of preschool children and disappear as children get older. The same child who at age two is calling a tomato a ball will have no problem grouping it with other fruits and vegetables at age six, and may very well become a botanist as an adult! It is important to keep in mind, however, that the kinds of errors I've described above are not the only ways that young children classify. As described next, children are in some ways much more capable than these early errors would suggest.

Early abilities

One way to observe early capabilities is to study infants. In the past 20 years, researchers have devised ingenious experimental methods for gauging what infants know. Researchers measure the very simple behaviors that infants can do, such as head-turns, sucking on a pacifier, gazing, facial expressions, and even heartbeats. Using these methods, researchers have consistently found that even newborns form sensible categories of simple sights, sounds, tastes, and smells (Mehler & Fox 1985). One-month-old babies group together speech sounds in much the same way as adults do, for example, perceiving that "bay" and "day" are different sounds. Before they are six months of age, infants categorize faces and emotional expressions (happy, sad, angry). They perceive colors, objects, even kinds of animals—all well before they can even speak (Quinn, Eimas, & Rosenkrantz 1993). It seems clear, then, that simple categories are not beyond the capacity of young children. In some ways babies seem to be born knowing how to carve up the world into categories.

Preschool children typically find it difficult to group together things in two different ways at the same time, such as realizing that someone can be both a boy and a brother.

Perhaps even more impressive is the behavior of children who are "experts." Chi, Mervis, and their colleagues have studied young children who are exceptionally interested in a particular topic, such as dinosaurs, birds, or the game of chess. For example, one dinosaur expert who was studied at age four-and-a-half had been exposed to dinosaur information since turning three, and his parents read dinosaur books to him for an average of three hours per week (Chi & Koeske 1983). Another child became expert in identifying and naming birds and could identify 118 different kinds of birds by four years of age (Johnson & Mervis 1994). The general finding from this research is that when children know a great deal about a specialized domain, their categories look remarkably like the categories one would find with older children or even adults. Age seems to present few barriers for a child who has become an expert on a certain topic. Chi, Hutchinson, and Robin (1989) studied four-year-old children who were highly knowledgeable about the domain of dinosaurs

and found that their categories of dinosaurs were detailed, factually correct, and chock-full of information. These results tell us that even preschoolers can form mature categories.

We turn next to the question of how children use categories to think about information that is not immediately obvious.

Children younger than about age two-and-a-half typically "overextend" their words by applying them in overly broad ways, such as calling any round object a ball or any four-legged animal a dog.

Beyond the obvious

In *Beyond the Information Given*, Bruner (1973) points out that most of what we know about the world around us is not directly shown or visible. Instead, we make inferences from whatever information is available to go beyond what is most immediate. One can intuitively appreciate this point by considering a few familiar proverbs: "Don't judge a book by its cover," "Beauty is only skin deep," "Appearances can be deceiving." In real life, as in proverbs, how something looks can be misleading. Consider the trick-or-treater at Halloween who looks like a witch but is really the second-grader down the street; the apple that looks luscious on the outside but is full of worms inside; the animal that flies in the sky and looks like a bird but is really a bat.

Notice that these examples involve contrasting categories: witch versus girl, edible versus inedible, bird versus bat. Much of "going beyond the information given" involves forming categories that are based on information that's neither obvious nor visible.

I would like to turn now to the question of how and when children realize that categories go beyond the obvious. I will review three areas of research evidence with preschool children: the appearance-reality distinction, the power of words, and the thinking on biological growth. The theme that will emerge is that by four years of age preschool children clearly understand that categories include nonobvious information. In the summary, I bring out the positive—and negative—implications of this understanding for young children.

The appearance-reality distinction

When do children realize that appearances can be deceiving? Past research finds that, although three-year-olds have some difficulties holding in mind the distinction between appearance and reality, these difficulties greatly subside during the preschool years. For example, some years ago deVries (1969) examined children's reactions to a docile cat wearing a dog mask. Children first saw that the cat was harmless; then the cat briefly disappeared behind a screen, reappearing a moment later with the dog mask in place. Some of the three-year-olds become quite frightened after viewing the transformation and insisted that the cat had turned into a dog. However, by age six the children typically reported that the animal wasn't really a dog; it was only a cat wearing a mask.

> **When do children realize that appearances can be deceiving? Research finds that, although three-year-olds have some difficulties holding in mind the distinction between appearance and reality, these difficulties greatly subside during the preschool years.**
> **When appearance-reality distinctions (for example, you are still you even if you have on a mask) are complex or tricky, young children are still more likely than older children to get confused.**

Flavell (1986) found a marked shift between ages three and four in how children reason about appearance-reality conflicts. He presented children with deceptive objects, such as a glass of milk taken from plain view and placed

behind an orange filter. Even though children saw for themselves that the filter changed the appearance of the object, the three-year-olds typically insisted that appearance and reality were one and the same—for example, that the liquid looked orange and that it was "really and truly" orange juice. In contrast, the four-year-olds understood that even though the liquid looked orange, it was "really and truly" milk. Part of the difficulty for three-year-olds seems to be keeping both appearance and reality in mind at the same time.

These are all tigers, even though they are wearing and doing different things.

Other researchers have found some awareness of the appearance-reality distinction at even younger ages. When children are able to view a costume change directly, even three-year-olds realize that wearing a costume doesn't affect identity (Keil 1989). So, for example, a horse wearing a zebra costume is still a horse.

In fact, by four years of age, children realize that the "insides" of an animal or object may be even more important than its "outsides" for identifying what it is. In our own work Wellman and I asked children to show us which items had the same outsides and which had the same insides (Gelman & Wellman 1991). By age four, children could tell us that items that were alike on the outside were not necessarily alike on the inside. For example, a piggy bank and a real pig were judged to be alike on the outside but not the inside. Conversely, a real pig and a cow were judged to be alike on the inside but not the outside. Furthermore, when we asked children what would happen if a dog, say, didn't have its blood and bones, four- and five-year-olds told us that it would no longer be a dog and would no longer bark or eat dog food. However, when we asked them what would happen if a dog didn't have its fur, they reported that it still would be a dog and still could bark. Even though children can't see an object's insides, they understand that insides can be more important than outward appearances.

One final note about the appearance-reality distinction: Although four-year-olds *can* appreciate the distinction, this does not mean that they always *do*. When appearance-reality distinctions are complex or tricky, young children still are more likely than older children to get confused. For example, early elementary school children continue to err when asked whether superficial changes affect animal identity, often reporting that operations, ingestion of pills, or injections that result in physical appearance changes also can change what an animal actually is (Keil 1989).

The power of words

Young children place great weight on the names we give to things. Piaget (1929) suggested that children at first think that names are linked to the "essence" of a category: "In learning the names of things the child at this stage believes it is doing much more." He observed that children have some difficulty recognizing that the words we assign to objects are arbitrary, and instead they attach special significance to the name itself.

More recently, research has shown that children use category names (bird, dinosaur, squirrel) as a guide to extending their knowledge and making inferences. Children tend to assume that animals with the same category name are alike in important, nonobvious ways (Gelman & Markman 1986). For example, preschool children as young as two-and-a-half years typically assume that different kinds of birds all live in nests, feed their babies the same kinds of food, and have the same kinds of bones inside. Even when we teach children biological facts that they've never heard before, three- and four-year-olds generalize these facts to other animals with the same name.

We found also that children make use of new names that they learn in the context of the research study. For example, Coley and I showed two-and-a-half-year-old children pictures of unfamiliar animals such as a pterodactyl and a leaf-insect (Gelman & Coley 1990). One group of children learned no names for these animals and tended to assume incorrect labels for them (for example, that the pterodactyl was a bird and the leaf-insect a leaf). A second group of children learned the correct category names for these animals, for example, "dinosaur" for the pterodactyl and "bug" for the leaf-insect. We then asked children various questions about the animals: whether or not the pterodactyl lived in a nest, whether or not the leaf-insect grew on a tree, and so forth. The children who had

not learned the correct names typically answered the questions incorrectly, assuming that the pterodactyl lived in a nest (like other flying animals) or the leaf-insect grew on a tree. But the children who had learned the new category names made appropriate inferences based on the names. They said that the pterodactyl, like other dinosaurs, did not live in a nest, for example. Simply providing a name for the animal changed how children thought about the animal and what inferences they made.

Sample Generalizations Expressed in Spontaneous Talk

Some generalizations expressed by mothers

"Remember, I told you cats like balls of yarn?"
"That's a chipmunk. And they eat the acorns."
"Did you know when pigs get big, they're called hogs?"
"A wok is how people in China cook. Well, actually, a wok is how people in America cook like Chinese people."

Some generalizations expressed by children*

"That shirt's not for girls." (Ross, two years, seven months)

"Animals eat berries and they eat mushrooms." (Abe, two years, nine months)

"Indians live in Africa." (Adam, three years, three months)

"Bad guys have some guns." (Mark, three years, seven months)

*Bloom (1970), Brown (1973), Kuczaj (1976), Mac Whinney and Snow (1985, 1990), and Sachs (1983) have made their transcripts of adult-child interactions available through the Child Language Data Exchange System (CHILDES).

Preschool children pay close attention to the words we apply not just to categories of animals but also to categories of people. Hearing a child labeled "boy" or "girl" has vast implications for the kinds of inferences children form (Gelman, Collman, & Maccoby 1986). Preschoolers expect that a child's behaviors, preferences, goals, physical properties, and future identity can all be predicted based on whether the child is referred to as a boy or a girl. Children make such inferences even if they are thinking about a child whose appearance is atypical, such as a boy with long hair or a girl with very short hair. What is important in these cases is that an adult supplies the gender category label (boy, girl). If an adult doesn't say whether the child in question is a boy or a girl, children often have difficulty coming up with the correct classification on their own and tend instead to make inferences based on appearances. So when they meet a long-haired boy, many four-year-olds will assume that the child is a girl and

These are all pigs, even though they are wearing and doing different things.

plays with dolls. As soon as they hear he is a boy, however, their way of thinking about the child shifts.

Recently my colleagues and I have started to look at the kinds of generalizations children spontaneously express in their everyday talk and the kinds of generalizations that mothers express when talking with their children (Gelman et al. in press). Our focus was on statements and questions referring to an entire category rather than those referring to only a portion of a category. For example, we examined those times that children and mothers talked about mice (as a general category) rather than *some* mice, *my* mouse, or *those* mice. In other words, we wished to see when children and parents go beyond the specific context they are in to think about the category as an abstract whole. The box "Sample Generalizations Expressed in Spontaneous Talk," lists some examples.

Rodriguez and I are finding that children begin making broad generalizations about categories as early as two-and-a-half years of age, but that these generalizations increase rather dramatically between two-and-a-half and four years. This result suggests that children may become increasingly attentive to categories during this period. We are also finding that the sorts of generalizations that both children and parents express are especially frequent for categories of people and animals (for example, in the box these categories include cats, chipmunks, pigs, girls, animals, Indians, and bad guys). Both mothers and children make many fewer generalizations about categories of inert objects such as shoes, books, chairs.

Children sometimes maintain these generalizations even in the face of conflicting information. For example, consider the conversation that I recently had with my three-and-a-half-year-old son:

> *Adam*: Kids don't like coffee. Grown-ups do.
> *Me*: I don't like coffee.
> *Adam*: Yes you do! You're not a kid.

Similarly, many children express strong gender-stereotyped beliefs in the preschool years, reporting, for example, that mommies can't be doctors or that boys can't play with dolls (Liben & Signorella 1987). These category-based generalizations seem somewhat rigid and inflexible at the preschool age and are not easily overcome simply by giving the child counterevidence.

It is not yet clear whether or how the talk that children hear from others and other caregivers affects the kinds of generalizations they form. Do children who hear many generalizations tend to generalize more broadly than children who do not? Do the sorts of categories that parents and other caregivers talk about in this way affect how children think about these particular categories? For example, if a caregiver expresses many generalizations about gender categories, does this lead children to notice gender more or to make more inferences based on gender? These are important questions that await future research.

Thinking about biological growth

Caterpillars turn into butterflies, tadpoles turn into frogs, babies become adults, and acorns become oak trees. These examples of growth and metamorphosis provide an interesting arena for looking at how children understand categories because in every case the category member undergoes dramatic change and yet in some sense remains the same.

> **When children know a great deal about a specialized domain, their categories look remarkably like the categories one would find with older children or even adults.**

Long before they have any detailed knowledge of biological processes children come to understand several fundamental points about growth (Rosengren et al. 1991; Hickling & Gelman 1995). Four-year-olds understand that an individual animal can change shape, color, and size over the course of growth yet still keep the same name and identity. They understand that every kind of plant comes from a specialized kind of seed; for example, apple trees come from apple sees. They understand that the growth cycle is predictable and repeating: from seed to plant to fruit to seed to plant to fruit, and so on. They recognize that growth itself comes about due to natural processes (such as sunshine and rain) and not due to artificial processes (such as human activities).

> **Preschoolers expect that a child's behaviors, preferences, goals, physical properties, and future identity can all be predicted based on whether the child is referred to as a boy or a girl. Children sometimes maintain these generalizations even in the face of conflicting information. Many children express strong gender-stereotyped beliefs in the preschool years, reporting, for example, that mommies can't be doctors or that boys can't play with dolls.**

Four-year-olds also realize that nature can "win out" over nurture. For example, if four-year-old children hear about an animal that is adopted by another species and raised in this atypical environment (e.g., a cow raised by pigs), they predict that the animal will continue to grow and develop just like the birth parents (Gelman & Wellman 1991)—the cow will moo and have a straight tail when it grows up, even though it has been raised by pigs. Preschool children make similar predictions about nature-nurture conflicts with seeds (e.g., a lemon seed planted in a cornfield) or people (e.g., a baby whose birth parents and adoptive parents differ in skin color or personality traits) (Hirschfeld 1996; Springer 1996; Taylor 1996).

Taken altogether, these studies suggest that four-year-old children view growth and development as natural processes (Gelman & Kremer 1991) unfolding inside the animal or plant rather than resulting from outside influences. They expect that a great deal of how an animal or plant grows and develops is fixed at birth in the infant animal or the seed of the plant.

Children at age three know a great deal less about biological growth (Gelman & Wellman 1991; Rosengren et al. 1991; Hickling & Gelman 1995). It may be that early experiences are contributing to the changes between ages three and four. One study found that children who care for a pet goldfish at home are more knowledgeable about biology than children who do not (Inagaki 1990). However, at this point little is known about the kinds of experiences that children have with growth and metamorphosis in their preschools and at home and how these experiences affect children's understanding of growth.

Summary

Children have an impressive understanding of categories by age four—they grasp the distinction between appearance and reality, they use names as a guide for making inferences, and they realize that growth is an orderly, natural process. To some extent, even two-and-a-half and three-year-old children show some of these same early understandings. However, there are also developmental changes during the preschool period (especially between two-and-a-half and four years of age). The youngest children are apt to have more difficulties with the appearance-reality distinction, are less apt to form spontaneous generalizations using the categories that they have, and are easily confused about the growth process.

Altogether the lesson we have learned from studying children's early categories is that categories are tremendously important tools for young children and have implications for how they view the world. Like any tools, categories can be used in either useful or inappropriate ways. We have already seen some of the dangers in early categories: children sometimes take names more seriously than they should and draw overly broad generalizations based on the categories that they know. Overall, however, we view the effects of categories as mostly positive. Children make use of categories to expand their knowledge. By simply naming objects we can encourage children to notice how different items are similar and help children gain new information about the world. Furthermore, because children expect items in a category to be alike in nonobvious ways, they are able to learn about "scientific" properties (such as the insides of animals) well before kindergarten age. Both of these implications illustrate that categories are the foundation for later learning in school.

References

Bloom, L. 1970. Language development: Form and function in emerging grammars. Cambridge, MA: MIT Press.

Brown, R. W. 1973. A first language: The early stages. Cambridge, MA: Harvard University Press.

Bruner, J. S. 1973. *Beyond the information given: Studies in the psychology of knowing*. New York: Norton.

Chi, M., J. Hutchinson, & A. Robin. 1989. How inference about novel domain-related concepts can be constrained by structured knowledge. *Merrill-Palmer Quarterly* 35: 27–62.

Chi, M. T. H., & R. D. Koeske. 1983. Network representation of a child's dinosaur knowledge. *Developmental Psychology* 19: 29–39.

Clark, E. V. 1973. What's in a word? On the child's acquisition of semantics in his first language. In *Cognitive development and the acquisition of language*, ed. T. E. Moore. New York: Academic.

deVries, R. 1969. *Constancy of generic identity in the years three to six*. Monographs of the Society for Research in Child Development, vol. 34, no. 3, serial no. 127. Chicago: University of Chicago Press.

Flavell, J. H. 1986. The development of children's knowledge about the appearance-reality distinction. *American Psychologist* 41: 418–25.

Gelman, S. A., & J. D. Coley. 1990. The importance of knowing a dodo is a bird: Categories and inferences in 2-year-old children. *Developmental Psychology* 26: 796–804.

Gelman, S.A., J. D. Coley, K. Rosengren, E. Hartman, & T. Pappas. In press. *Beyond labeling: The role of maternal input in the acquisition of richly-structured categories*. Monographs of the Society for Research in Child Development. Chicago: University of Chicago Press.

Gelman, S. A., P. Collman, & E. E. Maccoby. 1986. Inferring properties from categories versus inferring categories from properties: The case of gender. *Child Development* 57: 396–404.

Gelman, S. A., & K. E. Kremer. 1991. Understanding natural causes: Children's explanations of how objects and their properties originate. *Child Development* 62: 396–414.

Gelman, S. A., & E. M. Markman. 1986. Categories and induction in young children. *Cognition* 23: 183–209.

Gelman, S. A., & H. M. Wellman. 1991. Insides and essences: Early understandings of the non-obvious. *Cognition* 38: 213–44.

Hickling, A. K., & S. A. Gelman. 1995. How does your garden grow? Early conceptualization of seeds and their place in plant growth cycle. *Child Development* 66: 856–76.

Hirschfeld, L. A. 1996. *Race in the making: Cognition, culture, and the child's construction of human kinds*. Cambridge, MA: MIT Press.

Inagaki, K. 1990. The effects of raising animals on children's biological knowledge. *British Journal of Developmental Psychology* 8: 119–29.

Inhelder, B., & J. Piaget. 1964. *The early growth of logic in the child*. New York: Norton.

James, W. 1890. *The principles of psychology*. New York: Dover.

Johnson, K. E., & C. B. Mervis. 1994. Microgenetic analysis of first steps in children's acquisition of expertise on shorebirds. *Developmental Psychology* 30: 418–35.

Keil, F. C. 1989. *Concepts, kinds, and cognitive development*. Cambridge, MA: MIT Press.

Kuczaj, S. 1976. -ing, -s, and -ed: A study of the acquisition of certain verb inflections. Ph.D. diss., University of Minnesota.

Liben, L. S., & M. L. Signorella, eds. 1987, *Children's gender schemata*. San Francisco: Jossey-Bass.

MacWhinney, B., & C. Snow. 1985. The Child Language Data Exchange System. *Journal of Child Language* 12: 271–95.

MacWhinney, B., & C. Snow. 1990. The Child Language Data Exchange System: An update. *Journal of Child Language* 17: 457–72.

Markman, E. M. 1989. *Categorization and naming in children: Problems of induction*. Cambridge, MA: MIT Press.

Mehler, J., & R. Fox, eds. 1985. *Neonate cognition: Beyond the blooming, buzzing confusion*. Hillsdale, NJ: Erlbaum.

Piaget, J. 1928. *Judgement and reasoning in the child*. London: Routledge & Kegan Paul.

Piaget, J. 1929. *The child's conception of the world*. London: Routledge & Kegan Paul.

Quinn, P. C., P. D. Eimas, & S. L. Rosenkrantz. 1993. Evidence for representations of perceptually similar natural categories by 3-month-old and 4-month-old infants. *Perception* 22: 463–75.

Rosengren, K. S., S. A. Gelman, C. W. Kalish, & M. McCormick, 1991. As time goes by: Children's early understanding of growth in animals. *Child Development* 62: 1302–20.

Sachs, J. 1983. Talking about the there and then: The emergence of displaced reference in parent-child discourse. In *Children's language, vol. 4*, ed. K. E. Nelson. Hillsdale, NJ: Erlbaum.

Smiley, S. S., & A. L. Brown. 1979. Conceptual preference for thematic or taxonomic relations: A nonmonotonic age trend from preschool to old age. *Journal of Experimental Child Psychology* 28: 249–57.

Springer, K. 1996. Young children's understanding of a biological basis for parent-offspring relations. *Child Development* 67: 2841–56.

Taylor, M. G. 1996. The development of children's beliefs about social and biological aspects of gender differences. *Child Development* 67: 1555–71.

Copyright © 1998 by Susan A. Gelman, Department of Psychology, 525 E. University Ave., University of Michigan, Ann Arbor, MI 48109–1109. E-mail: gelman@umich.edu.

Susan A. Gelman, Ph.D., is professor of psychology at the University of Michigan. She has received awards from the American Psychological Association, the J. S. Guggenheim Foundation, and the National Science Foundation for her research on concept and language learning in children.

This is one of a regular series of Research in Review columns. The column in this issue was invited by Research in Review Editor, **Carol Seefeldt**, Ph.D., professor at the University of Maryland, College Park.

Illustrations © by Patti Argoff.

Do Young Children Understand What Others Feel, Want, and Know?

Angeline Lillard and Stephanie Curenton

Very young children can show surprising awareness of what other people feel, want, and know. By the time they are seven or eight months old, babies pay special attention to the emotional expressions of adults. By the second year of life, toddlers are beginning to know when others are feeling happy, angry, or sad. They may even try to comfort someone who is distressed. Toddlers also assume that others have desires and goals and may clutch a toy they are holding or try to hide it behind their backs when they see another child eyeing it.

From a very early age children appear to develop an intuitive or "folk" psychology in which they attribute wants and beliefs to others to account for people's actions. Young children, as well as adults, are very interested in what others are doing and feeling and why they do what they do.

Background

Learning to understand the feelings and intentions of other people is a critical part of becoming a functioning member of society. To get along well with others, interact cooperatively, and develop close social relationships, this learning must take place. The development of social understanding is so important to human development and it begins so early that psychologists are beginning to think of it as an innate potential, like the ability to learn language. This view differs from Piaget's theory that young children do not develop the ability to "take the perspective" of others and understand their feelings and intentions until at age six or seven they enter the "concrete operational" period of mental development.

People's understanding that others have mental states is a very interesting feat. When we see someone fall down and cry, we assume the person is *sad*, and *wants* comforting. When we see a child crouched over a piece of paper with a pencil in hand, sounding out letters, we guess that child is *trying* to write letters. An amazing aspect of these understandings is that mental states are usually not accompanied by any hard evidence of their existence. We have to make it up. It appears that even very young children, as early as 18 months of age, also make it up, inventing mental states in others (Meltzoff 1995).

Research suggests that humans are unique in this regard, since animals do not appear to invent mental states

(Povinelli & Eddy 1996). Animals simply respond to facial expressions, vocalizations, and body postures. People, on the other hand, attribute mental states with gusto, even applying them to cars and ovens and other entities in which they obviously do not belong.

Many observant toddler and preschool teachers know how sensitive some of these very young children can be to the thoughts and feelings of others.

The study of how and when we acquire an understanding of other's minds has taken developmental psychology by storm, with a tenfold increase over the past decade in the number of publications discussing these issues. The reason for this attention is that knowledge about minds has consequences for so many areas of human functioning. Human interactions from the nursery onward are often about what we think others are thinking.

For example, when children learn the meaning of new words, they need to notice the focus of attention of the adult who is supplying the new word. Even by 18 months, children who are busy playing with a new toy will look to an adult's face when she sounds like she is supplying a new word label ("It's a cyclops! Look at the cyclops!"). Further, children will assume the new word refers to whatever the adult is looking at rather than simply assume it refers to their own toy (Baldwin 1991). This suggests that children have some perspective-taking ability even in Piaget's sensorimotor stage.

Another example of how understanding minds is fundamental to human interactions concerns intentions. Dodge and Price (1994) have shown that boys with very aggressive behavior attribute mean intentions to others, while nonaggressive boys who are in the same situation do not. Other research has shown that children with delinquency problems have trouble taking others' perspectives, and that training them in role-taking by discussing how others view the world is associated with reductions in their aggressive behavior (Chandler 1975).

Children with autism also show marked deficits on many tasks requiring an understanding of minds. Some researchers have even claimed that "mindblindness," the inability to understand others' mental states, is the fundamental deficit of autism (Baron-Cohen 1995). Talking about others' intentions and mental states helps very young children, even those who are not abnormally aggressive or delinquent, to understand mental states. For example, when parents talk more with their children at age two about others' emotions, the children by age four have a better understanding of others' minds.

What do young children know about minds, and when do they know it?

Studies of young children developing understanding of mental states have focused on four areas: children's understanding of (1) the relationship between information from the senses (perception) and what people know, (2) the emotions of others, (3) others' desires, and (4) others' beliefs.

Perception

Three-year-olds have some rudimentary understandings of how sensory experience is related to what people know. Even before three years of age, a child knows to behave differently toward his mother if she is out of the room when a coveted item is hidden (and therefore needs some clues about where to find it) than if she is in the room when the item is hidden (O'Neill 1996). By four or five years of age, children realize how they learned something.

In one study, two objects identical except for their color were shown to children. One of the objects was placed in a tunnel, and the children felt it but did not see it. When asked what color it was, children under five tended to positively assert that the object was one of the colors ("It's blue!"). When asked how they knew, children often responded with the impossible: "It felt blue!" (O'Neill, Astington, & Flavell 1992). By age five, most children realized they could not know an object's color by feeling it.

Emotions

Simple emotions are understood very early. Happiness is usually the first emotion children master, followed by anger and sadness (Borke 1971) and fear (Michalson & Lewis 1985). Repacholi and Gopnik (1997) had 18-month-olds observe a woman looking at broccoli, smiling at it, and saying, "Mmm! Broccoli!" Next she made an ugly face and said, "Yuck!" while looking at the children's preferred food, Goldfish crackers. When asked to give the experimenter some food, most toddlers chose to give her broccoli instead of the crackers. Fourteen-month-olds, in contrast, tried to give her the Goldfish crackers.

This study suggests that by 18 months of age children realize that others' desires might differ from their own and they can use emotional expressions to interpret those desires. Children also learn early how situations relate to emotions. For example, by age three most children assume that people are happy at birthday parties and sad when a dog bites them (Harris 1989).

Now, new research validates what we see.

Although young children can understand emotions based on desires, they have difficulty understanding emotions, such as surprise, that are based on beliefs. Understanding surprise is difficult because the emotion is a mismatch between a person's beliefs and reality. Most children do not understand surprise until they have mastered belief, which occurs usually at age five (Hadwin & Perner 1991). They also find it hard to understand the notion that emotional expressions might not represent true feelings. For example, until age five or six, children do not seem to realize that one might smile upon receiving a gift even if one does not like the gift (Saarni 1984). Preschoolers also have difficulty understanding ambivalent feelings, such as being happy about getting a new bicycle but disappointed because it is the wrong color (Kestenbaum & Gelman 1995).

Desires

Children's earliest understanding of the mental states of others has been described as desire psychology (Wellman 1990), because they interpret someone's actions in terms of what that person might want. By age three children understand that desires are positive attitudes toward something outside of themselves. They can also understand the differences between what is wanted and what is reality. For example, when talking about ice cream, one young child said, "I don't want it cold. I wanted it warm" (Bartsch & Wellman 1995, 71).

Similarly, children realize that although one person might like something, another might not. They also have a grasp of how desires relate to actions. Three-year-olds predict that if someone wants something and does not succeed in finding it, the person will keep looking. Furthermore, they understand the link between desires and emotions: that if someone gets what she wants, she will be happy, and if someone does not get what she wants, she will be sad (Wellman & Woolley 1990).

Beliefs

A major development of the preschool years is an understanding that others have beliefs about the world that affect what they do. Until about age four, children have a tendency to act as if everyone knows and believes what they themselves know to be true. If a child falls down at school, she expects her mother to know about the event because she herself knows about it. If a child knows that the ladder on the slide has a broken rung, he believes that his friend knows it too (and will be careful without being told).

One way psychologists have studied children's understanding of belief has been by using *false-belief tasks*. In one such task, children are shown a doll and told that the doll has left a treasured candy bar in a drawer and gone out to play. Children see the doll's mother move the candy to a cupboard. The doll returns, and children are asked where the doll will look for his candy. Until they are four or five years old, children usually predict that the doll will go straight to the cupboard to retrieve the candy bar (Wimmer & Perner 1983). Older children usually understand that the doll would falsely believe the candy was in the drawer.

This error holds even in greatly simplified circumstances and even when the child herself is the actor. For example, in another type of false-belief task, children first are shown a cracker box and asked what is inside. Most respond, "Crackers!" Then the children are shown that the box actually contains leaves, not crackers, and they now are asked what they had thought was inside. Although the task is very simple and other children are asked about their own mental states rather than someone else's, until age four or five a child will usually respond, "Leaves!" (Gopnik & Astington 1988).

This outcome is not due to a problem with the word *think*, because the same error applies when the word *say* is used. It is not due to embarrassment, because the error holds if children are asked what a friend or parent would think. It is not due to misunderstanding the temporal aspect of the question, because when asked what someone else would think was inside if they were seeing the closed-up box for the first time, three-year-olds still usually say, "Leaves!"

It seems that until children are about four years old (perhaps a year later in children from families with low incomes ([Holmes, Black, & Miller 1996]), they have difficulty with the notion that our beliefs about the world are sometimes false. What appears to underlie this error is a failure to understand that our minds represent a version of the world, like a photograph represents some state of affairs at the time it was taken. Perhaps children view minds more like photographs that are updated to match reality.

Most young children act as if there is only one way to represent the world, an object, or a situation, and other lines of research support this. In *appearance-reality tasks*, for example, children are shown fake objects, like a candle that looks just like an apple. After discussing its appearance and reality, children are asked both what it is (really and truly) and what it looks like "to your eyes right now." Children older than four will give two answers: it is really a candle, but it looks like an apple. Younger children, however, give just one answer, usually claiming that the object looks like what it really is: a candle (Flavell, Green, & Flavell 1986).

Children do not understand that one reality can be represented in two different ways. This misconception about minds presumably has important effects. For example, children's lies before age four may be told only to influence behavior rather than with full understanding of the consequences for belief.

Psychologists' studies have suggested ages at which most children acquire certain understandings about minds. The fact is that even a two-year-old might make a comment that reflects a grasp of false belief. At age two, after answering the phone, one author's elder daughter announced, "I thought it was going to be Dad, but it was Sally!" What this suggests is that under highly supportive conditions children might occasionally evidence early insight about some concept, like mental representation, but mastery of that concept might be years off. Development is rarely all or none (Siegler 1998). Most children appear to have a pretty solid understanding of mental representation around age four or five.

How parents and teachers can support the development of children's understanding of others, and how culture might be important

When children have developed a *theory of mind*—an understanding that others have feelings and desires and beliefs—they are likely to engage in more positive interactions with others (Leekam 1993; Lalonde & Chandler 1995; Happe & Frith 1996). Since an ability to understand other minds is related to positive social relations, a major goal in both home and school settings becomes supporting this development. Researchers believe that to some degree the capacity for understanding other minds comes with biological maturation and accompanying increases in cognitive ability. In addition, studies suggest that engaging in pretend play (Youngblade & Dunn 1995) and having conversations about mental states (Dunn, Brown, & Beardsall 1991) may support the development of children's social understanding.

Encouraging pretend play

One reason that pretending may help children understand the mental states of others is that in social pretense the child must negotiate the pretend world and come face-to-face with others' representations of it. Piaget would endorse such a view, in which intense peer interaction promotes social understanding. Another aspect is that, in pretending to be other people, the child takes on others' views of the world. Regardless of why pretend play appears to help, it does seem that facilitating social pretense in children close to age four could helpfully boost them over the edge to understanding that people mentally represent their worlds.

Talking to children about minds

A second way of helping young children understand others' minds is by talking to them about minds and mental states. Dunn has found that talking more about emotional states in natural contexts to children at 33 months is associated with better performance on false-belief tasks at 40 months (Dunn, Brown, & Beardsall 1991).

Many children's books center on changes in feelings, and reading such books and discussing the feelings may also assist children's understanding that minds represent the world. Additionally, reading such books and discussing the feelings may also aid children's understanding of how other people think and feel.

Researchers have also found that younger siblings understand false beliefs earlier than do older siblings (Lewis

et al. 1996). Perhaps this is because the more siblings a child has, the more feelings there are to talk about, and younger siblings might be particularly influenced by such talk.

There is evidence that children who are deaf, whose parents do not use sign language, are delayed in passing false-belief tasks, whereas those children whose parents do sign pass tasks at the usual age. This finding further supports the role of conversation in developing social understanding.

Finally, although we may balk at the idea of organized lessons around mental states, some researchers have found that both explaining thoughts by using cartoon-type "thought bubbles" and discussing false beliefs with children after watching carefully constructed false-belief videotapes assists them in understanding false beliefs. Such methods are not being used to help children with autism.

The role of culture

Another powerful influence on children's growing understanding of others' minds is most likely culture, but research on this topic is relatively scarce. Most psychologists who have studied children's theories of mind have been guided by mainstream cognitive development approaches that pay little attention to the impact of culture. It has been generally assumed that certain basic understandings occur in children at about the same age everywhere in the world with only minor variations due to cultural practices. One study did find that children of Baka pygmies of Cameroon passed false-belief tasks at about the same age as did most of their European and American peers (Avis & Harris 1991).

Until about age four children have a tendency to act as if everyone knows and believes what they themselves know to be true. A major development of the preschool years is an understanding that others have beliefs about the world that affect what they do.

Yet different cultures do have different ways of understanding minds (Lillard 1998), and cultural understandings may well influence children. One prominent difference is how much attention is paid to minds. Although Northern Europeans and Americans (at least middle-class, more highly educated families) tend to focus a lot of attention on how minds and mental states cause behaviors, people from Asian cultures pay more attention to how the situations people are in dictate behavior.

Perhaps a subtle difference in the concept of the person underlies this distinction, some viewing the person as an autonomous unit seeking to fill her own desires and others considering the person as part of a larger social whole whose actions are dictated by the needs of the group, not the self. Such concept differences appear within the United States as well, with rural American children (whose parents most likely have no more than a high school education and a working-class income) resembling Asian children in that they refer more to context-based reasons for behaviors than to mental-state reasons (Lillard, Zeljo, & Harlan 1998; Lillard in press).

Cultures also differ in their attention to certain types of mental states. One study suggests that African American children engage in more emotion talk than do European American children (Blake 1994). Japanese families also talk more to their children about emotions, engaging in what could be seen as intensive empathy training (Azuma 1994). As one example, instead of telling children to eat their dinner so they will grow or because they are lucky not to be starving like children in some other part of the world, Japanese parents are apt to emphasize that a poor farmer worked hard to grow the food and that the children will hurt his feelings if they do not eat it. When a single sock was found in a classroom during a visit one author made to a Japanese preschool, the teacher said to the class, "This poor sock has no partner. Poor sock. Can we help the sock?"

Such cultural practices train children to respond with feeling to those around them as behooves one in Japanese society. Indeed, Japanese adults are not supposed to talk about mental states. References to mental state are taboo, because a truly sensitive person should know others' mental states without being told about them. These adult conventions may necessitate a great deal of talk about mental state with children, so they learn to be very good at making inferences about mental states before they become taboo topics.

Another apparent cultural difference related to how we understand minds is the extent to which children are allowed to live in mentally constructed worlds as opposed to a single-objective world. Middle-class European American parents appear to socialize children to see the priority of personal views over reality. One recent study reports that middle-class European American parents even accept their children's false statements, apparently to protect their children's self-esteem (Wiley et al. 1998). For example, when a child asserted that Santa Claus comes at Easter, her mother yielded, "Oh, I'm confused," rather than correcting her. Working-class European American parents, in contrast, tended to correct their children, expecting them to get the story right.

Such cultural differences probably lead children to think differently about minds and behaviors. Indeed, researchers have found that children from working-class rural homes tend to explain behaviors as being mandated by circumstances, while children from middle-class urban homes tend to explain them as arising from desires and emotions (Lillard, Zeljo, & Harlan 1998). If reality can be any way that you imagine it, minds become more im-

portant. Such views have implications for classroom behavior. In Mexican culture the teacher is revered, and children are expected to learn the teacher's way as the one right way (Delgado-Gaitan 1994); Asian culture is purportedly similar. In contrast, European American children are expected to learn to think critically and challenge the teacher, imposing their own reality on the topic.

Summary

Generally, research suggests that children who understand others' minds at an early age may be more able to get along well with others and that parents and teachers can support the development of this understanding by encouraging pretend play and discussing mental states with them from storybooks or real-life encounters. It is probably not worth discussing the concept of thoughts with toddlers because it may be beyond their understanding. However, some research suggests that by age three, discussions of what other people are thinking may be helpful.

The fact that discussion leads to understanding aspects of the mind, coupled with different approaches to minds across cultures, suggests that we need to be sensitive about minds and behavior. Every child develops ideas about minds and behaviors, but the ideas individual children have may be different depending on their cultural milieu.

References

Avis, J., & P. L. Harris, 1991. Belief-desire reasoning among Baka children: Evidence for a universal conception of mind. *Child Development* 62: 460–67.

Azuma, H. 1994. Two modes of cognitive socialization in Japan and the United States. In *Cross-cultural roots of minority child development*, eds. P. M. Greenfield & R. R. Cocking, 275–84. Hillsdale, NJ: Erlbaum.

Baldwin, D. A. 1991. Infants' contribution to the achievement of joint reference. *Child Development* 62: 875–90.

Baron-Cohen, S. 1995. *Mindblindness: An essay on autism and theory of mind.* London: MIT Press.

Bartsch, K., & H. M. Wellman. 1995. *Children talk about the mind.* Oxford: Oxford University Press.

Blake, I. K. 1994. Language development and socialization in young African-American children. In *Cross-cultural roots of minority child development*, eds. P. M. Greenfield & R. R. Cocking, 147–66. Hillsdale, NJ: Erlbaum.

Borke, H. 1971. Interpersonal perception of young children: Egocentrism or empathy? *Developmental Psychology* 5: 263–69.

Chandler, M. J. 1975. Egocentrism and anti-social behavior: The assessment and training of social perspective-taking skills. *Developmental Psychology* 9: 326–32.

Delgado-Gaitan, C. 1994. Socializing young children in Mexican-American families: An intergenerational perspective. In *Cross-cultural roots of minority child development*, eds. P. M. Greenfield & R. R. Cocking, 55–86. Hillsdale, NJ: Erlbaum.

Dodge, K. A., & J. M. Price. 1994. On the relation between social information processing and socially competent behavior in early school-aged children. *Child Development* 65: 1385–97.

Dunn, J., J. Brown, & L. Beardsall. 1991. Family talk about feeling states and children's later understanding of others' emotions. *Developmental Psychology* 27: 448–55.

Flavell, J. H., F. L. Green, & E. R. Flavell. 1986. *Development of knowledge about the appearance-reality distinction*. Monographs of the Society for Research in Child Development, vol. 51, no. 1, serial no. 212.

Gopnik, A., & J. W. Astington, 1988. Children's understanding of representational change and its relation to the understanding of false belief and the appearance-reality distinction. *Child Development* 59: 26–37.

Hadwin, J., & J. Perner. 1991. Pleased and surprised: Children's cognitive theory of emotion. *British Journal of Developmental Psychology* 9: 215–34.

Happe, F., & U. Frith. 1996. Theory of mind and social impairment in children with conduct disorder. *British Journal of Developmental Psychology* 14: 385–98.

Harris, P. L. 1989. *Children and emotion*. Oxford: Basil Blackwell.

Holmes, H., C. Black, & S. Miller. 1996. A cross-task comparison of false belief understanding in a Head Start population. *Journal of Experimental Child Psychology* 63: 263–85.

Kestenbaum, R., & S. A. Gelman. 1995. Preschool children's identification and understanding of mixed emotions. *Cognitive Development* 10: 443–58.

Lalonde, C. E., & M. J. Chandler. 1995. False belief understanding goes to school: On the social-emotional consequences of coming early or late to a first theory of mind. *Cognition and Emotion* 9: 167–85.

Leekam, S. 1993. Children's understanding of mind. In *The development of social cognition: The child as psychologist*, ed. M. Bennett, 26–61. New York: Guilford.

Lewis, C., N. Freeman, C. Kyriakidou, K. Maridaki-Kassotaki, & D. Berridge. 1996. Social influences on false belief access: Specific sibling influences or general apprenticeship? *Child Development* 67: 2930–47.

Lillard, A. S. 1998. Ethnopsychologies: Cultural variations in theory of mind. *Psychological Bulletin* 123: 3–33.

Lillard, A. S. In press. Developing a cultural theory of mind: The CIAO approach. *Current Directions in Psychological Science*.

Lillard, A. S., A. Zeljo, & D. Harlan. 1998. Developing cultural schemas: Behavior explanation in Taipei, the rural U.S., and the urban U.S. University of Virginia. Typescript paper.

Meltzoff, A. 1995. Understanding the intentions of others: Reenactment of intended acts by 18-month-old children. *Child Development* 31: 838–50.

Michalson, L., & M. Lewis. 1985. What do children know about emotions and when do they know it? In *The socialization of emotions*, eds. M. Lewis & C. Saarni, 117–39. New York: Plenum.

O'Neill, D. K. 1996. Two-year-old children's sensitivity to a parent's knowledge state when making requests. *Child Development* 67: 659–77.

O'Neill, D. K., J. Astington, & J. H. Flavell. 1992. Young children's understanding of the role that sensory experiences play in knowledge acquisition. *Child Development* 63: 474–90.

Povinelli, D. J., & T. J. Eddy. 1996. *What young chimpanzees know about seeing*. Monographs of the Society for Research in Child Development, vol. 61, no. 3, serial no. 247.

Repacholi, B. M., & A. Gopnik. 1997. Early reasoning about desires: Evidence from 14- and 18-month-olds. *Developmental Psychology* 33: 12–21.

Saarni, C. 1984. An observational study of children's attempts to monitor their expressive behavior. *Child Development* 55: 1504–13.

Siegler, R. S. 1998. *Children's thinking*. Upper Saddle River, NJ: Prentice-Hall.

Wellman, H. M. 1990. *The child's theory of mind*. Cambridge, MA: Bradford Books/MIT Press.

Wellman, H. M., & J. D. Woolley. 1990. From simple desires to ordinary beliefs: The early development of everyday psychology. *Cognition* 35: 245–275.

Wiley, A. R., A. J. Rose, L. K. Burger, & P. J. Miller. 1998. Constructing autonomous selves through narrative practices: A comparative study of working-class and middle-class families. *Child Development* 69: 833–47.

Wimmer, H., & J. Perner. 1983. Beliefs about beliefs: Representation and constraining function of wrong beliefs in young children's understanding of deception. *Cognition* 13: 103–28.

Youngblade, L. M., & J. Dunn. 1995. Individual differences in young children's pretend play with mother and sibling: Links to relationships and understanding of other people's feelings and beliefs. *Child Development* 66: 1472–92.

For further reading and information

Berk, L. E. 1994. Research in Review. Vygotsky's theory: The importance of make-believe play. *Young Children* 50 (1): 30–39.

Curry, N. E., & S. H. Arnaud. 1995. Personality difficulties in preschool children as revealed through play themes and styles. *Young Children* 50 (4): 4–9.

Dyson, A. H. 1990. Research in Review. Symbol makers, symbol weavers: How children link play, pictures, and print. *Young Children* 45 (2): 50–57.

Gowen, J. W. 1995. Research in Review. The early development of symbolic play. *Young Children* 50 (3): 75–83.

Katz, L. G., & D. E. McClellan. 1997. *Fostering children's social competence: The teacher's role*. Washington, DC: NAEYC.

Nourot, P. M., & J. L. Van Hoorn. 1991. Research in Review. Symbolic play in preschool and primary settings. *Young Children* 46 (6): 40–50.

Sawyers, J. K., & C. S. Rogers. 1988. *Helping young children develop through play: A practical guide for parents, caregivers, and teachers*. Washington, DC: NAEYC.

Slaby, R. G., W. C. Roedell, D. Arezzo, & K. Hendrix. 1995. *Early violence prevention: Tools for teachers of young children*. Washington, DC: NAEYC.

Stark County (Ohio) School District; North Central Regional Educational Laboratory; Iowa, Nebraska, and Ohio Departments of Education: Jennings Foundation; & NAEYC. 1996. *Play—The seed of learning*. The Early Childhood Program series. 30 min. Distributed by NAEYC, Washington, D.C. Videocassette.

Stone, J. G. 1990. *Teaching preschoolers: It looks like this… In pictures*. Washington, DC: NAEYC.

Zavitkovsky, D., K. R. Baker, J. R. Berlfein, & M. Almy. 1986. *Listen to the children*. Washington, DC: NAEYC.

Angeline Lillard, Ph.D., is assistant professor of psychology at the University of Virginia in Charlottesville. She has conducted many studies on children's theories of mind and was recently awarded the American Psychological Association's (Division 7) Boyd McCandless Young Scientist Award for distinguished contribution to developmental psychology.

Stephanie M. Curenton, M.A., is a graduate student at the University of Virginia. Her research interests include the development of theory of mind in low-income and ethnic minority populations.

This is one of a regular series of Research in Review columns. The column in this issue was edited by **Martha B. Bronson**, Ph.D., professor of early childhood education at Boston College.

Giftedness: Current Theory and Research

Ellen Winner[1]

Abstract

Gifted children, those with unusually high ability in one or more domains, not only develop more rapidly than typical children, but also appear to be qualitatively different. They have an intense drive to master, require little explicit tuition, and, if intellectually gifted, often pose deep philosophical questions. Although some psychologists have tried to account for the achievements of gifted individuals solely in terms of drive or "deliberate practice," no evidence allows us to rule out innate differences in talent. Profiles of gifted individuals are often uneven: Extremely high ability in one area can coexist with ordinary or even subnormal ability in another area. Scientific investigation of the gifted reveals the importance of drive and hard work in achievement of any kind, and the lack of necessary correlation among abilities in different areas.

Keywords

gifted; drive; innate; talent; savant

While mainstream psychology has sought to understand the universal in human mental processes, a respectable complementary tradition has investigated individual differences and the atypical. Like the study of retardation, psychopathology, and emotional disorders, research on the gifted belongs to the latter tradition. Psychologists have studied such populations not only in order to understand them on their own terms, but also in the hope that an understanding of the atypical may shed light on the typical.

Systematic study of the gifted began in the 1920s with Terman's (1925) longitudinal study of 1,528 children with IQs averaging 151. These children were surprisingly well rounded and socially well adjusted, and grew up to be successful professionals. However, none made widely recognized intellectual breakthroughs. Thus, even extraordinarily high IQs do not by themselves lead to creative eminence. Whether such IQs predict even professional success could not be determined because Terman did not control for possible effects of socioeconomic background.

Since Terman's time, there has developed a consensus that giftedness is often not captured by the unidimensional measure of IQ. Some researchers have differentiated mathematical and verbal giftedness and have shown how domain-specific tests (math and verbal Scholastic Assessment Tests) are more accurate than IQ tests in distinguishing such gifts (Stanley, 1973). Some have broadened giftedness to include high ability in any areas, including music, spatial reasoning, and interpersonal understanding (Gardner, 1993). The case has also been made that intellectual giftedness is more than high ability, and should include creativity and motivation (Renzulli, 1978). One understanding of giftedness is most likely to advance if we define giftedness simply as unusually high ability in any area (including domain-specific ability as well as high global IQ), and then proceed to investigate the correlates (e.g., drive, creativity) and developmental path of each type of high ability.

ARE GIFTED INDIVIDUALS QUALITATIVELY OR QUANTITATIVELY DIFFERENT?

Perhaps the most basic question about giftedness is its relationship to the typical. Do gifted individuals stand out chiefly in terms of the speed with which their abilities develop and with which they process information? Or do they develop and process information in a way that is qualitatively different from normal?

Strong claims have been made about qualitatively different modes of thinking in high-IQ children, but the evidence remains anecdotal. According to clinical observations, high-IQ children consider many possible interpretations of a question, grasp the essential elements of a complex problem, and often pose deep philosophical questions (Lovecky, 1994). Controlled studies are required to determine whether these observations are true of gifted children in general, only those with high IQs, or perhaps only a subset of IQ-gifted children (e.g., only those above a certain level of IQ, verbally but not mathematically gifted). These studies must compare gifted children with peers matched for mental age so that the effects of ability level and giftedness can be disentangled.

Gifted children also appear to be qualitatively different from ordinary children in motivation, but again the evidence remains anecdotal. The gifted children who come to the attention of teachers and parents display an intense drive, or "rage to master." They work for hours with no parental prodding or external reinforcement. As they work, they pose challenges for themselves. Such children also differ from ordinary children in the way they learn. They make discoveries on their own, and much of the time they appear to teach themselves. But we do not know how many children have high ability but low motivation to demonstrate that ability (or high motivation in an area in which they do not have high ability) and who thus do not come to our attention as gifted. Again, controlled studies are needed to compare gifted children with older children who have similar levels (but in their case, age-typical levels) of ability.

The strong drive that accompanies giftedness, the posing of challenges, the mastery orientation, and the ability to make discoveries independently together suggest that gifted children do not just develop more rapidly than others, but develop and think differently from others. But there is a clear need for systematic research so that we can move beyond anecdotal evidence and determine whether high ability is always accompanied by such qualitative cognitive and motivational differences.

THE ROLE OF INNATE TALENT

Giftedness provides an ideal arena in which to investigate the relation between inborn talent and learning (Simonton, 1999). According to the layperson's view, gifted children are endowed with innate talents that make themselves known from a very early age, a view echoed by researchers whose focus is giftedness, and who publish in journals devoted to the study of gifted children (typically IQ-gifted children). A contrasting environmental view has emerged among psychologists who identify their focus as the study of talent or expertise.

The evidence for the nurture position rests on retrospective studies of eminent individuals. An early study revealed the importance of drive as separate from ability. Roe (1952) showed that scientists who achieve the highest levels differ from their less eminent colleagues not in intellectual ability but in capacity for concentration and hard work. However, because all of Roe's scientists had high ability, this study tells us nothing about what one can accomplish with low inborn ability along with a strong drive to work.

The importance of a supportive environment and intensive training was demonstrated by Bloom (1985), who found that individuals of world-class status in the arts, mathematics, science, or athletics all reported strong family support and years of training. However, such a finding hardly rules out innate talent: Bloom's subjects also recalled signs of high ability at a very young age, prior to or at the very start of formal training. These memories of early signs of high ability are consistent with parental accounts of child prodigies whose extraordinary abilities seem to emerge from nowhere.

Most recently, studies have revealed the necessity of "deliberate practice"—effortful work designed to improve performance. Ericsson, Krampe, and Tesch-Romer (1993) demonstrated that level of achievement in piano, violin, ballet, chess, bridge, and athletics is predicted by sheer amount of deliberate practice. For example, the best musicians in this study had engaged in twice as many hours of deliberate practice over their lives as had the least successful ones. However, children who work the earliest and hardest may well be those with the highest levels of talent. Most children cannot be cajoled to play music or think about math problems for hours on end, but highly gifted children often cannot be cajoled away from such activities. Amount of deliberate practice is thus likely to be a function of drive and interest, temperamental factors associated with talent. That is, children with high ability in a given area are likely to have a high drive to master that area.

As pointed-out by Schneider (in press), Ericsson and his colleagues never measured ability levels, and thus there is no way to rule out ability differences among individuals of unequal levels of eminence. Independent assessments of the predictive power of ability and deliberate practice have shown that both are important (Schneider, in press). Simonton (1991) showed that the most eminent classical composers began to compose and made lasting contributions after fewer years of formal training than their less eminent peers. The fact that they achieved greater heights with less practice suggests that their success reflected another ingredient besides practice—and a likely candidate is a higher level of inborn musical talent.

Despite attempts to account for giftedness in terms of nurture, no evidence allows us to rule out the necessity of an innate component. Simonton (1999) proposed a model of innate talent that is multidimensional and dynamic. He argued that achievement in any domain requires various innate components, with some domains requiring far more than others; components develop independently over time; level of ability is determined by a multiplicative composite of these components; and giftedness is emergenic (i.e., it manifests itself only when all of the required components are inherited). This model can account for many of the complexities of giftedness, including the rarity of giftedness particularly in complex domains (because if only one component skill in a domain is assigned a weight of zero, the individual cannot be gifted in that domain). Of course, granting a role to nature does not rule out nurture. Whether nature or nurture accounts for more of the variance in giftedness remains to be determined, and the answer to this question is likely to differ across different domains of giftedness (Simonton, 1999).

HOW UNEVEN ARE THE COGNITIVE PROFILES OF GIFTED INDIVIDUALS?

If the components of giftedness within a given domain develop independently of one another, the profiles of individuals gifted in that domain should be uneven. There is some evidence for this. Adults with high IQs show lower correlations among subtests of the IQ than do those with ordinary IQs (Detterman & Daniel, 1989). In addition, the cognitive profiles of academically gifted children are often quite uneven, with mathematical ability far outstripping verbal ability, or the reverse (Benbow & Minor, 1990). Research is needed to determine how common such uneven profiles are among the gifted, and how common it is to have gifts accompanied by absolute rather than relative weaknesses.

Just as uneven profiles often characterize the abilities of high-IQ individuals, uneven profiles also characterize individuals gifted in music or art, who may have a strong gift in the presence of an unremarkable IQ. For example, Simonton (1999) noted that Beethoven had almost no mathematical ability; nor was he particularly strong verbally. And Csikszentmihalyi, Rathunde, and Whalen (1993) found that the artistically gifted adolescents they studied had poor academic skills.

In the case of savants, who present the most striking cases of unevenness, an extreme ability coexists with a subnormal IQ. Savants are retarded, autistic, or both, yet exhibit a strong gift in a particular domain (typically music, visual art, or numerical calculation). They have often been dismissed as mere imitators whose abilities are irrelevant to an understanding of giftedness in nonsavants. However, savants show an implicit understanding of the rules of their domain, revealing that they are not rote imitators. In addition, the drawings and musical works they produce can be expressive and have artistic merit. Because savant gifts are similar to nonsavant gifts in important respects, savants provide strong evidence that general intelligence, or what psychologists often call *g*, is unrelated to high levels of achievement in some domains.

UNANSWERED QUESTIONS

An understanding of what constitutes giftedness shows the importance of drive and hard work in achievement of any kind, and reveals that high abilities in some domains do not require a high IQ. A fundamental question not yet resolved is whether gifted children differ from average ones only in a quantitative way, or whether they differ qualitatively, in which case new principles are required to account for their performance. Several other perplexing questions that open the door to intriguing new lines of research include whether the heritability of gifts differs across domains, whether the role of practice and its interaction with innate talent differ across domains, what forms of early prodigiousness do and do not predict creative eminence in adulthood, and whether brain imaging can demonstrate similarities in the brain organization and functioning of savant and nonsavant gifted individuals working in the same domain.

Answers to some of these questions also have educational implications. The question of how gifted children should be educated (most often asked about the intellectually gifted) is of enormous practical importance. These children benefit cognitively and socially from ability grouping and acceleration (including early entrance to college programs; Janos, Robinson, & Lunneborg, 1989). Research on the long-term cognitive and social outcomes of these methods should continue, and policy should follow from research findings rather than ideological positions.

Recommended Reading

Heller, K. A., Monks, F. J., Sternberg, R. J., & Subotnik, R. F. (Eds.). (in press) *International handbook of research and development of giftedness and talent* (2nd ed.). London: Elsevier.

Miller, L. K. (1999). The savant syndrome. Intellectual impairment and exceptional skill. *Psychological Bulletin, 125,* 31–46.

Simonton, D. K. (1994). *Greatness: Who makes history and why.* New York: Guilford Press.

Sternberg, R. J., & Davidson, J. E. (1986). *Conceptions of giftedness.* New York: Cambridge University Press.

Winner, E. (1996). *Gifted children: Myths and realities.* New York: Basic Books.

Acknowledgments—I thank Howard Gardner, Deirdre Lovecky, Nancy Robinson, and Catya von Karolyi for helpful comments on an earlier draft of this article.

Note

1. Address correspondence to Ellen Winner, Department of Psychology, McGuinn Hall, Boston College, Chestnut Hill, MA 02467; e-mail: ewinner@ mediaone.net.

References

Benbow, C. P., & Minor, L. L. (1990). Cognitive profiles of verbally and mathematically precocious students: Implications for identification of the gifted. *Gifted Child Quarterly, 34,* 21–26.

Bloom, B. S. (Ed.), (1985). *Developing talent in young people.* New York: Ballantine Books.

Csikszentmihalyi, M., Rathunde, K., & Whalen, S. (1993). *Talented teenagers: The roots of success and failure.* New York: Cambridge University Press.

Detterman, D. K., & Daniel, M. H. (1989). Correlations of mental tests with each other and with cognitive variables are highest for low IQ groups. *Intelligence, 15,* 349–359.

Ericsson, K. A., Krampe, R., & Tesch-Romer, C. (1993). The role of deliberate practice in the acquisition of expert performance. *Psychological Review, 199,* 363–406.

Gardner, H. (1993). *Multiple intelligences: The theory in practice.* New York: Basic Books.

Janos, P. M., Robinson, N. M., & Lunneborg, C. E. (1989). Markedly early entrance to college. *Journal of Higher Education, 60,* 494–518.

Lovecky, D. V. (1994). Exceptionally gifted children: Different minds. *Roeper Review, 17,* 116–120.

Renzulli, J. (1978). What makes giftedness? Reexamining a definition. *Phi Delta Kappan, 60,* 180–184.

Roe, A. (1952). *The making of a scientist.* New York: Dodd, Mead.

Schneider, W. (in press). Giftedness, expertise, and (exceptional) performance: A developmental perspective. In K. A. Heller,

F. J. Monks, R. J. Sternberg & R. F. Subotnik (Eds.), *International handbook of research and development of giftedness and talent* (2nd ed.). London: Elsevier.

Simonton, D. K. (1991). Emergence and realization of genius: The lives and works of 120 classical composers. *Journal of Personality and Social Psychology, 61,* 829–840.

Simonton, D. K. (1999). Talent and its development: An emergenic and epigenetic model. *Psychological Review, 106,* 435–437.

Stanley, J. C. (1973). Accelerating the educational progress of intellectually gifted youths. *Educational Psychologist, 10,* 133–146.

Terman, L. M. (1925). *Genetic studies of genius: Vol. 1. Mental and physical traits of a thousand gifted children*. Stanford, CA: Stanford University Press.

Department of Psychology, Boston College, Chestnut Hill, Massachusetts, and Project Zero, Harvard Graduate School of Education, Cambridge, Massachusetts

From *Current Directions in Psychological Science*, October 2000, pp. 153-156. © 2000 by Current Directions in Psychological Science. Reprinted by permission of Blackwell Publishing Ltd., Osney Mead, Oxford, OX2 0EL, UK.

The First Seven...
and the Eighth

A Conversation with Howard Gardner

Human intelligence continues to intrigue psychologists, neurologists, and educators.
What is it? Can we measure it? How do we nurture it?

Kathy Checkley

Howard Gardner's theory of multiple intelligences, described in Frames of Mind *(1985), sparked a revolution of sorts in classrooms around the world, a mutiny against the notion that human beings have a single, fixed intelligence. The fervor with which educators embraced his premise that we have multiple intelligences surprised Gardner himself. "It obviously spoke to some sense that people had that kids weren't all the same and that the tests we had only skimmed the surface about the differences among kids," Gardner said.*

Here Gardner brings us up-to-date on his current thinking on intelligence, how children learn, and how they should be taught.

How do you define intelligence?

Intelligence refers to the human ability to solve problems or to make something that is valued in one or more cultures. As long as we can find a culture that values an ability to solve a problem or create a product in a particular way, then I would strongly consider whether that ability should be considered an intelligence.

First, though, that ability must meet other criteria: Is there a particular representation in the brain for the ability? Are there populations that are especially good or especially impaired in an intelligence? And, can an evolutionary history of the intelligence be seen in animals other than human beings?

I defined seven intelligences (see box) in the early 1980s because those intelligences all fit the criteria. A decade later when I revisited the task, I found at least one more ability that clearly deserved to be called an intelligence.

That would be the naturalist intelligence. What led you to consider adding this to our collection of intelligences?

Somebody asked me to explain the achievements of the great biologists, the ones who had a real mastery of taxonomy, who understood about different species, who could recognize patterns in nature and classify objects. I realized that to explain that kind of ability, I would have to manipulate the other intelligences in ways that weren't appropriate.

So I began to think about whether the capacity to classify nature might be a separate intelligence. The naturalist ability passed with flying colors. Here are a couple of reasons: First, it's an ability we need to survive as human beings. We need, for example, to know which animals to hunt and which to run away from. Second, this ability isn't restricted to human beings. Other animals need to have a naturalist intelligence to survive. Finally, the big selling point is that brain evidence supports the existence of the naturalist intelligence. There are certain parts of the brain particularly dedicated to the recognition and the naming of what are called "natural" things.

How do you describe the naturalist intelligence to those of us who aren't psychologists?

The naturalist intelligence refers to the ability to recognize and classify plants, minerals, and animals, including rocks and grass and all variety of flora and fauna. The ability to recognize cultural artifacts like cars or sneakers may also depend on the naturalist intelligence.

Now, everybody can do this to a certain extent—we can all recognize dogs, cats, trees. But, some people from an early age are extremely good at recognizing and classifying artifacts. For example, we all know kids who, at age

3 or 4, are better at recognizing dinosaurs than most adults.

Darwin is probably the most famous example of a naturalist because he saw so deeply into the nature of living things.

Are there any other abilities you're considering calling intelligences?

Well, there may be an existential intelligence that refers to the human inclination to ask very basic questions about existence. Who are we? Where do we come from? What's it all about? Why do we die? We might say that existential intelligence allows us to know the invisible, outside world. The only reason I haven't given a seal of approval to the existential intelligence is that I don't think we have good brain evidence yet on its existence in the nervous system—one of the criteria for an intelligence.

© Susie Fitzhugh

You have said that the theory of multiple intelligences may be best understood when we know what it critiques. What do you mean?

The standard view of intelligence is that intelligence is something you are born with; you have only a certain amount of it; you cannot do much about how much of that intelligence you have; and tests exist that can tell you how smart you are. The theory of multiple intelligences challenges that view. It asks, instead, "Given what we know about the brain, evolution, and the differences in cultures, what are the sets of human abilities we all share?"

My analysis suggested that rather than one or two intelligences, all human beings have several (eight) intelligences. What makes life interesting, however, is that we don't have the same strength in each intelligence area, and we don't have the same amalgam of intelligences. Just as we look different from one another and have different kinds of personalities, we also have different kinds of minds.

This premise has very serious educational implications. If we treat everybody as if they are the same, we're catering to one profile of intelligence, the language-logic profile. It's great if you have that profile, but it's not great for the vast majority of human beings who do not have that particular profile of intelligence.

School matters, but only insofar as it yields something that can be used once students leave school.

Can you explain more fully how the theory of multiple intelligences challenges what has become known as IQ?

The theory challenges the entire notion of IQ. The IQ test was developed about a century ago as a way to determine who would have trouble in school. The test measures linguistic ability, logical-mathematical ability, and, occasionally, spatial ability.

What the intelligence test does not do is inform us about our other intelligences; it also doesn't look at other virtues like creativity or civic mindedness, or whether a person is moral or ethical.

We don't do much IQ testing anymore, but the shadow of IQ tests is still with us because the SAT—arguably the most potent examination in the world—is basically the same kind of disembodied language-logic instrument.

The truth is, I don't believe there is such a general thing as scholastic aptitude. Even so, I don't think that the SAT will fade until colleges indicate that they'd rather have students who know how to use their minds well—students who may or may not be good test takers, but who are serious, inquisitive, and know how to probe and problem-solve. That is really what college professors want, I believe.

Can we strengthen our intelligences? If so, how?

We can all get better at each of the intelligences, although some people will improve in an intelligence area more readily than others, either because biology gave them a better brain for that intelligence or because their culture gave them a better teacher.

Teachers have to help students use their combination of intelligences to be successful in school, to help them learn whatever it is they want to learn, as well as what the teachers and society believe they have to learn.

Now, I'm not arguing that kids shouldn't learn the literacies. Of course they should learn the literacies. Nor am I arguing that kids shouldn't learn the disciplines. I'm a tremendous champion of the disciplines. What I argue against is the notion that there's only one way to learn how to read, only one way to learn how to compute, only one way to learn about biology. I think that such contentions are nonsense.

It's equally nonsensical to say that everything should be taught seven or eight ways. That's not the point of the MI theory. The point is to realize that any topic of importance, from any discipline, can be taught in more than one way. There are things people need to know, and educators have to be extraordinarily imaginative and persistent in helping students understand things better.

A popular activity among those who are first exploring multiple intelligences is to construct their own intellectual profile. It's thought that when teachers go through the process of creating such a profile, they're more likely to recognize and appreciate the intellectual strengths of their students. What is your view on this kind of activity?

My own studies have shown that people love to do this. Kids like to do it, adults like to do it. And, as an activity, I think it's perfectly harmless.

I get concerned, though, when people think that determining your intellectual profile—or that of someone else—is an end in itself.

You have to use the profile to understand the ways in which you seem to learn easily. And, from there, determine how to use those strengths to help you become more successful in other endeavors. Then, the profile becomes a way for you to understand yourself better, and you can use that understanding to catapult yourself to a better level of understanding or to a higher level of skill.

How has your understanding of the multiple intelligences influenced how you teach?

My own teaching has changed slowly as a result of multiple intelligences because I'm teaching graduate students psychological theory and there are only so many ways I can do that. I am more open to group work and to student projects of various sorts, but even if I wanted to be an "MI professor" of graduate students, I still have a certain moral obligation to prepare them for a world in which they will have to write scholarly articles and prepare theses.

As long as you can lose one ability while others are spared, you cannot just have a single intelligence.

Where I've changed much more, I believe, is at the workplace. I direct research projects and work with all kinds of people. Probably 10 to 15 years ago, I would have tried to find people who were just like me to work with me on these projects.

I've really changed my attitude a lot on that score. Now I think much more in terms of what people are good

at and in putting together teams of people whose varying strengths complement one another.

How should thoughtful educators implement the theory of multiple intelligences?

Although there is no single MI route, it's very important that a teacher take individual differences among kinds very seriously. You cannot be a good MI teacher if you don't want to know each child and try to gear how you teach and how you evaluate to that particular child. The bottom line is a deep interest in children and how their minds are different from one another, and in helping them use their minds well.

Now, kids can be great informants for teachers. For example, a teacher might say, "Look, Benjamin, this obviously isn't working. Should we try using a picture?" If Benjamin gets excited about that approach, that's a pretty good clue to the teacher about what could work.

The theory of multiple intelligences, in and of itself, is not going to solve anything in our society, but linking the multiple intelligences with a curriculum focused on understanding is an extremely powerful intellectual undertaking.

When I talk about understanding, I mean that students can take ideas they learn in school, or anywhere for that matter, and apply those appropriately in new situations. We know people truly understand something when they can represent the knowledge in more than one way. We have to put understanding up front in school. Once we have that goal, multiple intelligences can be a terrific handmaiden because understandings involve a mix of mental representations, entailing different intelligences.

People often say that what they remember most about school are those learning experiences that were linked to real life. How does the theory of multiple intelligences help connect learning to the world outside the classroom?

The theory of multiple intelligences wasn't based on school work or on tests. Instead, what I did was look at the world and ask, What are the things that people do in the world? What does it mean to be a surgeon? What does it mean to be a politician? What does it mean to be an artist or a sculptor? What abilities do you need to do those things? My theory, then, came from the things that are valued in the world.

So when a school values multiple intelligences, the relationship to what's valued in the world is patent. If you cannot easily relate this activity to something that's valued in the world, the school has probably lost the core idea of multiple intelligences, which is that these intelligences evolved to help people do things that matter in the real world.

School matters, but only insofar as it yields something that can be used once students leave school.

The Intelligences, in Gardner's Words

• Linguistic intelligence is the capacity to use language, your native language, and perhaps other languages, to express what's on your mind and to understand other people. Poets really specialize in linguistic intelligence, but any kind of writer, orator, speaker, lawyer, or a person for whom language is an important stock in trade highlights linguistic intelligence.

• People with a highly developed logical-mathematical intelligence understand the underlying principles of some kind of a causal system, the way a scientist or a logician does; or can manipulate numbers, quantities, and operations, the way a mathematician does.

• Spatial intelligence refers to the ability to represent the spatial world internally in your mind—the way a sailor or airplane pilot navigates the large spatial world, or the way a chess player or sculptor represents a more circumscribed spatial world. Spatial intelligence can be used in the arts or in the sciences. If you are spatially intelligent and oriented toward the arts, you are more likely to become a painter or a sculptor or an architect than, say, a musician or a writer. Similarly, certain sciences like anatomy or topology emphasize spatial intelligence.

• Bodily kinesthetic intelligence is the capacity to use your whole body or parts of your body—your hand, your fingers, your arms—to solve a problem, make something, or put on some kind of a production. The most evident examples are people in athletics or the performing arts, particularly dance or acting.

• Musical intelligence is the capacity to think in music, to be able to hear patterns, recognize them, remember them, and perhaps manipulate them. People who have a strong musical intelligence don't just remember music easily—they can't get it out of their minds, it's so omnipresent. Now, some people will say, "Yes, music is important, but it's a talent, not an intelligence." And I say, "Fine, let's call it a talent." But, then we have to leave the word *intelligent* out of *all* discussions of human abilities. You know, Mozart was damned smart!

• Interpersonal intelligence is understanding other people. It's an ability we all need, but is at a premium if you are a teacher, clinician, salesperson, or politician. Anybody who deals with other people has to be skilled in the interpersonal sphere.

• Intrapersonal intelligence refers to having an understanding of yourself, of knowing who you are, what you can do, what you want to do, how you react to things, which things to avoid, and which things to gravitate toward. We are drawn to people who have a good understanding of themselves because those people tend not to screw up. They tend to know what they can do. They tend to know what they can't do. And they tend to know where to go if they need help.

• Naturalist intelligence designates the human ability to discriminate among living things (plants, animals) as well as sensitivity to other features of the natural world (clouds, rock configurations). This ability was clearly of value in our evolutionary past as hunters, gatherers, and farmers; it continues to be central in such roles as botanist or chef. I also speculate that much of our consumer society exploits the naturalist intelligences, which can be mobilized in the discrimination among cars, sneakers, kinds of makeup, and the like. The kind of pattern recognition valued in certain of the sciences may also draw upon naturalist intelligence.

How can teachers be guided by multiple intelligences when creating assessment tools?

We need to develop assessments that are much more representative of what human beings are going to have to do to survive in this society. For example, I value literacy, but my measure of literacy should not be whether you can answer a multiple-choice question that asks you to select the best meaning of a paragraph. Instead, I'd rather have you read the paragraph and list four questions you have about the paragraph and figure out how you would answer those questions. Or, if I want to know how you can write, let me give you a stem and see whether you can write about that topic, or let me ask you to write an editorial in response to something you read in the newspaper or observed on the street.

The current emphasis on performance assessment is well supported by the theory of multiple intelligences. Indeed, you could not really be an advocate of multiple intelligences if you didn't have some dissatisfaction with the current testing because it's so focused on short-answer, linguistic, or logical kinds of items.

MI theory is very congenial to an approach that says: one, let's not look at things through the filter of a short-answer test. Let's look directly at the performance that we value, whether it's a linguistic, logical, aesthetic, or social performance; and, two, let's never pin our assessment of understanding on just one particular measure, but let's always allow students to show their understanding in a variety of ways.

You have identified several myths about the theory of multiple intelligences. Can you describe some of those myths?

One myth that I personally find irritating is that an intelligence is the same as a learning style. Learning styles are claims about ways in which individuals purportedly approach everything they do. If you are planful, you are supposed to be planful about everything. If you are logical-sequential, you are supposed to be logical-sequential about everything. My own research and observations suggest that that's a dubious assumption. But whether or not that's true, learning styles are very different from multiple intelligences.

© Susie Fitzhugh

Multiple intelligences claims that we respond, individually, in different ways to different kinds of content, such as language or music or other people. This is very different from the notion of learning style.

You can say that a child is a visual learner, but that's not a multiple intelligences way of talking about things. What I would say is, "Here is a child who very easily represents things spatially, and we can draw upon that strength if need be when we want to teach the child something new."

Another widely believed myth is that, because we have seven or eight intelligences, we should create seven or eight tests to measure students' strengths in each of those areas. That is a perversion of the theory. It's re-creating the sin of the single intelligence quotient and just multiplying it by a larger number. I'm personally against assessment of intelligences unless such a measurement is used for a very specific learning purpose—we want to help a child understand her history or his mathematics better and, therefore, want to see what might be good entry points for that particular child.

What experiences led you to the study of human intelligence?

It's hard for me to pick out a single moment, but I can see a couple of snapshots. When I was in high school, my uncle gave me a textbook in psychology. I'd never actually heard of psychology before. This textbook helped me understand color blindness. I'm color blind, and I became fascinated by the existence of plates that illustrated what color blindness was. I could actually explain why I couldn't see colors.

Another time when I was studying the Reformation, I read a book by Erik Erikson called *Young Man Luther* (1958).[1] I was fascinated by the psychological motivation of Luther to attack the Catholic Church. That fascination influenced my decision to go into psychology.

The most important influence was actually learning about brain damage and what could happen to people when they had strokes. When a person has a stroke, a certain part of the brain gets injured, and that injury can tell you what that part of the brain does. Individuals who lose their musical abilities can still talk. People who lose their linguistic ability still might be able to sing. That understanding not only brought me into the whole world of brain study, but it was really the seed that led ultimately to the theory of multiple intelligences. As long as you can lose one ability while others are spared, you cannot just have a single intelligence. You have to have several intelligences.

Note

1. See Erik Erikson, *Young Man Luther* (New York: W. W. Norton, 1958).

Howard Gardner is Professor of Education at Harvard Graduate School of Education and author of, among other books, *The Unschooled Mind: How Children Think and How Schools Should Teach* (1991). He can be reached at Roy B. Larsen Hall, 2nd Floor, Appian Way, Harvard Graduate School of Education, Cambridge, MA 02138. **Kathy Checkley** is a staff writer for *Update* and has assisted in the development of ASCD's new CD-ROM, *Exploring Our Multiple Intelligences*, pilot online project on multiple intelligences.

HOW SHOULD READING BE TAUGHT?

Educators have long argued over the best way to teach reading to children. The research, however, indicates that a highly popular method is inadequate on its own.

Keith Rayner, Barbara R. Foorman, Charles A. Perfetti, David Pesetsky and Mark S. Seidenberg

Most of us are a little fuzzy on how we learned to read, much as we cannot recall anything special about learning to talk. Although these skills are related, the ways we acquire them differ profoundly. Learning to speak is automatic for almost all children brought up in normal circumstances, but learning to read requires elaborate instruction and conscious effort. Remember how hard it once was? Reading this page with the magazine turned upside down should bring back some of the struggles of early childhood, when working through even a simple passage was a slog.

Well aware of the difficulties, educators have given a great deal of thought to how they can best help children learn to read. No single method has triumphed. Indeed, heated arguments about the most appropriate form of reading instruction continue to polarize the teaching community. To help forge a consensus, we recently came together under the aegis of the American Psychological Society to review the voluminous research on the mental processing that underlies skilled reading and on how reading should be taught. The results point strongly in directions that may disturb some parents.

Three general approaches have been tried. In one, called whole-word instruction (also known as the "looksay" method), children learn by rote how to recognize at a glance a vocabulary of 50 to 100 words. Then they gradually acquire other words, often through seeing them used over and over in the context of a story. ("Run, Spot, run," from the well-known Dick and Jane series of readers, is a classic example of a sentence designed to aid whole-word instruction.) This procedure could just as well be used to learn Chinese, in which each character in the written language corresponds to a word or word root.

Overview/ *Teaching Reading*

- Learning to read is a crucial step in children's education because those who fare poorly in the early grades are unlikely to catch up with their more skilled classmates, even after years of further schooling.
- During the 1990s many educators in America abandoned the traditional "phonics" method of reading instruction: teaching children directly the correspondences between spoken sounds and letters that represent them. Instead elementary school teachers turned to various "whole-language" methods, by which students learn the connections between letters and sounds incidentally in the course of literature-based activities.
- Evaluations of the effectiveness of the two methods have shown that children become skilled readers much more readily when their instruction includes phonics. Modern research in psychology and linguistics helps to explain why this is so.

Actually, for the past half a century, youngsters in China have followed a different prescription: as a first step toward literacy, they are taught to read Chinese words using the Roman alphabet. Similarly, speakers of most other languages learn the relationship between letters and the sounds associated with them (phonemes). That is, children are taught how to use their knowledge of the alphabet to sound out words. This procedure constitutes a second approach to teaching reading—the phonics so familiar to baby boomers.

The connections between letters and phonemes would appear simple enough. For example, the letter "b" almost always sounds the same as it does in the word "bat." Or consider the silent "e," which denotes that the preceding vowel has a long sound, as in the words "pave," "save" and "gave." Although the final "e" is not voiced, its role is straightforward. English, however, offers plenty of exceptions—take the word "have." There are, in fact, hundreds of deviations from the normal patterns, including "give," "said," "is," "was," "were," "done" and "some." Such problematic yet common words are among the first a child has to learn.

Clearly, the lack of perfect correspondence between letters and sounds is a source of confusion and a potential roadblock for the beginning reader. As a result, many schools have adopted a different approach: the whole-language method (also called literature-based instruction or guided reading). The strategy here is similar to whole-word instruction, but it relies more heavily on the child's experience with language. For example, students are offered engaging books and are encouraged to guess the words that they do not know by considering the context of the sentence or by looking for clues in the story line and illustrations, rather than trying to sound them out. Often children are given the opportunity to write stories of their own, in an effort to instill a love of words and reading.

The whole-language approach aims to make reading instruction enjoyable. One of its key principles is that the rules of phonics should *not* be taught directly. Rather the connection between letters and sounds should be learned incidentally through exposure to text. This methodology stipulates that students should not be corrected when they make errors reading words. The philosophical rationale is that learning to read, like learning to speak, is a natural act that children can essentially teach themselves how to do. Just how well that assumption holds up in practice often depends on the individual.

How Beginners Learn to Read

ALTHOUGH MANY PARENTS might think that innate intelligence will govern how well their kids learn to read no matter what type of instruction is given, the evidence suggests otherwise. Two separate studies from the 1960s and 1970s have shown that, in general, IQ has very little bearing on early reading ability. More recently, researchers have found that children who have difficulty learning to read often have above-average IQs.

It might also be tempting to believe that the differences in early reading ability wash out over time, but that, too, is a misconception. Keith E. Stanovich of the University of Toronto has, for example, shown that children's facility with reading in the first grade usually provides a good indication of what their 11th-grade reading proficiency will turn out to be. Why? Because reading re-

quires practice, and those who excel end up practicing the most. Hence, the gap between more and less able readers in the first few grades generally grows over the years.

Teaching children to read well early on obviously helps to develop a valuable lifetime habit; thus, it is no wonder that educators have placed enormous emphasis on finding the best way to teach these skills. At one time, a great deal of debate in educational circles centered on whether whole-word or phonics instruction was the most effective. But over the past decade or so, arguments have revolved around the relative merits of phonics and whole-word's successor, whole-language.

Many teachers adopted the whole-language approach because of its intuitive appeal. After all, making reading fun promises to keep children motivated, and learning to read depends more on what the student does than on what the teacher does. But the prospect of keeping kids interested would not have been enough by itself to convince teachers to use the whole-language method. What really sold it was an educational philosophy that empowered teachers to compose their own curricula and encouraged them to treat children as active participants, an enticing combination that was promoted with flair by some educator celebrities. The presumed benefits of whole-language instruction—and the stark contrast to the perceived dullness of phonics—led to its growing acceptance across America during the 1990s.

In Massachusetts, for example, whole-language almost became the official state method of instruction with passage of the Massachusetts Education Reform Act of 1993. That legislation changed what had been a tradition of little state involvement in school curriculum. The law promised to increase state funding for public education, and in exchange local school systems were required to meet new state standards.

Despite the previous lack of central control, the reading curricula in Massachusetts public schools were rather uniform—and it is not difficult to understand why. As in other places, teachers and administrators took the same courses at the same handful of universities, attended the same workshops, bought the same textbooks and responded to the same educational fashions. Hence, the committee of educators charged by the state government with framing a statement about how reading should be taught were heavily influenced by the whole-language approach. And naturally enough, the document they produced highlighted the idea that children could learn to read the same way they learned to talk. It presented a vision of language acquisition that attributed the process to curiosity and enthusiasm alone, and it seemed authoritative, claiming support from research.

As it happens, Massachusetts is home to hubs of research in linguistics and the psychology of reading—at the Massachusetts Institute of Technology and the University of Massachusetts at Amherst. After the content of the proposed curriculum document became known, a

How Phonics Is Taught

IN TEACHING PHONICS, instructors present the spellings for different sounds in a specific order, introducing the simplest (or most useful) patterns early on. They then practice these patterns with their students using engaging stories. Shown below are 20 of the 120 or so patterns presented to first graders in one modern phonics program *Open Court Reading*, from SRA/McGraw-Hill. Choosing another published system of phonics instruction would provide the students with a somewhat different scope and sequence, but the general strategy would be the same.

Some teachers prefer to dispense with such structured programs and to create phonics lessons on their own. Doing so is no small chore, because they have so may decisions to make. Should rules be taught for all the ways to spell each of the approximately 40 distinct sounds (phonemes) of American English? For the long "a" alone, there are eight spelling patterns, as in "make," "rain," "say," "they," "baby," "eight," "vein," and "great." And do all the phonemes need attention? For example, do the vowel sounds in "book" and "moon" both need to be taught?

Although some teachers can tackle these questions and create phonics lessons that are every bit as effective as those provided in a published program, most probably have too many demands on their time to take on that task. Just how much latitude phonics instructors should be given and how effectively they can make use of the flexibility remain points of debate in a number of school districts.

—*K.R., B.R.F., C.A.P., D.P., and M.S.S.*

Letter Pattern to Be Mastered (first 10 patterns taught)	One of the Words Used as Examples	Letter pattern to be Mastered (final 10 patterns taught)	One of the Words Used as Examples
m	monkey	ture	nature
a	lamb	ear	earn
t	time	or	worm
h	hound	ar	carry
p	popcorn	er	berry
n	nose	tion	nation
c	camera	ion	million
d	dinosaur	re	reheat
(contractions)	can't	ure	measure
s	sausages	ous	dangerous

number of scholars in these places (including two of us) reacted strongly. Dozens of linguists and psychologists signed a letter taking issue with the document's assertion that research supported whole-language instruction. They sent it to the state commissioner of education, who eventually saw to it that corrections were made and that state standards reflected the actual research results.

By chance, this incident took place just as debate about how to teach reading was heating up in other states (most notably, in California and Texas). Sides were often divided along political lines, with conservatives backing phonics and liberals favoring whole-language instruction. Consequently, the Massachusetts dispute drew national attention. In particular, conservative newsletters and Web sites created considerable publicity for the researchers' letter—an ironic twist, given that the list of professors who signed it included several well-known leftists.

Why Phonics?

WHY DID SO MANY LINGUISTS and psychologists object strongly to the abandonment of phonics? In short, because research had clearly demonstrated that understanding how letters relate to the component sounds of words is critically important in reading. Our recent review of the topic shows that there is no doubt about it: teaching that makes the rules of phonics clear will ultimately be more successful than teaching that does not. Admittedly, some children can infer these principles on their own, but most need explicit instruction in phonics, or their reading skills will suffer.

U.S. Government Studies Supporting Phonics Instruction

TITLE	ORGANIZER	SCOPE	SUMMARY STATEMENT
Preventing Reading Difficulties in Young Children	National Academy of Sciences/National Research Council (sponsored by the Department of Education); 1998	Literature review covering more than 700 publications	"Failure to grasp that written spellings systematically represent the sounds of spoken words makes it difficult not only to recognize printed words but also to understand how to learn and to profit from instruction. If a child cannot rely on the alphabetic principle, word recognition is inaccurate or laborious and comprehension of connected text will be impeded."
Teaching Children to Read: An Evidence-Based Assessment of the Scientific Research Literature on Reading and Its Implications for Reading Instruction	National Reading panel (convened by the National Institute of Child Health and Human Development, in consultation with the secretary of education); 2000	Includes a meta-analysis of 38 controlled studies of phonics instruction published since 1970	"The meta-analysis indicated that systematic phonics instruction enhances children's success in learning to read and that systematic phonics instruction is significantly more effective than instruction that teaches little or no phonics."

This conclusion rests, in part, on knowledge of how experienced readers make sense of words on a page—an understanding that psychologists have developed over many decades. One of the first researchers to investigate the nature of reading was James M. Cattell, an American psychologist of the Victorian era. To test whether proficient readers were taking in words letter by letter or all at once, he performed a pioneering experiment, exposing subjects very briefly to whole words or to individual letters and asking them what they saw. He found that they were better able to report words than letters. Thus, it seemed apparent to him that people do not absorb printed words one letter at a time. (Such findings helped to motivate the creation of the whole-word method later on.) More recent research has refined our knowledge of this phenomenon. For example, studies that track eye movements during reading show that although people register each letter in a word as a separate symbol, they normally perceive all the letters in a word simultaneously.

The question of whether accomplished readers mentally sound out words took longer to answer. Advocates of whole-language instruction have argued forcefully for more than 20 years that people often derive meanings directly from print without ever determining the sound of the word. Some psychologists today accept this view, but most believe that reading is typically a process of rapidly sounding out words mentally, even for the highly skilled.

The most compelling evidence for this last contention comes from clever experiments by Guy Van Orden of Arizona State University wherein a subject is first asked a question, such as "Is it a flower?" He or she is then presented with a target word (for example, "rose") and asked whether the word fits the category. Sometimes the subject is offered a word that sounds the same as a correct answer (called a homophone—say, "rows" instead of "rose"). Subjects often mistakenly identify such words as fitting the category, and these incorrect responses show that readers routinely convert strings of letters to sounds (or rather, to their unvoiced mental equivalents), which they then use to ascertain meanings.

Some eye-movement studies have used homophones to demonstrate that the process of sounding out words mentally begins very rapidly after a reader's gaze first fixes on a particular word. And recent brain studies show that the primary motor cortex is active during reading, presumably because it is involved with mouth movements used in reading aloud.

Consequently, psychologists now know that the process of mentally sounding out words is an integral part of silent reading, even for the highly skilled. This understanding suggests that learning the correspondences between letters and sounds—that is to say, phonics—is keenly important for beginners. Further support for phonics instruction comes from experiments designed to mimic the way people learn to read.

Investigators have, for example, trained English-speaking college students to read using unfamiliar symbols such as Arabic letters. One group learned the phonemes associated with individual Arabic letters (the phonics approach), while another group learned entire words associated with certain strings of Arabic letters (whole-word). Then both groups were required to read a new set of words constructed from the original characters. In general, readers who were taught the rules of phonics could read many more new words than those trained with a whole-word procedure. Research using computer programs that simulate how children read also indicates that gaining a command of phonics is easier than learning to associate whole words with their meanings.

Classroom studies comparing phonics with either whole-word or whole-language instruction are also quite illuminating. The late Jeanne S. Chall of Harvard University carried out a comprehensive review of such work, as subsequently did Marilyn J. Adams, who was also affiliated with Harvard. In a nutshell, their reviews, as well as our own, show that systematic phonics instruction produces higher achievement for beginning readers. The differences are greatest for students at risk of failing to learn to read, such as those living in homes where the value of literacy is not emphasized.

One particularly persuasive study was undertaken as long ago as 1985. Mary Ann Evans of the University of Guelph in Canada and Thomas H. Carr of Michigan State University compared two programs used in 20 first-grade classrooms. Half the students were offered traditional reading instruction, which included the use of specially designed readers, phonics drills and applications. The other half were taught using an individualized method that drew from their experiences with language; these children produced their own booklets of stories and developed sets of words to be recognized (common components of the whole-language approach). The two groups spent the same amount of time on reading, had similar socioeconomic profiles and were virtually identical on measures of intelligence and language maturity. Yet this study found that the first group scored higher at year's end on tests of reading and comprehension.

More recent investigations (namely, authoritative evaluations by the National Reading Panel and the National Research Council) examining all the available studies echo these results. Influenced by such findings, the Bush administration is now promoting the inclusion of phonics in reading programs nationwide.

A Delicate Balance

IF RESEARCHERS ARE SO CONVINCED about the need for phonics instruction, why does the debate continue? Because the controversy is enmeshed in the philosophical differences between traditional and progressive approaches, differences that have divided American educators for years. The progressives challenge the results of laboratory tests and classroom studies on the basis of a broad philosophical skepticism about the value of such research. They champion student-centered learning and teacher empowerment. Sadly, they fail to realize that these very admirable educational values are equally consistent with the teaching of phonics.

If schools of education insisted that would-be reading teachers learned something about the vast research in linguistics and psychology that bears on reading, and if these institutions regularly included a modern, high-quality course on phonics, their graduates would be more eager to use phonics and would be prepared to do so effectively.

They would nor have to follow scripted programs or rely on formulaic workbooks and could allow their pupils to apply the principles of phonics while reading for pleasure. Using whole-language activities to supplement phonics instruction certainly helps to make reading fun and meaningful for children, so no one would want to see such tools discarded. Indeed, recent work has indicated—and many teachers have discovered—that the combination of literature-based instruction and phonics is more powerful than either method used alone.

Teachers obviously need to strike a balance. But in doing so, we urge them to remember that reading must be grounded in a firm understanding of the connections between letters and sounds. Instructors should recognize the ample evidence that youngsters who are directly taught phonics become better at reading, spelling and comprehension than those who must pick up all the confusing rules of English on their own. Educators who deny this reality are neglecting decades of research. They are also neglecting the needs of their students.

MORE TO EXPLORE

Beginning to Read: Thinking and Learning about Print. Marilyn J. Adams. MIT Press, 1990.

Learning to Read: The Great Debate. Jeanne S. Chall. Harcourt Brace, 1996.

Preventing Reading Difficulties in Young Children. Edited by C. E. Snow et al. National Academy Press, 1998. Available at books.nap.edu/books/030906418X/html/index.html

Teaching Children to Read: An Evidence-Based Assessment of the Scientific Research Literature on Reading and Its Implications for Reading Instruction. National Reading Panel. National Institute of Child Health and Human Development, 2000. Available at www.nationalreadingpanel.org/Publications/publications.htm

How Psychological Science Informs the Teaching of Reading. Keith Rayner, Barbara R. Foorman, Charles A. Perfetti, David Pesetsky and Mark S. Seidenberg in Psychological Science in the Public Interest, Vol. 2, No. 2, pages 31–74; November 2001. Available at www.psychologicalscience.org/newsresearch/publications/journals/pspi2_2.html

THE AUTHORS KEITH RAYNER, BARBARA R. FOORMAN, CHARLES A. PERFETTI, DAVID PESETSKY and MARK S. SEIDENBERG collaborated on a paper surveying the teaching of reading for the November 2001 issue of Psychological Science in the Public Interest. Rayner, Distinguished Professor of Psychology at the University of Massachusetts at Amherst, is currently on sabbatical in England at the University of Durham. Foorman is a professor of pediatrics at the University of Texas–Houston Health Science Center, where she directs the Center for Academic and Reading Skills. Perfetti is University Professor of Psychology, and Linguistics at the University of Pittsburgh, where he is associate director of the Learning Research and Development Center. Pesetsky is Ferrari P. Ward Professor of Linguistics at the Massachusetts Institute of Technology. Seidenberg is a professor of psychology at the University of Wisconsin–Madison.

Where the Boys Are

Is America shortchanging
male children?

By Cathy Young

One day last September, there were two back-to-back events in adjacent rooms at the National Press Club in Washington, D.C. "Beyond the 'Gender Wars,'" a symposium organized by the American Association of University Women (AAUW), was followed by a rejoinder from the Independent Women's Forum (IWF), "The XY Files: The Truth Is Out There… About the Differences Between Boys and Girls." Each event largely followed a predictable script. On the AAUW side, there was verbiage about "gender, race, and class" and hand-wringing about the "conservative backlash"; despite an occasional nod to innate sex differences, "gender equity" was pointedly defined as "equal outcomes." On the IWF side, there were affirmations of *vive la différence* and warnings about the perils of trying to engineer androgyny; despite some acknowledgment that there are not only differences between the sexes but much overlap, the old-fashioned wisdom about men and women was treated as timeless truth. And yet both discussions shared one major theme: the suddenly hot issue of boys—to be more specific, boys as the victimized sex in American education and culture.

Just a few years ago, of course, girls were the ones whose victimization by sexist schools and a male-dominated society was proclaimed on the front pages of newspapers and lamented in editorials, thanks largely to widely publicized reports released by the AAUW in the early 1990s. It was probably only a matter of time before somebody asked, "But what about boys?" By the end of the decade, headlines like "How Boys Lost Out to Girl Power" began to crop up in the media, and boys-in-crisis books began to hit the shelves.

But as the two National Press Club panels underscored, two contrasting arguments are being made on behalf of boys. In one room, there was sympathy for boys who yearn to be gentle, nurturing, and openly emotional but live in a society that labels such qualities "sissy"; in the other, there was sympathy for boys who want only to be boys but live in a society that labels their natural qualities aggressive and patriarchal. Harvard psychiatrist William Pollack, author of the 1999 bestseller *Real Boys: Rescuing Our Sons From the Myths of Boyhood*, believes boys are suffering because our culture traps them in the rigid codes of traditional manhood. American Enterprise Institute scholar Christina Hoff Sommers, author of the controversial new volume *The War Against Boys: How Misguided Feminism Is Harming Our Young Men*, believes boys are suffering because our culture seeks to "feminize" them and devalues manhood. (Guess which of them spoke on which panel.) One camp wants to reform masculinity, the other to restore it; one seeks to rescue boys from patriarchy, the other from feminism.

Both sides, however, agree that something is rotten in the state of boyhood. *Real Boys* opens with the assertion that boys, including many who seem to be doing fine, are "in serious trouble" and "in a desperate crisis." Pollack and other gender reformers paint the typical American boy as an emotional cripple, if not a walking time bomb ready to explode into a school massacre. The shooters of Littleton and Jonesboro, Pollack has said, are merely "the tip of the iceberg."

In *The War Against Boys*, Sommers persuasively challenges this hysteria, noting that it's ludicrous to generalize from a few sociopaths to "millions of healthy male children" who manage to get through high school without gunning down a single person. (She fails to mention that some people in the pro-manhood camp have been just as eager to use homicidal boys as symbols of a male crisis: A couple of years ago in *Commentary*, Midge Decter wrote that "raging schoolyard murder" is what happens when boys are deprived of "manly instruction" and honorable ways to assert their masculinity.) Sommers argues that most children, male and female, are in fairly good psychological health and in no need of "fixing."

Yet Sommers herself refers to boys as "the gender at risk," and her book is hardly free of alarmism, from the title to an opening that rivals Pollack's: "It's a bad time to be a boy in America."

Gender Gap

The most tangible and effectively documented cause of concern is male academic underachievement:

• Girls make up 57 percent of straight-A students; boys make up 57 percent of high school dropouts.

• In 1998, 48 percent of girls but only 40 percent of boys graduating from high school had completed the courses in English, social studies, science, math, and foreign languages recommended as a minimum by the National Commission on Excellence in Education. (In 1987 there was no such gender gap, though only 18 percent of students met these requirements.) According to the National Center for Education Statistics, high school girls now outnumber boys in upper-level courses in algebra, chemistry, and biology; physics is the only subject in which males are still a majority.

• On the National Assessment of Educational Progress (NAEP) tests in 1996, 17-year-old girls, on average, outscored boys by 14 points in reading and 17 points in writing (on a scale of 0 to 500). While boys did better on the math and science tests, it was by margins of five and eight points, respectively.

• Women account for 56 percent of college enrollment in America. This is not due simply, as some feminists claim, to older women going back to school; among 1997 high school graduates, 64 percent of boys and 70 percent of girls went on to college. Female college freshmen are also more likely than men to get a degree in four years.

These differences do not cut across all racial and social lines. The gender gap in higher education has reached truly startling proportions among blacks. From 1977 to 1997, the number of bachelor's degrees awarded annually rose by 30 percent for black men but by 77 percent for black women; among 1996–97 college graduates, black women outnumbered men almost 2 to 1. The "man shortage" among college-educated blacks, which has contributed to tensions over interracial dating, is singled out as a

"cause for concern" in the Urban League's recent report *The State of Black America 1999*.

Among non-Hispanic whites, women now receive 55 percent of bachelor's degrees. Feminists are correct when they say this imbalance is partly due to older women going back to school after growing up in an era when girls were expected to pursue the "MRS degree." In 1998, according to the Census Bureau, 48 percent of white college students under 35 were male. But for blacks and Hispanics, a female-to-male ratio of about 3 to 2 persists even when older students are excluded.

For middle-class girls and boys, college is now as much of a given as a high school diploma. Girls from working-class and poor families, on the other hand, are significantly more likely to go to college than boys. There are complex reasons for this. About one-tenth of women in college are training for the health professions, "feminine" jobs similar in status to predominantly male skilled trades that don't require college studies. (Interestingly, female registered nurses and therapists now outearn male mechanics and construction workers.) There is also a theory that, in the new economy, a certificate from a high-tech company's training program may be worth more than a college degree, and that it's mostly young men who skip college to pursue such options. But this explanation, appealing to many feminists, remains speculative. No one knows how many people actually do this; generally, for men or women, the lack of a college degree is still a serious handicap in the marketplace.

In many cases, the "college gap" indisputably reflects a trend toward more upward mobility for women. In a 1999 Rutgers Marriage Project study of sex and relationships among noncollege men and women under 30, David Popenoe and Barbara Dafoe Whitehead report that the women in their focus groups came across as more confident and responsible, with "clear and generally realistic plans for moving up the career ladder," including plans for going back to school. The men seemed less focused and mature; when they talked about their plans for getting ahead, it was often in terms of such "goals" as winning the lottery.

Girls Rule

Perhaps the social changes of the past three decades have made young women more self-assured and eager to use their new opportunities, while leaving many men unnerved and confused about what's expected of them. It may also be that boys, particularly those from low-income families, often become alienated from school early—both because their slower developmental timetable causes them to fall behind girls and because school is a "feminized" environment with mostly female authority figures and boy-unfriendly rules that emphasize being quiet and sitting still.

Some teachers may be prejudiced against boys, regarding them as little brutes or rascals. In a 1990 survey commissioned by the AAUW, children were asked whom teachers considered smarter and liked better; the vast majority of boys and girls alike said "girls." Journalist Kathleen Parker recalls that her son, now a teenager, had a grade school teacher who openly said she liked girls more and singled out boys for verbal abuse—such as telling a student who had his feet up on the desk, "Put your feet down; I don't want to look at your genitalia."

Traditional schoolmarmish distaste for unruly young males may be amplified by modern gender politics. Some educators clearly see boys as budding sexists and predators in need of re-education. Some classrooms become forums for diatribes about the sins of white males, and some boys may be hit with absurd charges of misconduct—such as Jonathan Prevette, the Lexington, North Carolina, first-grader punished with a one-day suspension in 1996 for kissing a girl on the cheek.

"If you listen to 10- or 11-year-old boys, you will hear that school is not a very happy place for them," says Bret Burkholder, a counselor at Pierce College in Puyallup, Washington, who also works with younger boys as a baseball coach. "It's a place where they're consistently made to feel stupid, where girls can walk around in T-shirts that say 'Girls rule, boys drool,' but if a boy makes a negative comment about girls he'll have the book thrown at him."

Even apart from feminism, some "progressive" trends in education may have been detrimental to boys. For example, British researchers have found that "whole language" reading instruction, based on word recognition by shapes, pictures, and contextual clues rather than knowledge of letters, is particularly ineffective with male students.

Early "school turnoff" may cause many boys to develop an anti-learning mindset the British have labeled "laddism"—a mirror image of the prefeminist notion that it isn't cool for a girl to be too bright. "The boys become oppositional and band together in the belief that manly culture doesn't include grade grubbing," observes University of Alaska psychologist Judith Kleinfeld. For black boys, this attitude may be exacerbated by the notion that learning is a "white thing."

Sommers convincingly argues that boys' academic shortcomings have not received proper attention because the discussion of gender and education has been hijacked by "girl partisans." In the 1992 report *How Schools Shortchange Girls*, the AAUW brushed aside boys' disadvantages and explicitly warned against targeted efforts to remedy their deficits in literacy. A few years later, it effectively hushed up a study it had commissioned—*The Influence of School Climate on Gender Differences in the Achievement and Engagement of Young Adolescents*, by University of Michigan psychologist Valerie Lee and her associates—when the findings failed to support the shortchanged-girls premise.

These days, feminists are more willing to admit the good news about girls. The AAUW's new leitmotif, evident at the "Beyond the Gender Wars" symposium, is that we should stop pitting girls against boys in a victimhood contest and work to make the schools better for everyone—which sounds fine, except that it's a little disingenuous to trumpet girls' victimization and then shout, "Let's not play victim!" as soon as boys' problems are mentioned. What's more, the "gender equity" crowd still grasps for any excuse to discount young men's problems. If more women go to college, said some AAUW panelists, that's because they need it just to break even with men who finish high school. In fact, while female college graduates over 25 earn only 15 percent more than male high school graduates, that group includes older women who went to college with no plans for a career and were out of the labor force for years as well as women who went back to school after raising a family and have limited work experience. This hardly means that young women who are going to college today will do only slightly better financially than young men who are not.

Clash of the Stereotypes

"Boy partisans" can exaggerate too. In his remarks at the IWF's National Press Club event, Rutgers University anthropologist Lionel Tiger inflated the 2-to-1 female-to-male ratio among black college graduates to 5 to 1. (When pressed afterward, he could not recall the source for this surprising figure.) In *The War Against Boys*, Sommers asserts that recent data on high school and college students clearly lead to "the conclusion that girls and young women are thriving, while boys and young men are languishing." Yet this dramatic statement is contradicted further down the page by her own summary of Valerie Lee's study of gender and achievement, which she lauds as "responsible and objective." Lee reports that sex differences in school performance are "small to moderate" and "inconsistent in direction"—boys fare better in some areas, girls in others.

More boys flounder in school (and, as Sommers acknowledges, more of them reach the highest levels of excellence, from the best test scores to top rankings in prestigious law schools). But it's important to put things in perspective. Boys are twice as likely as girls to be shunted into special education with labels that may involve a high degree of subjectivity or even bias, but we are talking about a fairly small proportion of all children. About 7 percent of boys and 3 percent of girls are classified as learning disabled, 1.5 percent of boys and 1.1 percent of girls as mentally retarded; just over 1 percent of boys and fewer than half as many girls are diagnosed with severe emotional disturbances.

Clearly, many boys are doing well; just as clearly, it's an overstatement to say that girls in general are "thriving," since all too often the educational system serves no one well. Twelfth-grade girls may do better than boys on reading and writing tests, but their average scores still fall short of the level that indicates real competence—the ability to understand and convey complicated information.

There's quite a bit of exaggeration, too, in the notion of schools as a hostile environment for boys. Few would dispute that boys tend to be more physically active and less patient than girls; but these differences are far less stark than the clichés deployed in the "boy wars." In a 1998 Department of Education study, 65 percent of boys and 78 percent of girls in kindergarten were described by teachers as usually persistent at their tasks, and 58 percent of boys and 74 percent of girls as usually attentive—a clear yet far from interplanetary gap.

Still smaller are the differences between boys' and girls' views of the school climate. Surprisingly, in a 1995 survey by the Institute for Social Research at the University of Michigan, virtually the same percentages of female and male high school seniors said they liked school. When the question "Whom do teachers like more?" is posed in such a way that they must select one favored sex, kids are likely to answer "girls." Yet when asked about their own experiences, boys are only slightly less likely than girls to say that teachers listen to them, that they call on them often and encourage them, and that discipline and grading at their school are fair.

> ## "We used to think that the schools shortchanged girls; now the news is that schools are waging a war against boys," says psychologist Judith Kleinfeld. "Neither view is right."

Even the image of sexual harassment policies as a wholesale anti-boy witch hunt is too simplistic. For one thing, girls also get caught in the net; last fall, two eighth-grade girls in Euless, Texas, were punished for hugging in the hallway. The bizarre overreactions (which even the Department of Education cautions against) reflect not only gender warfare but the zero tolerance lunacy that has also caused children to be suspended under anti-drug policies for giving an aspirin to a friend. Moreover, these stories coexist with cases in which real sexual assaults are ignored or covered up by school officials.

Some critics of girls-as-victims mythology are uncomfortable with sweeping claims about the plight of boys. "All this haggling about who's the *real* victim is absurd—and unseemly, coming from Americans and describing what must be the most fortunate generation of young people ever to inhabit the planet," says Daphne Patai, a comparative literature scholar at the University of Massachusetts at Amherst and author of *Heterophobia: Sexual Harassment and the Future of Feminism.*

Judith Kleinfeld, who authored the 1996 paper "The Myth That Schools Shortchange Girls," published by the Washington, D.C.-based Women's Freedom Network (of which I am vice president), credits Sommers with drawing attention to an often-ignored problem but wishes her argument had been more nuanced. "We used to think that the schools shortchanged girls; now the news is that schools are waging a war against boys, that girls are on top and boys have become the second sex," says Kleinfeld. "Neither view is right. We should be sending a dual message: one, boys and girls do have characteristic problems, and we need to be aware of what they are; two, boys and girls are also individuals. Unfortunately, there's a lot of exaggeration going on, and a lot of destructive stereotyping by both sides."

Monolithic Manhood

Stereotypes and exaggerations fly just as freely when it comes to the larger debate about how boys should be raised in an age of sexual equality. Gender reformers like Pollack and his Harvard colleague Carol Gilligan, the psychologist and professor of gender studies who pioneered the notion of girls' failing self-esteem in the 1980s before turning her attention to boys, lament that patriarchal norms force boys to separate prematurely from their families, especially their mothers, and to deny their pain, sadness, vulnerability, and fear. As a result, Pollack argues, boys disconnect from their true selves and go into a kind of emotional deep freeze, or even become bullies to prove their manhood.

Real Boys is full of "gender straitjacket" horror stories in which boys barely out of diapers are called "wimps" and told to "act like a man" (usually by fathers) when they are scared or upset. Pollack's dismay is understandable, but how many American fathers really act out such John Wayne parodies? The generalizations are especially shaky since most of Pollack's conclusions seem to be based on troubled boys in his clinical practice. While he occasionally tempers his melodramatic claims, observing that "many, if not most, boys maintain an inner wellspring of emotional connectedness," this does little to change the bleak overall picture.

Mark Kiselica, a psychologist at the College of New Jersey and past president of the American Psychological Association's Society for the Psychological Study of Men and Masculinity, bristles at the notion of boys as "emotional mummies" cut off from relationships. In fact, recent studies by psychologist Susan Harter and her colleagues at the University of Denver, which refute Gilligan's theory that girls lose self-confidence as teenagers, also suggest that adolescent boys are only slightly less open about their thoughts and feelings with parents and friends than are girls. In a 1997 survey by Louis Harris and Associates for the Commonwealth Fund, only one in five teenage boys (and one in seven girls) said they talked to no one when they felt stressed or depressed.

If there's a truth in the arguments of would-be reformers of masculinity, it is that in the past 30 years "gender rules" have been loosened for women more than for men: A boy taking ballet classes raises more eyebrows than a girl playing hockey. But these issues shouldn't and won't be resolved by a bureaucracy of social engineers. The reformers, in any case, vastly overestimate the rigidity and the power of traditional male norms, depicting masculinity as far more monolithic than it has ever been. Most parents don't need Pollack to remind them that, when talking to sons about male family members or friends, they should praise these men's warm and nurturing qualities.

If the "save the males" crowd inflates the harm hypermasculine cultural values can do to American boys at the turn of the millennium, many conservatives probably underestimate it—and, in turn, inflate the perils of creeping androgyny. To be sure, there are educators eager to impose their egalitarian vision on other people's children by banning toy guns from preschools, prohibiting "segregated" play at recess, or herding boys into quilting groups and prodding them to talk about how they feel. It's difficult to tell how widespread this is outside the elite Eastern private schools from which Sommers gets several of her examples, where parents not only choose but pay big money to send their offspring. On the other hand, in many communities, boys still face strong pressure to be jocks—and the jock culture probably is more damaging to boys' learning than the occasional quilting circle.

Would conservative champions of boyhood also praise traditionally masculine fathers who came to honor and cherish their sons' "soft" qualities, even when those sons chose to become hairdressers?

Not unlike the feminists, many conservatives have a vision of a monolithic, virtually unchanging "culture of manhood" that boys must join. Yet one does not have to believe that gender is only a "social construct" to know that standards of male behavior and beliefs about male nature in different times and places have varied as greatly as male dress. Two hundred years ago, it wasn't unusual or inappropriate for men to weep at sentimental plays and for male friends to exchange letters with gushy expressions of affection.

The truth is, both efforts to produce "unisex" children and efforts to enforce traditional masculine or feminine norms are likely to warp children's individuality. Kleinfeld had a chance to observe this when raising her own children: a girl who liked mechanical tools and had an aptitude for

science, yet resisted efforts to get her interested in a scientific career and chose humanitarian work instead, and a quiet, gentle boy who was an avid reader. "We tried to get him active in sports, but we were fighting his individual nature," says Kleinfeld. "The one time he made a touchdown in football, he was running the wrong way."

In The War Against Boys, Sommers praises feminists who came to honor and cherish their sons' masculine qualities, among them a pacifist-liberal writer whose son chose a military career. But would conservative champions of boyhood also praise traditionally masculine fathers who came to honor and cherish their sons' "soft" qualities, even when those sons chose to become elementary school teachers or hairdressers?

Male Achievement Initiatives

While boys may not be a "second sex," there are clearly distinct educational problems that disproportionately affect male students. Surely it makes sense to look at these problems and consider some gender-specific solutions. Yet such efforts have been virtually nonexistent, largely, no doubt, because they are seen as politically incorrect. In November 1999, Goucher College in Baltimore held a conference called "Fewer Men on Campus: A Puzzle for Liberal-Arts Colleges and Universities." While the event was ostensibly free of any anti-feminist stridency, it drew hostile barbs from the AAUW and warnings about a "backlash" against women's gains from the American Council on Education's Office of Women in Higher Education. (ACE has no special office addressing the issues of men, the new minority on college campuses.) Government efforts to advance "gender equity" in education remain focused solely on inequities allegedly holding back girls and women.

While programs to remedy girls' underachievement in math, science, and computers have proliferated in recent years, funded by the government and by private groups such as the National Science Foundation, there are no programs targeting boys' deficits in reading and writing. (Such programs seem to be working well in England.) Literacy is a popular issue for politicians of both parties, and this year the U.S. Department of Education has given nearly $200 million in grants to state initiatives aimed at improving reading skills in elementary school as part of the Reading Excellence Program. But when I asked project coordinators in Pennsylvania, Illinois, and the District of Columbia if any of these programs would address the gender gap in literacy, it was obvious that the question took them by surprise.

Efforts to help boys can be regarded as suspect even if they target black boys, who have an acknowledged place in the pantheon of the oppressed. In 1996, acting on a complaint from a female student's mother, the Department of Education's Office of Civil Rights ruled that the Black Male Achievement Initiative, a mentoring network in the predominantly black schools of Prince George's County, Maryland, that matched boys with successful professional men, had to be opened to girls. Zack Berry, a staffer in the school district's Office of Youth Development, has no doubt that boys suffered as a result: "Once the program went coed, we found we were doing very well by the young ladies but we were losing our boys left and right, especially in high school." In a few schools, he says, male participation dwindled to less than one-fifth of the total.

This bias against male-only services may be waning. Even the story of Black Male Achievement Initiative has something of a happy ending. In 1999, after the school district collected data showing that boys did not fare as well as girls and presented them to the Office of Civil Rights, the OCR reversed itself and gave a green light to single-sex mentoring programs and activities. Another all-male program that has chapters in several mostly black public schools in Maryland, BROTHERS (Brothers Reaching Out To Help Each Reach Success), has met with no objections so far. "Faculty and adults have rallied around BROTHERS because it has helped a group of kids who just weren't buying into school," says Mike Durso, the principal of Springbrook High School in Silver Spring. The group, which arranges for teens to mentor and tutor younger boys, has been credited with improving discipline, graduation rates, and college enrollment.

Single-sex education, whose popularity for girls surged after the girl crisis hysteria of the early 1990s—leading to the somewhat controversial opening of an all-girl public charter school in New York in 1996 and a sister school in Chicago last fall—deserves more consideration for boys as well. True, there are few reliable data on how children fare in single-sex vs. coed classrooms; if single-sex schools often do better, it may be because they are the product of a conscious effort to create a more academically oriented, more orderly, more individually focused learning environment.

If there's an answer to the "boy question," it lies in getting away from a one-size-fits-all model and making sure that parents and children have as many choices as possible.

Nonetheless, single-sex schooling may be the best option for some boys and girls, not necessarily because the sexes are so radically different but because some teenagers learn best without the distracting presence of the other sex. Susan Harter and other researchers have found that the fear of looking stupid in front of opposite-sex classmates is a major deterrent to speaking in class for boys and girls alike. Boys in particular may try to impress girls by acting "cool" or goofy. Counterintuitively, many education experts believe that all-boy classrooms may also allow boys to show their gentle side—pursue interests in art or poetry, discuss the emotions of literary characters—without the fear of appearing "girly."

As for coeducational schools, it goes without saying that they should not be places where children are insulted because of their sex or turned into lab rats for social engineers bent on reinventing gender. Fortunately, unlike the parents of college students, people with children in primary or secondary schools usually have some idea of what's happening in classrooms, and they can help keep the gender warriors in check. Several years ago, a particularly noxious sexual harassment prevention curriculum introduced in Minnesota, which would have had 7-year-olds reciting a solemn pledge to combat harassment, was shelved because of parental opposition and adverse publicity.

Many of the "unmanly" educational fads conservatives deplore are bad for reasons that have little to do with gender. "Cooperative" teaching can turn off bright girls as well as competitive boys. Nor is touchy-feely pedagogy, such as writing assignments requiring students to explore intimate issues, necessarily "female-friendly." Girls who like sharing confidences with each other may balk at "sharing" with teachers. A 1994 Los Angeles Times story described reactions to a controversial statewide exam with essay questions about conflicts with parents and regrets about the past. Most of the students who were quoted as complaining about invasive questions were girls.

On the other hand, it's doubtful that many people will worry that their sons will be emasculated by making quilts at school, or by adopting the persona of a famous woman in a class presentation. It would be interesting, though, to see a feminist teacher's reaction if a boy chose Margaret Thatcher as his heroine instead of Anita Hill.

Answering the 'Boy Question'

If there's an answer to the "boy question," it lies in getting away from a one-size-fits-all model, whether feminist or traditionalist, and making sure that parents and children have as many choices as possible. Right now, parents with sexually egalitarian values can generally rely on free government schools to transmit these values to their children, while those who want their children's education to instill traditional beliefs about sex roles have to pay tuition at a private school (as well as taxes to help finance the public schools). Parents who want single-sex schooling for their children are also left with fewer and more expensive options than those satisfied with coeducation. This is one problem that school vouchers could address.

The more diversity there is in education, the more it can be tailored to each child's individuality. Even those who agree that boys have specific needs based on sex-linked traits may define these needs quite differently.

Sommers stresses strict discipline in a teacher-led, structured classroom; Kleinfeld suggests that active and nonconformist children, who are disproportionately male, would do well in "open classrooms where children move around a lot," with "teachers who enjoy wiseacres." Each prescription is undoubtedly right for some boys. And there are still other boys who, defying averages, do not thrive on competition and do better in cooperative settings.

We are still far away from a truly diverse educational system. But we have come a long way toward a diverse society that respects both the maleness and the individuality of boys and young men. This diversity will always have room for conservative subcultures that uphold traditional ideals of manhood, as well as for feminist-pacifist communes in which a little boy who uses a stick as a toy sword immediately has the weapon confiscated. But I'd like to think that the future belongs to the feminist who can respect her son the career soldier and to the career soldier who can respect his son the hairdresser.

Contributing Editor Cathy Young (CathyYoung2@cs.com) is the author of Ceasefire: Why Women and Men Must Join Forces to Achieve True Equality (*The Free Press*).

Reprinted with permission from *Reason* Magazine, February 2001, pp. 24-31. © 2001 by the Reason Foundation, 3415 S. Sepulveda Blvd. Suite, 400, Los Angeles, CA 90034.

UNIT 3
Social and Emotional Development

Unit Selections

Key Points to Consider

- Since the publication of Daniel Goleman's seminal book on emotional intelligence, or EQ, a whole host of researchers and writers have jumped on the EQ bandwagon. What is your best summary of the research on EQ? Do you think EQ is a better predictor of life success than IQ? Why or why not? Do you think emotional intelligence is something that can be learned or is inborn? Should schools be charged with increasing students' EQ? Why or why not?

- When you were a child, did you experience gender segregation—boys playing with boys, girls with girls? How might this have influenced your social and emotional development? Did your teachers encourage or discourage segregation between the sexes? What could a teacher or parents do to influence gender segregation? Recently, there is growing interest in schooling boys and girls in completely separate schools. What advantages or disadvantages might being educated separately have for boys and girls?

- Think back to what you did as a child when asked to play. Now compare this to the myriad of activities that many parents now schedule for their children. Explain your thoughts on the advantages and disadvantages of scheduling children for ever more activities, as opposed to providing children with free, unstructured play opportunities.

- Do you think girls are more interpersonally and verbally mean than boys? Explain. Do you remember girls having special cliques when you were in school? Do you remember any girls who fit the types of Queen Bees, Alpha Girls, or Really Mean Girls? Do you think these types continue into adulthood? Why or why not?

- When you were in school, did you know of any bullies? Were you ever the target of a bully? What, if anything, did your teacher or other school personnel do when a student was bullied? Did their intervention help the situation? Did you ever engage in bullying? If so, why? If you had a child who was bullied at school, what actions would you take?

 **Links: www.dushkin.com/online/**
These sites are annotated in the World Wide Web pages.

Max Planck Institute for Psychological Research
http://www.mpipf-muenchen.mpg.de/BCD/bcd_e.htm
National Child Care Information Center (NCCIC)
http://www.nccic.org
Serendip
http://serendip.brynmawr.edu/serendip/

One of the truisms about our species is that we are social animals. From birth, each person's life is a constellation of relationships, from family at home to friends in the neighborhood and school. This unit addresses how children's social and emotional development is influenced by important relationships with parents, peers, and teachers.

When John Donne in 1623 wrote, "No man is an island... every man is... a part of the main," he implied that all humans are connected to each other and that these connections make us who we are. Early in this century, sociologist C. H. Cooley highlighted the importance of relationships with the phrase "looking-glass self" to describe how people tend to see themselves as a function of how others perceive them. Personality theorist Alfred Adler, also writing in the early twentieth century, claimed that personal strength derived from the quality of one's connectedness to others: The stronger the relationships, the stronger the person. The notion that a person's self-concept arises from relations with others also has roots in developmental psychology. As Jean Piaget once wrote, "There is no such thing as isolated individuals; there are only relations." The articles in this unit respect these traditions by emphasizing the theme that a child's development occurs within the context of relationships.

Since the celebrated publication of Daniel Goleman's book on emotional intelligence, scores of programs and research in the area have emerged. In "Emotional Intelligence: What the Research Says," authors Casey Cobb and John Mayer caution against unbridled, wholesale untested acceptance of the concept. Instead, they argue for a more careful analysis of two models regarding the concept of emotional intelligence when implementing programs in the schools.

Another major influence in the landscape of childhood is friendship. When do childhood friendships begin? Friends become increasingly important during the elementary school years. If forming strong, secure attachments with family members is an important task of early childhood, then one of the major psychological achievements of middle childhood is a move toward the peer group. Across the elementary school years, children spend ever-increasing time with peers in the neighborhood and at school. The authors of "What Ever Happened to Play?" lament the loss of free, unscheduled playtime for children as parents continue to feel pressure to enroll their children in a whole host of scheduled after-school activities and lessons. Some child experts warn that this trend may have negative consequences for children.

Reknowned psychologist Eleanor Maccoby reviews emerging research examining how same-sex social groups and group processes influence and socialize children's sex typed behavior. She discusses the role of group size, playtime interactions among all-male and all-female groups, and the formation of sex-distinctive subcultures as powerful forces in shaping children's sex-typed behaviors, values, and interests.

Are girls or boys more aggressive? Typically, most people might nominate boys as being more aggressive. In "Girls Just Want to Be Mean," Margaret Talbot argues that while boys may

be more likely to resort to physical aggression, girls are more likely to engage in verbal and relational aggression. She observes the interactions among sixth grade girls at a private school to identify girl cliques such as Queen Bees, Alpha Girls, and the Really Mean Girls to get a better understanding of how these teen cliques operate.

Bullying is not a new phenomenon and many teachers and parents perceive bullying as a normal part of childhood. More recently however, some of the tragic school shootings appear to be linked to children who were teased and bullied at school. In "Bullying Among Children," Janis Bullock discusses research on common characteristics of bullies and the effects of bullying on their victims. Given the detrimental effects on children's development and adjustment, the author advocates strongly that school personnel engage in a number of specific interventions.

Article 13

Emotional Intelligence: What the Research Says

When integrating the concept of emotional intelligence into curriculum practice, educators need to understand the models, rely on solid research, and—as always—tread carefully.

Casey D. Cobb and John D. Mayer

Emotional intelligence was popularized by Daniel Goleman's 1995 best-selling book, *Emotional Intelligence*. The book described emotional intelligence as a mix of skills, such as awareness of emotions; traits, such as persistence and zeal; and good behavior. Goleman (1995) summarized the collection of emotional intelligence qualities as "character."

The public received the idea of emotional intelligence enthusiastically. To some, it de-emphasized the importance of general IQ and promised to level the playing field for those whose cognitive abilities might be wanting. To others, it offered the potential to integrate the reasoning of a person's head and heart. Goleman made strong claims: Emotional intelligence was "as powerful," "at times more powerful," and even "twice as powerful" as IQ (Goleman, 1995, p. 34; Goleman, 1998, p. 94). On its cover, *Time* magazine declared that emotional IQ "may be the best predictor of success in life, redefining what it means to be smart" (Gibbs, 1995). Goleman's book became a *New York Times*—and international—best-seller.

The claims of this science journalism extended easily to the schools. *Emotional Intelligence* concluded that developing students' emotional competencies would result in a "'caring community,' a place where students feel respected, cared about, and bonded to classmates" (Goleman, 1995, p. 280). A leader of the social and emotional learning movement referred to emotional intelligence as "the integrative concept" underlying a curriculum for emotional intelligence (Elias et al., 1997, pp. 27, 29). And the May 1997 issue of *Educational Leadership* extensively covered the topic of emotional intelligence.

Two Models

This popular model of emotional intelligence was based on, and added to, a 1990 academic theory and subsequent publications now referred to as the *ability* approach to emotional intelligence. The logic behind the ability model was that emotions are signals about relationships. For example, sadness signals loss. We must process emotion—perceive, understand, manage, and use it—to benefit from it; thus, emotional processing—or emotional intelligence—has great importance (Mayer & Salovey, 1997; Salovey & Mayer, 1990).

The concept of emotional intelligence legitimates the discussion of emotions in school.

The ability model argued for an emotional intelligence that involves perceiving and reasoning abstractly with information that emerges from feelings. This argument drew on research findings from areas of nonverbal perception, empathy, artificial intelligence, and brain research. Recent empirical demonstrations have further bolstered the case (Mayer, Caruso, & Salovey, 1999; Mayer, DiPaolo, & Salovey, 1993; 1990; Mayer & Salovey, 1993; Salovey & Mayer, 1990).

The ability model made no particular claims about the potential predictive value of emotional intelligence. In fact, even several years after the publication of Goleman's book, psychologists view the popular claims about predicting success as ill-defined, unsupported, and implausible (Davies, Stankov, & Roberts, 1998; Epstein, 1998). Rather, the ability version emphasizes that emotional intelligence exists. If emotional intelligence exists and qualifies as a traditional or standard intelligence (like general IQ), people who are labeled *bleeding hearts* or *hopeless romantics* might be actually engaged in sophisticated information processing. Moreover, the concept of emotional intelligence legitimates the discussion of emotions in schools and other organizations because emotions reflect crucial information about relationships.

Two models of emotional intelligence thus developed. The first, the ability model, defines emotional intelligence as a set of abilities and makes claims about the importance of emotional information and the potential uses of reasoning well with that information. The second, which we will refer to as the mixed model, is more popularly oriented. It mixes emotional intelligence as an ability with social competencies, traits, and behaviors, and makes wondrous claims about the success this intelligence leads to.

Educational leaders have experimented with incorporating emotional learning in schools. For the most part, emotional intelligence is finding its way into schools in small doses, through socioemotional learning and character education programs. But examples of grander plans are evolving, with a few schools organizing their entire curriculums around emotional intelligence. One state even attempted to integrate emotional learning into all its social, health, and education programs (Elias et al., 1997; Rhode Island Emotional Competency Partnership, 1998).

Educational practices involving emotional intelligence should be based on solid research, not on sensationalistic claims.

The problem is that some educators have implemented emotional intelligence programs and policies without much sensitivity to the idea that there is more than one emotional intelligence model. We have expressed concern that school practices and policies on emotional intelligence relied on popularizations that were, in some instances, far ahead of the science on which they were presumably based (Mayer & Cobb, 2000). The early claims of the benefits of emotional intelligence to students, schools, and beyond were made without much empirical justification.

We hope that emotional intelligence is predictive of life success or that it leads to good behavior, but we recognize that it is fairly early in the game. We are also wary of the sometimes faddish nature of school reform and the grave fate of other hastily implemented curricular innovations. Consider the rush by California to

implement self-esteem programs into its schools in the late 1980s (Joachim, 1996). Substantial resources were exhausted for years before that movement was deemed a failure. The construct of emotional intelligence comes at a time when educators are eager to find answers to problems of poor conduct, interpersonal conflict, and violence plaguing schools; however, educational practices involving emotional intelligence should be based on solid research, not on sensationalistic claims. So, what *does* the research say?

Identifying emotions in faces, pictorial designs, music, and stories are typical tasks for assessing the emotional perception area of emotional intelligence.

Measuring Emotional Intelligence

Emotional intelligence, whether academically or popularly conceived, must meet certain criteria before it can be labeled a psychological entity. One criterion for an intelligence is that it can be operationalized as a set of abilities. Ability measures—measures that ask people to solve problems with an eye to whether their answers are right or wrong—are the sine qua non of assessing an intelligence. If you measure intelligence with actual problems (such as, What does the word *season* mean?), you can assess how well a person can think. If you simply ask a student how smart she is (for example, How well do you solve problems?)—a so-called self-report—you cannot be certain that you are getting an authentic or genuine answer. In fact, the correlation between a person's score on an intelligence test and self-reported intelligence is almost negligible. Early evidence suggests that self-reported emotional intelligence is fairly unrelated to actual ability (Mayer, Salovey, & Caruso, 2000).

Ability-based testing of emotional intelligence has centered on the Mayer-Salovey-Caruso Emotional Intelligence Test (MSCEIT) and its precursor, the Multifactor Emotional Intelligence Scale (MEIS). Both tests measure the four areas of emotional intelligence: perception, facilitation of thought, understanding, and management (Mayer, Caruso, & Salovey, 1999). For example, look at the pictures of the faces on this page. Is the person happy? Sad? Are other emotions expressed? Identifying emotions in faces, pictorial designs, music, and stories are typical tasks for assessing the area of emotional intelligence called emotional perception.

Another type of MSCEIT question asks, When you are feeling slow and sour, which of the following emotions does this most closely resemble: (A) frustration, (B) jealousy, (C) happiness, or (D) joy? Most people would probably choose *frustration* because people become frustrated when they move too slowly and are disappointed (or sour) that things aren't going as planned. This kind of question measures the second area of emotional intelligence: emotional facilitation of thought.

A third type of MSCEIT question tests individuals' knowledge about emotions: Contempt is closer to which combination of emotions: *anger and fear* or *disgust and anger?* Such a question assesses emotional understanding.

The final type of MSCEIT questions measures emotional management. These questions describe a hypothetical situation that stirs the emotions (such as the unexpected break-up of a long-term relationship) and then ask how a person should respond to obtain a given outcome (for example, staying calm).

One crucial aspect of assessing emotional intelligence lies in the method by which answers are scored. Scoring a standard IQ test is fairly straightforward, with clear-cut, defensible answers for every item. The responses on a test of emotional intelligence are better thought of as *fuzzy sets*—certain answers are more right or plausible than others, and only some answers are absolutely wrong all the time. To assess the relative correctness of an answer, we can use consensus, expertise or target criteria (or some combination). A correct response by way of the consensus approach is simply the answer most frequently selected by test-takers. Answers can also be deemed correct by such experts as psychologists or other trained professionals. Finally, correct responses can be validated using a target criterion. For instance, the actual emotional reaction of an anonymously depicted spouse facing a difficult decision could serve as the targeted response in a test item that described his or her situation.

The MSCEIT and MEIS are undergoing considerable scrutiny from the scientific community. Although not everyone is convinced yet of their validity, the tests do provide the most dramatic evidence thus far for the existence of an emotional intelligence. Early findings provide strong evidence that emotional intelligence looks and behaves like other intelligences, such as verbal intelligence, but remains distinct enough to stand alone as a separate mental ability. Like other intelligences, emotional intelligence appears to develop with age (Mayer, Caruso, & Salovey, 1999).

Predictive Value

The first emotional intelligence tests were used two years *after* the popular claims of 1995, so the actual findings lag behind the popular perception of a well-established area of research. One important pattern is emerging, however. Preliminary research (primarily from unpublished studies and dissertations) from the MEIS suggests a modest relationship between emotional intelligence and lower levels of "bad" behaviors.

In one study, high scores in emotional intelligence moderately predicted the absence of adult bad behavior,

such as getting into fights and arguments, drinking, smoking, and owning firearms (Mayer, Caruso, Salovey, Formica, & Woolery, 2000). In a dissertation study, the MEIS-A measured the emotional intelligence of fifty-two 7th and 8th graders in an urban school district (Rubin, 1999). Analyses indicated that higher emotional intelligence was inversely related to teacher and peer ratings of aggression among students. In another study, researchers reported that higher MEIS-A scores among 200 high school students were associated with lower admissions of smoking, intentions to smoke, and alcohol consumption (Trinidad & Johnson, 2000). The conclusion suggested by such research is that higher emotional intelligence predicts lower incidences of "bad" behavior. As for the claims about success in life—those studies have yet to be done.

What Can Schools Do?

Educators interested in emotional intelligence of either the ability or mixed type are typically directed to programs in social and emotional learning (Goleman, 1995; Goleman, 1996; Mayer & Salovey, 1997). These programs had been around for years before the introduction of the emotional intelligence concept. Some aspects of the programs overlap with the ability approach to emotional intelligence. This overlap occurs when programs ask early elementary children to "appropriately express and manage" various emotions and "differentiate and label negative and positive emotions in self and others," or call for students to integrate "feeling and thinking with language" and learn "strategies for coping with, communicating about, and managing strong feelings" (Elias et al., 1997, p. 133–134). Other aspects of these programs are specifically more consistent with the mixed (or popular) models than the ability approach in that they include distinct behavioral objectives, such as "becoming assertive, self-calming, cooperative," and "understanding responsible behavior at social events" (p. 135). There is also an emphasis on such values as honesty, consideration, and caring.

What may work better, at least for some students, is helping them develop the capacity to make decisions on their own in their own contexts.

What would a curriculum based on an ability model look like? Basically, it would drop the behavioral objectives and values and focus on emotional reasoning.

Choosing Approaches

The emotional intelligence curriculum (or ability model) and the social and emotional learning curriculum (or mixed model) both overlap and diverge. The emotional ability approach focuses only on teaching emotional reasoning. The social and emotional learning curriculum mixes emotional skills, social values, and behaviors. In the case of these two approaches, less—that is, the pure ability model—may be better. What troubles us about the broader social and emotional learning approach is that the emphasis on students getting along with one another could stifle creativity, healthy skepticism, or sponta-neity—all valued outcomes in their own right. Teaching people to be tactful or compassionate as full-time general virtues runs counter to the "smart" part of emotional intelligence, which requires knowing when to be tactful or compassionate and when to be blunt or even cold and hard.

Moreover, a social and emotional approach that emphasizes positive behavior and attitudes can be a real turn-off for a negative thinker—often the very student that the teacher is trying to reach. Research supports this concern: Positive messages appear less believable and less sensible to unhappy people than sad messages do (Forgas, 1995). We suspect that troubled students will be alienated by insistent positivity. There may be nothing wrong with trying such approaches, but they may not work.

Correctly perceiving emotional information is part of the way that children make sense of things.

What may work better at least for some students, is helping them develop the capacity to make decisions on their own in their own contexts. This type of education is knowledge-based and is more aligned with an ability model of emotional intelligence. It involves teaching students emotional knowledge and emotional reasoning, with the hope that this combination would lead children to find their own way toward making good decisions.

Most children will require gentle guidance toward the good. We wonder, however, whether we can achieve this goal better by example and indirect teaching than by the direct, uniform endorsement of selected values in the curriculum.

How Might the Ability Curriculum Work?

The teaching of emotional knowledge has been a facet of some curriculums for years. For example, educators can help children perceive emotions in several ways. Elementary teachers could ask the class to name the feelings that they are aware of and then show what they look or feel like (for example, Show me sad). Similarly, teachers could ask students to identify the emotions depicted by various pictures of faces. Children can also

learn to read more subtle cues, such as the speed and intonation of voice, body posture, and physical gestures.

Correctly perceiving emotional information is one way children make sense of things. The ability to perceive emotions can be further fine-tuned as a student ages. Consider the level of sophistication required for an actor to put on a convincing expression of fear—and for the audience to recognize it as such.

Students can also learn to use emotions to create new ideas. For instance, asking students in English class to write about trees as if they were angry or delighted facil-itates a deeper understanding of these emotions.

Understanding emotions should also be a goal of the curriculum. For example, social studies expert Fred Newmann (1987) has suggested that higher-order thinking can be enhanced through empathic teaching. A social studies teacher could show images of the Trail of Tears, the forced exodus of the Cherokee from their homeland, and have students discuss the feelings involved. This could help students vicariously experience what those perilous conditions were like. In literature courses, teachers who point out the feelings of a story character, such as a triumphant figure skater or a despairing widow, can teach a great deal about what emotions tell us about relationships. Because the ability version of emotional intelligence legitimizes discussing emotions by considering them to convey information, it also supports emotionally evocative activities—such as theater, art, and interscholastic events—that help kids understand and learn from personal performance.

Emotional Intelligence in Schools

Educators looking to incorporate emotional intelligence into their schools should be aware that the two different models of emotional intelligence suggest two somewhat different curricular approaches. The model of emotional intelligence that makes its way into schools should be empirically defensible, measurable, and clear enough to serve as a basis for curriculum development. We believe that an ability-based curriculum, which emphasizes emotional knowledge and reasoning, may have advan-tages because it reaches more students.

References

Davies, M., Stankov, L., & Roberts, R. D. (1998). Emotional intelligence: In search of an elusive construct. *Journal of Personality & Social Psy-chology, 75*, 989–1015.

Elias, M. J., Zins, J. E., Weissberg, R. P., Frey, K. S., Greenberg, M. T., Haynes, N. M., Kessler, R., Schwab-Stone, M. E., & Schriver, T. P. (1997). *Promoting social and emotional learning: Guidelines for educators.* Alexandria, VA: ASCD.

Epstein, S. (1998). *Constructive thinking: The key to emotional intelligence.* Westport, CT: Praeger.

Forgas, J. P. (1995). Mood and judgement: The affect infusion model (AIM). *Psychological Bulletin, 117*(1), 39–66.

Gibbs, N. (1995, October 2). The EQ factor. *Time, 146*(14), 60–68.

Goleman, D. (1995). *Emotional intelligence.* New York: Bantam.

Goleman, D. (1996). *Emotional intelligence: A new vision for educators* [Videotape]. Port Chester, NY: National Professional Resources.

Goleman, D. (1998, November/December). What makes a leader? *Harvard Business Review, 76,* 93–102.

Joachim, K. (1996). The politics of self-esteem. *American Educational Research Journal, 33,* 3–22.

Mayer, J. D., Caruso, D. R., & Salovey, P. (1999). Emotional intelligence meets standards for a traditional intelligence. *Intelligence, 27,* 267–298.

Mayer, J. D., Caruso, D. R., Salovey, P., Formica, S., & Woolery, A. (2000). Unpublished raw data.

Mayer, J. D., & Cobb, C. D. (2000). Educational policy on emotional intelligence: Does it make sense? *Educational Psychology Review, 12*(2), 163–183.

Mayer, J. D., DiPaolo, M. T., & Salovey, P. (1990). Perceiving affective content in ambiguous visual stimuli: A component of emotional intelligence. *Journal of Personality Assessment, 54,* 772–781.

Mayer, J. D., & Salovey, P. (1993). The intelligence of emotional intelligence. *Intelligence, 17*(4), 433–442.

Mayer, J. D., & Salovey, P. (1997). What is emotional intelligence? In P. Salovey & D. Sluyter (Eds.), *Emotional development and emotional intelligence: Implications for educators* (pp. 3–31). New York: BasicBooks.

Mayer, J. D., Salovey, P., & Caruso, D. R. (2000). Models of emotional intelligence. In R. J. Sternberg (Ed.), *Handbook of Intelligence* (pp. 396–420). Cambridge: Cambridge University Press.

Newmann, F. M. (1987). *Higher order thinking in the teaching of social studies: Connections between theory and practice.* Madison, WI: National Center on Effective Secondary Schools. (ERIC Document Reproduction Service No. 332 880)

Rhode Island Emotional Competency Partnership. (1998). *Update on emotional competency.* Providence, RI: Rhode Island Partners.

Rubin, M. M. (1999). *Emotional intelligence and its role in mitigating aggression: A correlational study of the relationship between emotional intelligence and aggression in urban adolescents.* Unpublished manuscript, Immaculata College, Immaculata, PA.

Salovey, P., & Mayer, J. D. (1990). Emotional intelligence. *Imagination, Cognition, & Personality, 9*(3), 185–211.

Trinidad, D. R., & Johnson, A. (2000). *The association between emotional intelligence and early adolescent tobacco and alcohol use.* Unpublished manuscript, University of Southern California, Los Angeles, CA.

Casey D. Cobb (casey.cobb@unh.edu) is Assistant Professor of Education and **John D. Mayer** is Professor of Psychology at the University of New Hampshire, 62 College Rd., Durham, NH 03824.

What Ever Happened To
PLAY?

Kids are spending less time
frolicking freely, though fun is one
of the best things for them

By WALTER KIRN with WENDY COLE

Theresa Collins lives next to a park, but her kids don't play there all that often. For one thing, all three of her children lead busy lives, what with school, piano lessons, soccer practice and the constant distraction of the home computer. What's more, she fears that the park is dangerous. "I've heard of people exposing themselves there," says Theresa, a 42-year-old special-education teacher in Sarasota, Fla. And while she's not sure if the scary stories are true, she would rather be safe than sorry, like so many other contemporary parents. Her daughter Erica, 9, isn't allowed to visit the park without her brother Christopher, 11, who wasn't permitted to play alone there until about a month ago. As for Matthew, 16, who might have supervised Christopher, he avoids the park by choice. He favors video games. "It's a shame," says Theresa. So why doesn't she take the kids to the park? "It's boring. And I don't have time," she says.

"When I'm home, I have a lot to do here."

No wonder America's swing sets are feeling lonely. With so many roving flashers to elude, so many high-tech skills to master, so many crucial tests to pass and so many anxious parents to reassure, children seem to be playing less and less these days. Even hassled grown-ups are starting to notice. "We're taking away childhood," says Dorothy Sluss, a professor of early-childhood education at East Tennessee State University. "We don't value play in our society. It has become a four-letter word."

Statistics back her up. In 1981, according to University of Michigan researchers, the average school-age child had 40% of the day for free time—meaning hours left over after sleeping, eating, studying and engaging in organized activities. By 1997, the figure was down to 25%.

The very existence of research studies on play suggests that ours is a serious society that can take the fun out of almost anything, including the issue of fun itself. That's why any list of the enemies of play must begin with adults, who make the rules. If play is endangered, it's parents who have endangered it, particularly those who feel that less goofing off in the name of youthful achievement is a good thing. See Dick run. Well, that's fine for little Dick, but wouldn't most parents rather raise a Jane who sits still, studies and gets into Harvard?

If so, they're shortsighted, say the experts on play. Alvin Rosenfeld, co-author of *The Over-Scheduled Child: Avoiding the Hyper-Parenting Trap*, holds an old-fashioned view of play: it's joyful and emotionally nourishing. Stuart Brown, a retired psychiatrist and founder of the Institute for Play in Carmel Valley, Calif., believes that too little play may have a dark side. What Brown calls "play deprivation" can lead, he says, to depression, hostility and the loss of "the things that make us human beings."

Play doesn't just make kids happy, healthy and human. It may also make them smarter, says Rosenfeld. Today's mania for raising young Einsteins, he observes, might have destroyed the real Einstein—a notorious dreamer who earned poor grades in school but somewhere in his frolics divined the formula for the relationship between matter and energy. Play refreshes and stimulates the mind, it seems. And "frequent breaks may actually make kids more interested in learning," according to Rhonda Clements, a Hofstra University professor of physical education.

The case for play is simple and intuitive, which is what makes the decline of play a mystery. If Dick can run wild and get into Princeton too, then why isn't he out there running his little head off? That play has real value won't surprise most parents. That their kid horses around less than they did when they were young probably doesn't shock them either. The puzzle is, Where did all the playtime go?

Millie Wilcox, 60, thinks she knows. The retired nurse and mother of two grown boys (one of them being this writer) doesn't have a Ph.D. in child psychology, just a memory of her own Ohio childhood picking elderberries in the alley and once—imagine doing this today—playing house inside a cardboard box set smack dab in the middle of the street. "There wasn't so much traffic back then," says Wilcox, "and it seems like every neighborhood had a vacant lot. Vacant lots were important. Plus, our mothers were around during the day, and they knew everyone on the block, so they weren't scared for us."

There's common sense behind Wilcox's nostalgia for her old stamping grounds. After all, play needs to happen somewhere—preferably somewhere safe and open and not entirely dominated by grownups—but those idyllic somewheres are growing scarce. "In the huge rush to build shopping malls and banks," says Clements, "no one is thinking about where kids can play. That doesn't generate tax revenue."

What about those inviting vacant lots? "There's practically no such thing anymore," laments urban planner Robin Moore, a former president of the International Association for the Child's Right to Play. Thanks to sidewalk-free subdivisions, congested roads and ubiquitous commercial developments, "all the free space has been spoken for," says Moore. Roger Hart, an environmental psychologist at the City University of New York, cites a general "disinvestment in public space" as one reason children are playing less outdoors. Even public sandboxes are vanishing. Says Hart: "People have become paranoid about animal waste." What's more, as the average family size gets smaller and suburban houses are built farther apart, "kids have a harder time finding each other than they used to," Moore says.

Parental fear is also a factor. Fear of molesters, bacteria, zooming SUVS. Neighbors who own guns. Neighbors who let their kids eat refined sugar. The list is as lengthy as last Sunday's newspaper, and it grows longer with every new edition. "It used to be," Hart says, "that in the presence of one another, kids formed a critical mass to keep each other safe. Gone are the days when children make any of their own plans." Their fearful, ambitious parents made plans for them, but these plans don't always mesh, unfortunately. A suburban Chicago mom who wishes to remain anonymous called up a school friend of her daughter's to arrange a play date. The kindergartner was booked solid. "It seems like kids today are always on the way to somewhere," complains the disillusioned mom

One place kids keep rushing to is Chuck E. Cheese, the chain of video game–crammed pizzerias where families can frolic in air-conditioned safety, separated by turnstiles from the Big Bad Wolf. Such enterprises fill the play vacuum with something far more modern and secure—"edutainment." It's a growing industry. Randy White is CEO of White Hutchinson Leisure & Learning Group in Kansas City, Mo. His company develops cavernous play facilities, up to 30,000 sq. ft. in area, that are Xanadus of prefabricated diversion, offering art projects, costumes, blocks and even simulated fishing. "We're reintroducing free play to families," says White. Free play at a price, that is. His facilities charge up to $10 a head. "Parents feel that if they're not paying much for an experience, it's not worth it educationally," he says.

Screen Time

THESE DAYS, when kids do play, it's often indoors and with machines, limiting their opportunities for free exploration

When young fun has to prove itself in educational terms—when it's not sufficient that play be just playful—the world has reached a dreary spot. Yet here we are. Consider this: since the 1980s, with the rise of the academic-standards movement, hundreds of American elementary schools have eliminated recess. The Atlanta schools have dropped recess system-wide, and other districts are thinking of following suit. Does a no-recess day raise test scores or aid kids' mental performance? There's no evidence for it. There is plenty of evidence, however, that unbroken classwork drives children slightly batty, as Atlanta teachers are starting to note. Multiple studies show that when recess time is delayed, elementary-school kids grow increasingly inattentive. Goodbye recess, hello Ritalin.

Rebecca Lamphere, 25, of Virginia Beach, Va., is a play activist, to coin an awkward phrase. Her mission began three years ago after she noticed that the school playground adjacent to her house was always empty. School officials later instituted a "recess substitute" program called Walk 'n Talk that involved having children circle four orange cones set up on the grounds after lunchtime. "It was considered social time," Lamphere says, "but they all had to go in one direction and keep their voices down." Lamphere wasn't pleased—her daughter Charleen was about to start kindergarten—so she launched a protest. She circulated a petition, sought out experts in child development and ultimately attracted statewide attention. Last April, Virginia Beach mandated daily recess, and the state followed five months later.

Is that what we've come to—obligatory play? The defenders of unfettered recreation have a way of making it sound like broccoli, wholesome and vitamin packed but unenticing. "Kids need to learn how to navigate themselves and keep their bodies safe," says Richard Cohen, a child-development expert and play-programs manager at Brookfield Zoo outside Chicago. What fun! At their grimmest, the play scholars sound like Stuart Brown recounting a study of Texas prison inmates that found a common element in their childhoods. "They didn't engage in rough-and-tumble play," he says, offering anxious parents yet one more reason to live in mortal fear of almost everything.

Fear—the natural enemy of play. The fear that a French lesson missed is a Yale acceptance letter lost. The fear that sending junior outside to roam will end in reporting him missing to the police. Do we now have to add to these fears—some of them neurotic, others real—the fear that "play deprivation" will stunt kids' spirits, shrink their brains and even land them in jail? Such protective obsessing seems to be the problem, and doing more of it offers no solution. Parents should probably just tell kids that fooling around is bad for them, open the door and follow them outside. All work and no play can make adults dull too—sometimes even a little paranoid.

From *Time*, April 30, 2001, pp. 56-58. © 2001 by Time Inc. Reprinted by permission.

Gender and Group Process: A Developmental Perspective

Eleanor E. Maccoby[1]
Department of Psychology, Stanford University, Stanford, California

Abstract
Until recently, the study of gender development has focused mainly on sex typing as an attribute of the individual. Although this perspective continues to be enlightening, recent work has focused increasingly on children's tendency to congregate in same-sex groups. This self-segregation of the two sexes implies that much of childhood gender enactment occurs in the context of same-sex dyads or larger groups. There are emergent properties of such groups, so that certain sex-distinctive qualities occur at the level of the group rather than at the level of the individual. There is increasing research interest in the distinctive nature of the group structures, activities, and interactions that typify all-male as compared with all-female groups, and in the socialization that occurs within these groups. Next steps in research will surely call for the integration of the individual and group perspectives.
Keywords
   sex; gender; groups; socialization

Among researchers who study the psychology of gender, a central viewpoint has always been that individuals progressively acquire a set of behaviors, interests, personality traits, and cognitive biases that are more typical of their own sex than of the other sex. And the individual's sense of being either a male or a female person (*gender identity*) is thought to be a core element in the developing sense of self. The acquisition of these sex-distinctive characteristics has been called *sex typing*, and much research has focused on how and why the processes of sex typing occur. A favorite strategy has been to examine differences among individuals in how sex typed they are at a given age, searching for factors associated with a person's becoming more or less "masculine" or more or less "feminine" than other individuals. In early work, there was a heavy emphasis on the family as the major context in which sex typing was believed to take place. Socialization pressures from parents were thought to shape the child toward "sex-appropriate" behaviors, personality, and interests and a firm gender identity.

On the whole, the efforts to understand gender development by studying individual differences in rate or degree of sex typing, and the connections of these differences to presumed antecedent factors, have not been very successful. The various manifestations of sex typing in childhood—toy and activity preferences, knowledge of gender stereotypes, personality traits—do not cohere together to form a cluster that clearly represents a degree of sex typing in a given child. And whether or not a given child behaves in a gender-typical way seems to vary greatly from one situation to another, depending on the social context and other conditions that make an individual's gender salient at a given moment. Only weak and inconsistent connections have been found between within-family socialization practices and children's sex-typed behavior (Ruble & Martin, 1998). And so far, the study of individual variations in sex typing has not helped us to understand the most robust manifestation of gender during childhood: namely, children's strong tendency to segregate themselves into same-sex social groups. Although work on gender development in individual children continues and shows renewed vigor, a relatively new direction of interest is in children's groups. This current research and theorizing considers how gender is implicated in the formation, interaction processes, and socialization functions of childhood social groupings.

In some of this work, the dyad or larger group, rather than the individual child, is taken as the unit of analysis. Through the history of theoretical writings by sociologists and social psychologists, there have been claims that groups have emergent properties, and that their functioning cannot be understood in terms of the characteristics of their individual members (Levine & Moreland, 1998). Accumulating evidence from recent work suggests that in certain gender configurations, pairs or groups of children elicit certain behaviors from each other that are not characteristic of either of the participants when alone or in other social contexts (Martin & Fabes, 2001). Another possibility is that the group context amplifies what are only weak tendencies in the individual participants. For example, in their article "It Takes Two to Fight," Coie and his colleagues (1999) found that the probability of a fight occurring depended not only on the aggressive predispositions of the two individual boys involved, but also on the unique properties of the dyad itself. Other phenomena, such as social approach to another child, depend on the sex of the approacher and the approachee taken jointly, not on the sex of either child, when children's sociability is analyzed at the level of the individual (summarized in Maccoby, 1998). It is important, then, to describe and analyze children's dyads or larger groups as such, to see how gender is implicated in their characteristics and functioning.

GENDER COMPOSITION OF CHILDREN'S GROUPS

Beginning at about age 3, children increasingly choose same-sex playmates when in settings where their social groupings are not managed by adults. In preschools, children may play in loose configurations of several children, and reciprocated affiliation between same-sex pairs of children is common while such reciprocation between pairs of opposite sex is rare (Strayer, 1980; Vaughan, Colvin, Azria, Caya, & Krzysik, 2001). On school playgrounds, children sometimes play in mixed-sex groups, but increasingly, as they move from age 4 to about age 12, they spend a large majority of their free play time exclusively with others of their own sex, rarely playing in a mixed-sex dyad or in a larger group in which no other child of their own sex is involved. Best friendships in middle childhood and well into adolescence are very heavily weighted toward same-sex choices. These strong tendencies toward same-sex social preferences are seen in the other cultures around the world where gender composition of children's groups has been studied, and are also found among young nonhuman primates (reviewed in Maccoby, 1998).

GROUP SIZE

Naturally occurring face-to-face groups whose members interact with one another continuously over time tend to be small—typically having only two or three members, and seldom having more than five or six members. Some gender effects on group size can be seen. Both boys and girls commonly form same-sex dyadic friendships, and sometimes triadic ones as well. But from about the age of 5 onward, boys more often associate together in larger clusters. Boys are more often involved in organized group games, and in their groups, occupy more space on school playgrounds. In an experimental situation in which same-sex groups of six children were allowed to utilize play and construction materials in any way they wished, girls tended to split into dyads or triads, whereas boys not only interacted in larger groups but were much more likely to undertake some kind of joint project, and organize and carry out coordinated activities aimed at achieving a group goal (Benenson, Apostolaris, & Parnass, 1997). Of course, children's small groups—whether dyads or clusters of four, five, or six children—are nested within still larger group structures, such as cliques or "crowds."

Group size matters. Recent studies indicate that the interactions in groups of four or more are different from what typically occurs in dyads. In larger groups, there is more conflict and more competition, particularly in all-male groups; in dyads, individuals of both sexes are more responsive to their partners, and a partner's needs and perspectives are more often taken into account than when individuals interact with several others at once (Benenson, Nicholson, Waite, Roy, & Simpson, 2001; Levine & Moreland, 1998). The question of course arises: To what extent are certain "male" characteristics, such as greater competitiveness, a function of the fact that boys typically interact in larger groups than girls do? At present, this question is one of active debate and study. So far, there are indications that group size does indeed mediate sex differences to some degree, but not entirely nor consistently.

INTERACTION IN SAME-SEX GROUPS

From about age 3 to age 8 or 9, when children congregate together in activities not structured by adults, they are mostly engaged in some form of play. Playtime interactions among boys, more often than among girls, involve rough-and-tumble play, competition, conflict, ego displays, risk taking, and striving to achieve or maintain dominance, with occasional (but actually quite rare) displays of direct aggression. Girls, by contrast, are more often engaged in what is called collaborative discourse, in which they talk and act reciprocally, each responding to what the other has just said or done, while at the same time trying to get her own initiatives across. This does not imply that girls' interactions are conflict free, but rather that girls pursue their individual goals in the context of also striving to maintain group harmony (summary in Maccoby, 1998).

The themes that appear in boys' fantasies, the stories they invent, the scenarios they enact when playing with other boys, and the fictional fare they prefer (books, television) involve danger, conflict, destruction, heroic actions by male heroes, and trials of physical strength, considerably more often than is the case for girls. Girls' fantasies and play themes tend to be oriented around domestic or romantic scripts, portraying characters who are involved in social relationships and depicting the maintenance or restoration of order and safety.

Girls' and boys' close friendships are qualitatively different in some respects. Girls' friendships are more intimate, in the sense that girl friends share information about the details of their lives and concerns. Boys typically know less about their friends' lives, and base their friendship on shared activities.

Boys' groups larger than dyads are in some respects more cohesive than girls' groups. Boys in groups seek and achieve more autonomy from adults than girls do, and explicitly exclude girls from their activities more commonly than girls exclude boys. Boys more often engage in joint risky activities, and close ranks to protect a group member from adult detection and censure. And friendships among boys are more interconnected; that is, friends of a given boy are more likely to be friends with each other than is the case for several girls who are all friends of a given girl (Markovitz, Benenson, & Dolenszky, 2001). The fact that boys' friendships are more interconnected does not mean that they are closer in the sense of intimacy. Rather, it may imply that male friends are more accustomed to functioning as a unit, perhaps having a clearer group identity.

HOW SEX-DISTINCTIVE SUBCULTURES ARE FORMED

In a few instances, researchers have observed the process of group formation from the first meeting of a group over several subsequent meetings. An up-close view of the formation of gendered subcultures among young children has been provided by Nicolopoulou (1994). She followed classrooms of preschool children through a school year, beginning at the time they first entered the school. Every day, any child could tell a story to a teacher, who recorded the story as the child told it. At the end of the day, the teacher read aloud to the class the stories that were recorded that day, and the child author of each story was invited to act it out with the help of other children whom the child selected to act out different parts. At the beginning of the year, stories could be quite rudimentary (e.g., "There was a boy. And a girl. And a wedding."). By the end of the year, stories became greatly elaborated, and different members of the class produced stories related to themes previously introduced by others. In other words, a corpus of shared knowledge, meanings, and scripts grew up, unique to the children in a given classroom and reflecting their shared experiences.

More important for our present purposes, there was a progressive divergence between the stories told by girls and those told by boys. Gender differences were present initially, and the thematic content differed more and more sharply as time went on, with boys increasingly focusing on themes of conflict, danger, heroism, and "winning," while girls' stories increasingly depicted family, nonviolent themes. At the beginning of the year, children might call upon others of both sexes to act in their stories, but by the end of the year, they almost exclusively called upon children of their own sex to enact the roles in their stories. Thus, although all the children in the class

were exposed to the stories told by both sexes, the girls picked up on one set of themes and the boys on another, and two distinct subcultures emerged.

Can this scenario serve as a prototype for the formation of distinctive male and female "subcultures" among children? Yes, in the sense that the essence of these cultures is a set of socially shared cognitions, including common knowledge and mutually congruent expectations, and common interests in specific themes and scripts that distinguish the two sexes. These communalities can be augmented in a set of children coming together for the first time, since by age 5 or 6, most will already have participated in several same-sex groups, or observed them in operation on TV, so they are primed for building gender-distinct subcultures in any new group of children they enter. Were we to ask, "Is gender socially constructed?" the answer would surely be "yes." At the same time, there may well be a biological contribution to the nature of the subculture each sex chooses to construct.

SOCIALIZATION WITHIN SAME-SEX GROUPS

There has long been evidence that pairs of friends—mostly same-sex friends—influence one another (see Dishion, Spracklen, & Patterson, 1996, for a recent example). However, only recently has research focused on the effects of the amount of time young children spend playing with other children of their own sex. Martin and Fabes (2001) observed a group of preschoolers over a 6-month period, to obtain stable scores for how much time they spent with same-sex playmates (as distinct from their time spent in mixed-sex or other-sex play). They examined the changes that occurred, over the 6 months of observation, in the degree of sex typing in children's play activities. Martin and Fabes reported that the more time boys spent playing with other boys, the greater the increases in their activity level, rough-and-tumble play, and sex-typed choices of toys and games, and the less time they spent near adults. For girls, by contrast, large amounts of time spent with other girls was associated with increasing time spent near adults, and with decreasing aggression, decreasing activity level, and increasing choices of girl-type play materials and activities. This new work points to a powerful role for same-sex peers in shaping one another's sex-typed behavior, values, and interests.

WHAT COMES NEXT?

The recent focus on children's same-sex groups has revitalized developmental social psychology, and promising avenues for the next phases of research on gender development have appeared. What now needs to be done?

1. Investigators need to study both the variations and the similarities among same-sex groups in their agendas and interactive processes. The extent of generality across groups remains largely unexplored. The way gender is enacted in groups undoubtedly changes with age. And observations in other cultures indicate that play in same-sex children's groups reflects what different cultures offer in the way of materials, play contexts, and belief systems. Still, it seems likely that there are certain sex-distinctive themes that appear in a variety of cultural contexts.
2. Studies of individual differences need to be integrated with the studies of group process. Within each sex, some children are only marginally involved in same-sex

groups or dyads, whereas others are involved during much of their free time. And same-sex groups are internally differentiated, so that some children are popular or dominant while others consistently occupy subordinate roles or may even be frequently harassed by others. We need to know more about the individual characteristics that underlie these variations, and about their consequences.
3. Children spend a great deal of their free time in activities that are not gender differentiated at all. We need to understand more fully the conditions under which gender is salient in group process and the conditions under which it is not.

Recommended Reading

Benenson, J.F., Apostolaris, N. H., & Parnass, J. (1997). (See References)
Maccoby, E. E. (1998). (See References)
Martin, C. L., & Fabes, R. A. (2001). (See References)

Note

1. Address correspondence to Eleanor E. Maccoby, Department of Psychology, Stanford University, Stanford, CA 94305-2130.

References

Benenson, J. F., Apostolaris, N. H., & Parnass, J. (1997). Age and sex differences in dyadic and group interaction. *Developmental Psychology, 33,* 538–543.
Benenson, J. F., Nicholson, C., Waite, A., Roy, R., & Simpson, A. (2001). The influence of group size on children's competitive behavior. *Child Development, 72,* 921–928.
Cole, J. D., Dodge, K. A., Schwartz, D., Cillessen, A. H. N., Hubbard, J. A., & Lemerise, E. A. (1999). It takes two to fight: A test of relational factors, and a method for assessing aggressive dyads. *Developmental Psychology, 36,* 1179–1188.
Dishion, T. J., Spracklen, K. M., & Patterson, G. R. (1996). Deviancy training in male adolescent friendships. *Behavior Therapy, 27,* 373–390.
Levine, J. M., & Moreland, R. L. (1998). Small groups. In D. T. Gilbert, S. T. Fiske, & G. Lindzey (Eds.), *Handbook of social psychology* (Vol. 2, pp. 415–469). Boston: McGraw-Hill.
Maccoby, E. E. (1998). *The two sexes: Growing up apart, coming together.* Cambridge, MA: Harvard University Press.
Markovitz, H., Benenson, J. F., & Dolenszky, E. (2001). Evidence that children and adolescents have internal models of peer interaction that are gender differentiated. *Child Development, 72,* 879–886.
Martin, C. L., & Fabes, R. A. (2001). The stability and consequences of young children's same-sex peer interactions. *Developmental Psychology, 37,* 431–446.
Nicolopoulou, A. (1997). Worldmaking and identity formation in children's narrative play-acting. In B. Cox & C. Lightfoot (Eds.), *Sociogenic perspectives in internalization* (pp. 157–187). Hillsdale, NJ: Erlbaum.
Ruble, D. N., & Martin, D. L. (1998). Gender development. In W. Damon & N. Eisenberg (Eds.), *Handbook of child psychology* (5th ed., Vol. 3, pp. 933–1016). New York: John Wiley & Sons.
Strayer, F. F. (1980). Social ecology of the preschool peer group. In W. A. Collins (Ed.), *Minnesota Symposium on Child Psychology: Vol. 13. Development of cognitions, affect and social relations* (pp. 165–196). Hillsdale, NJ: Erlbaum.
Vaughn, B. E., Colvin, T. N., Azria, M. R., Caya, L., & Krzysik, L. (2001). Dyadic analyses of friendship in a sample of preschool-aged children attending Headstart. *Child Development, 72,* 862–878.

Girls Just Want to Be Mean

By MARGARET TALBOT

Today is Apologies Day in Rosalind Wiseman's class—so, naturally, when class lets out, the girls are crying. Not all 12 of them, but a good half. They stand around in the corridor, snuffling quietly but persistently, interrogating one another. "Why didn't you apologize to me?" one girl demands. "Are you stressed right now?" says another. "I am so stressed." Inside the classroom, which is at the National Cathedral School, a private girls' school in Washington, Wiseman is locked in conversation with one of the sixth graders who has stayed behind to discuss why her newly popular best friend is now scorning her.

"You've got to let her go through this," Wiseman instructs. "You can't make someone be your best friend. And it's gonna be hard for her too, because if she doesn't do what they want her to do, the popular girls are gonna chuck her out, and they're gonna spread rumors about her or tell people stuff she told them." The girl's ponytail bobs as she nods and thanks Wiseman, but her expression is baleful.

Wiseman's class is about gossip and cliques and ostracism and just plain meanness among girls. But perhaps the simplest way to describe its goals would be to say that it tries to make middle-school girls be nice to one another. This is a far trickier project than you might imagine, and Apologies Day is a case in point. The girls whom Wiseman variously calls the Alpha Girls, the R.M.G.'s (Really Mean Girls) or the Queen Bees are the ones who are supposed to own up to having back-stabbed or dumped a friend, but they are also the most resistant to the exercise and the most self-justifying. The girls who are their habitual victims or hangers-on—the Wannabes and Messengers in Wiseman's lingo—are always apologizing anyway.

But Wiseman, who runs a nonprofit organization called the Empower Program, is a cheerfully unyielding presence. And in the end, her students usually do what she wants: they take out their gel pens or their glittery feather-topped pens and write something, fold it over and over again into origami and then hide behind their hair when it's read aloud. Often as not, it contains a hidden or a not-so-hidden barb. To wit: "I used to be best friends with two girls. We weren't popular, we weren't that pretty, but we had fun together. When we came to this school, we were placed in different classes. I stopped being friends with

them and left them to be popular. They despise me now, and I'm sorry for what I did. I haven't apologized because I don't really want to be friends any longer and am afraid if I apologize, then that's how it will result. We are now in completely different leagues." Or: "Dear B. I'm sorry for excluding you and ignoring you. Also, I have said a bunch of bad things about you. I have also run away from you just because I didn't like you. A." Then there are the apologies that rehash the original offense in a way sure to embarrass the offended party all over again, as in: "I'm sorry I told everybody you had an American Girl doll. It really burned your reputation." Or: "Dear 'Friend,' I'm sorry that I talked about you behind your back. I once even compared your forehead/face to a minefield (only 2 1 person though.) I'm really sorry I said these things even though I might still believe them."

Wiseman, who is 32 and hip and girlish herself, has taught this class at many different schools, and it is fair to say that although she loves girls, she does not cling to sentimental notions about them. She is a feminist, but not the sort likely to ascribe greater inherent compassion to women or girls as a group than to men or boys. More her style is the analysis of the feminist historian Elizabeth Fox-Genovese, who has observed that "those who have experienced dismissal by the junior-high-school girls' clique could hardly, with a straight face, claim generosity and nurture as a natural attribute of women." Together, Wiseman and I once watched the movie "Heathers," the 1989 black comedy about a triad of vicious Queen Bees who get their comeuppance, and she found it "pretty true to life." The line uttered by Winona Ryder as Veronica, the disaffected non-Heather of the group, struck her as particularly apt: "I don't really like my friends. It's just like they're people I work with and our job is being popular."

Wiseman's reaction to the crying girls is accordingly complex. "I hate to make girls cry," she says. "I really do hate it when their faces get all splotchy, and everyone in gym class or whatever knows they've been crying." At the same time, she notes: "The tears are a funny thing. Because it's not usually the victims who cry; it's the aggressors, the girls who have something to apologize for. And sometimes, yes, it's relief on their part, but it's also somewhat manipulative, because if they've done something crappy, the person they've done it to can't get that mad at them if they're crying. Plus, a lot of the time they're using the apology to dump on somebody all over again."

Is dumping on a friend really such a serious problem? Do mean girls wield that much power? Wiseman thinks so. In May, Crown will publish her book-length analysis of girl-on-girl nastiness, "Queen Bees and Wannabes: Helping Your Daughter Survive Cliques, Gossip, Boyfriends and other Realities of Adolescence." And her seminars, which she teaches in schools around the country, are ambitious attempts to tame what some psychologists are now calling "relational aggression"—by which they mean the constellation of "Heathers"-like manipulations and exclusions and gossip-mongering that most of us remember from middle school and through which girls, more often than boys, tend to channel their hostilities.

"My life is full of these ridiculous little slips of paper," says Wiseman, pointing to the basket of apologies and questions at her feet. "I have read thousands of these slips of paper. And 95 percent of them are the same. 'Why are these girls being mean to me?' 'Why am I being excluded?' 'I don't want to be part of this popular group anymore. I don't like what they're doing.' There are lots of girls out there who are getting this incredible lesson that they are not inherently worthy, and from someone—a friend, another girl—who was so intimately bonded with them. To a large extent, their definitions of intimacy are going to be based on the stuff they're going through in sixth and seventh grade. And that stuff isn't pretty."

"Within the hidden culture of aggression, girls fight with body language and relationships instead of fists and knives."

Rachel Simmons, from *Odd Girl Out: The Hidden Culture of Agression in Girls*

This focus on the cruelty of girls is, of course, something new. For years, psychologists who studied aggression among schoolchildren looked only at its physical and overt manifestations and concluded that girls were less aggressive than boys. That consensus began to change in the early 90's, after a team of researchers led by a Finnish professor named Kaj Bjorkqvist started interviewing 11- and 12-year-old girls about their behavior toward one another. The team's conclusion was that girls were, in fact, just as aggressive as boys, though in a different way. They were not as likely to engage in physical fights, for example, but their superior social intelligence enabled them to wage complicated battles with other girls aimed at damaging relationships or reputations—leaving nasty messages by cellphone or spreading scurrilous rumors by e-mail, making friends with one girl as revenge against another, gossiping about someone just loudly enough to be overheard. Turning the notion of women's greater empathy on its head, Bjorkqvist focused on

the destructive uses to which such emotional attunement could be put. "Girls can better understand how other girls feel," as he puts it, "so they know better how to harm them."

Researchers following in Bjorkqvist's footsteps noted that up to the age of 4 girls tend to be aggressive at the same rates and in the same ways as boys—grabbing toys, pushing, hitting. Later on, however, social expectations force their hostilities underground, where their assaults on one another are more indirect, less physical and less visible to adults. Secrets they share in one context, for example, can sometimes be used against them in another. As Marion Underwood, a professor of psychology at the University of Texas at Dallas, puts it: "Girls very much value intimacy, which makes them excellent friends and terrible enemies. They share so much information when they are friends that they never run out of ammunition if they turn on one another."

In the last few years, a group of young psychologists, including Underwood and Nicki Crick at the University of Minnesota, has pushed this work much further, observing girls in "naturalistic" settings, exploring the psychological foundations for nastiness and asking adults to take relational aggression—especially in the sixth and seventh grades, when it tends to be worst—as seriously as they do more familiar forms of bullying. While some of these researchers have emphasized bonding as a motivation, others have seen something closer to a hunger for power, even a Darwinian drive. One Australian researcher, Laurence Owens, found that the 15-year-old girls he interviewed about their girl-pack predation were bestirred primarily by its entertainment value. The girls treated their own lives like the soaps, hoarding drama, constantly rehashing trivia. Owens's studies contain some of the more vivid anecdotes in the earnest academic literature on relational aggression. His subjects tell him about ingenious tactics like leaving the following message on a girl's answering machine—"Hello, it's me. Have you gotten your pregnancy test back yet?"—knowing that her parents will be the first to hear it. They talk about standing in "huddles" and giving other girls "deaths"—stares of withering condescension—and of calling one another "dyke," "slut" and "fat" and of enlisting boys to do their dirty work.

Relational aggression is finding its chroniclers among more popular writers, too. In addition to Wiseman's book, this spring will bring Rachel Simmons's "Odd Girl Out: The Hidden Culture of Aggression in Girls," Emily White's "Fast Girls: Teenage Tribes and the Myth of the Slut" and Phyllis Chesler's "Woman's Inhumanity to Woman."

In her book, the 27-year-old Simmons offers a plaintive definition of relational aggression: "Unlike boys, who tend to bully acquaintances or strangers, girls frequently attack within tightly knit friendship networks, making aggression harder to identify and intensifying the damage to the victims. Within the hidden culture of aggression, girls fight with body language and relationships instead of fists and knives. In this world, friendship is a weapon, and the sting of a shout pales in comparison to a day of someone's silence. There is no gesture more devastating than the back turning away." Now, Simmons insists, is the time to pull up the rock and really look at this seething underside of American girlhood. "Beneath a facade of female intimacy," she writes, "lies a terrain traveled in secret, marked with anguish and nourished by silence."

Not so much silence, anymore, actually. For many school principals and counselors across the country, relational aggression is becoming a certified social problem and the need to curb it an accepted mandate. A small industry of interveners has grown up to meet the demand. In Austin, Tex., an organization called GENaustin now sends counselors into schools to teach a course on relational aggression called Girls as Friends, Girls as Foes. In Erie, Pa., the Ophelia Project offers a similar curriculum, taught by high-school-aged mentors, that explores "how girls hurt each other" and how they can stop. A private Catholic school in Akron, Ohio, and a public-school district near Portland, Ore., have introduced programs aimed at rooting out girl meanness. And Wiseman and her Empower Program colleagues have taught their Owning Up class at 60 schools. "We are currently looking at relational aggression like domestic violence 20 years ago," says Holly Nishimura, the assistant director of the Ophelia Project. "Though it's not on the same scale, we believe that with relational aggression, the trajectory of awareness, knowledge and demand for change will follow the same track."

Whether this new hypervigilance about a phenomenon that has existed for as long as most of us can remember will actually do anything to squelch it is, of course, another question. Should adults be paying as much attention to this stuff as kids do or will we just get hopelessly tangled up in it ourselves? Are we approaching frothy adolescent bitchery with undue gravity or just giving it its due in girls' lives? On the one hand, it is kind of satisfying to think that girls might be, after their own fashion, as aggressive as boys. It's an idea that offers some relief from the specter of the meek and mopey, "silenced" and self-loathing girl the popular psychology of girlhood has given us in recent years. But it is also true that the new attention to girls as relational aggressors may well take us into a different intellectual cul-de-sac, where it becomes too easy to assume that girls do not use their fists (some do), that all girls are covert in their cruelties, that all girls care deeply about the ways of the clique—and that what they do in their "relational" lives takes precedence over all other aspects of their emerging selves.

After her class at the National Cathedral School, Wiseman and I chat for a while in her car. She has to turn down the India Arie CD that's blaring on her stereo so we can hear each other. The girl she had stayed to talk with after class is still on her mind, partly because she represents the social type for whom Wiseman seems to feel the profoundest sympathy: the girl left behind by a newly popular, newly dismissive friend. "See, at a certain point it becomes cool to be boy crazy," she explains. "That happens in sixth grade, and it gives you so much social status, particularly in an all-girls school, if you can go up and talk to boys.

"But often, an Alpha Girl has an old friend, the best-friend-forever elementary-school friend, who is left behind because she's not boy crazy yet," Wiseman goes on, pressing the accelerator with her red snakeskin boot. "And what she can't figure out is: why does my old friend want to be better friends with a girl who talks behind her back and is mean to her than with me, who is a good friend and who wouldn't do that?"

The subtlety of the maneuvers still amazes Wiseman, though she has seen them time and again. "What happens," she goes on, "is that the newly popular girl—let's call her Darcy—is hanging out with Molly and some other Alpha Girls in the back courtyard, and the old friend, let's call her Kristin, comes up to them. And what's going to happen is Molly's going to throw her arms around Darcy and talk about things that Kristin doesn't know anything about and be totally physically affectionate with Darcy so that she looks like the shining jewel. And Kristin is, like, I don't exist. She doesn't want to be friends with the new version of Darcy—she wants the old one back, but it's too late for that."

So to whom, I ask Wiseman, does Kristin turn in her loneliness? Wiseman heaves a sigh as though she's sorry to be the one to tell me an obvious but unpleasant truth. "The other girls can be like sharks—it's like blood in the water, and they see it and they go, 'Now I can be closer to Kristin because she's being dumped by Darcy.' When I say stuff like this, I know I sound horrible, I know it. But it's what they do."

Hanging out with Wiseman, you get used to this kind of disquisition on the craftiness of middle-school girls, but I'll admit that when my mind balks at something she has told me, when I can't quite believe girls have thought up some scheme or another, I devise little tests for her—I ask her to pick out seventh-grade Queen Bees in a crowd outside a school or to predict what the girls in the class will say about someone who isn't there that day or to guess which boys a preening group of girls is preening for. I have yet to catch her out.

Once, Wiseman mentions a girl she knows whose clique of seven is governed by actual, enumerated rules and suggests I talk with this girl to get a sense of what reformers like her are up against. Jessica Travis, explains Wiseman, shaking her head in aggravated bemusement at the mere thought of her, is a junior at a suburban Maryland high school and a member of the Girls' Advisory Board that is part of Wiseman's organization. She is also, it occurs to me when I meet her, a curious but not atypical social type—an amalgam of old-style Queen Bee-ism and new-style girl's empowerment, brimming over with righteous self-esteem and cheerful cattiness. Tall and strapping, with long russet hair and blue eye shadow, she's like a Powerpuff Girl come to life.

When I ask Jessica to explain the rules her clique lives by, she doesn't hesitate. "O.K.," she says happily. "No 1: clothes. You cannot wear jeans any day but Friday, and you cannot wear a ponytail or sneakers more than once a week. Monday is fancy day—like black pants or maybe you bust out with a skirt. You want to remind people how cute you are in case they forgot over the weekend. O.K., 2: parties. Of course, we sit down together and discuss which ones we're going to go to, because there's no point in getting all dressed up for a party that's going to be lame. No getting smacked at a party, because how would it look for the rest of us if you're drunk and acting like a total fool? And if you do hook up with somebody at the party, please try to limit it to one. Otherwise you look like a slut and that reflects badly on all of us. Kids are not that smart; they're not going to make the distinctions between us. And the rules apply to all of us—you can't be like, 'Oh, I'm having my period; I'm wearing jeans all week.' "

She pauses for a millisecond. "Like, we had a lot of problems with this one girl. She came to school on a Monday in jeans. So I asked her, 'Why you wearing jeans today?' She said, 'Because I felt like it.' 'Because you felt like it? Did you forget it was a Monday?' 'No.' She says she just doesn't like the confinement. She doesn't want to do this anymore. She's the rebel of the group, and we had to suspend her a couple of times; she wasn't allowed to sit with us at lunch. On that first Monday, she didn't even try; she didn't even catch my eye—she knew better. But eventually she came back to us, and she was, like, 'I know, I deserved it.' "

Each member of Jessica's group is allowed to invite an outside person to sit at their table in the lunch room several times a month, but they have to meet at the lockers to O.K. it with the other members first, and they cannot exceed their limit. "We don't want other people at our table more than a couple of times a week because we want to bond, and the bonding is endless," Jessica says. "Besides, let's say you want to tell your girls about some total fool thing you did, like locking your hair in the car door. I mean, my God, you're not going to tell some stranger that."

For all their policing of their borders, they are fiercely loyal to those who stay within them. If a boy treats one of them badly, they all snub him. And Jessica offers another example: "One day, another friend came to school in this skirt from Express—ugliest skirt I've ever seen—red and brown plaid, O.K.? But she felt really fabulous. She was like, Isn't this skirt cute? And she's my friend, so of course I'm like, Damn straight, sister! Lookin' good! But then, this other girl who was in the group for a while comes up and she says to her: 'Oh, my God, you look so stupid! You look like a giant argyle sock!' I was like, 'What is wrong with you?' "

Jessica gets good grades, belongs to the B'nai B'rith Youth Organization and would like, for no particular reason, to go to Temple University. She plays polo and figure-skates, has a standing appointment for a once-a-month massage and "cried from the beginning of 'Pearl Harbor' till I got home that night." She lives alone with her 52-year-old mother, who was until January a consultant for Oracle. She is lively and loquacious and she has, as she puts it, "the highest self-esteem in the world." Maybe that's why she finds it so easy to issue dictums like: "You cannot go out with an underclassman. You just cannot—end of story." I keep thinking, when I listen to Jessica talk about her clique, that she must be doing some kind of self-conscious parody. But I'm fairly sure she's not.

On a bleary December afternoon, I attend one of Wiseman's after-school classes in the Maryland suburbs. A public middle school called William H. Farquhar has requested the services of the Empower Program. Soon after joining the class, I ask the students about a practice Wiseman has told me about that I find a little hard to fathom or even to believe. She had mentioned it in passing—You know how the girls use three-way calling"—and when I professed puzzlement, explained: "O.K., so Alison and Kathy call up Mary, but only Kathy talks and Alison is just

lurking there quietly so Mary doesn't know she's on the line. And Kathy says to Mary, 'So what do you think of Alison?' And of course there's some reason at the moment why Mary doesn't like Alison, and she says, Oh, my God, all these nasty things about Alison—you know, 'I can't believe how she throws herself at guys, she thinks she's all that, blah, blah, blah.' And Alison hears all this."

Not for the first time with Wiseman, I came up with one of my lame comparisons with adult life: "But under normal circumstances, repeating nasty gossip about one friend to another is not actually going to get you that far with your friends."

"Yeah, but in Girl World, that's currency," Wiseman responded. "It's like: Ooh, I have a dollar and now I'm more powerful and I can use this if I want to. I can further myself in the social hierarchy and bond with the girl being gossiped about by setting up the conference call so she can know about it, by telling her about the gossip and then delivering the proof."

In the classroom at Farquhar, eight girls are sitting in a circle, eating chips and drinking sodas. All of them have heard about the class and chosen to come. There's Jordi Kauffman, who is wearing glasses, a fleece vest and sneakers and who displays considerable scorn for socially ambitious girls acting "all slutty in tight clothes or all snotty." Jordi is an honor student whose mother is a teacher and whose father is the P.T.A. president. She's the only one in the class with a moderately sarcastic take on the culture of American girlhood. "You're in a bad mood one day, and you say you feel fat," she remarks, "and adults are like, 'Oh-oh, she's got poor self-esteem, she's depressed, get her help!' "

Next to Jordi is her friend Jackie, who is winsome and giggly and very pretty. Jackie seems more genuinely troubled by the loss of a onetime friend who has been twisting herself into an Alpha Girl. She will later tell us that when she wrote a heartfelt e-mail message to this former friend, asking her why she was "locking her out," the girl's response was to print it out and show it around at school.

On the other side of the room are Lauren and Daniela, who've got boys on the brain, big time. They happily identify with Wiseman's negative portrayal of "Fruit-Cup Girl," one who feigns helplessness—in Wiseman's example, by pretending to need a guy to open her pull-top can of fruit cocktail—to attract male attention. There's Courtney, who will later say, when asked to write a letter to herself about how she's doing socially, that she can't, because she "never says anything to myself about myself." And there's Kimberly, who will write such a letter professing admiration for her own "natural beauty."

They have all heard of the kind of three-way call Wiseman had told me about; all but two have done it or had it done to them. I ask if they found the experience useful. "Not always," Jordi says, "because sometimes there's something you want to hear but you don't hear. You want to hear, 'Oh, she's such a good person' or whatever, but instead you hear, 'Oh, my God, she's such a bitch.' "

I ask if boys ever put together three-way calls like that. "Nah," Jackie says. "I don't think they're smart enough."

Once the class gets going, the discussion turns, as it often does, to Jackie's former friend, the one who's been clawing her way into the Alpha Girl clique. In a strange twist, this girl has, as Daniela puts it, "given up her religion" and brought a witch's spell book to school.

"That's weird," Wiseman says, "because usually what happens is that the girls who are attracted to that are more outside-the-box types—you know, the depressed girls with the black fingernails who are always writing poetry—because it gives them some amount of power. The girl you're describing sounds unconfident; maybe she's looking for something that makes her seem mysterious and powerful. If you have enough social status, you can be a little bit different. And that's where she's trying to go with this—like, I am so in the box that I'm defining a new box."

Jackie interjects, blushing, with another memory of her lost friend. "I used to tell her everything," she laments, "and now she just blackmails me with my secrets."

"Sounds like she's a Banker," Wiseman says. "That means that she collects information and uses it later to her advantage."

"Nobody really likes her," chimes in Jordi. "She's like a shadow of her new best friend, a total Wannabe. Her new crowd's probably gonna be like, 'Take her back, pulleeze!'"

"What really hurts," Jackie persists, "is that it's like you can't just drop a friend. You have to dump on them, too."

"Yeah, it's true," Jordi agrees matter-of-factly. "You have to make them really miserable before you leave."

After class, when I concede that Wiseman was right about the three-way calling, she laughs. "Haven't I told you girls are crafty?" she asks. "Haven't I told you girls are evil?"

It may be that the people most likely to see such machinations clearly are the former masters of them. Wiseman's anthropological mapping of middle-school society—the way she notices and describes the intricate rituals of exclusion and humiliation as if they were a Balinese cockfight—seems to come naturally to her because she remembers more vividly than many people do what it was like to be an adolescent insider or, as she puts it, "a pearls-and-tennis-skirt-wearing awful little snotty girl."

It was different for me. When I was in junior high in the 70's—a girl who was neither a picked-on girl nor an Alpha Girl, just someone in the vast more-or-less dorky middle at my big California public school—the mean girls were like celebrities whose exploits my friends and I followed with interest but no savvy. I sort of figured that their caste was conferred at birth when they landed in Laurelwood—the local hillside housing development peopled by dentists and plastic surgeons—and were given names like Marcie and Tracie. I always noticed their pretty clothes and haircuts and the smell of their green-apple gum and cherry Lip Smackers and their absences from school for glamorous afflictions like tennis elbow or skiing-related sunburns. The real Queen Bees never spoke to you at all, but the Wannabes would sometimes insult you as a passport to popularity. There was a girl named Janine, for instance, who used to preface every offensive remark with the phrase "No offense," as in "No offense, but you look like a woofing dog." Sometimes it got her the nod from the Girl World authorities and sometimes it didn't, and I could never figure out why or why not.

Which is all to say that to an outsider, the Girl World's hardcore social wars are fairly distant and opaque, and to somebody like Wiseman, they are not. As a seventh grader at a private school in Washington, she hooked up with "a very powerful, very scary group of girls who were very fun to be with but who could turn on you like a dime." She became an Alpha Girl, but she soon found it alienating. "You know you have these moments where you're like, 'I hate this person I've become; I'm about to vomit on myself'? Because I was really a piece of work. I was really snotty."

Teachers would "guide students to the realization that most girls don't maliciously compete or exclude each other, but within their social context, girls perceive that they must compete with each other for status and power, thus maintaining the status system that binds them all."

Rosalind Wiseman,
Empower Program

When I ask Wiseman to give me an example of something wicked that she did, she says: "Whoa, I'm in such denial about this. But O.K., here's one. When I was in eighth grade, I spread around a lie about my best friend, Melissa. I told all the girls we knew that she had gotten together, made out or whatever, with this much older guy at a family party at our house. I must have been jealous—she was pretty and getting all this attention from guys. And so I made up something that made her sound slutty. She confronted me about it, and I totally denied it."

Wiseman escaped Girl World only when she headed off to California for college and made friends with "people who didn't care what neighborhood I came from or what my parents did for a living." After majoring in political science, she moved back to Washington, where she helped start an organization that taught self-defense to women and girls. "I was working with girls and listening to them, and again and again, before it was stories about boys, it was stories about girls and what they'd done to them. I'd say talk to me about how you're controlling each other, and I wrote this curriculum on cliques and popularity. That's how it all got started."

Wiseman's aim was to teach classes that would, by analyzing the social hierarchy of school, help liberate girls from it. Girls would learn to "take responsibility for how they treat each other," as Wiseman's handbook for the course puts it, "and to develop strategies to interrupt the cycle of gossip, exclusivity and reputations." Instructors would not let comments like "we have groups but we all get along" stand; they would deconstruct them, using analytic tools familiar from the sociology of privilege and from academic discourse on racism. "Most often, the 'popular' students make these comments while the students who are not as high in the social hierarchy disagree. The comments by the popular students reveal how those who have privilege are so accustomed to their power that they don't recognize when they are dominating and silencing others." Teachers would "guide students to the realization that most girls don't maliciously compete or exclude each other, but within their social context, girls perceive that they must compete with each other for status and power, thus maintaining the status system that binds them all."

The theory was sober and sociological, but in the hands of Wiseman, the classes were dishy and confessional, enlivened by role-playing that got the girls giggling and by Wiseman's knowing references to Bebe jackets, Boardwalk Fries and 'N Sync. It was a combination that soon put Wiseman's services in high demand, especially at some of the tonier private schools in the Washington area.

"I was just enthralled by her," says Camilla Vitullo, who as a headmistress at the National Cathedral School in 1994 was among the first to hire Wiseman. "And the girls gobbled up everything she had to say." (Vitullo, who is now at the Spence School in Manhattan, plans to bring Wiseman there.) Soon Wiseman's Empower Program, which also teaches courses on subjects like date rape, was getting big grants from the Liz Claiborne Foundation and attracting the attention of Oprah Winfrey, who had Wiseman on her show last spring.

Wiseman has been willing to immerse herself in Girl World, and it has paid off. (Out of professional necessity, she has watched "every movie with Kirsten Dunst or Freddie Prinze Jr." and innumerable shows on the WB network.) But even if it weren't her job, you get the feeling she would still know more about all that than most adults do. She senses immediately, for example, that when the girls in her Farquhar class give her a bottle of lotion as a thank-you present, she is supposed to open it on the spot and pass it around and let everybody slather some on. ("Ooh, is it smelly? Smelly in a good way?") When Wiseman catches sight of you approaching, she knows how to do a little side-to-side wave, with her elbow pressed to her hip, that is disarmingly girlish. She says "totally" and "omigod" and "don't stress" and "chill" a lot and refers to people who are "hotties" or "have it goin' on." And none of it sounds foolish on her yet, maybe because she still looks a little like a groovy highschooler with her trim boyish build and her short, shiny black hair and her wardrobe—picked out by her 17-year-old sister, Zoe—with its preponderance of boots and turtlenecks and flared jeans.

Zoe. Ah, Zoe. Zoe is a bit of a problem for the whole Reform of Girl World project, a bit of a fly in the ointment. For years, Wiseman has been working on her, with scant results. Zoe, a beauty who is now a senior at Georgetown Day School, clearly adores her older sister but also remains skeptical of her enterprise. "She's always telling me to look inside myself and be true to myself—things I can't do right now because I'm too shallow and superficial" is how Zoe, in all her Zoe-ness, sums up their differences.

Once I witnessed the two sisters conversing about a party Zoe had given, at which she was outraged by the appearance of freshman girls—and not ugly, dorky ones, either! Pretty ones!"

"And what exactly was the problem with that?" Wiseman asked.

"As long as education is mandatory, we have a huge obligation to make it socially safe."

Michael Thompson, author of *Best Friends, Worst Enemies*

"If you're gonna be in high school," Zoe replied, with an attempt at patience, "you have to stay in your place. A freshman girl cannot show up at a junior party; disgusting 14-year-old girls with their boobs in the air cannot show up at your party going"—her voice turned breathy—Uh, hi, where's the beer?"

Wiseman wanted to know why Zoe couldn't show a little empathy for the younger girls.

"No matter what you say in your talks and your little motivational speeches, Ros, you are not going to change how I feel when little girls show up in their little outfits at my party. I mean, I don't always get mad. Usually I don't care enough about freshmen to even know their names."

Wiseman rolled her eyes.

"Why would I know their names? Would I go out of my way to help freshmen? Should I be saying, 'Hey, I just want you to know that I'm there for you'? Would that make ya happy, Ros? Maybe in some perfect Montessori-esque, P.C. world, we'd all get along. But there are certain rules of the school system that have been set forth from time immemorial or whatever."

"This," said Wiseman, "is definitely a source of tension between us."

A little over a month after the last class at Farquhar, I go back to the school to have lunch with Jordi and Jackie. I want to know what they've remembered from the class, how it might have affected their lives. Wiseman has told me that she will sometimes get e-mail messages from girls at schools where she has taught complaining of recidivism: "Help, you have to come back! We're all being mean again"—that kind of thing.

The lunchroom at Farquhar is low-ceilinged, crowded and loud and smells like frying food and damp sweaters. The two teachers on duty are communicating through walkie-talkies. I join Jordi in line, where she selects for her lunch a small plate of fried potato discs and nothing to drink. Lunch lasts from 11:28 to 11:55, and Jordi always sits at the same table with Jackie (who bounds in late today, holding the little bag of popcorn that is her lunch) and several other girls.

I ask Jackie what she remembers best about Wiseman's class, and she smiles fondly and says it was the "in and out of the box thing—who's cool and who's not and why."

I ask Jordi if she thought she would use a technique Wiseman had recommended for confronting a friend who had weaseled out of plans with her in favor of a more popular girl's invitation. Wiseman had suggested sitting the old friend down alone at some later date, "affirming" the friendship and telling her clearly what she wanted from her. Jordi had loved it when the class acted out the scene, everybody hooting and booing at the behavior of the diva-girl as she dissed her social inferiors in a showdown at the food court. But now, she tells me that she found the exercise "kind of corny." She explains: "Not many people at my school would do it that way. We'd be more likely just to battle it out on the Internet when we got home." (Most of her friends feverishly instant-message after school each afternoon.) Both girls agree that the class was fun, though, and had taught them a lot about popularity.

Which, unfortunately, wasn't exactly the point. Wiseman told me once that one hazard of her trade is that girls will occasionally go home and tell their moms that they were in a class where they learned how to be popular. "I think they're smarter than that, and they must just be telling their moms that," she said. "But they're such concrete thinkers at this age that some could get confused."

I think Wiseman's right—most girls do understand what she's getting at. But it is also true that in paying such close attention to the cliques, in taking Queen Bees so very seriously, the relational-aggression movement seems to grant them a legitimacy and a stature they did not have when they ruled a world that was beneath adult radar.

Nowadays, adults, particularly in the upper middle classes, are less laissez-faire about children's social lives. They are more vigilant, more likely to have read books about surviving the popularity wars of middle school or dealing with cliques, more likely to have heard a talk or gone to a workshop on those topics. Not long ago, I found myself at a lecture by the best-selling author Michael Thompson on "Understanding the Social Lives of our Children." It was held inside the National Cathedral on a chilly Tuesday evening in January, and there were hundreds of people in attendance—attractive late-40's mothers in cashmere turtlenecks and interesting scarves and expensive haircuts, and graying but fit fathers—all taking notes and lining up to ask eager, anxious questions about how best to ensure their children's social happiness. "As long as education is mandatory," Thompson said from the pulpit, "we have a huge obligation to make it socially safe," and heads nodded all around me. He made a list of "the top three reasons for a fourth-grade girl to be popular," and parents in my pew wrote it down in handsome little leather notebooks or on the inside cover of Thompson's latest book, "Best Friends, Worst Enemies." A red-haired woman with a fervent, tremulous voice and an elegant navy blue suit said that she worried our children were socially handicapped by "a lack of opportunities for unstructured cooperative play" and mentioned that she had her 2-year-old in a science class. A serious-looking woman took the microphone to say that she was troubled by the fact that her daughter liked a girl "who is mean and controlling and once wrote the word murder on the bathroom mirror—and this is in a private school!"

I would never counsel blithe ignorance on such matters—some children are truly miserable at school for social reasons,

truly persecuted and friendless and in need of adult help. But sometimes we do seem in danger of micromanaging children's social lives, peering a little too closely. Priding ourselves on honesty in our relationships, as baby-boomer parents often do, we expect to know everything about our children's friendships, to be hip to their social travails in a way our own parents, we thought, were not. But maybe this attention to the details can backfire, giving children the impression that the transient social anxieties and allegiances of middle school are weightier and more immutable than they really are. And if that is the result, it seems particularly unfortunate for girls, who are already more mired in the minutiae of relationships than boys are, who may already lack, as Christopher Lasch once put it, "any sense of an impersonal order that exists independently of their wishes and anxieties" and of the "vicissitudes of relationships."

I think I would have found it dismaying if my middle school had offered a class that taught us about the wiles of Marcie and Tracie: if adults studied their folkways, maybe they were more important than I thought, or hoped. For me, the best antidote to the caste system of middle school was the premonition that adults did not usually play by the same rigid and peculiar rules—and that someday, somewhere, I would find a whole different mattering map, a whole crowd of people who read the same books I did and wouldn't shun me if I didn't have a particular brand of shoes. When I went to college, I found it, and I have never really looked back.

And the Queen Bees? Well, some grow out of their girly sense of entitlement on their own, surely; some channel it in more productive directions. Martha Stewart must have been a Q.B. Same with Madonna. At least one of the Q.B.'s from my youth—albeit the nicest and smartest one—has become a pediatrician on the faculty of a prominent medical school, I noticed when I looked her up the other day. And some Queen Bees have people who love them—dare I say it?—just as they are, a truth that would have astounded me in my own school days but that seems perfectly natural now.

On a Sunday afternoon, I have lunch with Jessica Travis and her mother, Robin, who turns out to be an outgoing, transplanted New Yorker—born in Brighton Beach, raised in Sheepshead Bay." Over white pizza, pasta, cannoli and Diet Cokes, I ask Robin what Jessica was like as a child.

"I was fabulous," Jessica says.

"She was," her mother agrees. "She was blond, extremely happy, endlessly curious and always the leader of the pack. She didn't sleep because she didn't want to miss anything. She was just a bright, shiny kid. She's still a bright, shiny kid."

After Jessica takes a call on her pumpkin-colored cellphone, we talk for a while about Jessica's room, which they both describe as magnificent. "I have lived in apartments smaller than her majesty's two-bedroom suite," Robin snorts. "Not many single parents can do for their children what I have done for this one. This is a child who asked for a pony and got two. I tell her this is the top of the food chain. The only place you can go from here is the royal family."

I ask if anything about Jessica's clique bothers her. She says no—because what she calls "Jess's band of merry men" doesn't "define itself by its opponents. They're not a threat to anyone. Besides, it's not like they're an A-list clique."

"Uh, Mom," Jessica corrects. "We are definitely an A-list clique. We are totally A-list. You are giving out incorrect information."

"Soooorry," Robin says. "I'd fire myself, but there's no one else lining up for the job of being your mom."

Jessica spends a little time bringing her mother and me up to date on the elaborate social structure at her high school. The cheerleaders' clique, it seems, is not the same as the pom-pom girls' clique, though both are A-list. All sports cliques are A-list, in fact, except—of course"—the swimmers. There is a separate A-list clique for cute preppy girls who "could play sports but don't." There is "the white people who pretend to be black clique" and the drama clique, which would be "C list," except that, as Jessica puts it, "they're not even on the list."

"So what you are saying is that your high school is littered with all these groups that have their own separate physical and mental space?" Robin says, shaking her head in wonderment.

When they think about it, Jessica and her mom agree that the business with the rules—what you can wear on a given day of the week and all that—comes from Jessica's fondness for structure. As a child, her mom says she made up games with "such elaborate rules I'd be lost halfway through her explanation of them." Besides, there was a good deal of upheaval in her early

life. Robin left her "goofy artist husband" when Jessica was 3, and after that they moved a lot. And when Robin went to work for Oracle, she "was traveling all the time, getting home late. When I was on the road, I'd call her every night at 8 and say: 'Sweet Dreams. I love you. Good Night.'"

"Always in that order," Jessica says. "Always at 8. I don't like a lot of change."

Toward the end of our lunch, Jessica's mother—who says she herself was more a nerd than a Queen Bee in school—returns to the subject of cliques. She wants, it seems, to put something to rest. "You know I realize there are people who stay with the same friends, the same kind of people, all their life, who never look beyond that," she says. "I wouldn't want that for my daughter. I want my daughter to be one of those people who lives in the world. I know she's got these kind of narrow rules in her personal life right now. But I still think, I really believe, that she will be a bigger person, a person who spends her life in the world." Jessica's mother smiles. Then she gives her daughter's hair an urgent little tug, as if it were the rip cord of a parachute and Jessica were about to float away from her.

Margaret Talbot, a contributing writer for the magazine, is a fellow at the New America Foundation.

Bullying Among Children

Most teachers are aware that bullying begins early, yet many appear to believe the myth that children "picking on" or teasing one another is a "normal" part of childhood.

Janis R. Bullock

Six-year-old Sam is barely eating. When asked by his dad what is wrong, he bursts into tears. "The kids at school keep calling me a nerd, and they poke and push me," he sobs.

"There's a kid at school no one likes," 7-year-old Anika shares with her parents. "We all tease her a lot. She is a total dork. I would never invite her to my birthday party."

Bullying is a very old phenomenon; European researchers have studied its effects for decades (Olweus, 1991). Until recently, however, the issue has received less attention from researchers in the United States, perhaps because of the prevailing belief that bullying among children is inevitable. Considering that bullying often is a sign that aggressive or violent behavior is present elsewhere in children's lives—young children may be acting out at school what they have observed and learned in the home—and the fact that bullying among primary school-age children is now recognized as an antecedent to progressively more violent behavior in later grades (Saufler & Gagne, 2000), it behooves teachers to take notice.

Unfortunately, teachers have differing attitudes toward children who bully. Most teachers are aware that bullying begins early, yet many appear to believe the myth that children "picking on" or teasing one another is a "normal" part of childhood. They also may believe that these conflicts are best resolved by the children themselves. Consequently, some teachers do not intervene.

CHARACTERISTICS OF BULLIES AND THEIR VICTIMS

Bullying refers to repeated, unprovoked, harmful actions by one child or children against another. The acts may be physical or psychological. Physical, or direct, bullying includes hitting, kicking, pushing, grabbing toys from other children, and engaging in very rough and intimidating play. Psychological bullying includes name calling, making faces, teasing, taunting, and making threats. Indirect, or less obvious and less visible, bullying includes exclusion and rejection of children from a group (Olweus, 1991).

Children who bully are impulsive, dominate others, and show little empathy. They display what Olweus (1991) defines as an "aggressive personality pattern combined with physical strength" (p. 425). Without intervention, the frequency and severity of the bullying behaviors may increase. Even more disturbing, it appears that the patterns of bullying learned in the early years can set children on a course of violence later in life (Batsche & Knoff, 1994; Baumeister, 2001).

Although a longstanding characterization of children who bully points to their low self-esteem, there is little empirical evidence to support this view. In fact, more recent research (Baumeister, 2001; Bushman & Baumeister, 1998) suggests that an inflated self-esteem increases the odds of aggressive behavior. When a bully's self-regard is seriously threatened by insults or criticisms, for example, his or her response will be more aggressive than normal. Furthermore, bullies often report that they feel powerful and superior, and justified in their actions.

Research on family dynamics suggests that many children already have learned to bully others by preschool age. Many young children who bully lack empathy and problem-solving skills, and learn from their parents to hit back in response to problems (Loeber & Dishion, 1984; Vladimir & Brubach, 2000).

Children who are bullied, on the other hand, are often younger, weaker, and more passive than the bully. They appear anxious, insecure, cautious, sensitive and quiet, and often react by crying and withdrawing. They are often lonely and lack close friendships at school. Without adult intervention, these children are likely to be bullied repeatedly, putting them at-risk for continued social rejection, depression, and impaired self-esteem (Schwartz, Dodge, & Coie, 1994). A smaller subset of these children, known as "provocative victims," have learned to respond aggressively to perceived threats by retaliating not only against the aggressor, but also against others (Olweus, 1993).

INCIDENCES OF BULLYING AMONG CHILDREN

Evidence suggests that, in the United States, the incidence of bullying among children is increasing and becoming a nationwide problem. One out of five children admits to being a bully (Noll & Carter, 1997). In general, boys engage in more physical, direct means of bullying, whereas girls engage in the more psychological and indirect bullying, such as exclusion. Roland (1989) reported that girls may be involved in bullying as much as boys, but are less willing to acknowledge their involvement. In addition, because indirect bullying is often less apparent, girls' bullying may be underestimated. Girls tend to bully less as they get older. The percentage of boys who bully, however, is similar at different age levels (Smith & Sharp, 1994).

Twenty-five to 50 percent of children report being bullied. The great majority of boys are bullied by other boys, while 60 percent of girls report being bullied by boys. Eight percent of children report staying away from school one day per month because they fear being bullied. Forty-three percent of children have a fear of being harassed in the school bathroom (Noll & Carter, 1997). Children report that many incidents of bullying occur in situations that are difficult for the teacher to monitor, such as during playground activity.

THE EFFECTS OF BULLYING ON CHILDREN

To succeed in school, children must perceive their environment as being safe, secure, and comfortable. Yet, for many children, bullying and teasing begins as soon as children first form peer groups. For some children, this is a time when patterns of victimizing and victimization become established. Consequently, the victims perceive school as a threatening place and experience adjustment difficulties, feelings of loneliness, and a desire to avoid

school. These feelings may linger even when bullying ceases (Kochenderfer & Ladd, 1996).

Children desire and need interaction with peers, physical activity, and time outdoors. Consequently, they often consider outside recess to be their favorite part of the school day. Sadly, however, many children who are bullied report that problems occur on the playground and view the playground as a lonely, unhappy, and unsafe environment.

If children are fearful or feel intimidated, they cannot learn effectively. They may react by skipping school, avoiding certain areas of the school (the bathroom or the playground), or, in extreme, yet increasingly common, cases, they may bring weapons to school (Noll & Carter, 1997). Olweus (1991) reminds us that "every individual should have the right to be spared oppression and repeated, intentional humiliation in school, as in society at large" (p. 427). As early exposure to bullying can produce both immediate and delayed effects in children's ability to adjust to school, school staff need to intervene as soon as problems are detected.

RECOMMENDATIONS FOR TEACHERS TO SUPPORT CHILDREN

A comprehensive plan to address the problems of bullying and teasing must involve school personnel, teachers, children, and families. Intervention must occur on three levels: school-wide, in specific classrooms, and with individuals.

School-wide Intervention

School personnel must recognize the pervasiveness of bullying and teasing and its detrimental effects on children's development. Inservice training can be developed that outlines a clear policy statement against bullying and intervention strategies for addressing it. The school also can develop a comprehensive plan geared to teach children prosocial behaviors and skills. The children may be involved in the development of such policies and strategies, providing their input on what behavior is appropriate and identifying sanctions against bullies (Lickona, 2000; Olweus, 1997).

School personnel could enlist families' support and involvement by sharing details of the policy through parent-teacher conferences and newsletters. Families need to be aware of the specific sanctions that will be imposed on children who bully, and they need opportunities to offer feedback and suggestions. It is important to encourage parents to talk with their children about bullying. Children who are bullied often believe that their parents are unaware of the situation, and that their concerns are not being addressed or discussed. Children *do* want adults to intervene, however (Gropper & Froschl, 1999). If families are kept informed, they can work as a "team member" with school counselors and teachers to change the school environment.

Additional sources of school-wide support for children who are bullied and teased may be developed, including mentoring programs. Teachers can identify children who need support, and find them a mentor. Children may feel more at ease and less anxious when they have a "buddy," such as an older student, who can help intervene (Noll & Carter, 1997). Counselors at one elementary school selected, trained, and supervised high school students to teach the younger children how to deal with bullying and harassment. After implementation of this program, the teachers observed a decline in reports of harassment (Frieman & Frieman, 2000).

Bullying frequently occurs on the playground (Whitney, Rivers, Smith, & Sharp, 1994), yet many children believe that teachers do little to stop it. Consequently, "play-time… is more of a prison sentence than an opportunity to play and socialize" (Slee, 1995, p. 326). Therefore, school personnel may need to review playground design and space, children's access to these spaces, teacher supervision, and the role of the school in early intervention on the playground (Lambert, 1999). Yard monitors and lunch time supervisors can be trained to watch for signs of bullying. In addition, children can be asked to identify those places where bullying most frequently occurs.

Intervention in Specific Classrooms

Clearly, bullying and hurtful teasing affects children's ability to learn and enjoy play, as well as the teacher's ability to teach. Within the classroom, teachers can begin addressing the problem by creating times for children to talk about their concerns. Interestingly, one study showed that when children ages 5 to 7 years of age were asked about assisting someone who was being bullied, 37 percent replied that it was none of their business to help (Slee & Rigby, 1994).

Teachers can ask children to talk about what makes them feel unsafe or unwelcome in school. The teacher then can make a list of the children's responses, discuss them (e.g., "I don't like it when someone hits me or calls me a name"), and create corresponding rules (e.g., "Hitting and name calling are not allowed in the classroom"). When necessary, the discussions can be continued during class meetings so that the rules can be reviewed, revised, and updated. The teacher can also show children what to do to help themselves or other children, and remind them of the consequences of breaking the rules. Teachers can reduce children's anxiety by setting firm limits on unacceptable behavior (Froschl & Sprung, 1999).

If the bullying continues, teachers may need to make referrals to school counselors who will work with children, either individually or in groups, to talk about concerns, discuss solutions and options, and give suggestions on how to form friendships. Children without close friends are more likely to be victimized and may benefit from specific suggestions for building friendships (e.g., invite a friend to your house, work together on a school project, share a common interest, play a favorite game together).

Certain types of curricula, especially those that provide opportunities for cooperative learning experiences, may make bullying less likely to flourish. Children need to be engaged in worthwhile, authentic learning activities that encourage their interests and abilities (Katz, 1993). When they are intellectually motivated, they are less likely to bully. For example, project work (Katz & Chard, 2000) involves children's in-depth investigations into topics of their own choosing. As they explore events and objects around them in the classroom, in the school yard, in the neighborhood, and in the community, they learn to cooperate, collaborate, and share responsibilities. Project work can be complemented by noncompetitive games, role playing, and dramatization to raise awareness of bullying and increase empathy for those who experience it. Some teachers use children's literature to help create caring and peaceful classrooms (Morris, Taylor, & Wilson, 2000).

Intervention With Individuals

Developing both immediate and long-term strategies for identifying and working with bullies may be necessary. When teachers observe an incident of bullying, they can intervene by asking the bully to consider the consequences of his or her actions and think about how others feel. By talking calmly, yet firmly, to the bully, the teacher can make it clear that such behavior is unacceptable. Teachers can show the bully alternate ways to talk, interact, and negotiate; at the same time, they can encourage victims to assert themselves. By doing so, the teacher is showing the bully and the victim that action is being taken to stop the bullying. Acting promptly can prevent the bullying from escalating.

When interacting with children on a one-on-one basis, teachers should provide encouragement that acknowledges specific attributes, rather than dispensing general praise, approval, or admiration ("I am so glad that you have done a great job; it is wonderful; yours is one of the best projects") that may appear to be contrived. Expressions of specific encouragement ("You seem to be pleased and very interested in your project, and it appears you have worked on it for many days and used many resources to find answers to your questions"), as opposed to general praise, are descriptive, sincere, take place in private, focus on the process, and help children to develop an appreciation for their efforts and work. While developing children's self-esteem is a worthwhile goal, false praise may instead promote narcissism and unrealistic self-regard. Teachers should avoid encouraging children to think highly of themselves when they have not earned it (Baumeister, 2001; Hitz & Driscoll, 1988).

Additional long-term strategies may include encouraging children to resolve their own problems and using peers to mediate between bullies and their targets. Furthermore, teachers can spend time helping children to form ties with peers who can offer protection, support, security, and safety, thus helping to reduce children's exposure to bullying (Kochenderfer & Ladd, 1997; Ladd, Kochenderfer, & Coleman, 1996).

Summary

Bullying and teasing are an unfortunate part of too many children's lives, leading to trouble for both bullies and their victims. Children who are bullied come to believe that school is unsafe and that children are mean. They may develop low self-esteem and experience loneliness. Children who continue to bully will have difficulty developing and maintaining positive relationships. A comprehensive intervention plan that addresses the needs of the school, the classroom, teachers, children, and families can be developed and implemented to ensure that all children learn in a supportive and safe environment.

References

Batsche, G. M., & Knoff, H. M. (1994). Bullies and their victims: Understanding a pervasive problem in the schools. *School Psychology Review, 23*, 165–174.

Baumeister, R. (2001). Violent pride: Do people turn violent because of self-hate, or self-love? *Scientific American, 284*, 96–101.

Bushman, B. J., & Baumeister, R. F. (1998). Threatened egotism, narcissism, self-esteem, and direct and displaced aggression: Does self-love or self-hate lead to violence? *Journal of Personality and Social Psychology, 75*, 219–229.

Frieman, M., & Frieman, B. B. (2000). *Reducing harassment in elementary school classrooms using high school mentors.* (ERIC Document Reproduction Service No. ED 439 797).

Froschl, M., & Sprung, B. (1999). On purpose: Addressing teasing and bullying in early childhood. *Young Children, 54*, 70–72.

Gropper, N., & Froschl, M. (1999). The role of gender in young children's teasing and bullying behavior. Montreal, Canada. (ERIC Document Reproduction Service No. ED 431 162).

Hitz, R., & Driscoll, A. (1988). Praise or encouragement? New insights into praise: Implications for early childhood teachers. *Young Children, 42*, 6–13.

Katz, L. G. (1993). *Distinctions between self-esteem and narcissism: Implications for practice.* Urbana, IL: ERIC Clearinghouse on Elementary and Early Childhood Education.

Katz, L., & Chard, S. (2000). *Engaging children's minds: The project approach* (2nd ed.). Stamford, CT: Ablex.

Kochenderfer, B. J., & Ladd, G. W. (1996). Peer victimization: Cause or consequence of school maladjustment? *Child Development, 67*, 1305–1317.

Kochenderfer, B. J., & Ladd, G. W. (1997). Victimized children's responses to peers' aggression: Behaviors associated with reduced versus continued victimization. *Development and Psychopathology, 9*, 59–73.

Ladd, G. W., Kochenderfer, B. J., & Coleman, C. (1996). Friendship quality as a predictor of young children's early school adjustment. *Child Development, 67*, 1103–1118.

Lambert, E. B. (1999). Do school playgrounds trigger playground bullying? *Canadian Children, 42*, 25–31.

Lickona, T. (2000). Sticks and stones may break my bones AND names WILL hurt me. Thirteen ways to prevent peer cruelty. *Our Children, 26*, 12–14.

Loeber, R., & Dishion, T. J. (1984). Boys who fight at home and school: Family conditions influencing cross-setting consistency. *Journal of Consulting and Clinical Psychology, 52*, 759–768.

Morris, V. G., Taylor, S. I., & Wilson, J. T. (2000). Using children's stories to promote peace in classrooms. *Early Childhood Education Journal, 28*, 41–50.

Noll, K., & Carter, J. (1997). *Taking the bully by the horns.* Reading, PA: Unicorn Press.

Olweus, D. (1991). Bully/victim problems among schoolchildren: Basic facts and effects of a school based intervention program. In D. J. Pepler & K. H. Rubin (Eds.), *The development and treatment of childhood aggression* (pp. 441–448). Hillsdale, NJ: Lawrence Erlbaum.

Olweus, D. (1993). Victimization by peers: Antecedents and long-term outcomes. In K. H. Rubin & J. B. Asendorf (Eds.), *Social withdrawal, inhibition, and shyness in childhood* (pp. 315–341). Hillsdale, NJ: Lawrence Erlbaum.

Olweus, D. (1997). Bully/victim problems in school: Facts and intervention. *European Journal of Psychology of Education, 12*, 495–510.

Roland, E. (1989). Bullying: The Scandinavian research tradition. In D. P. Tattum & D. A. Lane (Eds.), *Bullying in schools* (pp. 21–32). London: Trentham Books.

Saufler, C., & Gagne, C. (2000). *Maine project against bullying. Final report.* Augusta, ME: Maine State Department of Education. (ERIC Document Reproduction Service No. ED 447 911).

Schwartz, D., Dodge, K. A., & Coie, J. D. (1994). The emergence of chronic peer victimization in boys' play groups. *Child Development, 64*, 1755–1772.

Slee, P.T. (1995). Bullying in the playground: The impact of interpersonal violence on Australian children's perceptions of their play environment. *Children's Environments, 12*, 320–327.

Slee, P. T., & Rigby, K. (1994). Peer victimisation at school. *AECA Australian Journal of Early Education, 19*, 3–10.

Smith, P. K., & Sharp, S. (1994). The problem of school bullying. In P. K. Smith & S. Sharp (Eds.), *School bullying* (pp. 1–19). London: Routledge.

Vladimir, N., & Brubach, A. (2000). *Teasing among school-aged children.* (ERIC Document Reproduction Service No. 446 321).

Whitney, I., Rivers, I., Smith, P. K., & Sharp, S. (1994). The Sheffield project: Methodology and findings. In P. K. Smith & S. Sharp (Eds.), *School bullying* (pp. 20–56). London: Routledge.

Janis R. Bullock is Professor, Early Childhood Education, Department of Health and Human Development, Montana State University, Bozeman.

UNIT 4

Parenting and Family Issues

Unit Selections

Key Points to Consider

• Where did you get your ideas, values, and beliefs about how a parent behaves? If you were unsure about how to respond to a particular parenting situation, whom would you consult? How do you think your own experience of parenting has affected your attitudes or possible parenting practices? Do you think your parents had a significant effect on your growing up? Do you think America is raising more spoiled children? Explain.

• Today, virtually no one has a family network that has not been touched by divorce and remarriage. Since divorce and remarriage affect boys and girls differently and at different ages, how might you handle these transitions in the best interest of a child?

• When you were growing up, were you ever in child care? What was the experience like? If you were to put your own children in child care, how would you know what features to look for that signal a high-quality experience? Do you think raising a child at home with the mother is always the best situation? Why or why not?

 **Links: www.dushkin.com/online/**
These sites are annotated in the World Wide Web pages.

Facts for Families
http://www.aacap.org/publications/factsfam/index.htm

Families and Work Institute
http://www.familiesandworkinst.org

The National Academy for Child Development
http://www.nacd.org

National Council on Family Relations
http://www.ncfr.com

The National Parent Information Network (NPIN)
http://ericps.ed.uiuc.edu/npin/

Parenting and Families
http://www.cyfc.umn.edu

Parentsplace.com: Single Parenting
http://www.parentsplace.com/family/archive/0,10693,239458,00.html

Stepfamily Association of America
http://www.stepfam.org

Few people today realize that the potential freedom to choose parenthood—deciding whether or not to become a parent, deciding when to have children, or deciding how many children to have—is a development due to the advent of reliable methods of contraception and other recent sociocultural changes. Moreover, unlike any other significant job to which we may aspire, few, if any, of us will receive any formal training or information about the lifelong responsibility of parenting. For most of us, our behavior is generally based on our own conscious and subconscious recollections of how we were parented as well as on our observations of the parenting practices of others around us. In fact, our society often behaves as if the mere act of producing a baby automatically confers upon the parents an innate parenting ability and as if a family's parenting practices should remain private and not be subjected to scrutiny or criticism by outsiders.

Given this climate, it is not surprising that misconceptions about many parenting practices continue to persist today. Only within the last 40 years or so have researchers turned their lenses on the scientific study of the family. Social, historical, cultural, and economic forces also have dramatically changed the face of the American family today. For example, significant numbers of children in our country will experience the divorce and/or remarriage of their parents at some point during their lifetimes. In "What Matters? What Does Not? Five Perspectives on the Association Between Marital Transitions and Children's Adjustment," E. Mavis Hetherington and colleagues describe the effects of divorce and remarriage on children.

Most parents never take courses or learn of the research on parenting. In the seminal article "Contemporary Research on Parenting: The Case for Nature *and* Nurture" a distinguished panel of researchers summarize recent parenting research and describe the importance of considering the interaction of genetics and environment, a child's temperament, and peer and neighborhood interactions when determining parental influence. Similarly, in "Who's in Charge Here?" the author discusses how parents today are struggling to find balance in the way they discipline their children.

The majority of mothers in the United States rely on some form of child care. Sandra Scarr, a leading scholar on the issue, reviews the research on the effects of child care on children's social, academic, and emotional development in "American Child Care Today." Ellen Galinsky interviewed children from their per-

spective about their views and wishes of their working parents in "Do Working Parents Make the Grade?"

With alarming frequency, news reports bring us accounts of tragedies and other unspeakable acts that are committed increasingly by young adults and now even by children. How do children and adults learn to behave in a moral and responsible way? In "The Moral Development of Children" William Damon discusses research on the origins of morality in children and the key role that parents play in promoting their children's moral development.

Contemporary Research on Parenting

The Case for Nature and Nurture

W. Andrew Collins *University of Minnesota,* **Eleanor E. Maccoby** *Stanford University,*
Laurence Steinberg *Temple University,* **E. Mavis Hetherington** *University of Virginia,*
Marc H. Bornstein *National Institute of Child Health and Human Development*

Current findings on parental influences provide more sophisticated and less deterministic explanations than did earlier theory and research on parenting. Contemporary research approaches include (a) behavior-genetic designs, augmented with direct measures of potential environmental influence; (b) studies distinguishing among children with different genetically influenced predispositions in terms of their responses to different environmental conditions; (c) experimental and quasi-experimental studies of change in children's behavior as a result of their exposure to parents' behavior, after controlling for children's initial characteristics; and (d) research on interactions between parenting and nonfamilial environmental influences and contexts, illustrating contemporary concern with influences beyond the parent-child dyad. These approaches indicate that parental influences on child development are neither as unambiguous as earlier researchers suggested nor as insubstantial as current critics claim.

> The heredity and environment of an organism can be completely separated only in analytic thinking, for in actual nature such separation would lead to instant death of the organism, even though the philosopher making the analysis might himself survive. (Gesell & Thompson, 1934, p. 293)

Research on parenting has been the centerpiece of long-standing efforts in psychology to understand socialization processes. As the field moves into its second century, however, this focus on parental influence faces several high-profile challenges. One challenge comes from the charge that there is little compelling evidence of parents' influence on behavior and personality in adolescence and adulthood (Harris, 1995, 1998; Rowe, 1994). Another is the allegation that socialization researchers have neglected significant forces other than parenting—forces that may contribute more extensively than parenting to individual differences in adult behavior. The most commonly cited sources of alternative influences are heredity (Harris, 1995, 1998; Rowe, 1994) and peers (Harris, 1995, 1998), although some writers emphasize the relatively greater importance of concurrent environmental forces more generally (e.g., Lewis, 1997).

These criticisms of socialization research generally invoke studies of parenting published before the early 1980s. Neither the assumptions nor the research paradigms that dominated the field as recently as a decade ago, however, represent research on parenting today. Contemporary students of socialization largely agree that early researchers often overstated conclusions from correlational findings; relied excessively on singular, deterministic views of parental influence; and failed to attend to the potentially confounding effects of heredity. Contemporary researchers have taken steps to remedy many of those shortcomings. Unfortunately, the weaknesses of old studies still permeate presentations of socialization research in introductory textbooks and the mass media, partly because they appeal to preferences for simple generalizations instead of the conditional effects that capture the reality of socialization.

Leading-edge approaches to social development and personality no longer rely exclusively on correlational designs, overly simple laboratory analogs, or additive models for assigning variance to one source or another. Contemporary studies, including research on parenting, turn on complex statistical methods and research designs that capture real-world complexity without sacrificing the rigor necessary to infer causal relations. Moreover, conceptual models increasingly encompass multiple sources of influence. Researchers draw on emerging knowledge in behavior genetics, neuroendocrine studies, studies of animal behavior, and intervention and prevention science to recognize the complex interplay between inherited and experiential components of individual development. The result is both a more complete and a more differentiated picture of parenting and its likely effects (for comprehensive reviews of contemporary socialization research, see Bornstein, 1995b; Eisenberg & Damon, 1998).

One goal of this article is to outline key features of contemporary approaches to studies of parental socialization. We also show how current researchers have, for some time, been identifying and responding to the very challenges pointed to by recent critics. We pay particular attention to research designs that estimate inherited and other dispositional factors, as well as experiential ones, in estimating influence. We describe several lines of evidence that address issues of causality regarding the scope and nature of parental influences. Finally, we propose that responsible conclusions about the significance of parenting can be based on only the emerging body of research findings that incorporate both individual and social factors and their interrelations.

Contemporary Approaches to Parenting Research

Research during the past two decades has undermined the once tacit assumption that environment should be the sole starting point in explaining individual differences in development. The relevant evidence comes from comparisons of the degree of similarity between individuals who vary in degree of genetic relatedness (e.g., identical vs. fraternal twins). Typical results imply that heredity accounts for a substantial proportion of this similarity, even though a recent meta-analysis (McCartney, Harris, & Bernieri, 1990) concluded that heredity rarely accounts for as much as 50% of the variation among individuals in a particular population, perhaps even less when personality characteristics are the focus. Although these findings also imply that environment contributes substantially to individual differences, behavior-genetics researchers typically infer environmental effects from the residual after estimates of genetic contributions are computed. The sources of the apparent environmental influences are not specified.

Efforts to understand the role of parents in socialization are constrained severely by the traditional analytic model on which the most cited behavior-genetic findings are based. This "additive" model regards hereditary and environmental components as independent and separable and holds that these two components together account for 100% of the variance in a characteristic (Plomin, 1990). Consequently, most behavior-genetic research has allowed for only main effects of genes and environment, ignoring the possibility that genes may function differently in different environments. A primary problem in disentangling heredity and measures of environmental influences, however, is that genetic and environmental factors are correlated (Plomin, 1990). Researchers consis-

tently find that parenting of identical twins is more similar than parenting of fraternal twins and that two biological siblings typically experience more similar parenting than do two adopted children (Dunn & Plomin, 1986; Plomin, DeFries, & Fulker, 1988; Reiss, Niederhiser, Hetherington, & Plomin, in press; Rowe, 1983). Parents' genotypes, as well as children's genotypes, contribute to these contrasting patterns. That individuals who are more closely related genetically also have more similar shared parental environments means that observed associations between parenting and measures of child characteristics cannot be assumed to be either entirely genetic or entirely environmental in origin. As Rose (1995) stated it, the central question in development is "how genetic effects are modulated across lifespans of environmental interactions" (p. 627).

A related problem further limits the usefulness of traditional behavior-genetic approaches to research on parenting. Estimating the effects of heredity versus environment ignores the potential for malleability, even in characteristics heavily influenced by heredity. When environmental conditions change substantially over time, mean levels of a characteristic also may change, although heritability coefficients (which are based on correlations) may or may not change (Plomin & Rutter, 1998). The problem comes from the failure to recognize that means and correlations can vary independently. Thus, although intelligence has been shown to have a high heritability coefficient, individuals' cognitive abilities can improve or decline as a function of experience (for an explanation of this point, see Weinberg, 1989).

Migration studies often reveal similar paradoxes. For example, height is highly heritable, with heritability coefficients in the 90s, showing that within a given population, the variation in children's heights is closely linked with the variations in their parents' heights. By inference, very little variance remains to be attributed to environmental factors. At the same time, grandparents born in Japan are, on the average, considerably shorter than their grandchildren born and reared in the United States (Angoff, 1988). In the same way, genetic factors that are highly important in a behavior do not show up in a study of the heritability of that behavior because this genetic factor is uniform for all members of a population. Thus, analyzing the variation of a factor within a population does not provide exhaustive information concerning either the genetic or the environmental contributions to the factor. Large-scale societal factors, such as ethnicity or poverty, can influence group means in parenting behavior—and in the effects of parenting behaviors—in ways that are not revealed by studies of within-group variability. In addition, highly heritable traits also can be highly malleable. Like traditional correlational research on parenting, therefore, commonly used behavior-genetic methods have provided an incomplete analysis of differences among individuals.

To acknowledge the importance of the interplay of heredity and environment, four lines of contemporary research on parenting have emerged. One line of research adopts the additive model of behavior-genetics research but augments it with direct measures of potential environmental influences in an effort to document environmental effects more precisely (Plomin et al., 1988; Reiss et al., in press). A second line of research addresses the insensitivity of additive models to Gene 5 Environment effects (Plomin & Rutter, 1998; Rutter et al., 1997) by distinguishing among children with different genetic predispositions on a characteristic to see whether they respond differently to different environmental conditions. The distinctions among genetically different groups often rely on measures of temperament or the parent's carrying a known genetic risk factor. A third line of research examines the effect of parental practices after controlling for any initial dispositional characteristics of children. This kind of research is intended to permit inferences about the direction of effects when parent and child characteristics are initially correlated. Evidence on this point comes from three types of research designs: (a) longitudinal studies in which child characteristics at Time 1 are controlled statistically, (b) experiments in which nonhuman animals are exposed to selected rearing environments, and (c) intervention studies either in which "experiments of nature" have resulted in marked changes in parenting experiences or in which families are randomly assigned to different treatment programs designed to improve parenting with resulting changes in child behavior. A fourth line of contemporary studies addresses the possibility that extrafamilial environmental conditions with which parenting is correlated contribute to individual differences in development and behavior.

Augmented Behavior-Genetic Designs

Traditional behavior-genetic designs give primacy to the effects of heredity, relying on a series of computations to reveal which portions of the variance should be labeled as contributions of the shared environment or assigned to nonshared, "other," or "unknown" sources. Although evidence of shared family influences and experiences has appeared for some characteristics such as health habits, alcohol patterns, smoking patterns (McGue, 1994), depression in later life (Gatz, Pedersen, Plomin, Nesselroade, & McLearn, 1992), delinquency as reported by siblings (Rowe, Chassin, Presson, Edwards, & Sherman, 1992), and autonomy and sociability (Reiss et al., in press), the most frequent conclusion has been that shared environments play a small, inconsequential role in children's development.

Many scholars, however, have challenged this inference. One criticism is that the assumptions, methods, and truncated samples used in behavior-genetic studies maximize the effects of heredity and features of the environment that are different for different children and minimize the effects of shared family environments (Goodman, 1991; Hoffman, 1991; Patterson, 1999; Rose, 1995; Stoolmiller, 1999). For example, Stoolmiller (1999) noted that recent adoption studies have been impaired by pronounced range restrictions (about 67%) in the family environments sampled. Stoolmiller argued that the estimated contribution of shared environment likely would be as much as 50% higher if appropriate corrections for range restriction were applied to data from such studies.

A second criticism is that estimates of the relative contributions of environment and heredity vary greatly depending on the source of data (Turkheimer & Waldron, in press). Twin studies typically yield higher heritability estimates for a trait than adoption studies do (Wachs & Plomin, 1991). Moreover, in both types of studies, heritability estimates vary considerably depending on the measures used to assess similarity between children or between parents and children. The largest effect sizes for environmental influences on social development are found with the relatively rarely used method of direct behavioral observations, whereas the smallest effect sizes for environmental influences are found with parental reports, which are the most commonly used measure in behavior-genetic studies of behavioral outcomes (Emde et al., 1992; Ghodsion-Garpey & Baker, 1997; Miles & Carey, 1997; Rutter et al., 1997; Wachs, 1992). The sizable variability in estimates of genetic and environmental contributions depending on the paradigms and measures used means that no firm conclusions can be drawn about the relative strength of these influences on development.

Traditional twin and adoption studies have been criticized on the grounds that they estimate environmental effects only as a residual: the effects remaining after genetic effects have been estimated and subtracted from 100%. Efforts to rectify this problem by measuring environment directly, however, have failed to clarify the contributions of environment relative to heredity. Most such efforts were stimulated by Plomin and Daniels's (1987) proposal that the environmental variance in behavior-genetic studies emanates largely from experiences that differ for children in the same family. By measuring such differences, researchers hoped to better understand the portion of the variance in behavior-genetic studies not attributed specifically to genetic relatedness. Behavior-genetic analyses, however, can establish that nonshared environment contributes to individual differences in a domain but cannot document the connections between objectively measured nonshared environmental events and development (Turkheimer & Waldron, in press). Most studies with direct measures of the environment and of the development of multiple siblings within a family, moreover, have not used designs that permit heritability estimates (e.g., Brody & Stoneman, 1994; Tejerina-Allen, Wagnere, & Cohen, 1994).

Thus, researchers' attempts to work within the traditional additive model, while augmenting it with direct measures of environment, have yielded findings that are conditional on a series of methodological problems in assessing the relevant environmental factors and in the inherent limitations of the additive model for identifying Gene X Environment interactions. The remainder of this article is devoted to recent investigations of how processes of influence operate and interact.

The Search for Gene X Environment Effects

Traditional behavior-genetic models do not afford comparisons of the effects of differing environments on individuals who vary on genetically influenced characteristics. For example, in twin and adoption studies, degree of biological relatedness between individuals, not specific markers of genetically linked characteristics in the two individuals, is the primary focus, and variations in environments are rarely assessed. The most likely possibility is that the forced estimates of main effects for genetic relatedness and environment in the additive model mask virtually ubiquitous correlations and statistical interactions between the two in existing research. Such interactions are notably difficult to detect because of low statistical power in most relevant studies (McCall, 1991; McClelland & Judd, 1993; Wahlsten, 1990). Although some writers (e.g., Harris, 1998) have elected to subsume evidence of Gene X Environment correlations and interactions under genetic contributions to behavioral development, responsible scholarship requires closer attention to emerging evidence that these effects involve direct parental influences as well (O'Connor, Deater-Deckard, Fulker, Rutter, & Plomin, 1998; Plomin & Rutter, 1998).

The search for Gene X Environment effects often takes the form of using measures of temperament for the purpose of distinguishing among children with different genetic predispositions to see whether they respond differently to given environmental conditions (Bornstein, 1995b; Plomin & Rutter, 1998; Rutter et al., 1997). Studies that pool parenting effects across children with very different temperaments inevitably obscure actual parental effects. Even when parenting effects are apparent, it is not reasonable to expect that a given style or quality of parenting would have the same effect on every child. Moreover, different parental strategies or degrees of parental effort may be required to bring about the same outcome in different children. Two types of recent studies attempt to disentangle individual children's heredity and the nature of their rearing experiences: (a) studies of the effect of rearing experiences on the behavior of children who differ on measures of temperament and (b) studies comparing the effect of high- versus low-risk environments on children of differing vulnerability.

Temperament and parenting. Temperamental characteristics, defined as "constitutionally based individual differences in reactivity and self-regulation" (Rothbart & Ahadi, 1994, p. 55), are thought to emerge early, to show some stability over time, but to be modifiable by experience. In general, statistical associations between early temperamental characteristics and later adjustment are modest (see Rothbart & Bates, 1998, for a review), suggesting that these associations also may be moderated by environmental factors. A difficult temperament, characterized by intense negative affect and repeated demands for attention, is associated with both later externalizing and internalizing disorders (Bates & Bayles, 1988; Bates, Bayles, Bennett, Ridge, & Brown, 1991). Early resistance to control, impulsivity, irritability, and distractibility predicts later externalizing and social alienation (Caspi, Henry, McGee, Moffitt, & Silva, 1995; Hagekull, 1989, 1994), whereas early shy, inhibited, or distress-prone behaviors predict later anxiety disorders, harm avoidance, and low aggression and social potency (Caspi & Silva, 1995).

Correlations between temperamental characteristics and parental behavior reflect bidirectional interactive processes, as well as genetic linkages between parent and child characteristics. Temperamental characteristics may set in motion a chain of reactions from others that put children at risk or protect them from developing behavior and psychological problems (Caspi & Elder, 1988; Hetherington, 1989, 1991; Quinton, Pickles, Maughan, & Rutter, 1993; Rutter, 1990; Rutter & Quinton, 1984; Werner, 1990). Difficultness, irritability, and distress proneness in infants evoke hostility, criticism, a tendency to ignore the child, avoidance, coercive discipline, and a lack of playfulness in mothers (Lee & Bates, 1985; Rutter & Quinton, 1984; Van den Boom, 1989). These reactions, in turn, are associated with avoidant (Grossman, Grossman, Spangler, Suess, & Unzner, 1985; Van den Boom, 1989) or insecure-ambivalent attachment (Goldsmith & Alansky, 1987; Miyake, Chen & Campos, 1985). Bates, Pettit, and Dodge (1995), in a longitudinal study, found that infants' characteristics (e.g., hyperreactivity, impulsivity, and difficult temperament) significantly predicted externalizing problems 10 years later. Although this finding at first seems to support the lasting effects of physiologically based characteristics, Bates et al. (1995) also showed that predictive power increased when they added information about parenting to the equation. Infants' early characteristics elicited harsh parenting at age 4, which in turn predicted externalizing problems when the children were young adolescents, over and above the prediction from infant temperament. Similarly, this and other findings imply that even though parental behavior is influenced by child behavior, parents' actions contribute distinctively to the child's later behavior. For example, in a longitudinal adoption design, O'Connor et al. (1998) confirmed that children at genetic risk for antisocial behavior elicited more negative parenting from adoptive parents than did children not at risk. They also found, however, that "most of the association between negative parenting and children's externalizing behavior was not explicable on the basis of an evocative gene-environment correlation and that an additional environmentally mediated parental effect on children's behavior was plausible" (p. 970).

Bidirectional and interactive effects of this kind now appear to carry significant implications for distinctive effects of parenting variations on children who differ in temperamental characteristics. In longitudinal work on the socialization of "conscience," Kochanska (1995, 1997) found that maternal use of gentle childrearing techniques that deemphasized power assertion was more effective with temperamentally fearful children than with bolder, more exploratory children in promoting the development of conscience. With bolder children, maternal responsiveness and a close emotional bond with the child were more important in fostering conscience. Similarly, the quality of parenting to some extent moderates associations between early temperamental characteristics of difficultness, impulsivity, and unmanageability and later externalizing disorders (Bates, Pettit, Dodge, & Ridge, 1998; Rothbart & Bates, 1998). Firm, restrictive parental control has been linked to lower levels of later externalizing in early difficult, unmanageable children (Bates et al., 1998). Although only a few studies have examined the moderating effects of parenting on the links between temperamental predispositions and later adjustment, and although not all of these studies have had positive results (Rothbart & Bates, 1998), the evidence nevertheless suggests that parenting moderates these associations.

Studies of risk and resiliency. Parallels to these differential relations between parenting and child behavior can be found in studies of risk and resiliency. Children who showed early developmental problems because of risk factors such as perinatal damage (Werner & Smith, 1992) improved in adjustment under authoritative parenting. Parenting, moreover, appears to play a mediating role between parental psychopathology and child symptoms of disorder (R. Conger, Ge, Elder, Lorenz, & Simons, 1994; Ge, Conger, Lorenz, Shanahan, & Elder, 1995; Ge, Lorenz, Conger, Elder, & Simons, 1994). For example, Downey and Walker (1992) demonstrated that children with a psychiatrically ill parent who were not exposed to parental maltreatment, in contrast to those who were, showed very low levels of both externalizing and internalizing. That different outcomes for children are associated with differential parental responses to the same risk factor implies parental influence, although Downey and Walker cannot rule out evocative behavior on the part of the child.

A Finnish adoption study (Tienari et al., 1994) further illustrates how a genetic predisposition can either manifest itself or not, depending on whether certain triggering environmental conditions are present. Adoptees who had a schizophrenic biological parent were more likely to develop a range of psychiatric disorders (including schizophrenia) than were adoptees not at genetic risk, but only if they were adopted into dysfunctional families (see also Cadoret, 1985). Similar findings have been reported from studies of adopted children whose biological parents had

a history of criminality (Bohman, 1996). If adopted into well-functioning homes, 12% of these children displayed petty criminality in adulthood. However, if adopted into families carrying environmental risk, their rate of petty criminality in adulthood rose to 40%. These findings suggest that well-functioning parents can buffer children at genetic risk and circumvent the processes that might ordinarily lead from genotype to phenotype. The more general point is that genetic vulnerabilities (or strengths) may not be manifested except in the presence of a pertinent environmental trigger such as parenting.

Studies of Parental Influence, Controlling for Initial Child Characteristics

A third line of research attempts to provide a basis for examining instances in which parental behavior may exert a causal influence in changing children's behavior. Studies of this type subsume several research strategies. One strategy is longitudinal research in which children's initial characteristics can be observed to change over time in relation to specific parenting experiences. Even more compelling evidence for determining the causal status of parenting, however, involves experimental manipulations. In some recent experiments, young nonhuman animals were exposed to measurably different rearing conditions. Some experiments of nature with humans also have provided evidence of this kind. The most compelling evidence, however, comes from interventions in which parents are assigned randomly to behavior-change treatment groups, with resulting changes in the behavior of both the parents and their otherwise untreated children. Random assignment is the means for ensuring that treatment groups are not initially different.

Longitudinal studies of parenting and child development. The most widely used strategy in contemporary studies of socialization uses short-term longitudinal designs to better distinguish parenting effects from the characteristics of the child (e.g., Ge et al., 1996; Steinberg, Lamborn, Darling, Mounts, & Dornbusch, 1994). In these studies, aspects of child functioning and development are measured at more than one point in time. Statistical procedures, such as the analysis of covariance or multiple regression, are then used to estimate the relation between parenting at one point in time and child outcomes at some subsequent point, after taking into account characteristics of the child at the time that parenting was assessed. Studies showing that the over-time effect of parenting on child development holds even after controlling for earlier child characteristics are important for several reasons. First, in the absence of a randomized experimental design, this strategy provides indirect evidence that parenting conceivably affects—rather than simply accompanying or following from—child adjustment. Such indirect evidence is important because one cannot randomly assign children to different home environments. These analyses do not rule out the possibility that different children elicit different parental responses, but they do provide evidence that the correlation between child adjustment and parenting is not due *solely* to the effect of children on parenting behavior.

Significant longitudinal relations between parenting and child adjustment after taking into account their concurrent relation also help rule out a number of third-variable explanations, including the possibility that the observed association is due to factors that parents and their children share, such as genes or socioeconomic status. To be a viable explanation for the observed association, a third variable would have to be correlated with the measures of child adjustment at the time of the longitudinal follow-up but not correlated with the same measures taken earlier. Any genetically mediated link between parenting and child adjustment, for example, would be taken into account by controlling for the concurrent relation between parenting and child adjustment before examining their relation over time.

Rearing experiments with animals. Recent work with nonhuman animals points clearly to the fact that experience—that is, encountering or engaging with the environment—influences brain development in young organisms and that these changes in the brain are associated with changes in behavior (Greenough & Black, 1992). Although some of the relevant environmental events must occur during a sensitive period to affect development (Bornstein, 1989), the mammalian brain generally remains malleable by environmental inputs well into adulthood (Huttenlocher, 1994; Nelson, in press). Environmental events that have to do with the amount or kind of "parenting" that a young organism receives are essential for survival in all mammalian species. The presence and activities of the infant stimulate a set of maternal behaviors needed by the infant (including but not confined to feeding), and these reciprocal maternal behaviors serve to facilitate the infant's adaptation and development (e.g., Stern, 1985). Studies of higher mammals confirm that, as these interactions continue to occur, an intense emotional bond is formed such that separation of the pair produces distress and behavioral disruption in each member of the pair. Studies in which young animals have been deprived of "mothering" have shown clearly that such deprivation not only disrupts the ongoing behavior of the young animal at the time of deprivation but also leads to dysfunctional outcomes for the offspring in the long term.

Current animal work is addressing implications of naturally occurring variation, within the "normal" range, in maternal behavior. Meaney and Plotsky and their colleagues (Caldji et al., 1998; Liu et al., 1997) have studied styles of mothering in rats, relating variations in these styles to behavioral outcomes in their offspring. Maternal animals differ considerably in the frequency with which they lick and groom their newborn pups and in whether they arch their backs to facilitate nursing or lie passively on top of or next to the pups. Individual differences in

these mothering styles have been shown to be quite stable. In adulthood, moreover, the offspring of mothers who had done more licking and grooming and had nursed with arched backs (high LG-ABN mothers, whom we can call *nurturant*) were less timid in leaving their home cages to obtain food or explore a novel environment than were the offspring of low LG-ABN mothers. These outcomes are correlated with neuroendocrine processes. As adults, rats who had experienced high levels of maternal licking and grooming as newborns showed reduced levels of adrenocorticotropic hormone and corticosterone in response to a stressful condition (close restraint). Furthermore, differences emerged in the densities of receptors for stress hormones in several loci in the brains of animals that had experienced the two different kinds of maternal styles in their first 10 days of life. Thus, early mothering styles apparently affected the neural circuitry that governs behavioral stress responses in the offspring as they grow into adulthood.

To determine whether there is an independent effect of maternal styles per se on these outcomes, apart from any genetic mediation, researchers have cross-fostered infants born to a low-nurturant mother to rearing by a high-nurturant mother. Early findings (Anisman, Zaharia, Meaney, & Merali, 1998) show that these infants manifest the benefits of their early rearing in their modified adult stress reactions, by comparison with infants born to low-nurturant mothers and reared by them.

Corroborating evidence comes from studies with nonhuman primates (Suomi, 1997). Suomi and colleagues initially observed naturally occurring individual differences in "emotional reactivity" among Rhesus monkeys. In early life, some animals are hesitant about exploring new environments and show extreme reactions to separation from their mothers, whereas others characteristically react more calmly. Individual animals' reactivity patterns remain quite stable over many years. These patterns of behavior are accompanied by distinctive neuroendocrine patterns. The behavioral and physiological indicators that distinguish highly reactive animals from less reactive ones are especially apparent under environmentally stressful conditions (Suomi, 1997).

When young Rhesus monkeys with clearly different reactivity patterns are cross-fostered to mothers who are either reactive (easily distressed) or nonreactive (calm), their adult behavior is quite different from that shown by the biological offspring of each type of mother. Genetically reactive young animals that are reared by calm mothers for the first six months of their lives and then placed in large social groups made up of peers and nonrelated older adults develop normally and indeed rise to the top of their dominance hierarchy. Further, these cross-fostered animals are adept at avoiding stressful situations and at recruiting social support that enables them to cope with stress. By contrast, genetically reactive infants who are raised by reactive mothers typically are socially incompetent when placed in the larger living group at the age of six months and are particularly vulnerable to stress. In general, the introduction of stressful conditions seems to make the effects of early rearing experience especially perceptible (Suomi, 1997). Thus, variations in mothering style have a lasting effect on the reactivity of the young animals when they move into new social contexts. Moreover, the quality of early mothering now has been found to affect the way genetically at-risk females parent their own offspring. If cross-fostered to low-reactive mothers, they are competent parents with their own offspring; if raised by high-reactive mothers, they manifest mothering deficits.

Recent work (Suomi, in press) has shown that the genetic make-up of young monkeys influences how large an effect early rearing conditions will have. A gene has been identified for which one allele is associated with a highly reactive temperament and the other allele with a calmer temperament. Certain aspects of the neuroendocrine system (i.e., serotonergic functioning) are controlled by this gene. Maternal deprivation has a powerful effect on the genetically reactive monkeys, producing deficits in their neuroendocrine functioning and in their behavioral and emotional reactions. For the animals not carrying the genetically risky allele, however, maternal deprivation has little effect.

These recent studies trace some of the complex steps in the long pathway between genes and phenotypic behavior. The findings show that both genes and parenting affect brain processes and neuroendocrine systems. These studies point to a future in which researchers will be able to provide more detailed information about the interplay of heredity and parenting influences than traditional twin and adoption studies can yield.

Experiments of nature. No extensively controlled rearing experiments have been conducted with human children, but several natural experiments have yielded information that is strikingly parallel to the findings of the cross-fostering work. A recent example is found with the children who lived in Romanian orphanages for some months or years in early childhood, during which time they were deprived of the opportunity to form a close bond with a single trusted adult caregiver. Some of these children have been adopted into middle-class homes in other cultures. The effects of the early deprivation appear to depend on its duration. Recent follow-up measures at age six in a group of Romanian orphans adopted by Canadian families show that children adopted during approximately the first half-year of life manifest no lasting effects of their early experience. But children adopted later have been found to have abnormally high levels of cortisol during the ordinary daily routine of their adoptive homes, indicating that the neuroendocrine system involved in stress regulation has not developed normally (Chisholm, 1998; Chisholm, Carter, Ames, & Morison, 1995; Gunnar, in press; see also Rutter & the ERA study team, 1998).

An example of variations in parenting that are more within the normal range comes from France, where 20 children were located who had been abandoned in infancy by their low-socioeconomic-status parents and adopted by upper-middle-class parents (Schiff, Duyme, Dumaret, & Tomkiewitz, 1982). These children all had biological siblings or half-siblings who remained with the biological mother and were reared by her in impoverished circumstances. The researchers were unable to find any selective factors that might have made the abandoned children more genetically promising than the ones retained at home. When tested in middle childhood, however, the adopted children's IQs averaged 14 points higher than those of their natural siblings. By contrast, children who remained with their biological mothers were four times more likely to exhibit failures in their school performance. These results are consistent with those of several other early adoption studies (e.g., Skodak & Skeels, 1949; Scarr & Weinberg, 1976, 1978) showing that adoption into well-functioning middle-class homes can provide a "bonus" in cognitive functioning for the children involved.

What aspects of living in more advantaged homes were responsible for these children's cognitive and educational gains is not known. Was it the more stimulating, more cultured, more educated environments provided by the adoptive parents, or were there greater amounts of parent-child interaction or more secure attachments? We can only suspect that something about the way these adoptive parents dealt with the children contributed to the effect. Evidence from the Colorado Adoption Project provides some suggestive evidence for a bidirectional process. The Colorado project included data on rates of communicative development in groups of 12-month-olds either born or adopted into intact families (Hardy-Brown, 1983; Hardy-Brown & Plomin, 1985; Hardy-Brown, Plomin, & DeFries, 1981). Biological mothers' verbal intelligence correlated with the language competencies of children they had not seen since birth. Reciprocally, however, adoptive mothers' activities, like imitating their infants' vocalizations and vocalizing responsively and contingently to infants' vocalizations, also predicted child language competencies. Similarly, another comparison of children with their biological and their adoptive parents (Scarr & Weinberg, 1978) showed that correlations between the vocabulary scores of adoptive mothers and children were as high as those between the vocabulary scores of biological mothers and their children. Like other examples cited earlier, these findings clearly show the distinct contribution of parental behavior over and above the contribution of heredity.

Interventions with human parents. Finally, interventions that seek to change the mean level of a behavioral or personality characteristic in children provide additional evidence of the efficacy of parenting. Efforts to manipulate parental behavior for the purpose of influencing child behavior are surprisingly rare. Laboratory analog studies (e.g., Kuczynski, 1984), although documenting short-term effects of specific behaviors of parents, cannot establish that such behaviors significantly influence broadband outcomes for offspring. The primary source of relevant information for human children comes from evaluations of programs designed to remediate or prevent socialization problems. Such programs typically target the behavior of either children alone or both children and parents. Of particular relevance to socialization, however, are studies in which the behavior of parents, but not the children, is the target of the manipulation. If the manipulation produces desired changes in the parent's behavior and if the degree of change, in turn, is associated with changes in the child's behavior, the evidence for the causal influence of parents is compelling. Unfortunately, only a few such programs focus on improving parental behavior, and even fewer estimate the causal influences of changes in parental behavior on child outcomes (for reviews, see Cowan, Powell, & Cowan, 1998; McMahon & Wells, 1998).

An exception is a recent prevention program intended to foster more effective parenting following divorce (Forgatch & DeGarmo, 1999). School-age sons of recently divorced single mothers often manifest increased academic, behavioral, social, and emotional problems relative to sons of nondivorced mothers, and the divorced mothers themselves commonly behave toward their sons in a more coercive and less positive manner than nondivorced mothers do (Chase-Lansdale, Cherlin, & Kiernan, 1995; Hetherington, 1993; Zill, Morrison, & Coiro, 1993). In most reports, however, the direction of causality is unclear. Forgatch and DeGarmo sought both to address the causality issue and to test a method for preventing these apparently negative sequelae of divorce. They designed group-intervention and individual follow-up procedures for 153 recently divorced mothers who met three criteria: they had been separated from their partners within the prior 3 to 24 months, they resided with a biological son in Grades 1 through 3, and they did not cohabit with a new partner. Initial observational, self-report, and teacher report measures of both mothers' parenting and children's behaviors were used to control for possible genetically influenced differences among parent-child pairs. Random assignment ensured that the treatment group was not systematically different from the control group of 85 mothers and sons who also met the screening criteria. No intervention was provided to the children. At the end of 12 months, treatment-group mothers generally showed less coercive behavior toward children and less decline in positive behavior than control-group mothers did (although both treatment- and control-group mothers manifested at least temporary declines in positive behavior during the year following divorce). Moreover, the degree of change in the mothers' behavior over the course of 12 months significantly predicted the degree of change in the children's behaviors. Changes in parenting practices were associated significantly with changes in teacher-reported school adjustment and with changes in both child-reported and parent-reported maladjustment. Estimated effect sizes for these correlated changes ranged from .032 to .144 (M. Forgatch, personal communication, November 1, 1999). These effect sizes are small to medium, according to Cohen's (1988) criteria.

Other intervention attempts with parents have yielded similarly impressive evidence. Cowan and Cowan (in press), in a randomized design, showed that parents' participation in a 16-week series of discussion groups on effective parenting just prior to their children's kindergarten entry resulted in better school adjustment and higher academic achievement for children in kindergarten and first grade, compared with children whose parents attended a series of discussion groups without the effective-parenting emphasis. The relative advantage for the children of intervention-group parents has persisted through age 10, a period of six years. With parents of infants, Van den Boom (1989, 1994) demonstrated that an intervention to train lower-class mothers to respond sensitively to their infants irritability and reduced the extent of avoidant attachment in distress-prone infants. Similarly, Belsky, Goode, and Most (1980) found that interventions to increase mothers' didactic interactions with infants during play resulted in significantly higher exploratory play among infants, compared with a no-treatment control group. In interventions to improve the behavioral-training skills of parents of noncompliant children, Forehand and colleagues demonstrated both improvements in parental behavior and behavioral changes in the children, as well as increased parental perceptions of improved child behavior and decreased parental depression (Forehand & King, 1977; Forehand, Wells, & Griest, 1980). Depending on the content of the maternal training, children have been shown to manifest differing patterns of competence. Riksen-Walraven (1978) showed that infants of mothers trained in responding demonstrated higher levels of exploratory competence, whereas infants of mothers trained on improving sensory stimulation habituated more efficiently. When interventions are effective, behavior change tends to be long-lasting (Patterson, 1975).

Findings from studies of parenting-focused interventions provide the strongest evidence available on the efficacy of parenting behavior in humans. Whether naturally occurring behaviors of the kind encouraged by these experimental programs account for behavioral development is more difficult to establish. Nevertheless, the increasing use of multimethod, multi-informant assessments and structural equation modeling is helping to overcome some of the shortcomings of traditional correlational studies of socialization and behavior-genetic studies using single informants (Rutter et al., 1997). These more methodologically rigorous studies (e.g., R. Conger & Elder, 1994; Forgatch, 1991; Kim, Hetherington, & Reiss, 1999) generally yield associations between parenting and child outcomes, with appropriate controls for Time 1 status on outcome measures, that meet Cohen's (1988) criteria for small or medium effect sizes. Some studies (e.g., Kochanska, 1997) yield impressively large effect sizes. Even small effects of parenting, however, are likely to become large effects over time (Abelson, 1985). Parental behavior has been shown to be highly stable across time (Holden & Miller, 1999). Thus, specific parental influences, consistently experienced, likely accumulate to produce larger meaningful outcomes over the childhood and adolescent years.

Studies of Links Between Parenting and Other Influences

Current investigations address a further challenge from recent critics of parenting research as well: the need to consider environmental influences other than parents in accounting for differences among children. Socialization research today is guided by an ecological perspective on human development (Bronfenbrenner, 1979; for recent reviews, see Bornstein 1995a, 1995b; Bronfenbrenner & Morris, 1998). Families are seen as important influences on children, the effect of which can be understood only in light of the simultaneous influence of social spheres such as peer groups and schools. These influences occur within broad contexts (e.g., neighborhood, cultural context, historical epoch) that add to, shape, and moderate the effect of the family. The ecological perspective not only emphasizes the potential significance of extrafamilial influences on the child's development but also, more importantly, stresses the interactive and synergistic, rather than additive and competitive, nature of the links between the family and other influences. In this section we consider the implications of this view for parenting in relation to two extrafamilial influences on socialization: peers and macrocontexts of parent-child relations.

Relations of parental and peer influence. In an earlier era, socialization researchers cast families and peers as opposing forces vying for influence over the child's behavior. In much the same way that recent developments in behavior genetics have challenged the wisdom of attempting to estimate how much variance in a trait is attributable to genes versus the environment, contemporary models of socialization no longer ask whether children are influenced more by parents or by peers. Today, socialization researchers develop and test models that examine how parents and peers exert conjoint influence on the developing child (e.g., Brown, Mounts, Lamborn, & Steinberg, 1993; Cairns & Cairns, 1994; Kishion, Patterson, Stoolmiller, & Skinner, 1991; Fuligni & Eccles, 1993; Mounts & Steinberg, 1995).

This new direction rests on four findings that have emerged consistently from research on parent and peer influences. The first finding is that the observed similarity between adolescents and their friends across a wide array of variables, including school achievement (Epstein, 1983), aggression (Cairns, Cairns, Neckerman, Gest, & Gariepy, 1988), internalized distress (Hogue & Steinberg, 1995), and drug use (Kandel, 1978), is due mostly to the tendency for individuals to select like-minded friends, as well as to the influence that friends have over each other (Berndt, 1999; Berndt, Hawkins, & Jiao, 1999). Children are not randomly assigned to peer groups. Although unambiguous estimates of the relative effect of selection and influence effects are not available, a child with antisocial inclinations may be far more likely to fall into a similarly inclined peer group than an antisocial peer group is to corrupt a well-behaved youngster. Similarly, an academically oriented child may be more likely to select academically oriented friends than a child who is not interested in school is to develop a passion for achievement because his or her friends are so inclined. Equating peer influence with peer similarity overstates considerably the extent of peer influence, because the equation fails to take account of the selection effect (Bauman & Fisher, 1986).

The second finding is that peer influence often operates with respect to everyday behaviors and transient attitudes, not enduring personality traits or values (Brown, 1990). Most studies examining individuals' religiosity, educational plans, and occupational choices, for example, reveal that parental influence on adolescent personality development is deeper and more enduring than that of peers (Brown, 1990). To be sure, even transient peer influences over day-to-day behaviors can have enduring sequelae that are opposed to what parents might desire (e.g., peer influence to become sexually active can result in an unplanned pregnancy and foreshortened educational attainment; peer influence to engage in criminal activity can result in a jail sentence). However, because peer influence tends to be immediate, its content changes with shifts in friendships. Studies that track individuals through adolescence often reveal that young adults are more similar to their parents than they had appeared to be as teenagers (J. Conger, 1971).

The third finding is evidence of the significance of parents and parent-child relationships in influencing which peers children select. Any psychological snapshot taken during adolescence, when peers are undeniably an important force in children's lives, rightly should be viewed as the end of a long process of socialization that began early in childhood and most likely has its origins in the family. Parke and Bhavnagri (1989) indicated that parents influence children's peer experiences in two general ways. During elementary school parents propel their children toward certain peers by managing their youngsters' social activities (which has the effect of increasing contact with some peers and diminishing it with others); during both childhood and adolescence, parents actively steer children toward certain friends and away from others. In addition, throughout the child's development parents indirectly influence the child's attitudes, values, personality, and motives, which in turn affect the child's interactions and affiliations with particular peers (Brown et al., 1993). For all of these reasons, parental and peer influence tend to be complementary, not antithetical (Brown, 1990).

Finally, and perhaps most importantly, adolescents differ considerably in their susceptibility to peer influence, and one of the most important contributors to this differential susceptibility is the quality of the parent-child relationship. Adolescents whose parents are authoritative (i.e., responsive and demanding) are less swayed by peer pressure to misbehave than are adolescents whose parents are permissive (Devereux, 1970) or authoritarian (Fuligni & Eccles, 1993). Indeed, adolescents from authoritative homes are more susceptible to prosocial peer pressure (e.g., pressure to do well in school) but less susceptible to antisocial peer pressure (e.g., pressure to use illicit drugs and alcohol; Mounts & Steinberg, 1995). In other words, the particular peers a youngster selects as friends and the extent to which he or she is susceptible to their influence are both affected by parenting.

A compelling illustration of indirect effects of parents comes from research on the development of antisocial behavior and aggression (DeBaryshe, Patterson, & Capaldi, 1993; Dishion et al., 1991; Patterson, DeBaryshe, & Ramsey, 1989). Researchers consistently have confirmed that adolescents' involvement in antisocial activity is influenced significantly by their relationships with antisocial peers but that the chain of events that leads some adolescents into antisocial peer groups begins at home during childhood. The links in this chain include exposure to harsh and coercive parenting, which contributes to the development of aggression and to academic difficulties in school; these problems, in late childhood, lead to the selection of antisocial peers. Even when selection effects are controlled, much of what appears to be peer influence is actually the end result of familial influence at an earlier point in the child's development.

Macrocontexts of parenting. Parents also mediate the association between broader social, cultural, economic, and historical contexts and children's behavior and personality. These broad contextual forces affect how parents behave and may accentuate or attenuate the effect of parental behavior on children's development. R. Conger (e.g., R. Conger et al., 1994) and McLoyd (1990), for example, have demonstrated that many of the deleterious effects of poverty on children's development are mediated through the effect of poverty on parenting; economic stress and disadvantage increase parental punitiveness, which in turn adversely affects the child. One implication of this for understanding the results of research on parenting is that estimates of the strength of parental influence are likely specific to particular communities in particular cultures at particular points in time. Many apparent "effects" of social class or economic disadvantage are mediated through the effect of these factors on parenting practices.

An example comes from recent research on the effects of neighborhood contexts on children's behavior and personality (Brooks-Gunn, Duncan, & Aber, 1997; Brooks-Gun, Duncan, Klebanov, & Sealand, 1993; Chase-Lansdale & Gordon, 1996). Neighborhood characteristics have been shown both to influence parents' behavior and to moderate the effect of parenting practices on the child's development (Klebanov, Brooks-Gunn, & Duncan, 1994). The effect of neighborhoods on parental practices is evident in the finding that parents adjust their management strategies to suit the demands of the neighborhood context within which they live (Furstenberg, Eccles, Elder, Cook, & Sameroff, 1997). Parents who live in dangerous neighborhoods tend to be more controlling and restrictive, which protects the child's physical well-being but which also may have the unintended consequence of squelching the child's sense of autonomy. With respect to moderating effects, Darling and Steinberg (1997) have shown that the links between parental involvement in school and children's achievement vary as a function of the behavior of other parents in the neighborhood, with parental involvement having more potent effects within neighborhoods with high concentrations of involved parents. Similarly, the beneficial effects of authoritative parenting are accentuated when adolescents affiliate with peers who themselves have authoritative parents (Fletcheer, Darling, Steinberg, & Dornbusch, 1995).

The documented relations between parental and other influences are consistent with recent criticisms (e.g., Harris, 1995, 1998) that socialization researchers have overemphasized the role of parents and underemphasized the role of nonfamilial influences, most notably, the peer group. Studies of the broader context of parental socialization, however, neither support nor refute claims about the potency of parental influence. These studies do amply illustrate that, far from a myopic focus on the influence of parents, contemporary researchers have for some time amassed evidence that socialization can be fully understood only by examining the role of parents in light of the influence of other settings in which children and families function.

Conclusions

The lines of research just described imply a concept of parenting and parental influence that is more differentiated and complex than the dominant models of earlier eras. Whereas socialization researchers often depicted parents as "molding" children to function adequately in the society (Hartup, 1989; Maccoby, 1992), contemporary evidence clearly points toward multiple roles for parents that often do not imply the deterministic effect once attributed to them. Whereas researches using behavior-genetic paradigms imply determinism by heredity and correspondingly little parental influence (e.g., Rowe, 1994), contemporary evidence confirms that the expression of heritable traits depends, often strongly, on experience, including specific parental behaviors, as well as predispositions and age-related factors in the child. Whereas both older traditions typically limited ideas about environmental effects to parents, contemporary researchers have shown the interrelated effects of parenting, nonfamilial influences, and the role of the broader context in which families live (e.g., Bronfenbrenner, 1979; Bronfenbrenner & Ceci, 1994; Brooks-Gunn et al., 1997; Darling & Steinberg, 1997; Wachs, 1999).

This new generation of evidence on the role of parenting should add to the conviction, long held by many scholars, that broad, general main effects for either heredity or environment are unlikely in research on behavior and personality. Statistical interactions and moderator effects are the rule, not the exception. Information of this kind, unfortunately, fits poorly with the desire of the popular media for facile sound bites about parenting or the yearning of some writers of introductory textbooks for general, causal statements about behavioral development. Contrary to criticisms of socialization research, the difficulty today is not that the evidence is inadequate to show parenting effects but that the evidence has revealed a reality that is far more complex than critics expected or that writers can convey in most popular media outlets. For psychologists, the challenge is to make that reality a compelling foundation for the science and practice of the future and to find ways of disseminating this knowledge to a public eager to understand the forces that shape children's development.

REFERENCES

Abelson, R. (1985). A variance explanation paradox: When a little is a lot. *Psychological Bulletin, 97,* 129–133.

Angoff, W. H. (1988). The nature-nurture debate, aptitudes, and group differences. *American Psychologist, 43,* 713–720.

Anisman, H., Zaharia, M. D., Meaney, M. J., & Merali, Z. (1998). Do early-life events permanently alter behavioral and hormonal responses to stressors? *International Journal of Developmental Neuroscience, 16,* 149–164.

Bates, J., & Bayles, K. (1988). The role of attachment in the development of behavior problems. In J. Belsky & T. Nezworski (Eds.), *Clinical implications of attachment* (pp. 253–299). Hillsdale, NJ: Erlbaum.

Bates, J., Bayles, K., Bennett, D. S., Ridge, B., & Brown, M. M. (1991). Origins of externalizing behavior problems at eight years of age. In E. J. Pepler & K. H. Rubin (Eds.), *The development and treatment of childhood aggression* (pp. 197–216). New York: Academic Press.

Bates, J., Pettit, G., & Dodge, K. (1995). Family and child factors in stability and change in children's aggressiveness in elementary school. In J. McCord (Ed.), *Coercion and punishment in long-term perspectives* (pp. 124–138). New York: Cambridge University Press.

Bates, J., Pettit, G., Dodge, K., & Ridge, B. (1998). Interaction of temperamental resistance to control and restrictive parenting in the development of externalizing behavior. *Developmental Psychology, 34,* 982–995.

Bauman, K., & Fisher, L. (1986). On the measurement of friend behavior in research on friend influence and selection: Findings from longitudinal studies of adolescent smoking and drinking. *Journal of Youth and Adolescence, 15,* 345–353.

Belsky, J., Goode, M. K., & Most, R. K. (1980). Maternal stimulation and infant exploratory competence: Cross-sectional, correlational, and experimental analyses. *Child Development, 51,* 1168–1178.

Berndt, T. J. (1999). Friends' influence on children's adjustment to school. In W. A. Collins & B. Laursen (Eds.), *Relationships as developmental contexts: The Minnesota Symposia on Child Psychology* (Vol. 30, pp. 85–108). Mahwah, NJ: Erlbaum.

Berndt, T. J., Hawkins, J. A., & Jiao, Z. (1999). Influence of friends and friendship on adjustment to junior high school. *Merrill-Palmer Quarterly, 45,* 13–41.

Bohman, M. (1996). Predispositions to criminality: Swedish adoption studies in retrospect. In G. R. Bock & J. A. Goode (Eds.), *Genetics of criminal and antisocial behavior, Ciba Foundation Symposium 194* (pp. 99–114). Chichester, England: Wiley.

Bornstein, M. H. (1989). Sensitive periods in development: Structural characteristics and causal interpretations. *Psychological Bulletin, 105,* 179–197.

Bornstein, M. H. (1995a). Form and function: Implications for studies of culture and human development. *Culture and Psychology, 1,* 123–137.

Bornstein, M. H. (Ed.). (1995b). *Handbook of parenting.* Mahwah, NJ: Erlbaum.

Brody, G., & Stoneman, Z. (1994). Sibling relations and their association with parental differential treatment. In E. M. Hetherington, D. Reiss, & R. Plomin (Eds.), *Separate social worlds of siblings: The impact of nonshared environment on development* (pp. 129–142). Hillsdale, NJ: Erlbaum.

Bronfenbrenner, U. (1979). *The ecology of human development.* Cambridge, MA: Harvard University Press.

Bronfenbrenner, U., & Ceci, S. J. (1994). Nature-nurture reconceptualized in developmental perspective: A bioecological model. *Psychological Review, 101,* 568–586.

Bronfenbrenner, U., & Morris, P. A. (1998). The ecology of developmental processes. In W. Damon & R. M. Lerner (Eds.), *Handbook of child psychology: Theoretical models of human development* (5th ed., Vol. 1, pp. 993–1028). New York: Wiley.

Brooks-Gunn, J., Duncan, G., & Aber, L. (Eds.). (1997). *Neighborhood poverty: Context and consequences for children.* New York: Russell Sage Foundation.

Brooks-Gunn, J., Duncan, G., Klebanov, P., & Sealand, N. (1993). Do neighborhoods influence child and adolescent development? *American Journal of Sociology, 99,* 353–395.

Brown, B. (1990). Peer groups. In S. Feldman & G. Elliott (Eds.), *At the threshold: The developing adolescent* (pp. 171–196). Cambridge, MA: Harvard University Press.

Brown, B., Mounts, N., Lamborn, S., & Steinberg, L. (1993). Parenting practices and peer group affiliation in adolescence. *Child Development, 64,* 467–482.

Cadoret, R. (1985). Genes, environment and their interaction in the development of psychopathology. In T. Sakai & T. Tsuboi (Eds.), *Genetic aspects of human development* (pp. 165–175). Tokyo: Igaku-Shoin.

Cairns, R., & Cairns, B. (1994). *Lifelines and risks: Pathways of youth in our time.* New York: Cambridge University Press.

Cairns, R., Cairns, B., Neckerman, H., Gest, S., & Gariepy, J. L. (1988). Social networks and aggressive behavior: Peer support or peer rejection? *Developmental Psychology, 24,* 815–823.

Caldjii, C., Tannenbaum, B., Sharma, S., Francis, D., Plotsky, P. M., & Meaney, M. J. (1998). Maternal care during infancy regulates the development of neural systems mediating the expression of fearfulness in the rat. *Proceedings of the National Academy of Science, 95,* 5335–5340.

Caspi, A., & Elder, G. (1988). Emergent family patterns: The intergenerational construction of problem behavior and relationships. *International Journal of Behavioral Development, 5,* 81–94.

Caspi, A., Henry, B., McGee, R. O., Moffitt, T. E., & Silva, P. A. (1995). Temperamental origins of child and adolescent behavior problems: From age 3 to age 15. *Child Development, 66,* 55–68.

Caspi, A., & Silva, P. (1995). Temperamental qualities at age 3 predict personality traits in young adulthood: Longitudinal evidence from a birth cohort. *Child Development, 66,* 486–498.

Chase-Lansdale, P. L., Cherlin, A., & Kiernan, K. (1995). The long-term effects of parental divorce on the mental health of young adults: A developmental perspective. *Child Development, 66,* 1614–1634.

Chase-Lansdale, P. L., & Gordon, R. A. (1996). Economic hardship and the development of five- and six-year-olds: Neighborhood and regional perspectives. *Child Development, 67,* 3338–3367.

Chisholm, K. (1998). A three-year follow-up of attachment and indiscriminate friendliness in children adopted from Romanian orphanages. *Child Development, 69,* 1092–1106.

Chisholm, K., Carter, M., Ames, E. W., & Morison, S. J. (1995). Attachment security and indiscriminately friendly behavior in children adopted from Romanian orphanages. *Development and Psychopathology, 7,* 283–294.

Cohen, J. (1988). *Statistical power analysis for the behavioral sciences* (2nd ed.). Hillsdale, NJ: Erlbaum.

Conger, J. (1971). A world they never knew: The family and social change. *Daedalus, 100,* 1105–1138.

Conger, R., & Elder, G. E. (1994). *Families in troubled times: Adapting to change in rural America.* New York: Aldine.

Conger, R., Ge, X., Elder, G. H., Lorenz, F., & Simons, R. (1994). Economic stress, coercive family process and developmental problems of adolescents. *Child Development, 65,* 541–561.

Cowan, P. A., & Cowan, C. P. (in press). What an intervention design reveals about how parents affect their children's academic achievement and social competence. In J. Borkowski, S. Landesman-Ramey, & M. Bristol (Eds.), *Parenting and the child's world: Multiple influences on intellectual and social-emotional development.* Hillsdale, NJ: Erlbaum.

Cowan, P. A., Powell, D., & Cowan, C. P. (1998). Parenting interventions: A family systems perspective. In W. Damon, I. Sigel, & K. A. Renninger (Eds.), *Handbook of child psychology: Child psychology in practice* (Vol. 4, pp. 3–72). New York: Wiley.

Darling, N., & Steinberg, L. (1997). Community influences on adolescent achievement and deviance. In J. Brooks-Gunn, G. Duncan, & L. Aber (Eds.), *Neighborhood poverty: context and consequences for children: Conceptual, methodological, and policy approaches to studying neighborhoods* (Vol. 2, pp. 120–131). New York: Russell Sage Foundation.

DeBaryshe, B., Patterson, G., & Capaldi, D. (1993). A performance model for academic achievement in early adolescent boys. *Developmental Psychology, 29,* 795–804.

Devereux, E. C. (1970). The role of peer group experience in moral development. In J. P. Hill (Ed.), *Minnesota Symposia on Child Psychology* (Vol. 4, pp. 94–140). Minneapolis: University of Minnesota Press.

Dishion, T., Patterson, G., Stoolmiller, M., & Skinner, M. (1991). Family, school, and behavioral antecedents to early adolescent involvement with antisocial peers. *Developmental Psychology, 27,* 172–180.

Downey, G., & Walker, E. (1992). Distinguishing family-level and child-level influences on the development of depression and aggression. *Development and Psychopathology 4,* 81–96.

Dunn, J., & Plomin, R. (1986). Determinants of maternal behavior toward three-year-old siblings. *British Journal of Developmental Psychology, 57,* 348–356.

Eisenberg, N., & Damon, W. (Eds.), (1998). *Handbook of child psychology: Social, emotional, and personality development* (Vol. 3). New York: Wiley.

Emde, R., Plomin, R., Robinson, J., Corley, R., DeFries, J., Fulker, D., Reznick, J. S., Campos, J., Kagan, J., & Zahn-Waxler, C. (1992). Temperament, emotion, and cognition at fourteen months: The MacArthur longitudinal twin study. *Child Development, 63,* 1437–1455.

Epstein, J. L. (1983). The influence of friends on achievement and affective outcomes. In J. L. Epstein & N. Karweit (Eds.), *Friends in school* (pp. 177–200). New York: Academic Press.

Fletcher, A., Darling, N., Steinberg, L., & Dornbusch, S. (1995). The company they keep: Relation of adolescents' adjustment and behavior to their friends' perceptions of authoritative parenting in the social network. *Developmental Psychology, 31,* 300–310.

Forehand, R., & King, H. E. (1977). Noncompliant children: Effects of parent training on behavior and attitude change. *Behavior Modification, 1,* 93–108.

Forehand, R., Wells, K. C., & Griest, D. L. (1980). An examination of the social validity of a parent training program. *Behavior Therapy, 11,* 488–502.

Forgatch, M. S. (1991). The clinical science vortex: A developing theory of antisocial behavior. In D. Pepler & K. Rubin (Eds.), *The development and treatment of childhood aggression* (pp. 291–315). Hillsdale, NJ: Erlbaum.

Forgatch, M. S., & DeGarmo, D. S. (1999). Parenting through change: An effective prevention program for single mothers. *Journal of Consulting and Clinical Psychology, 67,* 711–724.

Fuligni, A., & Eccles, J. (1993). Perceived parent-child relationships and early adolescents' orientation toward peers. *Developmental Psychology, 29,* 622–632.

Furstenberg, F., Jr., Eccles, J., Elder, G., Jr., Cook, T., & Smaeroff, A. (1997). *Managing to make it.* Chicago: University of Chicago Press.

Gatz, M., Pedersen, N. L., Plomin, R., Nesselroade, J. R., & McLearn, G. E. (1992). Importance of shared genes and shared environments for symptoms of depression in older adults. *Journal of Abnormal Psychology, 101,* 701–708.

Ge, X., Conger, R., Cadoret, R., Neiderhiser, J., Yates, W., Troughton, E., & Stewart, M. (1996). The developmental interface between nature and nurture: A mutual influence model of child antisocial behavior and parent behavior. *Developmental Psychology, 32,* 547–598.

Ge, X., Conger, R., Lorenz, F., Shanahan, M., & Elder, G. (1995). Mutual influences in parent and adolescent psychological distress. *Developmental Psychology, 31,* 406–419.

Ge, X., Lorenz, F., Conger, R., Elder, G., & Simons, R. (1994). Trajectories of stressful life events and depressive symptoms during adolescence. *Developmental Psychology, 30,* 467–483.

Gesell, A., & Thompson, H. (1934). *Infant behavior: Its genesis and growth.* New York: McGraw-Hill.

Ghodsion-Carpey, J., & Baker, L. A. (1997). Genetic and environmental influences on aggression in 4- to 7-year-old twins. *Aggressive Behavior, 13,* 173–186.

Goldsmith, H., & Alansky, J. (1987). Maternal and infant temperamental predictors of attachment: A meta-analytic review. *Journal of Consulting and Clinical Psychology, 55,* 805–816.

Goodman, R. (1991). Growing together and growing apart: The non-genetic forces on children in the same family. In R. McGuffin & R. Murry (Eds.), *The new genetics of mental illness* (pp. 212–224). Oxford, England: Oxford University Press.

Greenough, W., & Black, J. (1992). Induction of brain structure by experience: Substrates for cognitive development. In M. R. Gunnar & C. A. Nelson (Eds.), *Developmental neuroscience: Minnesota Symposia on Child Psychology* (Vol. 24, pp. 155–200). Hillsdale, NJ: Erlbaum.

Grossmann, K., Grossman, K., Spangler, G., Suess, G., & Unzner, L. (1985). Maternal sensitivity and newborns' orientation responses as related to quality of attachment in Northern Germany. *Monographs of the Society for Research in Child Development, 50*(1–2, Serial No. 209), 233–256.

Gunnar, M. (in press). Early adversity and the development of stress reactivity and regulation. In C. A. Nelson (Ed.), *The effects of adversity on neurobehavioral development: Minnesota Symposia on Child Psychology* (Vol. 31). Mahwah, NJ: Erlbaum.

Hagekull, B. (1989). Longitudinal stability of temperament within a behavioral style framework. In G. A. Kohnstamm, J. E. Bates, & M. K. Rothbart (Eds.), *Temperament in childhood* (pp. 283–297). Chichester, England: Wiley.

Hagekull, B. (1994). Infant temperament and early childhood functioning: Possible relations to the five-factor models. In C. J. Halverson, Jr., G. A. Kohnstamm, & R. P. Martin (Eds.), *The developing structure of temperament and personality* (pp. 227–240). Hillsdale, NJ: Erlbaum.

Hardy-Brown, K. (1983). Universals in individual differences: Disentangling two approaches to the study of language acquisition. *Developmental Psychology, 19,* 610–624.

Hardy-Brown, K., & Plomin, R. (1985). Infant communicative development: Evidence from adoptive and biological families for genetic and environmental influences on rate differences. *Developmental Psychology, 21,* 378–385.

Hardy-Brown, K., Plomin, R., & DeFries, J. C. (1981). Genetic and environmental influences on rate of communicative development in the first year of life. *Developmental Psychology, 17,* 704–717.

Harris, J. R. (1995). Where is the child's environment? A group socialization theory of development. *Psychological Review, 102,* 458–489.

Harris, J. R. (1998). *The nurture assumption: Why children turn out the way they do.* New York: Free Press.

Hartup, W. W. (1989). Social relationships and their developmental significance. *American Psychologist, 44,* 120–126.

Hetherington, E. M. (1989). Coping with family transitions: Winners, losers, and survivors. *Child Development, 60,* 1–14.

Hetherington, E. M. (1991). The role of individual differences in family relations in coping with divorce and remarriage. In P. Cowan & E. M. Hetherington (Eds.), *Advances in family research: Family transitions* (Vol. 2, pp. 165–194). Hillsdale, NJ: Erlbaum.

Hetherington, E. M. (1993). A review of the Virginia Longitudinal Study of Divorce and Remarriage: A focus on early adolescence. *Journal of Family Psychology, 7,* 39–56.

Hoffman, L. W. (1991). The influence of the family environment on personality: Accounting for sibling differences. *Psychological Bulletin, 110,* 187–203.

Hogue, A., & Steinberg, L. (1995). Homophily of internalized distress in adolescent peer groups. *Developmental Psychology, 31,* 897–906.

Holden, G. W., & Miller, P. C. (1999). Enduring and different: A meta-analysis of the similarity in parents' child rearing. *Psychological Bulletin, 125,* 223–254.

Huttenlocher, P. R. (1994). Synaptogenesis, synapse elimination, and neural plasticity in human cerebral cortex. In C. A. Nelson (Eds.), *Minnesota Symposia on Child Psychology: Threats to optimal development: Integrating biological, psychological, and social risk factors* (Vol. 27, pp. 35–54). Hillsdale, NJ: Erlbaum.

Kandel, D. (1978). Homophily, selection, and socialization in adolescent friendships. *American Journal of Sociology, 84,* 427–436.

Kim, J. E., Hetherington, E. M., & Reiss, D. (1999). Associations between family relationships, antisocial peers and adolescent's externalizing behaviors: Gender and family type differences. *Child Development, 70,* 1209–1230.

Klebanov, P. K., Brooks-Gunn, J., & Duncan, G. T. (1994). Does neighborhood and family poverty affect mothers' parenting, mental health and social support? *Journal of Marriage and the Family, 56,* 441–455.

Kochanska, G. (1995). Children's temperament, mothers' discipline, and the security of attachment: Multiple pathways to emerging internalization. *Child Development, 66,* 597–615.

Kochanska, G. (1997). Multiple pathways to conscience for children with different temperaments: From toddlerhood to age 5. *Developmental Psychology, 33,* 228–240.

Kuczynski, L. (1984). Socialization goals and mother-child interaction: Strategies for long-term and short-term compliance. *Developmental Psychology, 20,* 1061–1073.

Lee, C. L., & Bates, J. (1985). Mother-child interaction at age two years and perceived difficult temperament. *Child Development, 56,* 1314–1325.

Lewis, M. (1997). *Altering fate: Why the past does not predict the future,* New York: Guilford Press.

Liu, D., Diorio, J., Tannenbaum, B., Caldji, C., Francis, D., Freedman, M. A., Sharma, S., Pearson, P., Plotsky, P. M., & Meaney, M. J. (1997, September 12). Maternal care, hippocampal glucocorticoid receptors and hypothalamic-pituitary-adrenal responses to stress. *Science, 277,* 1659–1662.

Maccoby, E. E. (1992). The role of parents in the socialization of children: An historical overview. *Developmental Psychology, 28,* 1006–1017.

McCall, R. (1991). So many interactions, so little evidence: Why? In T. Wachs & R. Plomin (Eds.), *Conceptualization and measurement of organism-environment interactions* (pp. 142–161). Washington, DC: American Psychological Association.

McCartney, K., Harris, M., & Bernieri, F. (1990). Growing up and growing apart: A developmental meta-analysis of twin studies. *Psychological Bulletin, 107,* 226–237.

McClelland, G., & Judd, C. (1993). Statistical difficulties of detecting interactions and moderator effects. *Psychological Bulletin, 114,* 376–390.

McGue, M. (1994). Genes, environment, and the etiology of alcoholism. In R. Zucker, G. Boyd, & J. Howard (Eds.), *The development of alcohol problems: Exploring the biopsychosocial matrix of risk* (National Institute of Alcohol Abuse and Alcoholism Research Monograph No. 26, pp. 1–40). Rockville, MD: U. S. Department of Health and human Services.

McLoyd, V. (1990). The impact of economic hardship on Black families and children: Psychological distress, parenting, and socioemotional development. *Child Development, 61,* 311–346.

McMahon, R. J., & Wells, K. C. (1998). Conduct problems. In E. J. Mash & R. A. Barkley (Eds.), *Treatment of childhood disorders* (2nd ed., pp. 111–151). New York: Guilford Press.

Miles, D., & Carey, G. (1997). Genetic and environmental architecture of human aggression. *Journal of Personality and Social Psychology, 72,* 207–217.

Miyake, K., Chen, S. J., & Campos, J. (1985). Infant temperament, mother's mode of interaction and attachment in Japan: An interim report. *Monographs of the Society for Research in Child Development, 50* (1–2, Serial No. 209), 276–297.

Mounts, N., & Steinberg, L. (1995). An ecological analysis of peer influence on adolescent grade point average and drug use. *Developmental Psychology, 31,* 915–922.

Nelson, C. A. (in press). The neurobiological bases of early intervention. In S. J. Meisels & J. P. Shonkoff (Eds.), *Handbook of early childhood intervention* (2nd ed.). New York: Cambridge University Press.

O'Connor, T. G., Deater-Deckard, K., Fulker, D., Rutter, M. L., & Plomin, R. (1998). Genotype-environment correlations in late childhood and early adolescence: Antisocial behavioral problems and coercive parenting. *Developmental Psychology, 34,* 970–981.

Parke, R., & Bhavnagri, N. P. (1989). Parents as managers of children's peer relationships. In D. Belle (Ed.), *Children's social networks and social support* (pp. 241–259). New York: Wiley.

Patterson, G. R. (1975). Multiple evaluations of a parent-training program. In T. Thompson & W. S. Dockens (Eds.), *Applications of behavior modification* (pp. 299–322). New York: Academic Press.

Patterson, G. R. (1999). *Recent news concerning the demise of parenting may be a bit premature.* Unpublished manuscript, Oregon Social Learning Center, Eugene, OR.

Patterson, G. R., DeBaryshe, B. D., & Ramsey, E. (1989). A developmental perspective on antisocial behavior. *American Psychologist, 44,* 329–335.

Plomin, R. (1990). *Nature and nurture: An introduction to human behavioral genetics.* Pacific Grove, CA: Brooks/Cole.

Plomin, R., & Daniels, D. (1987). Why are children in the same family so different from each other? *Behavioral and Brain Science, 10,* 1–16.

Plomin, R., DeFries, J., & Fulker, D. (1988). *Nature and nurture during infancy and early childhood.* New York: Cambridge University Press.

Plomin, R., & Rutter, M. (1998). Child development, molecular genetics, and what to do with genes once they are found. *Child Development, 69,* 1223–1242.

Quinton, D., Pickles, A., Maughan, B., & Rutter, M. (1993). Partners, peers, and pathways: Assortative pairing and continuities in conduct disorder. *Development and Psychopathology, 5,* 763–783.

Reiss, D., Niederhiser, J., Hetherington, E. M., & Plomin, R. (in press). *The relationship code: Deciphering genetic and social patterns in adolescent development.* Cambridge, MA: Harvard University Press.

Riksen-Walraven, J. (1978). Effects of caregiver behavior on habituation rate and self-efficacy in infants. *International Journal of Behavioral Development, 1,* 105–130.

Rose, R. (1995). Genes and human behavior. *Annual Review of Psychology, 46,* 625–654.

Rothbart, M., & Ahadi, S. (1994). Temperament and the development of personality. *Journal of Abnormal Psychology, 103,* 55–66.

Rothbart, M., & Bates, J. (1998). Temperament. In W. Damon & N. Eisenberg (Eds.), *Handbook of child psychology: Social, emotional, and personality development* (Vol. 3, pp. 105–176). New York: Wiley.

Rowe, D. (1983). A biometrical analysis of perceptions of family environment: A study of twin and singleton sibling kinship. *Child Development, 54,* 416–423.

Rowe, D. (1994). *The limits of family influence: Genes, experience, and behavior.* New York: Guilford Press.

Rowe, D., Chassin, L., Presson, C., Edwards, D., & Sherman, S. J. (1992). An "epidemic" model of adolescent cigarette smoking. *Journal of Applied Social Psychology, 22,* 261–285.

Rutter, M. (1990). Psychosocial resilience and protective mechanisms. In J. Rolf, A. S. Masten, D. Cicchetti, K. H. Nuechterlein, & S. Weintraub (Eds.), *Risk and protective factors in the development of psychopathology* (pp. 181–214). New York: Cambridge University Press.

Rutter, M., Dunn, J., Plomin, R., Simonoff, E., Pickles, A., Maughan, B., Ormel, H., Meyer, J., & Eaves, L. (1997). Integrating nature and nurture: Implications of person-environment correlations and interactions for developmen-

tal psychopathology. *Development and Psychopathology, 9,* 335–364.

Rutter, M., & the English and Romanian Adoptees (ERA) study team. (1998). Developmental catch-up, and deficit, following adoption after severe global early privation. *Journal of Child Psychology and Psychiatry and Allied Disciplines, 39,* 465–476.

Rutter, M., & Quinton, D. (1984). Parental psychiatric disorder: Effects on children. *Psychological Medicine, 14,* 853–880.

Scarr, S., & Weinberg, R. A. (1976). IQ test performance of Black children adopted by White families. *American Psychologist, 31,* 726–739.

Scarr, S., & Weinberg, R. A. (1978). The influence of "family background" on intellectual attainment. *American Sociological Review, 43,* 674–692.

Schiff, M., Duyme, M., Dumaret, A., & Tomkiewitz, S. (1982). How much could we boost scholastic achievement and IQ scores? A direct answer from a French adoption study. *Cognition, 12,* 165–196.

Skodak, M., & Skeels, H. (1949). A final follow-up of one hundred adopted children. *Journal of Genetic Psychology, 75,* 85–125.

Steinberg, L., Lamborn, S., Darling, N., Mounts, N., & Dornbusch, S. (1994). Over-time changes in adjustment and competence among adolescents from authoritative, authoritarian, indulgent, and neglectful families. *Child Development, 65,* 754–770.

Stern, D. N. (1985). *The interpersonal world of the infant.* New York: Basic Books.

Stoolmiller, M. (1999). Implications of the restricted range of family environments for estimates of heritability and nonshared environment in behavior-genetic adoption studies. *Psychological Bulletin, 125,* 392–409.

Suomi, S. J. (1997). Long-term effects of different early rearing experiences on social, emotional and physiological development in nonhuman primates. In M. S. Kesheven & R. M. Murra (Eds.), *Neurodevelopmental models of adult psychopathology* (pp. 104–116). Cambridge, England: Cambridge University Press.

Suomi, S. J. (in press). A biobehavioral perspective on developmental psychopathology: Excessive aggression and serotonergic dysfunction in monkeys. In A. J. Sameroff, M. Lewis, & S. Miller (Eds.), *Handbook of developmental psychopathology.* New York: Plenum.

Tejerina-Allen, M., Wagner, B. M., & Cohen, P. (1994). A comparison of across-family and within-family parenting predictors of adolescent psychopathology and suicidal ideation. In E. M. Hetherington, D. Reiss, & R. Plomin (Eds.), *Separate social worlds of siblings: The impact of nonshared environment on development* (pp. 143–158). Hillsdale, NJ: Erlbaum.

Tienari, P., Wynne, L. C., Moring, J., Lahti, I., Naarala, M., Sorri, A., Wahlberg, K. E., Saarento, O., Seitma, M., Kaleva, M., & Lasky, K. (1994). The Finnish adoptive family study of schizophrenia: Implications for family research. *British Journal of Psychiatry, 23* (Suppl. 164), 20–26.

Turkheimer, E., & Waldron, M. C. (in press). Nonshared environment: A theoretical, methodological, and quantitative review. *Psychological Bulletin.*

Van den Boom, D. C. (1989). Neonatal irritability and the development of attachment. In G. A. Kohnstamm, J. E. Bates, & M. K. Rothbart (Eds.), *Temperament in childhood* (pp. 299–318). Chichester, England: Wiley.

Van den Boom, D. C. (1994). The influence of temperament and mothering on attachment and exploration: An experimental manipulation of sensitive responsiveness among lower-class mothers with irritable infants. *Child Development, 65,* 1457–1477.

Wachs, T. D. (1992). *The nature of nurture.* Newbury Park, CA: Sage.

Wachs, T. D. (1999). Celebrating complexity: Conceptualization and assessment of the environment. In S. Friedman & T. D. Wachs (Eds.), *Measuring environment across the life span: Emerging methods and concepts* (pp. 357–392). Washington, DC: American Psychological Association.

Wachs, T. D., & Plomin, R. (1991). *Conceptualization and measurement of organism–environment interaction.* Washington, DC: American Psychological Association.

Wahlsten, D. (1990). Insensitivity of the analysis of variance to heredity-environment interaction. *Behavior and Brain Science, 13,* 109–161.

Weinberg, R. A. (1989). Intelligence and IQ: Landmark issues and great debates. *American Psychologist, 44,* 98–104.

Werner, E. (1990). Protective factors and individual resilience. In S. Meisels & J. Shonkoff (Eds.), *Handbook of early childhood intervention* (pp. 97–116). Cambridge, MA: Harvard University Press.

Werner, E., & Smith, R. (1992). *Overcoming the odds: High risk children from birth to adulthood.* Ithaca, NY: Cornell University Press.

Zill, N., Morrison, D., & Coiro, M. (1993). Long-term effects of parental divorce on parent-child relationships, adjustment, and achievement in young adulthood. *Journal of Family Psychology, 7,* 91–103.

Editor's note. Jerome Kagan served as action editor for this article.

Authors' note. W. Andrew Collins, Institute of Child Development, University of Minnesota; Eleanor E. Maccoby, Department of Psychology, Stanford University; Laurence Steinberg, Department of Psychology, Temple University; E. Mavis Hetherington, Department of Psychology, University of Virginia; Marc H. Bornstein, Child and Family Research, National Institute of Child Health and Human Development.

Preparation of this article was supported in part by the Rodney S. Wallace Professorship for the Advancement of Teaching and Learning, College of Education and Human Development, University of Minnesota. We thank the following for helpful comments on the manuscript: Marion S. Forgatch, Ben Greenberg, Megan R. Gunnar, Willard W. Hartup, Jerome Kagan, Gerald Patterson, Stephen Suomi, Deborah Vandell, Theodore Wachs, and Richard A. Weinberg.

Correspondence concerning this article should be addressed to W. Andrew Collins, Institute of Child Development, University of Minnesota, 51 East River Road, Minneapolis, MN 55455–0345. Electronic mail may be sent to wcollins@tc.umn.edu.

What Matters? What Does Not?

Five Perspectives on the Association Between Marital Transitions and Children's Adjustment

E. Mavis Hetherington, Margaret Bridges, and Glendessa M. Insabella
University of Virginia

This article presents an analysis of 5 views of factors that contribute to the adjustment of children in divorced families or stepfamilies. These perspectives are those that emphasize (a) individual vulnerability and risk; (b) family composition; (c) stress, including socioeconomic disadvantage; (d) parental distress; and (e) disrupted family process. It is concluded that all of these factors contribute to children's adjustment in divorced and remarried families and that a transactional model examining multiple trajectories of interacting risk and protective factors is the most fruitful in predicting the well-being of children.

In the past 30 years, there has been a significant decline in the proportion of two-parent families in first marriages and a complementary increase in the number of single-parent households and stepfamilies. These changes are the result of a rapid rise in the divorce rate that began during the 1960s (Simons, 1996) and also, to a lesser extent, of an increase in births to single mothers. Although there has been a modest decrease in the divorce rate since the late 1970s, almost one half of marriages end in divorce in the United States, and one million children experience their parents' divorce each year (U.S. Bureau of the Census, 1992). It is projected that between 50% and 60% of children born in the 1990s will live, at some point, in single-parent families, typically headed by mothers (Bumpass & Sweet, 1989; Furstenberg & Cherlin, 1991). Currently, stepfamilies make up approximately 17% of all two-parent families with children under 18 years of age (Glick, 1989).

Although the high divorce rate has been interpreted as a rejection of the institution of marriage, 75% of men and 66% of women eventually will remarry, suggesting that although people are rejecting specific marital partners, most are not rejecting marriage itself (Booth & Edwards, 1992; Bumpass, Sweet, & Castro-Martin, 1990; Cherlin & Furstenberg, 1994; Ganong & Coleman, 1994). Since the 1960s, however, the annual rate of remarriage has actually declined as the divorce rate has increased. Moreover, divorces are more frequent in remarriages and occur at a rate 10% higher than that in first marriages (Bumpass et al., 1990; Cherlin & Furstenberg, 1994). Couples with remarried wives are almost twice as likely to divorce as are couples with remarried husbands. This association may be attributable to the 50% higher rate of dissolution in remarriages in which children from previous marriages are present (Tzeng & Mare, 1995), although the presence of children appears to be less relevant to the marital quality of African American couples (Orbuch, Veroff, & Hunter, in press). As a result of their parents' successive marital transitions, about half of all children whose parents divorce will have a stepfather within four years of parental separation, and 1 out of every 10 children will experience at least two divorces of their residential parent before turning 16 years of age (Furstenberg, 1988). These numbers underestimate the actual number of household reorganizations to which children are exposed because many couples cohabit before remarriage or cohabit as an alternative to remarriage (Bumpass & Raley, 1995; Bumpass, Sweet, & Cherlin, 1991; Cherlin & Furstenberg, 1994; Ganong & Coleman, 1994).

The national figures for marital transitions and family structure mask very different patterns among racial and ethnic groups because the social context of marriage varies across communities (Orbuch et al., in press). African American children are twice as likely as White children to experience at least one parental divorce (National Center for Health Statistics, 1988) and also are more likely to bear children out of wedlock in adolescence and adulthood (Demo & Acock, 1996; Tzeng & Mare, 1995; U.S. Bureau of the Census, 1992). In addition, African Americans and Hispanic Whites are less likely to divorce after separation and to remarry than are non-Hispanic Whites (Castro-Martin & Bumpass, 1989; Cherlin, 1992). Thus, in comparison with White children, more African American children spend longer periods of time in single-parent households, which often include kin and cohabiting partners.

As marriage has become a more optional, less permanent institution in contemporary American society, children in all ethnic groups are encountering stresses and adaptive challenges associated with their parents' marital transitions. Children from divorced and remarried families, in contrast to those from never-divorced families, exhibit more problem behaviors and lower psychological well-being. Little agreement exists, however, about the extent, severity, and duration of these problems because there is great diversity in children's responses to parental marital transitions (Amato & Keith, 1991a; Emery & Forehand, 1994; Hetherington, 1991b; McLanahan & Sandefur, 1994). Furthermore, although it is clear that marital dissension and dissolution, life in single-parent households, and remarriage present families and children with new experiences, risks, and resources, there is some disagreement on how these factors undermine or enhance the well-being of children.

Theoretical Perspectives on Marital Transitions and the Adjustment of Children

Five main theoretical perspectives have been proposed to explain the links between divorce and remarriage and children's adjustment. These perspectives are those emphasizing (a) individual risk and vulnerability; (b) family composition; (c) stress, including socioeconomic disadvantage; (d) parental distress; and (e) family process.

Individual Risk and Vulnerability

It has been proposed that some characteristics of parents and children may influence their exposure and vulnerability to adversity. Some adults possess characteristics (e.g., antisocial behavior) that place them at increased risk for marital discord, multiple marital transitions, and other adverse life experiences (Capaldi & Patterson, 1991; Kitson & Morgan, 1990; Patterson & Dishion, 1988; Simons, Johnson, & Lorenz, 1996). Adults with psychological problems such as depression or antisocial behavior often select partners who also experience psychological difficulties (Merikangas, Prusoff, & Weissman, 1988), thereby increasing their risk for marital problems and dissolution. This is called the marital selectivity hypothesis.

In addition, some children have attributes that increase their vulnerability or protect them from deleterious consequences of stresses associated with their parents' marital transitions (Amato & Keith, 1991a; Emery & Forehand, 1994; Hetherington, 1989, 1991b).

Family Composition

It is commonly assumed that two biological parents provide the optimal family environment for healthy child development and that any deviation from this family structure, such as single-parent families or stepfamilies, is problematic for children (Amato & Keith, 1991a; Kitson & Holmes, 1992; Simons, 1996). Much of the early theorizing about divorce and family structure focused on father absence.

Stress and Socioeconomic Disadvantage

This perspective emphasizes that marital transitions trigger a series of negative social and economic changes, stresses, and practical problems that can interfere with the well-being of parents and children. For custodial mothers and their children, divorce is related to a notable economic decline that is associated with living conditions that make raising children more difficult (McLanahan & Sandefur, 1994), whereas remarriage is associated with an increase in household income for single mothers. Although much of the research on stress has focused on economic stresses, both divorced and remarried families encounter other stresses related to changing family roles and relationships (Cherlin & Furstenberg, 1994; Hetherington & Stanley Hagen, 1995; Simons, 1996).

Parental Distress

This perspective suggests that stressful life experiences, including economic decline and adaptive challenges associated with divorce and remarriage, lead to parental strain, distress, and diminished well-being, which are reflected in psychological problems such as depression, anxiety, irritability, and antisocial behaviors, as well as stress-related health problems (Capaldi & Patterson, 1991; Forgatch, Patterson, & Ray, 1995; Hetherington, 1989, 1991b; Kiecolt-Glaser et al., 1987; Lorenz, Simons, & Chao, 1996; Simons & Johnson, 1996). There is great individual variability in response to negative life changes; some parents cope with such changes with apparent equanimity, whereas others exhibit marked affective disruption and distress.

Family Process

Finally, many researchers have emphasized that differences between nondivorced families and divorced and remarried families on process variables such as conflict, control, expression of positive and negative affect, and problem solving largely explain the effects of divorce and remarriage. It is argued that more proximal variables, such as discipline and child-rearing practices, are most important in affecting children's adjustment.

Although these perspectives often are presented as competing with each other, empirical support can be found for each, suggesting that they may best be considered as complementary hypotheses (Amato & Keith, 1991a; Simons, 1996). In this article, research on the five perspectives is reviewed, and the direct and indirect effects of the five factors on the adjustment of children and parents in divorced and remarried families are examined. Finally, a transactional model of marital transitions involving relationships among the factors is presented.

Adjustment of Children in Divorced and Remarried Families

There is general agreement among researchers that children, adolescents, and adults from divorced and remarried families, in comparison with those from two-parent, nondivorced families, are at increased risk for developing problems in adjustment (for meta-analyses, see Amato & Keith, 1991a, 1991b) and that those who have undergone multiple divorces are at a greater risk (Capaldi & Patterson, 1991; Kurdek, Fine, & Sinclair, 1995). For the most part, the adjustment of children from divorced and remarried families is similar (Amato & Keith, 1991a; Cherlin & Furstenberg, 1994). Children from divorced and remarried families are more likely than children from nondivorced families to have academic problems, to exhibit externalizing behaviors and internalizing disorders, to be less socially responsible and competent, and to have lower self-esteem (Amato & Keith, 1991a; Cherlin & Furstenberg, 1994; Hetherington, 1989). They have problems in their relationships with parents, siblings, and peers (Amato & Keith, 1991b; Hetherington, 1997).

Normative developmental tasks of adolescence and young adulthood, such as attaining intimate relationships and increasing social and economic autonomy, seem to be especially difficult for youths from divorced and remarried families. Adolescents from divorced and remarried families exhibit some of the same behavior problems found in childhood and, in addition, are more likely to drop out of school, to be unemployed, to become sexually active at an earlier age, to have children out of wedlock, to be involved in delinquent activities and substance abuse, and to associate with antisocial peers (Amato & Keith, 1991a; Conger & Chao, 1996; Demo & Acock, 1996; Elder & Russell, 1996; Hetherington & Clingempeel, 1992; McLanahan & Sandefur, 1994; Simons & Chao, 1996; Whitbeck, Simons, & Goldberg, 1996). Increased rates of dropping out of high school and of low socioeconomic attainment in the offspring of divorced and remarried families extend across diverse ethnic groups (Amato

& Keith, 1991b); however, the effect is stronger for females than for males (Hetherington, in press).

Adult offspring from divorced and remarried families continue to have more adjustment problems (Chase-Lansdale, Cherlin, & Kiernan, 1995; Hetherington, in press), are less satisfied with their lives, experience lower socioeconomic attainment, and are more likely to be on welfare (Amato & Keith, 1991b). Marital instability also is higher for adults from divorced and remarried families (Amato & Keith, 1991b; Glenn & Kramer, 1985; Hetherington, in press; McLanahan & Bumpass, 1988; Tzeng & Mare, 1995), in part because of the presence of a set of risk factors for divorce, including early sexual activity, adolescent childbearing and marriage, and cohabitation (Booth & Edwards, 1990; Hetherington, 1997). In addition, in comparison with young adults from nondivorced families, young adults from divorced and remarried families exhibit more reciprocated, escalating, negative exchanges, including denial, belligerence, criticism, and contempt, and less effective problem solving during their marital interactions (Hetherington, in press). This pattern is probably related to the intergenerational transmission of divorce, which is reported to be 70% higher in the first five years of marriage from adult women from divorced families than for those whose parents have remained married (Bumpass, Martin, & Sweet, 1991).

Although there is considerable consensus that, on average, offspring from divorced and remarried families exhibit more problems in adjustment than do those in nondivorced, two-parent families, there is less agreement on the size of these effects. Some researchers report that these effects are relatively modest, have become smaller as marital transitions have become more common (Amato & Keith, 1991a), and are considerably reduced when the adjustment of children preceding the marital transition is controlled (Block, Block, & Gjerde, 1986, 1988; Cherlin et al., 1991). However, others note that approximately 20%–25% of children in divorced and remarried families, in contrast to 10% of children in nondivorced families, have these problems, which is a notable twofold increase (Hetherington, 1989, 1991b; Hetherington & Clingempeel, 1992; Hetherington & Jodl, 1994; McLanahan & Sandefur, 1994; Simons & Associates, 1996; Zill, Morrison, & Coiro, 1993). Because these difficulties in adjustment tend to co-occur and appear as a single behavior-problem cluster (Jessor & Jessor, 1977; Mekos, Hetherington, & Reiss, 1996), the vast majority of children from divorced families and stepfamilies do not have these problems and eventually develop into reasonably competent individuals functioning within the normal range of adjustment (Emery & Forehand, 1994). This argument is not intended to minimize the importance of the increase in adjustment problems associated with divorce and remarriage nor to belittle the fact that children often report their parents' marital transitions to be their most painful life experience. It is intended to underscore the research evidence supporting the ability of most children to cope

117

with their parents' divorce and remarriage and to counter the position that children are permanently blighted by their parents' marital transitions.

We turn now to an examination of some of the individual, social, economic, and family factors that contribute to the diversity in children's adjustment in divorced and remarried families. Each factor is discussed as it relates to the five perspectives on marital transitions.

Individual Risk and Vulnerability of Parents Associated With Divorce and Remarriage

Some adults have attributes that increase their probability not only of having dysfunctional marital relationships but also for having other problematic social relationships within and outside of the family, displaying inept parenting behaviors, encountering stressful life events, and having decreased psychological well-being (Amato & Booth, 1996; Block et al., 1986). Longitudinal studies have found that, in adults as well as in children, many of the problems attributed to divorce and remarriage and their concomitant life changes were present before these transitions occurred.

Although psychological distress and disorders may increase after divorce, parents who later divorce are more likely preceding divorce to be neurotic, depressed, antisocial, or alcoholic; to have economic problems (Amato, 1993; Capaldi & Patterson, 1991; Forgatch et al., 1995; Gotlib & McCabe, 1990); and to have dysfunctional beliefs about relationships (Baucom & Epstein, 1990; Kelly & Conley, 1987; Kurdek, 1993). In their marital interactions, they exhibit poor problem-solving and conflict resolution skills, thus escalating reciprocation of negative affect, contempt, denial, withdrawal, and stable, negative attributions about their spouses' behavior, which in turn significantly increase their risk for marital dissolution and multiple divorces (Bradbury & Fincham, 1990; Fincham, Bradbury, & Scott, 1990; Gottman, 1993, 1994; Gottman & Levenson, 1992; Matthews, Wickrama, & Conger, 1996). Sometimes these patterns are later found in the marital relationships of their adult offspring (Hetherington, in press). In relationships with their children, parents whose marriages will later be disrupted are more irritable, erratic, and nonauthoritative as much as 8–12 years prior to divorce (Amato & Booth, 1996; Block et al., 1988). These factors contribute to problems in children's adjustment and family relations in nondivorced families, single-parent families, and stepfamilies.

Children's Individual Risk, Vulnerability, and Resiliency Associated With Adjustment to Divorce and Remarriage

In accord with the individual risk perspective, characteristics of children may make them vulnerable or protect them from the adverse consequences or risks associated with their parents' divorce or remarriage. Some of these attributes influence the experiences and adjustment of children long before marital transitions occur.

Children's Adjustment Preceding Divorce and Remarriage

Children whose parents later divorce exhibit poorer adjustment before the breakup (Amato & Booth, 1996; Amato & Keith, 1991a; Block et al., 1986; Cherlin et al., 1991). When antecedent levels of problem behaviors are controlled, differences in problem behaviors between children from divorced and nondivorced families are greatly reduced (Cherlin et al., 1991; Guidubaldi, Perry, & Nastasi, 1987). Several alternative interpretations of these findings can be made. First, it is likely that maladapted parents, dysfunctional family relationships, and inept parenting already have taken their toll on children's adjustment before a divorce occurs. Second, divorce may be, in part, a result of having to deal with a difficult child. Third, personality problems in a parent, such as emotionality and lack of self-regulation, that lead to both divorce and inept socialization practices also may be genetically linked to behavior problems in children (Jockin, McGue, & Lykken, 1996; McGue & Lykken, 1992).

Children in stepfamilies also exhibit more behavior problems before remarriage occurs, and some researchers have speculated that the adaptive difficulties of stepchildren may be largely the result of experiences in divorced families (Furstenberg, 1988). This seems unlikely, because there is an increase in adjustment problems immediately after a marital transition, and because children in newly married families show more problems than those in stabilized, divorced, one-parent households (Hetherington & Clingempeel, 1992) or than those in longer remarried, stabilized stepfamilies (Hetherington & Jodl, 1994).

Personality and Temperament

Children who have easy temperaments; who are intelligent, socially mature, and responsible; and who exhibit few behavior problems are better able to cope with their parents' marital transitions. Stresses associated with divorce and remarriage are likely to exacerbate existing problems in children (Block et al., 1986; Elder, Caspi, & Van Nguyen, 1992; Hetherington, 1989, 1991b). In particular, children with difficult temperaments or behavior problems may elicit negative responses from their parents who are stressed in coping with their marital transitions. These children also may be less able to adapt to parental negativity when it occurs and may be less adept at gaining the support of people around them (Hetherington, 1989, 1991b; Rutter, 1987). Competent, adaptable children with social skills and attractive personal characteristics, such as an easy temperament and a sense of humor, are more likely to evoke positive responses and support and to maximize the use of available resources that help them negotiate stressful experiences (Hetherington, 1989; Werner, 1988).

Developmental Status

Developmental status and gender are the child characteristics most extensively researched in relation to adaptation to divorce and remarriage; however, the results of these studies have been inconsistent. Investigations of children's age at divorce must consider both age at the time of the marital transition and age at the time of assessment. In most studies, these variables are confounded with the length of time since the divorce or remarriage occurred. Some researchers have found that preschool-age children whose parents divorce are at greater risk for long-term problems in social and emotional development than are older children (Allison & Furstenberg, 1989; Zill et al., 1993). It has been suggested that younger children may be less able to appraise realistically the causes and consequences of divorce, may be more anxious about the possibility of total abandonment, may be more likely to blame themselves for the divorce, and may be less able to utilize extrafamilial protective resources (Hetherington, 1989). This greater vulnerability of young children to divorce has not been reported by other investigators (Amato & Keith, 1991a).

In contrast, early adolescence seems to be an especially difficult time in which to have a remarriage occur. Early adolescents are less able to adapt to parental remarriage than are younger children or late adolescents (Hetherington, 1993; Hetherington & Clingempeel, 1992), perhaps because the presence of a stepparent exacerbates normal early adolescent concerns about autonomy and sexuality. In addition, adolescence and young adulthood are periods in which problems in adjustment may emerge or increase, even when divorce or remarriage has occurred much earlier (Amato & Keith, 1991a, 1991b; Bray & Berger, 1993; Hetherington, 1993, in press; Hetherington & Clingempeel, 1992; Hetherington & Jodl, 1994).

Gender

Although earlier studies frequently reported gender differences in response to divorce and remarriage, with divorce being more deleterious for boys and remarriage for girls (Hetherington, 1989), more recent studies have found that gender differences in response to divorce are less pronounced and consistent than was previously believed (Amato & Keith, 1991a). Some of the inconsistencies may be attributable to the fact that fathers' custody, joint custody, and the involvement of noncustodial fathers are increasing and that involvement of fathers may be more important for boys than for girls (Amato & Keith,

1991a; Clarke-Stewart & Hayward, 1996; Lindner-Gunnoe, 1993; Zill, 1988).

Some research has shown that boys respond to divorce with increases in conduct disorders and girls with increases in depression (Emery, 1982); however, both male and female adolescents from divorced and remarried families show higher rates of conduct disorders and depression than do those from nondivorced families (Amato & Keith, 1991a; Hetherington, 1993; Hetherington & Clingempeel, 1992; Hetherington & Jodl, 1994). Female adolescents and young adults from divorced and remarried families are more likely than their male counterparts to drop out of high school and college. Male and female adolescents are similarly affected in the likelihood of becoming teenage parents; however, single parenthood has more adverse effects on the lives of female adolescents (McLanahan & Sandefur, 1994). Female young adults from divorced and remarried families are vulnerable to declining socioeconomic status because of the sequelae of adolescent childbearing and school dropout. These sequelae are compounded in stepdaughters by early home leaving, which they attribute to family conflict (Cherlin & Furstenberg, 1994; Hetherington, 1997, in press).

Some girls in divorced, mother-headed families emerge as exceptionally resilient individuals, enhanced by confronting the increases in challenges and responsibilities that follow divorce (Hetherington, 1989, 1991b; Werner, 1993). Such enhancement is not found for boys following marital transitions or for girls in stepfamilies (Hetherington, 1989, 1991b). Boys, especially preadolescent boys, are more likely than girls to benefit from being in stepfather families (Amato & Keith, 1991a; Hetherington, 1993). Close relationships with supportive stepfathers are more likely to reduce antisocial behavior and to enhance the achievement of stepsons than of stepdaughters (Amato & Keith, 1991a; Hetherington, 1993; Lindner-Gunnoe, 1993; Zimiles & Lee, 1991). Girls are at greater increased risk than are boys for poor adjustment and low achievement when they are in either stepfather or stepmother families rather than in nondivorced families (Lee, Burkam, Zimiles, & Ladewski, 1994; Zimiles & Lee, 1991).

Some research suggests that living in stepfamilies is more beneficial to Black adolescents than to White adolescents, although these effects vary by gender. In contrast to the findings for White youths, young Black women in stepfamilies have the same rate of teenage parenthood as do those in two-parent, nondivorced families, and young Black men in stepfamilies are at no greater risk to drop out of high school than are those in two-parent families (McLanahan & Sandefur, 1994). McLanahan and Sandefur proposed that the income, supervision, and role models provided by stepfathers may be more advantageous for Black children because they are more likely than White children to live in more disorganized neighborhoods with fewer resources and social controls.

Family Composition-Parental Absence and the Adjustment of Children

The family composition or parental absence perspective proposed that a deviation in structure from a family with two first-married parents, biologically related to their children, is associated with increases in problem behavior in children. Two parents can provide support to each other, especially in their child rearing, as well as multiple role models and increased resources, supervision, and involvement for their children (Amato, 1995; Demo & Acock, 1996; Dornbusch et al., 1985; Furstenberg, Morgan, & Allison, 1987; Lamb, 1997). If father unavailability or absence is a critical factor in divorce, father custody or contact with a noncustodial parent, stepfather, or father surrogate should enhance children's adjustment. Furthermore, children who experience loss of their fathers through divorce or death should exhibit similar adjustment problems. Less theorizing has focused on mother absence, although similar hypotheses might be proposed for mothers.

Children and adults from homes with an absent parent due to either divorce or death have more problems in adjustment than do those in nondivorced families; however, significantly more problems are found in academic achievement, socioeconomic attainment, and conduct disorders for offspring from divorced families (Amato & Keith, 1991a; Felner, Ginter, Boike, & Cowen, 1981; Felner, Stolberg, & Cowen, 1975; Hetherington, 1972). Although children of both divorced and widowed women suffer the loss of their fathers and economic declines, the finding suggests that other factors moderate the differences in their outcomes. One of these factors may be greater support and involvement with the extended family, especially that of the lost parent's family, following death but not divorce (Hetherington, 1972). Another may be the greater conflict in families preceding divorce but not the death of a parent (Amato & Keith, 1991a).

The parental absence hypothesis also suggests that contact with noncustodial parents or joint custody should promote children's well-being; however, contact with both noncustodial mothers and fathers diminishes rapidly following divorce. More than 20% of children have no contact with their noncustodial fathers or see them only a few times a year, and only about one quarter of children have weekly visits with their divorced fathers (Seltzer, 1991). Black noncustodial fathers have higher rates of both regular contact and no contact with their children than do non-Hispanic White fathers (McLanahan & Sandefur, 1994). Decreased paternal involvement is related to residential distance, low socioeconomic status, and parental remarriage (Seltzer, 1991). Seltzer and Brandreth (1994) noted that custodial mothers serve as "gatekeepers" (Ahrons, 1983), controlling noncustodial fathers' access to and the conditions of visits with their children. When conflict, resentment, and anger are high, the "gate" may be closed, and fathers may be discouraged or shut out. In contrast, when there is low conflict between divorced spouses, when mediation is used (Dillon & Emery, 1996), or when noncustodial fathers feel they have some control over decisions in their children's lives (Braver et al., 1993; Seltzer, 1991), paternal contact and child support payments are more likely to be maintained.

In contrast, noncustodial mothers are more likely than noncustodial fathers to sustain contact with their children and to rearrange their living situations to facilitate children's visits. They maintain approximately twice as much contact with their children as noncustodial fathers do and are less likely to completely drop out of their children's lives or to diminish contact when either parent remarries (Furstenberg & Nord, 1987; Furstenberg, Nord, Peterson, & Zill, 1983; Lindner-Gunnoe, 1993; Santrock, Sitterle, & Warshak, 1988; White, 1994; Zill, 1988). In addition, there is some evidence that noncustodial mothers, like noncustodial fathers, are more likely to maintain contact with sons than with daughters (Lindner-Gunnoe, 1993), although the preferential contact of fathers with sons is larger and more consistently obtained than that of mothers (Amato & Booth, 1991).

There is little support for the position that sheer frequency of contact facilitates positive adjustment in children (Amato & Keith, 1991a; King, 1994a, 1994b). However, as we discuss at greater length in the Family Process and the Adjustment to Divorce and Remarriage section, under conditions of low interparental conflict, contact with competent, supportive, authoritative noncustodial parents can have beneficial effects for children, and these effects are most marked for noncustodial parents and children of the same sex (Hetherington, 1989; Lindner-Gunnoe, 1993; Zill, 1988) Thus, it is the quality of contact, rather than the frequency, that is important (Amato, 1993; Emery, 1988; Furstenberg & Cherlin, 1991).

Research on custodial arrangements also has found few advantages of joint custody over sole residential custody. In a large study of custody in California, Maccoby and Mnookin (1992) found adolescents in the custody of their fathers had higher rates of delinquency, perhaps because of poorer monitoring by fathers. A meta-analysis of divorce by Amato and Keith (1991a), however, did not support the findings of poorer adjustment in children in families in which fathers have custody.

A corollary to the parental absence hypothesis would suggest that the addition of a stepparent might compensate for the loss of a parent. However, the family composition perspective implies that it is not only the presence of two parents but also biological relatedness to the parents that matter. Although divorce involves the exit of a family member, remarriage involves the restructuring of the family constellation with the entrance of a stepparent and sometimes stepsiblings. Predictions made about stepfamilies on the basis of the family composition hypothesis are unclear. On the one hand, the presence of a stepparent might compensate for the loss of the noncustodial parent by restoring a two-parent household. On the other hand, the child must confront an additional transition to another family with a nontraditional composition involving the addition of nonbiologically related family members to the household. In a family in which both divorced parents remarry, much more complex kin networks are created within and outside the household in a linked family system (Jacobson, 1982) or a binuclear family (Ahrons, 1979). A child's expanded kin networks may include stepsiblings, half siblings, and stepgrandparents, as well as stepparents and biologically related kin, and represent a marked deviation from the composition of the nondivorced nuclear family (Booth & Edwards, 1992; Bray, 1987, 1988; Bray, Berger, & Boethel, 1994; Burrell, 1995; Cherlin & Furstenberg, 1994; Giles-Sims, 1987).

Stress, Socioeconomic Disadvantage, and the Adjustment to Divorce and Remarriage

The stress perspective attributes problems in the adjustment of children from divorced and remarried families to the increased stresses experienced in these families. Parents and children living in divorced families encounter a diverse array of stressful life events (Hetherington, Cox, & Cox, 1985; Simons et al., 1996). Both custodial mothers and fathers complain of task overload and social isolation as they juggle household, child-care, and financial responsibilities that are usually dealt with by two parents (Hetherington & Stanley Hagan, 1997). Noncustodial parents express concerns associated with the establishment of new residences, social networks, and intimate relationships; loss of children; problems with visitation arrangements; and continued difficulties in relations with their ex-spouses (Hetherington, 1989, 1991b; Hetherington & Stanley Hagan, 1997; Hoffman, 1995; Minton & Pasley, 1996).

In spite of the diversity in stresses associated with divorce, most attention by sociologists and economists has focused on the marked decrement in the income of custodial mothers following marital dissolution and its accompanying risk factors. Those investigators who support a socioeconomic disadvantage perspective suggest that controlling for income will eliminate or greatly diminish the association between family structure and children's well-being (McLanahan & Sandefur, 1994). In addition, because custodial fathers do not encounter the financial decrements experienced by custodial mothers and because remarriage is the fastest way out of poverty for single mothers, it might be expected that children in father-custody families and stepfamilies will exhibit fewer behavior problems than those in divorced mother-custody households.

Because of increased enforcement of noncustodial fathers' child support payments and changes in the labor force for women, it has been speculated that custodial mothers and their children may no longer experience such drastic economic declines following divorce. A recent review (Bianchi, Subaiya, & Kahn, 1997) suggests, however, that custodial mothers still experience the loss of approximately one quarter to one half of their predivorce income in comparison to only 10% by custodial fathers following divorce (Arendell, 1986; Cherlin, 1992; Emery, 1994; McLanahan & Booth, 1989). For custodial mothers, this loss in income is accompanied by increased workloads; high rates of job instability; and residential moves to less desirable neighborhoods with poor schools, inadequate services, often high crime rates, and deviant peer populations (McLanahan & Booth, 1989; McLanahan & Sandefur, 1994).

Although father-only families have substantially higher incomes than do families with divorced custodial mothers, a significant number of father-only families (18%) live in poverty, and fathers rarely receive child support (Meyer & Garasky, 1993). However, most father-custody families have financial, housing, child-care, and educational resources not available to divorced custodial mothers. Custodial fathers report less child-rearing stress than do custodial mothers, and their children show fewer problems (Amato & Keith, 1991a; Clarke-Stewart & Hayward, 1996). This could be attributed to economic advantages in father-custody families; however, even with income controlled, children in father-custody families—especially boys—show greater well-being than those in mother-custody families (Clarke-Stewart & Hayward, 1996).

Newly repartnered parents and their children report higher levels of both positive and negative life changes than do those in never-divorced families (Forgatch et al., 1995; Hetherington et al., 1985). Although there is a marked increase in income for divorced mothers following remarriage, conflicts over finances, child rearing, and family relations remain potent problems in stepfamilies (Bray & Berger, 1993; Hetherington, 1993; Hetherington & Jodl, 1994). The economic improvement conferred by remarriage is not reflected in the improved adjustment of children in stepfamilies, and the new stresses associated with remarriage often counter the benefits associated with increased income (Amato & Booth, 1991; Bray & Berger, 1993; Cherlin & Furstenberg, 1994; Demo & Acock, 1996; Forgatch et al., 1995; Hetherington & Clingempeel, 1992; Hetherington & Jodl, 1994).

Parental Distress and the Adjustment to Divorce and Remarriage

Investigators taking the parental distress perspective propose that stressors affect children's adjustment through parental distress and diminished well-being

(Bank, Duncan, Patterson, & Reid, 1993; Forgatch et al., 1995; Lorenz et al., 1996; Simons & Beaman, 1996; Simons, Beaman, Conger, & Chao, 1992; Simons & Johnson, 1996). In this view, it is the parents' response to stress, rather than the stress itself, that is most salient for children's adjustment.

Signs of diminished parental well-being and distress, including anger, anxiety, depression, loneliness, impulsivity, feelings of being externally controlled, and emotional liability, may emerge or increase in the immediate aftermath of divorce (Hetherington, 1989, 1993; Pearlin & Johnson, 1977). In addition, newly remarried parents are often depressed or preoccupied as they cope with the challenges of their new family life (Hetherington & Clingempeel, 1992; Hetherington & Jodl, 1994). The mental health of parents in divorced and remarried families is related to children's adjustment through diminished competence in their parenting (Clarke-Stewart & Hayward, 1996; Forgatch et al., 1995; Hetherington, 1993; Lorenz et al., 1996; Simons, 1996).

The stresses associated with marital transitions place both residential and nonresidential parents at risk not only for psychological disorders (Hetherington, 1989, 1991b; Kitson & Morgan, 1990; Stack, 1989; Travato & Lauris, 1989) but also for disruption in immune system functioning (Kiecolt-Glaser et al., 1988) and concomitant increased rates of illness and morbidity, which are notable in divorced adults, especially in men (Burman & Margolin, 1992; Hu & Goldman, 1990; Riessman & Gerstel, 1985). Nonresidential fathers engage in more health-compromising and impulsive behaviors, such as alcohol consumption, than do fathers in any other family type (Umberson, 1987; Umberson & Williams, 1993) and are overrepresented among suicides and homicides (Bloom, Asher, & White, 1978).

Although depression remains higher in divorced women than in nondivorced women, by two years after divorce, women show less depression and more psychological well-being than do those who remain in conflict-ridden marriages with husbands who undermine their discipline and feelings of competence. The well-being of both men and women increases after the formation of a mutually caring, intimate relationship, such as a remarriage (Hetherington, 1993). Most parents do adapt to their new marital situation, with concomitant decreases in psychological and physical problems. In support of the parental distress perspective, even temporary disruptions in parents' health, social, and psychological functioning may make it difficult to be competent in parenting children who may be confused, angry, and apprehensive about a divorce or remarriage, and this inept parenting adversely affects children's adjustment (Chase-Lansdale & Hetherington, 1990; Emery, 1988; Emery & Dillon, 1994; Hetherington, 1989; Hetherington & Stanley Hagan, 1995; Maccoby & Mnookin, 1992).

Family Process and the Adjustment to Divorce and Remarriage

Divorce and remarriage confront families with changes and challenges associated with pervasive alterations in family roles and functioning. The changes in family relationships can support or undermine the efforts of children to adapt to their new family situations. Proponents of the family process perspective argue that the impact of parental attributes, changes in family structure, socioeconomic disadvantage, and parental distress on children's adjustment is largely mediated by disruptions in family relationships and interactions, such as those involved in discipline and child-rearing practices (Demo & Acock, 1996; Forgatch et al., 1995; Hetherington, 1993; Simons & Beaman, 1996; Simons & Johnson, 1996). Without disruptions in family functioning, the former risk factors are less likely to compromise children's adjustment.

Relationships Between Divorced Couples

Marital conflict is associated with a wide range of deleterious outcomes for children, including depression, poor social competence and academic performance, and conduct disorders (Amato & Keith, 1991a; Cowan & Cowan, 1990; Davies & Cummings, 1994; Forehand, Brody, Long, Slotkin, & Fauber, 1986; Gottman & Katz, 1989; Peterson & Zill, 1986). Conflict, contempt, anger, and acrimony often antecede divorce, and in the immediate aftermath of marital disruption, conflict may escalate. Consequently, one of the most frequently asked questions about divorce is whether parents should stay together in an unhappy, conflict-ridden marriage for the sake of the children.

The hypothesis that conflict is a major contributor to problems in divorced families is substantiated by evidence that children in high-conflict, nondivorced families have more problems in psychological adjustment and self-esteem than do those in divorced families or in low-conflict, nondivorced families (Amato & Keith, 1991a; Amato, Loomis, & Booth, 1995). In addition, longitudinal prospective studies of divorce indicate that divorce improves the adjustment of children removed from contentious marriages but is deleterious for children whose parents had less overtly conflictual relationships preceding divorce (Amato et al., 1995). When measures of marital dissatisfaction rather than conflict are used, the advantages of divorce over unhappy marital situations are less marked (Simons, 1996) because many couples in unsatisfying marriages may not exhibit overt conflict (Gottman, 1994).

Although contact and conflict between divorced couples diminish over time, they remain higher for couples with children as they attempt to negotiate coparenting relationships and economic responsibilities (Masheter, 1991). Despite the fact that cooperative, mutually supportive, and nonconfrontational coparenting relationships are advantageous to parents and children, only about one quarter of divorced parents attain such relationships and an approximately equal number maintain acrimonious relationships (Maccoby & Mnookin, 1992). Most coparenting relationships after divorce evolve into parallel coparenting relationships not only with little communication or coordination of parenting but also with lessened conflict because of the disengaged relationships. Cooperative coparenting is most likely to occur when family size is small and when there was little conflict at the time of divorce (Maccoby, Buchanan, Mnookin, & Dornbusch, 1993). With little conflict and cooperative coparenting, children adapt better not only to their parents' divorce but also to their parents' remarriages, and they tend to have more positive relations with their stepparents (Bray & Berger, 1993; Crosbie-Burnett, 1991).

The sheer frequency of conflict may not be as detrimental as the type of conflict. Conflicts in which children are caught in the middle while parents denigrate each other, precipitate loyalty conflicts, communicate through the children, or fight about the children are most destructive to children's well-being (Buchanan, Maccoby, & Dornbusch, 1991; Maccoby et al., 1993; Maccoby & Mnookin, 1992). Children in highly conflicted families not only are more distressed but also may learn to exploit and mislead their parents and to escape monitoring of their activities when they are older (Hetherington, Law, & O'Connor, 1992). Even when children are not directly involved in their parents' conflicts, the adverse effects of conflicts may be experienced through increased parental irritability and diminished monitoring, support, and involvement (Patterson, 1991).

Relationships of Custodial Mothers and Children

Children in both mother- and father-custody families show more problems than do children in nondivorced families; however, most offspring in both types of divorced families eventually are reasonably well-adjusted. Because approximately 84% of children reside with their mothers following divorce (Seltzer, 1994), most studies of parent-child relations following marital dissolution have involved custodial mothers. Close relationships with supportive, authoritative mothers who are warm but exert firm, consistent control and supervision are generally associated with positive adjustment in children and adolescents (Bray & Berger, 1993; Forehand, Thomas, Wierson, Brody, & Fauber, 1990; Hetherington, 1989, 1993; Hetherington & Clingempeel, 1992; Maccoby et al., 1993; Simons & Johnson, 1996). In the immediate aftermath of divorce, there is a period of disrupted parenting characterized by irritability and coercion and diminished communication, affection, consistency, control, and monitoring (Hetherington, 1991a, 1991b, 1993; Simons & Johnson, 1996).

The parenting of divorced mothers improves over the course of the two years following divorce but remains less authoritative than that of nondivorced mothers, and problems in control and coercive exchanges between divorced mothers and sons may remain high (Hetherington, 1991a). Even in adulthood, relationships between sons and divorced mothers are less close than those in nondivorced families, whereas differences in closeness are not found for daughters (Booth & Amato, 1994). Preadolescent girls and their divorced mothers often have close, companionate, confiding relationships; however, in adolescence, there is a notable increase in conflict in these relationships (Hetherington, 1991a; Hetherington & Clingempeel, 1992). In comparison with adolescents in nondivorced, two-parent families, adolescents in divorced families and in stepfamilies experience the highest levels of mother-adolescent disagreements and the lowest levels of parental supervision (Demo & Acock, 1996). Both conflictive, negative parent-adolescent relationships and lack of monitoring are associated with involvement with antisocial peers—one of the most potent pathways to the development of delinquency, alcoholism, substance abuse, and teenage sexual activity and childbearing (Conger & Reuter, 1996; Hetherington, 1993; Simons & Chao, 1996; Whitbeck et al., 1996).

About one quarter to one third of adolescents in divorced and remarried families, in comparison with 10% of adolescents in nondivorced families, become disengaged from their families, spending as little time at home as possible and avoiding interactions, activities, and communication with family members (Hetherington, 1993; Hetherington & Jodl, 1994). This incidence is greater for boys in divorced families and for girls in stepfamilies. If disengagement is associated with lack of adult support and supervision and with involvement in a delinquent peer group, it leads to both antisocial behavior and academic problems in adolescents (Hetherington, 1993; Patterson, DeBaryshe, & Ramsey, 1989). However, if there is a caring adult involved with the adolescent outside of the home, such as the parent of a friend, a teacher, a neighbor, or a coach, disengagement may be a positive solution to a disrupted, conflictual family situation (Hetherington, 1993).

It has been noted that children in divorced families grow up faster, in part, because of early assignment of responsibilities (Weiss, 1979), more autonomous decision making (Dornbusch et al., 1985), and lack of adult supervision (Hetherington, 1991a; Thomson, McLanahan, & Curtin, 1992). Assignment of responsibility may be associated with resilience and unusual social competence in girls from divorced families; yet, if the task demands are beyond the children's capabilities, they also may be associated with low self-esteem, anxiety, and depression (Hetherington, 1989, in press). Furthermore, if adolescents perceive themselves as being unfairly burdened with responsibilities that interfere with their other activities, they may respond with resentment, rebellion, and noncompliance.

The restablilizing of family relations following a remarriage takes considerably longer than that following a divorce (Cherlin & Furstenberg, 1994). Whereas a new homeostasis is established in about two to three years following divorce, it has been estimated that the adjustment to remarriage may take as long as five to seven years (Cherlin & Furstenberg, 1994; Papernow, 1988; Visher & Visher, 1990). Because more than one quarter of remarriages are terminated within five years, with higher rates for families with children, restablization never occurs in many stepfamilies.

In the first year following a remarriage, custodial mothers engage in less affective involvement, less behavior control and monitoring, and more negativity than nondivorced mothers (Bray & Berger, 1993; Hetherington, 1993; Hetherington & Clingempeel, 1992). Negative mother-child interactions are related to more disengagement, dysfunctional family roles, poorer communication, and less cohesion in stepfamilies (Bray, 1990). However, in long-established remarriages, the parenting of custodial mothers with their biological offspring becomes increasingly similar to that in nondivorced families (Bray & Berger, 1993; Hetherington, 1993; Hetherington & Clingempeel, 1992; Hetherington & Jodl, 1994).

Relationships of Custodial Fathers and Children

Although children usually live with their mothers following the dissolution of their parents' marriage, father-headed families have tripled since 1974, making them the fastest growing family type in the United States (Meyer & Garasky, 1993). Arrangements about physical custody are often made on the basis of personal decisions by parents and not on judicial decree, and the preponderance of maternal physical custody, even when joint legal custody has been granted, may reflect concerns fathers have about assuming full-time parenting (Maccoby et al., 1993; Maccoby & Mnookin, 1992). Boys and older children are more likely to be placed in father-only custody, but some girls and young children do live with their fathers. In contrast to custodial mothers, custodial fathers are a very select group of fathers who may be more child-oriented than most fathers. Fathers who seek custody of their children are more involved and capable than those fathers who have custody thrust on them because the mothers were unwilling or incompetent to parent (Hanson, 1988; Mendes, 1976a, 1976b). Once their families have restabilized, custodial fathers report less child-rearing stress, better parent-child relations, and fewer behavior problems in their children than do custodial mothers (Amato & Keith, 1991a; Clarke-Stewart & Hayward, 1996; Furstenberg, 1988).

There are different strengths and weaknesses in the parenting of custodial mothers and fathers. Although

custodial mothers and custodial fathers are perceived to be similarly warm and nurturing with younger children (Warshak, 1986), mothers have more problems with control and with assignment of household tasks, whereas fathers have more problems with communication, self-disclosure, and monitoring of their children's activities (Chase-Lansdale & Hetherington, 1990; Furstenberg, 1988; Warshak, 1986). Moreover, fathers have special difficulties with monitoring adolescents' behavior, especially that of daughters (Buchanan, Maccoby, & Dornbusch, 1992; Maccoby et al., 1993).

Recent evidence indicates that adolescent adjustment is more predictable from the parenting of a custodial parent of the same sex than one of the opposite sex (Lindner-Gunnoe, 1993). This evidence parallels findings of the greater salience of same-sex parents in the adjustment of adolescents in nondivorced families (Furman & Buhrmester, 1992; Kurdek & Fine, 1993). In spite of this greater influence of same-sex custodial parents, both sons and daughters report feeling closer to their custodial parent than their noncustodial parent, regardless of whether the parent is a mother or a father (Hetherington & Clingempeel, 1992; Maccoby et al., 1993; White, Brinkerhoff, & Booth, 1985).

As has been found with mothers, when custodial fathers remarry, there are disruptions in father-child relationships, especially with daughters (Clingempeel, Brand, & Ievoli, 1984). Fathers may alter their caretaking relationships more radically than mothers do because fathers are more likely to expect a stepmother to play a major role in household tasks and parenting (Hetherington & Stanley Hagen, 1995). However, in long-established stepfamilies, there are few differences in parent-child relations between remarried fathers and their residential biological children and those fathers and children in nondivorced families (Hetherington & Jodl, 1994).

Relationships of Noncustodial Mothers and Children

Although less is known about noncustodial mothers than noncustodial fathers, nonresidential mothers maintain more contact with their children than do nonresidential fathers. It is not only in the quantity but also in the quality of parent-child relationships that these mothers and fathers differ. Noncustodial mothers are less adept than custodial mothers in controlling and monitoring their children's behavior, but they are more effective in these parenting behaviors than are noncustodial fathers (Furstenberg & Nord, 1987; Lindner-Gunnoe, 1993). Children report that noncustodial mothers are more interested in and informed about their activities; are more supportive, sensitive, and responsive to their needs; and are more communicative than noncustodial fathers (Furstenberg & Nord, 1987; Lindner-Gunnoe, 1993; Santrock & Sitterle, 1987). Therefore, it is not surprising that children report talking more about their problems and activities and feeling closer to noncustodial mothers than to noncustodial fathers (Lindner-Gunnoe, 1993), nor that noncustodial mothers have more influence over their children's development, especially their daughters' adjustment, than do noncustodial fathers (Brand, Clingempeel, & Bowen-Woodward, 1988; Lindner-Gunnoe, 1993; Zill, 1988). Noncustodial mothers' warmth, support, and monitoring enhance their children's scholastic achievement and diminish antisocial, externalizing problems (Lindner-Gunnoe, 1993). In appraising some research findings that children have fewer problems in the custody of fathers than in the custody of mothers (Amato & Keith, 1991a; Clarke-Stewart & Hayward, 1996), it must be considered that part of this effect may be attributable to the more active involvement of noncustodial mothers.

When a custodial father remarries, closeness to the noncustodial mother can have some disadvantages because it is related to children's lack of acceptance of a stepmother. In contrast, there is no association between the relationship with a noncustodial father and building a close relationship with a stepfather (Hetherington, 1993; Hetherington & Jodl, 1994; White, 1994).

Relationships of Noncustodial Fathers and Children

In contrast to mothers' behavior, the postdivorce parenting behavior of fathers is less predictable from their predivorce behavior (Hetherington et al., 1985). Some previously attached and involved fathers find the enforced marginality and intermittent contact in being noncustodial fathers to be painful, and they drift away from their children. Other fathers, especially custodial fathers, rise to the occasion and increase their involvement and parenting competence. However, most nonresidential fathers have a friendly, egalitarian, companionate relationship rather than a traditional parental relationship with their children (Arendell, 1986; Furstenberg & Nord, 1987; Hetherington, Cox, & Cox, 1979; Munsch, Woodward, & Darling, 1995). They want their visits to be pleasant and entertaining and are hesitant to assume the role of disciplinarian or teacher. They are less likely than nondivorced fathers to criticize, control, and monitor their children's behavior or to help them with tasks such as homework (Bray & Berger, 1993; Furstenberg & Nord, 1987; Hetherington, 1991b).

Frequency of contact with noncustodial fathers and the adjustment of children are usually found to be unrelated (Amato & Keith, 1991a). Although obviously some degree of contact is essential, it seems to be the quality of the relationship and the circumstances of contact rather than frequency of visits that are most important (Amato, 1993; Emery, 1988; Furstenberg & Cherlin, 1991; Simons & Beaman, 1996). When noncustodial fathers are not just "tour guide" fathers but maintain more parent-like contact,

participate in a variety of activities with their children, and spend holidays together, the well-being of children is promoted (Clarke-Stewart & Hayward, 1996). Under conditions of low conflict, the involvement of authoritative noncustodial fathers can enhance children's adjustment (Hetherington, 1989), especially that of boys (Lindner-Gunnoe, 1993). It can even, to some extent, protect the children from the adverse consequences of rejecting or incompetent noncustodial mothers (Hetherington, 1989). In contrast, under conditions of high conflict, frequent contact with noncustodial parents may exacerbate children's problems (Kline, Johnston, & Tschann, 1991).

Relationships Between Stepparents and Stepchildren

Papernow (1998) commented that the typical starting point for a stepfamily involving "a weak couple subsystem, a tightly bonded parent-child alliance, and potential interference in family functioning from an outsider" (p. 56) would be considered problematic in a traditional nondivorced family. Clinicians have remarked that any stepfamily that uses a traditional nuclear family as its ideal is bound for disappointment (Visher & Visher, 1990). Similar patterns of relationships in traditional families and stepfamilies may lead to different outcomes. Patterns of functioning and family processes that undermine or promote positive adjustment may differ in the two types of families (Bray & Berger, 1993). The complex relationships between families following remarriage may require less rigid family boundaries and more open, less integrated relations among the family subsystems.

Although both stepfathers and stepmothers feel less close to stepchildren than do nondivorced parents to their children, they, if not the stepchildren, want the new marriage to be successful (Brand et al., 1988; Bray & Berger, 1993; Hetherington, 1993; Kurdek & Fine, 1993). In the early stages of a remarriage, stepfathers have been reported to be like polite strangers, trying to ingratiate themselves with their stepchildren by showing less negativity but also less control, monitoring, and affection than do fathers in nondivorced families (Bray & Berger, 1992; Hetherington & Clingempeel, 1992). In longer established stepfamilies, a distant, disengaged parenting style remains the predominant one for stepfathers, but conflict and negativity, especially between stepparents and stepdaughters, can remain high or increase, especially with adolescents (Brand et al., 1988; Bray & Berger, 1993; Hetherington, 1993; Hetherington & Jodl, 1994). Some of the conflict in stepfamilies is due to the negative rejecting behavior of stepchildren toward stepparents (Bray & Berger, 1993; Hetherington & Clingempeel, 1992; Hetherington & Jodl, 1994). Even stepparents with the best intentions may give up in the face of persistent hostile behavior by stepchildren.

Conflict between stepfathers and stepchildren is not necessarily precipitated by the children. In fact, rates of physical abuse perpetrated by stepfathers on their stepchildren are 7 times higher than those by fathers on their biological children, and homicide rates for stepfathers are 100 times higher than those for biological fathers (Daly & Wilson, 1996; Wilson, Daly, & Weghorst, 1980). These differential rates are most marked with infants and preschool-age children (Daly & Wilson, 1996).

Stepmothers have a more difficult time integrating themselves into stepfamilies than do stepfathers. Remarried fathers often expect that the stepmothers will participate in child rearing, forcing the stepmothers into more active, less distant, and more confrontational roles than those required of stepfathers (Brand et al., 1988). Support by the fathers for the stepmothers' parenting and parental agreement on child rearing are especially important in promoting effective parenting in stepmothers (Brand et al., 1988). The assumption of the dominant disciplinarian role is fraught with problems for stepparents (Brand et al., 1988; Bray & Berger, 1993; Hetherington, 1991a), and although authoritative parenting can have salutary effects on stepchildren's adjustment, especially with stepfathers and stepsons, authoritative parenting is not always a feasible option in stepfamilies (Bray & Berger, 1993). When custodial parents are authoritative and when stepparents are warm and involved and support the custodial parents' discipline rather than making independent control attempts, children can be responsive and adjust well (Bray & Berger, 1993; Hetherington, 1989).

It is not only parent-child relationships but also relationships between siblings that are more conflictual and less supportive in divorced families and stepfamilies than in nondivorced families (Hetherington, 1991a). These effects are more marked for biologically related siblings than for stepsiblings (Hetherington & Jodl, 1994). Less involved, harsher parenting is associated with rivalrous, aggressive, and unsupportive sibling relationships in divorced and remarried families (Conger & Conger, 1996; Hetherington, 1991a, 1993; Hetherington & Clingempeel, 1992), and, in turn, these negative sibling relations lead to low social competence and responsibility and to more behavior problems in children (Hetherington & Clingempeel, 1992).

Conclusion: What Matters? What Doesn't

In reviewing the five perspectives, it is clear that each may influence children's adjustment. The first perspective, the individual risk and vulnerability hypothesis, is supported by evidence suggesting that children and their parents have attributes that directly contribute to their experiencing marital transitions and to having more difficulties in adjusting to them. These problems may be transmitted genetically from parents to children, or the effect on children's adjustment may be indirect, due to

parents' ineffective child-rearing strategies. However, individual vulnerability to the adverse outcomes of divorce and remarriage seems to involve a complex interaction among an array of individual attributes, including personality, age, gender, and ethnicity, and the effects of these interactions have been difficult to differentiate.

The family composition—parental absence hypothesis is not as well supported by the evidence. Generally, children in never-divorced families with two parents are more competent than children whose parents have divorced. However, this theory would suggest that children's adjustment should benefit from the addition of a stepparent, yet there are few indications of lower levels of problems in children in stepfamilies as compared with children in divorced families. Furthermore, some studies indicate that especially in the early stages of a remarriage, stepchildren exhibit more difficulties than do children in stabilized, divorced, single-parent families (Amato & Keith, 1991a; Hetherington, 1993; Hetherington & Clingempeel, 1992; Hetherington & Jodl, 1994).

These comments must be qualified by findings indicating that the presence of a stepfather, especially with preadolescent boys, can attenuate problems in adjustment for stepsons, whereas the presence of either a stepmother or a stepfather may be associated with higher levels of problem behaviors for girls (Amato & Keith, 1991a; Hetherington, 1989; Hetherington & Jodl, 1994; Lee et al., 1994). These results, in conjunction with the somewhat inconsistent evidence that boys may also fare better in a father-custody family than in a mother-custody family (Amato & Keith, 1991a; Clarke-Stewart & Hayward, 1996; Zill, 1988), indicate that the presence of a father may have positive effects on the well-being of boys. Rather than rejecting the family composition-parental absence perspective, it should be concluded that there is not a simple main effect of family composition or parental absence but that it is modified by the reason for parental unavailability, the quality of family relationships, and the child's gender.

The findings thus far yield only modest support for marked direct effects of life stress and economic deprivation on children's adjustment. Even when income is controlled, children in divorced families show more problems than do those in nondivorced families (Amato & Keith, 1991a; Clarke-Stewart & Hayward, 1996; Demo & Acock, 1996; Guidubaldi et al., 1987; Hetherington, 1997, in press; Simons & Associates, 1996). In addition, although the income in stepfamilies is only slightly lower than that in nondivorced families, children in these families show a similar level of problem behavior to that in divorced mother-custody families (Amato & Keith, 1991a; Demo & Acock, 1996; Forgatch et al., 1995; Henderson, Hetherington, Mekos, & Reiss, 1996; Simons & Johnson, 1996). Thus, the effects of income do not seem to be primary and are largely indirect.

Some investigators using large-scale survey data report that as much as half of the effects of divorce on children's adjustment is attributable to economic factors (McLanahan & Sandefur, 1994); others find no direct effects of income but a major effect of the quality of family relationships that may alter children's adjustment (Demo & Acock, 1996). Furthermore, in studies in which income has been controlled, differences between offspring in divorced and nondivorced families remain (Amato & Keith, 1991a; Clarke-Stewart & Hayward, 1996; Demo & Acock, 1996; Guidubaldi et al., 1987; Hetherington, in press; Simons & Associates, 1996). Some of the inconsistencies in findings are due to methodological differences in studies. Surveys often have large representative samples but inadequate measures, sometimes involving only two or three items and single informants, to assess parental and family characteristics and family process variables. Studies using smaller, less representative samples but more reliable multimethod, multi-informant assessment, including observations, have found that much of the effects of family structure and economic stress are mediated by inept parenting (Forgatch et al., 1995; Simons & Johnson, 1996). Furthermore, there is some support in the research on stress, economic deprivation, and marital transitions for the individual risk position. As stated earlier, antisocial individuals are at greater risk not only for job instability, economic problems (Simons et al., 1992), and stressful life events but also for divorce (Capaldi & Patterson, 1991; Kitson & Holmes, 1992; Lahey et al., 1988), problems in successive marital relationships (Capaldi & Patterson, 1991), and incompetent parenting (Forgatch et al., 1995; Simons & Johnson, 1996).

Although it is true that parental distress increases in the aftermath of a divorce, research indicates that the effect of parents' well-being is largely mediated through their parenting. Even temporary disruptions in parents' physical and psychological functioning due to a marital transition interfere with their ability to offer support and supervision at a time when children need them most.

Although attributes of parents and children, family composition, stress and socioeconomic disadvantage, and parental distress impact children's adjustment, their effects may be mediated through the more proximal mechanism of family process. Dysfunctional family relationships, such as conflict, negativity, lack of support, and nonauthoritative parenting, exacerbate the effects of divorce and remarriage on children's adjustment. Certainly if divorced or remarried parents are authoritative and their families are harmonious, warm, and cohesive, the differences between the adjustment of children in these families and those in nondivorced families are reduced. However, marital transitions increase the probability that children will not find themselves in families with such functioning. Research on the relationships between family members in nondivorced families and stepfamilies supports the family process hypothesis, suggesting that, in large part, it is negative, conflictual, dysfunctional family relationships between parents, parents and children, and siblings that account for differences in children's adjustment.

It has become fashionable to attempt to estimate the relative contributions of individual attributes, family structure, stresses, parental distress, and family process

Figure 1

A Transactional Model of the Predictors of Children's Adjustment Following Divorce and Remarriage

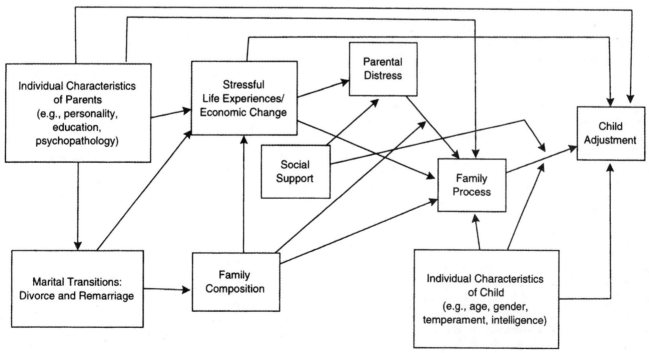

to the adjustment of children in divorced and remarried families. These attempts have led to conflicting results, futile controversies, and misleading conclusions because the amount of variance explained by the factors differs from sample to sample and varies with the methods and the data analytic strategies used. Moreover, different risk and vulnerability factors are likely to come into play and to vary in salience at different points in the transitions from an unhappy marriage to divorce, to life in a single-parent household, through remarriage, and into subsequent marital transitions. These risk factors will be modified by shifting protective factors and resources.

A transactional model of risks associated with marital transitions is perhaps most appropriate (see Figure 1). Divorce and remarriage increase the probability of parents and children encountering a set of interrelated risks. These risks are linked, interact, and are mediated and moderated in complex ways. These effects are illustrated in the model in different ways. For example, parental distress (e.g., maternal depression) does not have a direct effect on children's adjustment, which is not to say it does not have an impact. Instead, its influence is mediated through its link to family process, specifically the depressed mothers' diminished ability to effectively parent. In contrast, some variables moderate the relationship between other variables, such that the relationship depends on the level of the moderator. For example, children with difficult temperaments are expected to be more adversely affected by disruptions in family functioning than are children with easy temperaments. Thus, individual variables such as temperament can moderate the effect of family process on children's adjustment.

All family members encounter stresses associated with marital transitions, and it may be the balance between risks and resources that determines the impact of stresses on divorced and remarried parents and their children. All five of the factors described at the beginning of this article are associated with divorce and remarriage and with adverse outcomes for children. Studies using path analyses (e.g., Conger & Conger, 1996; Forgatch et al., 1995; Simons & Associates, 1996) have helped illuminate the patterns of linkages among these risks and have suggested that many of the risk factors are mediated by proximal experiences such as disruptions in parent-child or sibling relationships. However, the fact that a path is indirect does not reduce its importance. Figure 1 presents the theoretical model describing the linkages among these factors. A set of individual attributes, such as antisocial behavior, is associated with an increased risk of divorce and an unsuccessful remarriage; problems in social relationships, including parent-child relationships; and stressful life events. All family members encounter stresses as they deal with the changes, challenges, and restructuring of the family associated with marital transitions, but these vary for different family members and for divorce and remarriage. Divorce usually leads to the loss or the diminished availability of a father and the economic, social, and

emotional resources he can provide, which increases the probability of poverty and its concomitant environmental and experiential adversities for divorced custodial mothers and their children. Although some of the effects of stresses, such as living in neighborhoods with high crime rates, poor schools, antisocial peers, and few job opportunities or resources, may impact directly on children's adjustment and attainment, other effects of stress in divorced families may be indirect and mediated through parental psychological distress, inept or altered parenting, and disrupted family processes. Stresses associated with the changes and complexities in stepfamilies may also lead to distress and dysfunctional family functioning. Children, because of individual characteristics such as gender, temperament, personality, age, and intelligence, vary in their influence on family process and their vulnerability or resilience in dealing with their parents' divorce and remarriage and concomitant changes in family roles, relationships, and process. Thus, effects of the earlier risk factors on children's adjustment are mediated or moderated by associated transactional risk factors and often eventually by disruptions in family functioning. These indirect or mediated effects do not negate the importance of the earlier risk factors as a link in the transactional path of adversity leading to problems in child adjustment.

Static, cross-sectional slices out of the lives of parents and children in divorced or remarried families give a misleading picture of how risk and protective factors combine to influence the adjustment of children. An examination of the dynamic trajectories of interacting risk and protective factors associated with divorce and remarriage will yield a more valid and fruitful view of the multiple pathways associated with resiliency or adverse outcomes for children who have experienced their parents' marital transactions.

REFERENCES

Ahrons, C. R. (1979). The binuclear family: Two households, one family. *Alternative Lifestyles, 2,* 499–515.

Ahrons, C. R. (1983). Predictors of paternal involvement postdivorce: Mothers' and fathers' perceptions. *Journal of Divorce, 6,* 55–69.

Allison, P. D., & Furstenberg, F. F., Jr. (1989). How marital dissolution affects children: Variations by age and sex. *Developmental Psychology, 25,* 540–549.

Amato, P. R. (1993). Children's adjustment to divorce: Theories, hypotheses, and empirical support. *Journal of Marriage and the Family, 55,* 23–38.

Amato, P. R. (1995). Single-parent households as settings for children's development, well-being, and attainment: A social network/resources perspective. *Sociological Studies of Children, 7,* 19–47.

Amato, P. R., & Booth, A. (1991). Consequences of parental divorce and marital happiness for adult well-being. *Social Forces, 69,* 895–914.

Amato, P. R., & Booth, A. (1996). A prospective study of divorce and parent-child relationships. *Journal of Marriage and the Family, 58,* 356–365.

Amato, P. R. & Keith, B. (1991a). Parental divorce and adult well-being: A meta-analysis. *Journal of Marriage and the Family, 53,* 43–58.

Amato, P. R., & Keith, B. (1991b). Parental divorce and the well-being of children: A meta-analysis. *Psychological Bulletin, 110,* 26–46.

Amato, P. R., Loomis, L. S., & Booth, A. (1995). Parental divorce, marital conflict, and offspring well-being during early adulthood. *Social Forces, 73,* 895–915.

Arendell, T. (1986). *Mothers and divorce: Legal, economic, and social dilemmas.* Berkeley: University of California Press.

Bank, L., Duncan, T., Patterson, G. R., & Reid, J. (1993). Parent and teacher ratings in the assessment and prediction of antisocial and delinquent behaviors. *Journal of Personality, 61,* 693–709.

Baucom, D. H., & Epstein, N. (1990). *Cognitive-behavioral marital therapy.* New York: Brunner/Mazel.

Bianchi, S. M., Subaiya, L., & Kahn, J. (1997, March). *Economic well-being of husbands and wives after marital disruption.* Paper presented at the annual meeting of the Population Association of America, Washington, DC.

Block, J. H., Block, J., & Gjerde, P. F. (1986). The personality of children prior to divorce: A prospective study. *Child Development, 57,* 827–840.

Block, J. H., Block, J., & Gjerde, P. F. (1988). Parental functioning and the home environment in families of divorce: Prospective and concurrent analyses. *Journal of the American Academy of Child and Adolescent Psychiatry, 27,* 207–213.

Bloom, B. L., Asher, S. J., & White, S. W. (1978). Marital disruption as a stressor: A review and analysis. *Psychological Bulletin, 85,* 867–894.

Booth, A., & Amato, P. R. (1994). Parental marital quality, parental divorce, and relations with parents. *Journal of Marriage and the Family, 56,* 21–34.

Booth, A., & Edwards, J. N. (1990). Transmission of marital and family quality over the generations: The effects of parental divorce and unhappiness. *Journal of Divorce, 13,* 41–58.

Booth, A., & Edwards, J. N. (1992). Starting over: Why remarriages are more unstable. *Journal of Family Issues, 13,* 179–194.

Bradbury, T. N., & Fincham, F. D. (1990). Attributions in marriage: Review and critique. *Psychological Bulletin, 107,* 3–33.

Brand, E., Clingempeel, W. G., & Bowen-Woodward, K. (1988). Family relationships and children's psychosocial adjustment in stepmother and stepfather families. In E. M. Hetherington & J. D. Arasteh (Eds.), *Impact of divorce, single parenting, and stepparenting on children* (pp. 299–324). Hillsdale, NJ: Erlbaum.

Braver, S. L., Wolchik, S. A., Sandler, I. N., Sheets, V. L., Fogas, B., & Bay, R. C. (1993). A longitudinal study of noncustodial parents: Parents without children. *Journal of Family Psychology, 7,* 9–23.

Bray, J. H. (1987, August–September). *Becoming a stepfamily: Overview of The Developmental Issues in Stepfamilies Research Project.* Paper presented at the 95th Annual Convention of the American Psychological Association, New York.

Bray, J. H. (1988). Children's development during early remarriage. In E. M. Hetherington & J. D. Arasteh (Eds.), *Impact of divorce, single parenting, and stepparenting on children* (pp. 279–288). Hillsdale, NJ: Erlbaum.

Bray, J. H. (1990, August). *The developing stepfamily II: Overview and previous findings.* Paper presented at the 98th Annual Convention of the American Psychological Association, Boston.

Bray, J. H., & Berger, S. H. (1992). Nonresidential family-child relationships following divorce and remarriage. In C. E. Depner & J. H. Bray (Eds.), *Nonresidential parenting: New vistas in family living* (pp. 156–181). Newbury Park, CA: Sage.

Bray, J. H., & Berger, S. H. (1993). Developmental Issues in Stepfamilies Research Project: Family relationships and parent-child interactions. *Journal of Family Psychology, 7,* 76–90.

Bray, J. H., Berger, S. H., & Boethel, C. L. (1994). Role integration and marital adjustment in stepfather families. In K. Pasley & M. Ihinger-Tallman (Eds.), *Stepparenting: Issues in theory, research, and practice* (pp. 69–86). Westport, CT: Greenwood Press.

Buchanan, C. M., Maccoby, E. E., & Dornbusch, S. M. (1991). Caught between parents: Adolescents' experience in divorced homes. *Child Development, 62,* 1008–1029.

Buchanan, C. M., Maccoby, E. E., & Dornbusch, S. M. (1992). Adolescents and their families after divorce: Three residential arrangements compared. *Journal of Research on Adolescence, 2,* 261–291.

Bumpass, L. L., Martin, T. C., & Sweet, J. A. (1991). The impact of family background and early marital factors on marital disruption. *Journal of Family Issues, 12,* 22–42.

Bumpass, L. L., & Raley, R. K. (1995). Redefining single-parent families: Cohabitation and changing family reality. *Demography, 32,* 97–109.

Bumpass, L. L., & Sweet, J. A. (1989). *Children's experience in single-parent families: Implications of cohabitation and marital transitions* (National Study of Families and Households Working Paper No. 3). Madison: University of Wisconsin, Center for Demography and Ecology.

Bumpass, L. L., Sweet, J. A., & Castro-Martin, T. (1990). Changing patterns of remarriage. *Journal of Marriage and the Family, 52,* 747–756.

Bumpass, L. L., Sweet, J. A., & Cherlin, A. (1991). The role of cohabitation in declining rates of marriage. *Journal of Marriage and the Family, 53,* 913–927.

Burman, P., & Margolin, G. (1992). Analysis of the association between marital relationships and health problems: An interactional perspective. *Psychological Bulletin, 112,* 39–63.

Burrell, N. A. (1995). Communication patterns in stepfamilies: Redefining family roles, themes, and conflict styles. In M. A. Fitzpatrick & A. L. Vangelisti (Eds.), *Explaining family interactions* (pp. 290–309). Thousand Oaks, CA: Sage.

Capaldi, D. M., & Patterson, G. R. (1991). Relation of parental transitions to boys' adjustment problems: I. A linear hypothesis. II. Mothers at risk for transitions and unskilled parenting. *Developmental Psychology, 27,* 489–504.

Castro-Martin, T., & Bumpass, L. (1989). Recent trends and differentials in marital disruption. *Demography, 26,* 37–51.

Chase-Lansdale, P. L., Cherlin, A. J., & Kiernan, K. E. (1995). The long-term effects of parental divorce on the mental health of young adults: A developmental perspective. *Child Development, 66,* 1614–1634.

Chase-Lansdale, P. L., & Hetherington, E. M. (1990). The impact of divorce on life-span development: Short and long term effects. In P. B. Baltes, D. L. Featherman, & R. M. Lerner (Eds.), *Life-span development and behavior* (Vol. 10, pp. 105–150). Hillsdale, NJ: Erlbaum.

Cherlin, A. (1992). *Marriage, divorce, remarriage: Social trends in the U.S.* Cambridge, MA: Harvard University Press.

Cherlin, A. J., & Furstenberg, F. F. (1994). Stepfamilies in the United States: A reconsideration. In J. Blake & J. Hagen (Eds.), *Annual review of sociology* (pp. 359–381). Palo Alto, CA: Annual Reviews.

Cherlin, A. J., Furstenberg, F. F., Chase-Lansdale, P. L., Kiernan, K. E., Robins, P. K., Morrison, D. R., & Teitler, J. O. (1991). Longitudinal studies of effects of divorce in children in Great Britain and the United States. *Science, 252,* 1386–1389.

Clarke-Stewart, K. A., & Hayward, C. (1996). Advantages of father custody and contact for the psychological well-being of school-age children. *Journal of Applied Developmental Psychology, 17,* 239–270.

Clingempeel, W. G., Brand, E., & Ievoli, R. (1984). Stepparent-stepchild relationships in stepmother and stepfather families: A multimethod study. *Family Relations, 33,* 465–473.

Conger, R. D., & Chao, W. (1996). Adolescent depressed mood. In R. L. Simons & Associates (Eds.), *Understanding differences between divorced and intact families: Stress, interaction, and child outcome* (pp. 157–175). Thousand Oaks, CA: Sage.

Conger, R. D., & Conger, K. J. (1996). Sibling relationships. In R. L. Simons & Associates (Eds.), *Understanding differences between divorced and intact families: Stress, interaction, and child outcome* (pp. 104–124). Thousand Oaks, CA: Sage.

Conger, R. D., & Reuter, M. A. (1996). Siblings, parents, and peers: A longitudinal study of social influences in adolescent risk for alcohol use and abuse. In G. H. Brody (Ed.), *Sibling relationships: Their causes and consequences* (pp. 1–30). Norwood, NJ: Ablex.

Cowan, P. A., & Cowan, C. P. (1990). Becoming a family: Research and intervention. In I. Sigel & G. A. Brody (Eds.), *Family research* (pp. 246–279). Hillsdale, NJ: Erlbaum.

Crosbie-Burnett, M. (1991). Impact of joint versus sole custody and quality of the co-parental relationship on adjustment of adolescents in remarried families. *Behavioral Sciences and the Law, 9,* 439–449.

Daly, M., & Wilson, M. I. (1996). Violence against stepchildren. *Current Directions in Psychological Science, 5,* 77–81.

Davies, P. T., & Cummings, E. M. (1994). Marital conflict and child adjustment: An emotional security hypothesis. *Psychological Bulletin, 116,* 387–411.

Demo, D. H., & Acock, A. C. (1996). Family structure, family process, and adolescent well-being. *Journal of Research on Adolescence, 6,* 457–488.

Dillon, P. A., & Emery, R. E. (1996). Divorce mediation and resolution of child custody disputes: Long-term effects. *American Journal of Orthopsychiatry, 66,* 131–140.

Dornbusch, S. M., Carlsmith, J. M., Bushwall, S. J., Ritter, P. L., Liederman, H., Hastrof, A. H., & Gross, R. T. (1985). Single parents, extended households, and the control of adolescents. *Child Development, 56,* 326–341.

Elder, G., Caspi, A., & Van Nguyen, R. (1992). Resourceful and vulnerable children: Family influences in stressful times. In R. K. Silbereisen & K. Eyferth (Eds.), *Development in context: Integrative perspectives on youth development* (pp. 165–194). New York: Springer.

Elder, G. H., Jr., & Russell, S. T. (1996). Academic performance and future aspirations. In R. L. Simons & Associates (Eds.), *Understanding differences between divorced and intact families: Stress, interaction, and child outcome* (pp. 176–192). Thousand Oaks, CA: Sage.

Emery, R. E. (1982). Interpersonal conflict and the children of discord and divorce. *Psychological Bulletin, 92,* 310–330.

Emery, R. E. (1988). *Marriage, divorce, and children's adjustment.* Newbury Park, CA: Sage.

Emery, R. E. (1994). *Renegotiating family relationships.* New York: Guilford Press.

Emery, R. E., & Dillon, P. A. (1994). Conceptualizing the divorce process: Renegotiating boundaries of intimacy and power in the divorced family system. *Family Relations, 43,* 374–379.

Emery, R. E., & Forehand, R. (1994). Parental divorce and children's well-being: A focus on resilience. In R. J. Haggerty, L. R. Sherrod, N. Garmezy, & M. Rutter (Eds.), *Stress, risk, and resilience in children and adolescents* (pp. 64–99). Cambridge, England: Cambridge University Press.

Felner, R. D., Ginter, M. A., Boike, M. F., & Cowen, E. L. (1981). Parental death or divorce and the school adjustment of young children. *American Journal of Community Psychology, 9,* 181–191.

Felner, R. D., Stolberg, A., & Cowen, E. L. (1975). Crisis events and school mental health referral patterns of young children. *Journal of Consulting and Clinical Psychology, 43,* 305–310.

Fincham, F. D., Bradbury, T. N., & Scott, C. K. (1990). Cognition in marriage. In F. D. Fincham & T. N. Bradbury (Eds.), *The psychology of marriage* (pp. 118–149). New York: Guilford Press.

Forehand, R., Brody, G., Long, N., Slotkin, J., & Fauber, R. (1986). Divorce/divorce potential and interparental conflict: The relationship to early adolescent social and cognitive functioning. *Journal of Adolescent Research, 1,* 389–397.

Forehand, R., Thomas, A. M., Wierson, M., Brody, G., & Fauber, R. (1990). Role of maternal functioning and parenting skills in adolescent functioning following divorce. *Journal of Abnormal Psychology, 99,* 278–283.

Forgatch, M. S., Patterson, G. R., & Ray, J. A. (1995). Divorce and boys' adjustment problems: Two paths with a single model. In E. M. Hetherington & E. A. Blechman (Eds.), *Stress, coping, and resiliency in children and families* (pp. 67–105). Mahwah, NJ: Erlbaum.

Furman, W., & Buhrmester, D. (1992). Age and sex differences in perceptions of networks of personal relationships. *Child Development, 63,* 103–115.

Furstenberg, F. F., Jr. (1988). Child care after divorce and remarriage. In E. M. Hetherington & J. D. Arasteh (Eds.), *Impact of divorce, single parenting, and stepparenting on children* (pp. 245–261). Hillsdale, NJ: Erlbaum.

Furstenberg, F. F., Jr., & Cherlin, A. J. (1991). Divided families: *What happens to children when parents part.* Cambridge, MA: Harvard University Press.

Furstenberg, F. F., Jr., Morgan, S. P., & Allison, P. D. (1987). Paternal participation and children's well-being after marital dissolution. *American Sociological Review, 52,* 695–701.

Furstenberg, F. F., Jr., & Nord, C. W. (1987). Parenting apart: Patterns of childrearing after marital disruption. *Journal of Marriage and the Family, 47,* 893–904.

Furstenberg, F. F., Jr., Nord, C. W., Peterson, J. L., & Zill, N. (1983). The life course of children of divorce: Marital disruption and parental contact. *American Sociological Review, 48,* 656–668.

Ganong, L. H., & Coleman, M. (1994). *Remarried family relationships.* Thousand Oaks, CA: Sage.

Giles-Sims, J. (1987). Social exchange in remarried families. In K. Pasley & M. Ihinger-Tallman (Eds.), *Remarriage and stepparenting: Current research and theory* (pp. 141–163). New York: Guilford Press.

Glenn, N. D., & Kramer, K. B. (1985). The psychological well-being of adult children of divorce. *Journal of Marriage and the Family, 47,* 905–912.

Glick, P. C. (1989). Remarried families, stepfamilies, and stepchildren: A brief demographic profile. *Family Relations, 38,* 24–27.

Gotlib, I., & McCabe, S. B. (1990). Marriage and psychopathology. In F. D. Fincham & T. N. Bradbury (Eds.), *The psychology of marriage* (pp. 226–257). New York: Guilford Press.

Gottman, J. M. (1993). A theory of marital dissolution and stability. *Journal of Family Psychology, 7,* 57–75.

Gottman, J. M. (1994). *What predicts divorce?* Hillsdale, NJ: Erlbaum.

Gottman, J. M., & Katz, L. F. (1989). Effects of marital discord on young children's peer interaction and health. *Developmental Psychology, 25,* 373–381.

Gottman, J. M., & Levenson, R. W. (1992). Marital processes predictive of later dissolution: Behavior, physiology, and health. *Journal of Personality and Social Psychology, 63,* 221–233.

Guidubaldi, J., Perry, J. D., & Nastasi, B. K. (1987). Growing up in a divorced family: Initial and long-term perspectives on children's adjustment. In S. Oskamp (Ed.) *Applied social psy-*

chology annual: Vol. 7. Family processes and problems (pp. 202–237). Newbury Park, CA: Sage.

Hanson, S. M. H. (1988). Single custodial fathers and the parent-child relationship. Nursing Research, 30, 202–204.

Henderson, S. H., Hetherington, E. M., Mekos, D., & Reiss, D. (1996). Stress, parenting, and adolescent psychopathology in nondivorced and stepfamilies: A within-family perspective. In E. M. Hetherington & E. H. Blechman (Eds.), Stress, coping, and resiliency in children and families (pp. 39–66). Mahwah, NJ: Erlbaum.

Hetherington, E. M. (1972). Effects of father absence on personality development in adolescent daughters. Developmental Psychology, 7, 313–326.

Hetherington, E. M. (1989). Coping with family transitions: Winners, losers, and survivors. Child Development, 60, 1–14.

Hetherington, E. M. (1991a). Families, lies, videotapes. Journal of Research on Adolescence, 1, 323–348.

Hetherington, E. M. (1991b). The role of individual differences in family relations in coping with divorce and remarriage. In P. Cowan & E. M. Hetherington (Eds.), Advances in family research: Vol. 2, Family transitions (pp. 165–194). Hillsdale, NJ: Erlbaum.

Hetherington, E. M. (1993). An overview of the Virginia Longitudinal Study of Divorce and Remarriage with a focus on early adolescence. Journal of Family Psychology, 7, 39–56.

Hetherington, E. M. (1997). Teenaged childbearing and divorce. In S. Luthar, J. A. Burack, D. Cicchetti, & J. Wiesz (Eds.), Developmental psychopathology: Perspectives on adjustment, risk, and disorders (pp. 350–373). Cambridge, England: Cambridge University Press.

Hetherington, E. M. (in press). Social capital and the development of youth from nondivorced, divorced, and remarried families. In A. Collins (Ed.), Relationships as developmental contexts: The 29th Minnesota Symposium on Child Psychology. Hillsdale, NJ: Erlbaum.

Hetherington, E. M., & Clingempeel, W. G. (1992). Coping with marital transitions: A family systems perspective. Monographs of the Society for Research in Child Development, 57, (2–3, Serial No. 227).

Hetherington, E. M., Cox, M., & Cox, R. (1979). Family interaction and the social, emotional, and cognitive development of children following divorce. In V. Vaughn & T. Brazelton (Eds.), The family: Setting priorities (pp. 89–128). New York: Science and Medicine.

Hetherington, E. M. Cox, M., & Cox, R. (1985). Long-term effects of divorce and remarriage on the adjustment of children. Journal of the American Academy of Child Psychiatry, 24, 518–539.

Hetherington, E. M., & Jodl, K. M. (1994). Stepfamilies as settings for child development. In A. Booth & J. Dunn (Eds.), Stepfamilies: Who benefits? Who does not? (pp. 55–79). Hillsdale, NJ: Erlbaum.

Hetherington, E. M., Law, T. C., & O'Connor, T. G. (1992). Divorce: Challenges, changes, and new chances. In F. Walsh (Ed.), Normal family processes (2nd ed., pp. 219–246). New York: Guilford Press.

Hetherington, E. M., & Stanley Hagan, M. S. (1995). Parenting in divorced and remarried families. In M. Bornstein (Ed.), Handbook of parenting (pp. 233–255). Hillsdale, NJ: Erlbaum.

Hetherington, E. M., & Stanley Hagan, M. S. (1997). The effects of divorce on fathers and their children. In M. Bornstein (Ed.), The role of the father in child development (pp. 191–211). New York: Wiley.

Hoffman, C. D. (1995). Pre- and post-divorce father-child relationships and child adjustment: Noncustodial fathers' perspectives. Journal of Divorce and Remarriage, 23, 3–20.

Hu, Y., & Goldman, N. (1990). Mortality differentials by marital status: An international comparison. Demography, 27, 233–250.

Jacobson, D. S. (1982, August). Family structure in the age of divorce. Paper presented at the 90th Annual Convention of the American Psychological Association, Washington, DC.

Jessor, R., & Jessor, S. L. (1977). Problem behavior and psycho-social development. New York: Academic Press.

Jockin, V., McGue, M., & Lykken, D. T. (1996). Personality and divorce: A genetic analysis. Journal of Personality and Social Psychology, 71, 288–299.

Kelly, E. L., & Conley, J. J. (1987). Personality and compatibility: A prospective analysis of marital stability and marital satisfaction. Journal of Personality and Social Psychology, 52, 27–40.

Kiecolt-Glaser, J. K., Fisher, L. D., Ogrocki, P., Stout, J. C., Speicher, C. E., & Glaser, R. (1987). Marital quality, marital disruption, and immune function. Psychosomatic Medicine, 49, 13–34.

Kiecolt-Glaser, J. K., Kennedy, S., Malkoff, S., Fisher, L. D., Speicher, C. E., & Glaser, R. (1988). Marital discord and immunity in males. Psychosomatic Medicine, 50, 213–229.

King, V. (1994a). Nonresidential father involvement and child well-being: Can dads make a difference? Journal of Family Issues, 15, 78–96.

King, V. (1994b). Variation in the consequences of nonresidential father involvement for children's well-being. Journal of Marriage and the Family, 56, 964–972.

Kitson, G. C., & Holmes, W. M. (1992). Portrait of divorce: Adjustment to marital breakdown. New York: Guilford Press.

Kitson, G. C., & Morgan, L. A. (1990). The multiple consequences of divorce. Journal of Marriage and the Family, 52, 913–924.

Kline, M., Johnston, J. R., & Tschann, J. M. (1991). The long shadow of marital conflict: A model of children's post-divorce adjustment. Journal of Marriage and the Family, 53, 297–309.

Kurdek, L. A. (1993). Predicting marital dissolution: A 5-year prospective longitudinal study of newlywed couples. Journal of Personality and Social Psychology, 64, 221–242.

Kurdek, L. A., & Fine, M. A. (1993). Parent and nonparent residential family members as providers of warmth, support, and supervision to young adolescents. Journal of Family Psychology, 7, 245–249.

Kurdek, L. A., Fine, M. A., & Sinclair, R. J. (1995). School adjustment in sixth graders: Parenting transitions, family climate, and peer norm effects. Child Development, 66, 430–445.

Lahey, B. B., Hartdagen, S. E., Frick, P. J., McBurnett, K., Connor, R., & Hynd, G. W. (1988). Conduct disorder: Parsing the confounded relation to parental divorce and antisocial personality. Journal of Abnormal Psychology, 97, 334–337.

Lamb, M. E. (1997). Fathers and child development: An introductory overview and guide. In M. E. Lamb (Ed.), The role of the father in child development (pp. 1–18). New York: Wiley.

Lee, V. E., Burkam, D. T., Zimiles, H., & Ladewski, B. (1994). Family structure and its effect on behavioral and emotional problems in young adolescents. Journal of Research on Adolescence, 4, 405–437.

Lindner-Gunnoe, M. (1993). Noncustodial mothers' and fathers' contributions to the adjustment of adolescent stepchildren. Unpublished doctoral dissertation. University of Virginia.

Lorenz, F. O., Simons, R. L., & Chao, W. (1996). Family structure and mother's depression. In R. L. Simons & Associates (Eds.), Understanding differences between divorced and intact families: Stress, interaction, and child outcome (pp. 65–77). Thousand Oaks, CA: Sage.

Maccoby, E. E., Buchanan, C. M., Mnookin, R. H., & Dornbusch, S. M. (1993). Post-divorce roles of mothers and fathers in the lives of their children. Journal of Family Psychology, 7, 24–38.

Maccoby, E. E., & Mnookin, R. H. (1992). *Dividing the child: Social and legal dilemmas of custody.* Cambridge, MA: Harvard University Press.

Masheter, C. (1991). Post-divorce relationships between ex-spouses: The roles of attachment and interpersonal conflict. *Journal of Marriage and the Family, 53,* 101–110.

Matthews, L. S., Wickrama, K. A. S., & Conger, R. D. (1996). Predicting marital instability from spouse and observer reports of marital interaction. *Journal of Marriage and the Family, 58,* 641–655.

McGue, M., & Lykken, D. T. (1992). Genetic influence on risk of divorce. *Psychological Science, 6,* 368–373.

McLanahan, S. S., & Booth, K. (1989). Mother-only families: Problems, prospects, and politics. *Journal of Marriage and the Family, 51,* 557–580.

McLanahan, S. S., & Bumpass, L. (1988). Intergenerational consequences of family disruption. *American Journal of Sociology, 94,* 130–152.

McLanahan, S., & Sandefur, G. (1994). *Growing up with a single parent: What hurts, what helps?* Cambridge, MA: Harvard University Press.

Mekos, D., Hetherington, E. M., & Reiss, D. (1996). Sibling differences in problem behavior and parental treatment in nondivorced and remarried families. *Child Development, 67,* 2148–2165.

Mendes, H. A. (1976a). Single fatherhood. *Social Work, 21,* 308–312.

Mendes, H. A. (1976b). Single fathers. *Family Coordinator, 25,* 439–444.

Merikangas, K. R., Prusoff, B. A., & Weissman, M. M. (1988). Parental concordance for affective disorders: Psychopathology in offspring. *Journal of Affective Disorders, 15,* 279–290.

Meyer, D. R., & Garasky, S. (1993). Custodial fathers: Myths, realities, and child support policy. *Journal of Marriage and the Family, 55,* 73–89.

Minton, C., & Pasley, K. (1996). Fathers' parenting role identity and father involvement: A comparison of nondivorced and divorced, nonresident fathers. *Journal of Family Issues, 17,* 26–45.

Munsch, J., Woodward, J., & Darling, N. (1995). Children's perceptions of their relationships with coresiding and non-custodial fathers. *Journal of Divorce and Remarriage, 23,* 39–54.

National Center for Health Statistics. (1988). *Current estimates from the National Health Interview Survey: United States, 1987* (DHHS Publication No. 88–1594). Washington, DC: U.S. Government Printing Office.

Orbuch, T. L., Veroff, J., & Hunter, A. G. (in press). Black couples, White couples: The early years of marriage. In E. M. Hetherington (Ed.), *Coping with divorce, single-parenting, and remarriage: A risk and resiliency perspective.* Mahwah, NJ: Erlbaum.

Papernow, P. L. (1988). Stepparent role development: From outsider to intimate. In W. R. Beer (Ed.), *Relative strangers: Studies of stepfamily processes* (pp. 54–82). Totowa, NJ: Rowman & Littlefield.

Patterson, G. (1991, March). *Interaction of stress and family structure and their relation to child adjustment.* Paper presented at the biennial meetings of the Society for Research on Child Development, Seattle, WA.

Patterson, G., DeBaryshe, B., & Ramsey, E. (1989). A developmental perspective on antisocial behavior. *American Psychologist, 44,* 329–335.

Patterson, G., & Dishion, T. J. (1988). Multilevel family process models: Traits, interactions, and relationships. In R. Hinde & J. Stevenson-Hinde (Eds.), *Relationships within families: Mutual influences* (pp. 283–310). Oxford, England: Clarendon Press.

Pearlin, L. I., & Johnson, J. S. (1977). Marital status, life-stresses and depression. *American Sociological Review, 42,* 704–715.

Peterson, J. L., & Zill, N. (1986). Marital disruption, parent-child relationships, and behavior problems in children. *Journal of Marriage and the Family, 48,* 295–307.

Riessman, C. K., & Gerstel, N. (1985). Marital dissolution and health: Do males or females have greater risk? *Social Science and Medicine, 20,* 627–635.

Rutter, M. (1987). Psychosocial resilience and protective mechanisms. *American Journal of Orthopsychiatry, 57,* 316–331.

Santrock, J. W., & Sitterle, K. A. (1987). Parent-child relationships in stepmother families. In K. Pasley & M. Ihinger-Tallman (Eds.), *Remarriage and stepparenting: Current research and theory* (pp. 273–299). New York: Guilford Press.

Santrock, J. W., Sitterle, K. A., & Warshak, R. A. (1988). Parent-child relationships in stepfather families. In P. Bronstein & C. P. Cowan (Eds.), *Fatherhood today: Men's changing roles in the family* pp. 144–165). New York: Wiley.

Seltzer, J. A. (1991). Relationships between fathers and children who live apart: The father's role after separation. *Journal of Marriage and the Family, 53,* 79–101.

Seltzer, J. A. (1994). Consequences of marital dissolution for children. *Annual Review of Sociology, 20,* 235–266.

Seltzer, J. A., & Brandreth, Y. (1994). What fathers say about involvement with children after separation. *Journal of Family Issues, 15,* 49–77.

Simons, R. L. (1996). The effect of divorce on adult and child adjustment. In R. L. Simons & Associates (Eds.), *Understanding differences between divorced and intact families: Stress, interaction, and child outcome* (pp. 3–20). Thousand Oaks, CA: Sage.

Simons, R. L., & Associates. (Eds. (1996). *Understanding differences between divorced and intact families: Stress, interaction, and child outcome.* Thousand Oaks, CA: Sage.

Simons, R. L., & Beaman, J. (1996). Father's parenting. In R. L. Simons & Associates (Eds.), *Understanding differences between divorced and intact families: Stress, interaction, and child outcome* (pp. 94–103). Thousand Oaks, CA: Sage.

Simons, R. L., Beaman, J., Conger, R. D., & Chao, W. (1992). Childhood experience, conceptions of parenting, and attitudes of spouse as determinants of parental behavior. *Journal of Marriage and the Family, 55,* 91–106.

Simons, R. L., & Chao, W. (1996). Conduct problems. In R. L. Simons & Associates (Eds.), *Understanding differences between divorced and intact families: Stress, interaction, and child outcome* (pp. 125–143). Thousand Oaks, CA: Sage.

Simons, R. L., & Johnson, C. (1996). Mother's parenting. In R. L. Simons & Associates (Eds.), *Understanding differences between divorced and intact families: Stress, interaction, and child outcome* (pp. 81–93). Thousand Oaks, CA: Sage.

Simons, R. L., Johnson, C., & Lorenz, F. O. (1996). Family structure differences in stress and behavioral predispositions. In R. L. Simons & Associates (Eds.), *Understanding differences between divorced and intact families: Stress, interaction, and child outcome* (pp. 45–63). Thousand Oaks, CA: Sage.

Stack, S. (1989). The impact of divorce on suicide in Norway, 1951–1980. *Journal of Marriage and the Family, 51,* 229–238.

Thomson, E., McLanahan, S. S., & Curtin, R. B. (1992). Family structure, gender, and parental separation. *Journal of Marriage and the Family, 54,* 368–378.

Travato, F., & Lauris, G. (1989). Marital status and mortality in Canada: 1951–81. *Journal of Marriage and the Family, 51,* 907–922.

Tzeng, J. M., & Mare, R. D. (1995). Labor market and socioeconomic effects on marital stability. *Social Science Research, 24,* 329–351.

Umberson, D. (1987). Family status and health behaviors: Social control as a dimension of social integration. *Journal of Health and Social Behavior, 28,* 306–319.

132

Umberson, D., & Williams, C. L. (1993). Divorced fathers: Parental role strain and psychological distress. *Journal of Family Issues, 14,* 378–400.

U.S. Bureau of the Census. (1992). *Marital status and living arrangements: March, 1992* (No. 468, Tables G & 5, Current Population Reports, Series P–20). Washington, DC: U.S. Government Printing Office.

Visher, E. B., & Visher, J. S. (1990). Dynamics of successful stepfamilies. *Journal of Divorce and Remarriage, 14,* 3–11.

Warshak, R. A. (1986). Father custody and child development: A review and analysis of psychological research. *Behavioral Sciences and the Law, 4,* 185–202.

Weiss, R. S. (1979). Growing up a little faster: The experience of growing up in a single-parent household. *Journal of Social Issues, 35,* 97–111.

Werner, E. E. (1988). Individual differences, universal needs: A 30-year study of resilient high-risk infants. *Zero to Three: Bulletin of National Center for Clinical Infant Programs, 8,* 1–15.

Werner, E. E. (1993). Risk, resilience, and recovery: Perspectives from the Kauaii Longitudinal Study. *Development and Psychopathology, 54,* 503–515.

Whitbeck, L. B., Simons, R. L., & Goldberg, E. (1996). Adolescent sexual intercourse. In R. L. Simons & Associates (Eds.), *Understanding differences between divorced and intact families: Stress, interaction, and child outcome* (pp. 144–156). Thousand Oaks, CA: Sage.

White, L. (1994). Stepfamilies over the life course: Social support. In A. Booth & J. Dunn (Eds.), *Stepfamilies: Who benefits? Who does not?* (pp. 109–137). Hillsdale, NJ: Erlbaum.

White, L. K., Brinkerhoff, D. B., & Booth, A. (1985). The effect of marital disruption on children's attachment to parents. *Journal of Family Issues, 6,* 5–22.

Wilson, M. I., Daly, M., & Weghorst, S. J. (1980). Household composition and the risk of child abuse and neglect. *Journal of Biosocial Science, 12,* 333–340.

Zill, N. (1988). Behavior, achievement, and health problems among children in stepfamilies. In E. M. Hetherington & J. D. Arasteh (Eds.), *Impact of divorce, single parenting, and stepparenting on children* (pp. 324–368). Hillsdale, NJ: Erlbaum.

Zill, N. Morrison, D. R., & Coiro, M. J. (1993). Long-term effects of parental divorce on parent-child relationships, adjustment, and achievement in young adulthood. *Journal of Family Psychology, 7,* 91–103.

Zimiles, H., & Lee, V. E. (1991). Adolescent family structure and educational progress. *Developmental Psychology, 27,* 314–320.

E. Mavis Hetherington, Margaret Bridges, and Glendessa M. Insabella, Department of Psychology, University of Virginia.

Correspondence concerning this article should be addressed to E. Mavis Hetherington, Department of Psychology, University of Virginia, 102 Gilmer Hall, Charlottesville, VA 22903–2477. Electronic mail may be sent to emh2f@virginia.edu.

Who's In Charge Here?

Parents agree that children today are spoiled. But a rising number are fighting the tendency to indulge and coddle them

By NANCY GIBBS

HERE IS A PARENTING PARABLE FOR OUR AGE. CARLA WAGner, 17, of Coral Gables, Fla., spent the afternoon drinking the tequila she charged on her American Express Gold Card before speeding off in her high-performance Audi A4. She was dialing her cell phone when she ran over Helen Marie Witty, a 16-year-old honor student who was out Rollerblading. Charged with drunken driving and manslaughter, Carla was given a trial date—at which point her parents asked the judge whether it would be O.K. if Carla went ahead and spent the summer in Paris, as she usually does.

That settled it, as far as Mark Marion and Diane Sanchez, also of Coral Gables, were concerned. Their daughter Ariana, then 17, knew Carla, who was described in the local papers as the "poster child for spoiled teens." Ariana too had wanted a sports car for her 16th birthday, not an unreasonable expectation for a girl with a $2,000 Cartier watch whose bedroom had just had a $10,000 makeover. But Ariana's parents had already reached that moment that parents reach, when they wage a little war on themselves and their values and their neighbors and emerge with a new resolve.

Maybe Ariana would just have to wait for a car, they decided, wait until she had finished school and earned good grades and done volunteer work at the hospital. "We needed to get off the roller coaster," says Diane, and even her daughter agrees. "For my parents' generation, to even have a car when you were a teenager was a big deal," Ariana says. "Today, if it's not a Mercedes, it's not special." She pauses. "I think," she observes, "we lost the antimaterialistic philosophy they had... But then, it seems, so did they."

Even their children level the charge at the baby boomers: that members of history's most indulged generation are setting new records when it comes to indulging their kids. The indictment gathered force during the roaring '90s. A TIME/CNN poll finds that 80% of people think kids today are more spoiled than kids

of 10 or 15 years ago, and two-thirds of parents admit that their kids are spoiled. In New York City it's the Bat Mitzvah where 'N Sync was the band; in Houston it's a catered $20,000 pink-themed party for 50 seven-year-old girls who all wore mink coats, like their moms. In Morton Grove, Ill., it's grade school teachers handing out candy and yo-yos on Fridays to kids who actually managed to obey the rules that week. Go to the mall or a concert or a restaurant and you can find them in the wild, the kids who have never been told no, whose sense of power and entitlement leaves onlookers breathless, the sand-kicking, foot-stomping, arm-twisting, wheedling, whining despots whose parents presumably deserve the company of the monsters they, after all, created.

It is so tempting to accept the cartoon version of modern boomer parenting that it is easy to miss the passionate debate underneath it. Leave aside the extremes, the lazy parents who set no bounds and the gifted ones who are naturally wise when it comes to kids. In between you hear the conversation, the unending concern and confusion over where and how to draw the lines. Have we gone too far, given kids more power than they can handle and more stuff than they can possibly need? Should we negotiate with our children or just inform them of the rules? Is $20 too much for lunch money? What chores should kids have to do, and which are extra credit? Can you treat them with respect without sacrificing your authority? Cheer them on without driving them too hard? Set them free—but still set limits?

Some of these are eternal questions. Today's parents may often get the answers wrong, but it's also wrong to say they're not even trying. You don't have to get far into a conversation with parents to hear them wrestling with these issues. And you don't have to look hard to see a rebellion brewing. Just as the wobbling economy of the past year made conspicuous consumption a little less conspicuous, it also gave parents an excuse

HOW ONE FAMILY MANAGES

For all the parenting literature within arm's reach, Natalie and David Bontumasi, who live in the suburbs of Chicago, know that no book can tell them exactly the best way to raise their sons Lucian, 4 and Eliot, 17 months, the journey involves daily—if not hourly—tests of judgment. TIME correspondent Wendy Cole and photographer Steve Liss dropped in on the Bontumasis over four days to chronicle their efforts to do right by their sons. Reluctant to say no too often, graphic designer Natalie and marketing manager David also worry about the costs of being overly permissive. Working for the right balance can be a wearying exercise, even for these most patient of parents.

The Little Lawyer

Lucian tries to cajole his mom and dad to accompany him outside to play.

NATALIE: "I said no, and that should be the final answer."

DAVID: "I had said yes. Now that he's learned to play us off each other, we have to be more careful about what we agree to."

Bathtime Bargaining

Never enthusiastic about getting into the tub, Lucian can usually be talked into it.

NATALIE: "We plan for him to take a bath every night, but sometimes it's not worth the fight. He was so dirty that night, we didn't want to give in."

Tussling over the Telephone

Unable to tune out Eliot's screaming, mom surrenders.

NATALIE: "He shouldn't have the power to prevent me from talking to my mother. This phase just started, and I'm afraid I'll never get to talk on the phone again."

DAVID: "Sometimes I feel like Eliot does, and I want to pull the phone away from her too."

Diversionary Tactic

Against her better judgment, mom lets Lucian rifle through her purse so she can focus on shopping and not on him.

NATALIE: "I regretted it as soon as I let him play with my wallet. He was just as happy later with a twist tie."

DAVID: "I would never give him my wallet. There's got to be something else to give him."

Plaid or Checks?

As the family prepares for church, mom lets Lucian select from two shirts.

NATALIE: "When I give Lucian a choice of what to wear, it keeps him from saying he doesn't want to go. He feels like a participant."

DAVID: "He'd prefer to wear shorts and sandals if we let him, but we want him to look nice."

No Ham, No Way!

Trying to broaden the picky eater's palate is usually futile.

DAVID: "I know he likes it. He's had it before. But I'm disappointed when he doesn't expand his food horizons."

NATALIE: "I'm not really sure he needs to eat that cancer-causing protein."

Nighty Night

Bedtime, the last hurdle of the day, is also the most exhausting.

NATALIE: "I'm hoping for some time to relax before I pass out, but I let him get away with one more stalling tactic. He asks to look at one more thing, and I don't say no."

DAVID: "She's got a much more tiring, demanding day than I have."

to do what they have wanted to do anyway: say no to the $140 sneakers, fire the gardener, have junior mow the lawn. The *Wall Street Journal* calls it the Kid Recession: overall consumer spending rose slightly last year, but it dropped about a third among 8- to 24-year-olds. The *Journal* cited a November survey that found that 12% of kids said their allowance had been cut in recent months, while 16% received fewer gifts.

This is a war waged block by block, house by house. If it is too much to try to battle the forces of Hollywood or Madison Avenue or the Nintendo Corp., at least you can resolve that just because the kids down the street watch unlimited TV doesn't mean your kids should too. You can enforce a curfew, assign some chores and try hard to have dinner together regularly. And then hope that the experts are right when they say that what kids

KEEPING IT SIMPLE

The Rev. John Ohmer knew the parents in his congregation wanted help weaning themselves from the habit of overindulging their children. But as a father of three who has to ration Nintendo in his own home, Ohmer, rector of St. James Episcopal Church in Leesburg, Va., also knew it wasn't as simple as just telling families to buy less. So he revved up what he calls an "underground Christian resistance movement" for parents, offering parish workshops that urged them to make an inventory of their lives and holidays and then imagine the ideal version. Their dreams, it turned out, entailed a lot less Visa debt and a lot more intangible stuff. What they needed to do, he advised, was "build a bridge between the two."

That effort has become a bigger parish hit than bingo. St. James parents like James and Colleen Wheaton now set limits on the number and prices of Christmas gifts for their kids, whether from relatives or from Santa. They use the savings to buy construction material to make more of their own family decorations—together. Ohmer's workshop, says Colleen, "was the first place we could finally legitimize our frustrations."

Across the country, groups with Ohmer's spirit are leading a middle-class exodus out of the 90210 lifestyle. For example, more than 100 U.S. cities today host "simplicity circles" affiliated with the Cornell University–created Seeds of Simplicity program based in Los Angeles. Then there is the Center for a New American Dream, a Takoma Park, Md., group whose motto is "More fun, less stuff!" Says director Betsy Taylor: "This isn't just about unspoiling kids. It's about reclaiming our kids from a toxic commercial culture that has spun out of control."

At St. James last month, parishioner Mary Pellicano talked about the excesses of a "Dragontails" birthday party she and her husband George recently gave for their son Kieran, 4. "All the paraphernalia, the goody bags—it was over the top," Mary recalled. "Then Kieran hinted he'd have been just as happy playing hide-and-seek with a few friends before the cake. I realized I wasn't doing this for him—I was doing it for me! It was just another way of trying to keep up with the new SUV next door."

The night before, a simplicity circle in Silver Spring, Md., brainstormed solutions to the birthday angst. Jennifer Shields, a mother of children ages 3 and 4, said she explicitly asks on party invitations that guests give only art supplies—and she keeps her kids' gift expectations low by making her home TV-free during the day. Shields got applause—but also sparked debate. "We have to raise our kids to confront commercial realities," said Leningber. "We're not Amish."

There was consensus, however, over the Seeds of Simplicity proposal to resurrect household chores. "My kids have friends who have never had to help empty a dishwasher," said Erin Fulham. "Once a week now, my 11-year-old makes dinner, and my eight-year-old does the laundry."

Seeds of Simplicity's other core recommendations include making only planned trips to the mail—so kids view shopping as a more scheduled, less impulsive exercise—and consulting kids about any simplification decisions. Otherwise, says Seeds director Carol Holst, "you'll just have more screaming tantrums in the Toys'R' Us cash-register line."

New American Dream suggests teaching kids money management. Karen Bakuzonis in Gainesville, Fla., was working long hours to pay for extras like a lawn service—though she and her husband have two strapping sons. She has stopped working and has made her boys earn an allowance by doing chores—including the mowing. These days they have to pony up for goodies like Air Jordan sneakers. Bakuzonis says they now "realize how much life costs—and that it's a bit ridiculous to have a limousine take you and your date to a junior high dance," as some classmates recently did.

If that kind of talk sounds subversive, it's meant to: the savvy of the antispoiling movement is its revival of old counterculture instincts—which may be the best way to get the attention of baby-boomer parents.

—By Tim Padgett/Leesburg

mainly need is time and attention and love, none of which takes American Express.

THE HISTORIANS AND PSYCHOLOGISTS HAVE LOTS OF THEORIES about how we got here, but some perennial truths persist: every generation thinks the next one is too slack; every parent reinvents the job. Parenthood, like childhood, is a journey of discovery. You set off from your memories of being a kid, all the blessings, all the scars. You overreact, improvise and over time maybe learn what works; with luck you improve. It is characteristic of the baby boomers to imagine themselves the first to take this trip, to pack so many guidebooks to read along the way and to try to minimize any discomfort.

But a lot about being a millennial parent is actually new, and hard. Prosperity is a great gift, and these are lucky, peaceful times, but in some respects it is more difficult to be a parent now than when our parents were at the wheel. Today's prosperity has been fueled by people working longer hours than ever, and it is especially challenging to parent creatively and well when you're strung out and exhausted. The extended-family structure that once shared the burdens and reinforced values has frayed. Nothing breeds wretched excess like divorced parents competing with each other and feeling guilty to boot. It's not an option, as it once was, to let kids roam free outside after school, bike over to a friend's house, hang out with cousins or

TIME/CNN POLL

■ Are children today more or less spoiled than children 10 or 15 years ago?		■ Are your own children spoiled are not spoiled?*	
		Very/somewhat spoiled	
More	80%	**Not very/not at all spoiled**	68%
Less	3%		
About the same	15%		32%
■ Do children today have to do fewer or more chores?		■ Are your children exposed to too much advertising when it comes to toys and games they might buy?*	
Fewer	75%		
More	9%		
About the same	13%	**Too much advertising**	71%
		Too little	3%
		About the right amount	25%

From a telephone poll of 1,015 adult Americans taken on July 17-18 for TIME/CNN by Harris Interactive. Sampling error is ±3.1%.
*Asked of 351 parents. Sampling error is ±5.2%.

grandparents. The streets are not safe and the family is scattered, so kids are often left alone, inside, with the TV and all its messages.

Advertising targets children as never before, creating cravings that are hard to ignore but impossible to satisfy. These days $3 billion is spent annually on advertising that is directed at kids—more than 20 times the amount a decade ago. Nearly half of all U.S. parents say their kids ask for things by brand names by age 5. "I might mention to a child that the dress she is wearing is cute," says Marci Sperling Flynn, a preschool director in Oak Park, Ill., "and she'll say, 'It's Calvin Klein.' Kids shouldn't know about designers at age 4. They should be oblivious to this stuff."

Children have never wielded this much power in the marketplace. In 1984 children were estimated to influence about $50 billion of U.S. parents' purchases; the figure is expected to approach $300 billion this year. According to the Maryland-based Center for a New American Dream, which dispenses antidotes for raging consumerism, two-thirds of parents say their kids define their self-worth in terms of possessions; half say their kids prefer to go to a shopping mall than to go hiking or on a family outing; and a majority admit to buying their children products they disapprove of—products that may even be bad for them—because the kids said they "needed" the items to fit in with their friends.

Peer pressure can hit lower-income families especially hard. George Valadez, a hot-dog and beer vendor at Chicago's Wrigley Field, has sole custody of his three young kids. His concept of being a good provider is to pour every spare cent into them. The family's two-bedroom apartment is crammed with five television sets, three video-game consoles and two VCRs. Next month his kids want to attend a church camp in Michigan that costs $100 a child. So two weeks ago, abandoning their custom of giving away outgrown clothes and toys to neighbors, the family held its first yard sale to raise cash.

Technology also contributes to the erosion of parental authority. Video games are about letting kids manipulate reality, bend it to their will, which means that when they get up at last from the console, the loss of power is hard to handle. You can't click your little brother out of existence. Plus, no generation has had access to this much information, along with the ability to share it and twist it. Teenagers can re-create themselves, invent a new identity online, escape the boundaries of the household into a very private online world with few guardrails. As Michael Lewis argues in his new book, *Next: The Future Just Happened*, a world in which 14-year-olds can manipulate the stock market and 19-year-olds can threaten the whole music industry represents a huge shift in the balance of power.

In some ways the baby boomers were uniquely ill equipped to handle such broad parenting challenges. So eager to Question Authority when they were flower children, the boomers are reluctant to exercise it now. "This is overly harsh, overly cynical, but there's a reason why the baby-boom generation has been called the Me generation," says Wade Horn, a clinical child psychologist and President Bush's assistant secretary for family support at the Department of Health and Human Services. "They spent the 1950s being spoiled, spent the 1960s having a decade-long temper tantrum because the world was not precisely as they wanted it to be, spent the 1970s having the best sex and drugs they could find, the 1980s acquiring things and the 1990s trying to have the most perfect children. And not because they felt an obligation to the next generation to rear them to be healthy, well-adjusted adults, but because they wanted to have bragging rights."

That's the baby-boomer indictment in a nutshell, but there's a more benign way to interpret this generation's parenting. Those who grew up with emotionally remote parents who rarely got right down on the floor to play, who wouldn't think of listening respectfully to their six-year-old's opinions or explain why the rules are what they are, have tried to build a very different bond with their children. They are far more fluent in the language of emotional trauma and intent on not repeating their parents' mistakes. What's more, having prolonged childhoods, many parents today identify powerfully with their kids. But as Horn notes, "It's difficult to set limits with your children if your primary goal is to be liked. What parents need to understand is that their primary job is being a parent, not being their kids' friend."

It is a natural, primitive instinct to want to make your child happy and protect him from harm or pain. But that instinct, if not tempered, also comes with a cost. Adolescents can't learn to become emotionally resilient if they don't get any practice with frustration or failure inside their protective cocoons. Sean Stevenson, a fifth-grade teacher in Montgomery County, Md., says parents always say they want discipline and order in the classroom, but if it's their child who breaks the rules, they want an exemption. "They don't want the punishment to be enforced," says Stevenson. "They want to excuse the behavior. 'It's something in the child's past. Something else set him off. He just needs to be told, and it won't happen again.'"

In September, Harvard psychologist Dan Kindlon, co-author of the best-selling 1999 book *Raising Cain*, will publish *Too Much of a Good Thing: Raising Children of Character in an Indulgent Age*, in which he warns parents against spoiling their children either materially or emotionally, against trying to make kids' lives perfect. Using the body's immune system as a metaphor, Kindlon argues, "The body cannot learn to adapt to stress unless it experiences it. Indulged children are often less able to cope with stress because their parents have created an atmosphere where their whims are indulged, where they have always assumed… that they're entitled and that life should be a bed of roses."

The parents Kindlon interviewed expressed the bewilderment that many parents reveal in the face of today's challenging parenting environment. Almost half said they were less strict than their parents had been. And they too, like the parents in the TIME/CNN poll, pleaded overwhelmingly guilty to indulging their children too much. "It's not just a little ironic," Kindlon writes, "that our success and newfound prosperity—the very accomplishments and good fortune that we so desperately desire to share with our children—put them at risk."

SO THE JOB OF PARENTING IS HARDER THAN EVER, PARENTS SAY they don't think they are doing it very well, and lots of people on the sidelines are inclined to agree. But for all the self-doubt, it is still worth asking: Are today's parents really doing such a terrible job? Are kids today actually turning out so bad?

As far as one can register these things, the evidence actually suggests the opposite. Today's teenagers are twice as likely to do volunteer work as teens 20 years ago, they are drinking less, driving drunk less, having far fewer babies and fewer abortions, and committing considerably less violence. Last year math SAT scores hit a 30-year high, and college-admissions officers talk about how tough the competition is to get into top schools because the applicants are so focused and talented. "We have a great generation of young people right under our noses right now," observes Steven Culbertson, head of Youth Service America, a Washington resource center for volunteering, "and nobody knows it."

THE BOOK MONSTER ALERT!

After Dan Kindlon co-wrote the 1999 best seller about modern boys, *Raising Cain*, he suddenly had what so many others suddenly had in the 1990s: bucks. But Kindlon, 48, a Harvard child-psychology professor and family therapist, also had two children—and his clinical concerns about kids got personal. "My kids would do something bratty, like scream about a topping on their pizza," he says, "and I'd worry, 'Am I creating monsters?'"

He says he knows he isn't. Still, researching his new book, *Too Much of a Good Thing: Raising Children of Character in an Indulgent Age* (Talk Miramax Books), led to a tightening of some of his looser parenting policies. "As a family, we are happier for it," he writes. Kindlon thinks there's a lesson in this for a lot of parents. Some of them probably know it at some level: two-thirds of the 1,078 affluent parents he surveyed across the country said they were spoiling their kids. "You usually get underreporting when you ask a question that challenges their child raising that way," he says. "This was surprising."

Kindlon argues that as parents, his fellow baby boomers rely too much on their permissive behavioral values and too little on the antimaterialistic values that shaped their youth. They tend to coddle their children in an effort to insulate them from any discomfort. It's no coincidence, Kindlon suggest, that some educators recently decided that "dodge ball wasn't good (for kids)." Kindlon would never wish World War II or Vietnam on today's children—but he does believe they could use a few character-building lumps, if only from a rubber ball.

—T.P.

Maybe this is some kind of uncanny coincidence, that kids are doing this well despite the way they are being raised rather than because of it. Maybe virtue is their form of adolescent rebellion against parents who indulged every vice. Or it could be that the get-down-on-the-floor, consult-the-child, share-the-power, cushion-the-knocks approach isn't entirely wrong-headed. Perhaps those tendencies have done a lot of good for kids, and what's called for is not a reversal but a step back from extremes.

Certainly that is what many parents are starting to do. "I had one over-the-top birthday party for my child, and I'll never do it again," says Carrie Fisher, daughter of Hollywood star Debbie Reynolds and now the mother of nine-year-old Billie. "She got an elephant, and that's all I'll have to say. It will never happen again. I felt like the biggest ass." Fisher had her epiphany when she heard her daughter bragging to a friend, "My swimming pool is bigger than yours." That prompted some new rules. Among other things, Billie has to clean up her room, a change from Princess Leia's own childhood. "I always thought the fairies did it," she says, laughing. "When I moved into my first apartment, I didn't understand how there were rings in the tub and hair in the sink."

Miami interior decorator Nury Feria, the mother of two teenagers, launched her own little crusade within her job as a designer of children's bedrooms. She was finding herself creating rooms that were more like separate apartments. "Large-screen TVs, computers with individual Internet access, refrigerators, sound systems, video-game centers, leather sofas—the only thing missing was a pool," she says. "I realized that as the designer, I'm also supposed to help shape the lifestyle of the kids, and I didn't like a lot of what I was doing in that regard." So she began subtly trying to guide her clients away from certain amenities, advising some parents to scale back on the queen-size beds for seven-year-old girls or the themed bathrooms that rivaled the Small World ride at Disney World.

Despite incessant requests for a Nintendo system by her twin nine-year-old boys, one mom says she compromises by renting a Nintendo console from Blockbuster a few times a year for $30 each time. "It costs me more to do this, and we could afford to buy it. But I don't want video games in my house all the time. This is our compromise," she says. "My boys are the type to sit there with it all the time."

DAWN MAYNARD, 44, IS A PERSONAL trainer AND THE MOTHER of two boys, 14 and 15. An immigrant from Guyana, she lives in Bethesda, Md., and admits that she spoils her sons with electronics, even though she wishes she didn't. Still, she sees the war being fought all around her and counts the ways she has not surrendered. Some neighbors rented their son a limo to go to the prom. It seated 24. "My kids are in a county-run math camp that costs less than $200 for the entire three weeks. My sons' best friend is at golf camp for $4,000. I'm always fighting peer pressure with my sons."

All parents have to navigate these social, commercial and psychic pressures; it is how they respond that sets them apart. Many parents talk about this as the great struggle of their households. They find themselves quietly shedding old friends when they diverge over discipline; they shop online to avoid the temptation their kids face up and down the endless aisles; they attend workshops and buy books to help bolster their resolve. If you

doubt the guerrilla war, just check in with groups like the Center for a New American Dream: three years ago its website had fewer than 15,000 hits a month; today it gets more than 1.5 million.

Parents joke about looking for other "Amish" parents who will reinforce the messages they are trying to send. "Family dating" is an art form all its own, a feat of social chemistry that makes being 25 and single seem easy. In some circles family dating is still driven by traditional hierarchies of status and class, or off-hours' professional networking, or a shared love of sailing or baseball. But for today's concerned parents, it is increasingly driven by values, by sharing a general worldview on everything from TV watching to candy distribution to curfews. Otherwise, time spent together is just too stressful and explosive.

Of course, families engaged in a rollback still have to live in a world where plenty of other children are overindulged. If you live next door to such a kid, or he's thrown together with yours at school or soccer, it can be a challenge always to be explaining why Johnny gets to have marshmallows for breakfast and your kids don't. But the rules send your kids a message all their own, beyond the fact that marshmallows rot their teeth. The rules are a constant reminder that Mom and Dad care, that the kids' health is important to you, that kids are not home alone. And most of all, that it's O.K. to be different.

Parents who give up and back off leave their children at the mercy of a merciless culture. The ones who stand firm and stay involved often find their families grow closer, their kids stronger from being exposed to the toxins around them and building resistance to them. Ariana Marion ended up getting her car. She graduated with honors in June and heads to Wellesley in the fall. "There's a part of us that says we've still given them too much," says her mother Diane, "that wants to take them to live on a farm for a few years and drive a tractor. But we definitely feel we did the right thing by making her earn the car, by making her wait. And the best thing for us as parents was to learn that she was the kind of girl, and now woman, who could step up to the challenge."

—With reporting by Melissa August/Washington, Wendy Cole/Chicago, Lina Lofaro/New York, Tim Padgett/Miami, Jeffrey Ressner/Los Angeles and Rebecca Winters/New York

American Child Care Today

Sandra Scarr

University of Virginia and KinderCare Learning Centers, Inc.

Child care has 2 purposes: mothers' employment and children's development. These are conflicting goals, because the first focuses on the quantity and affordability of child care whereas the second favors expensive quality services. Affordable child care fosters maternal employment and gender equality. With welfare reform demanding more child-care places to move mothers from welfare to work, the pressure for larger quantities of child care is great. Demanding regulations raise the quality of care and give more assurance of children's well-being, but they also increase the cost. More expensive regulations price more working parents out of licensed care and force them to use unregulated home care. Widely varying qualities of child care have been shown to have only small effects on children's current development and no demonstrated long-term impact, except on disadvantaged children, whose homes put them at developmental risk. Parents have far greater impact on their children's development through both the genes and environments they provide. Thus, greater quantities of affordable, regulated child care may be possible.

Care of American children by anyone other than their own mothers needs to have a name. Even care of children by their own fathers is counted by the U.S. Labor Department as "other relative care." Cultural anxiety about nonmaternal child care is revealed in every aspect of research, practices, and policies that are reviewed in this article.

Terms for the care of children by people other than mothers include *child care, family day care, home care, center care, nanny care, babysitting, preschool education, after-school care,* and others. *Day care* is probably the most frequently used term, although early childhood professionals prefer the term *child care,* because "we take care of *children,* not *days*" (M. Guddemi, personal communication, July 6, 1996). Different terms relate to the age of the child (infant, toddler, preschool or school age), the setting (e.g., home versus center), and the primary purpose (babysitting, when the focus is on working mothers' needs, versus preschool education, when the focus is on benefits to the

child). The term *child care* is used throughout this article to include all varieties of nonmaternal care of children who reside with their parent(s) or close family members; it excludes foster care and institutional care.

The assumption of all the nomenclature is that child care provided by anyone other than the child's mother deserves special notice, because it is a nonnormative event that needs definition. In fact, shared child care is the normative experience for contemporary American children, the vast majority of whose mothers are employed. More than half the mothers of infants under 12 months of age are in the labor force; three quarters of school-age children's mothers are working (Behrman, 1996).

History of Child Care

Nonmaternal shared child care is, in fact, normative for the human young, both historically and worldwide: "Nonparental care is a universal practice with a long history, not a dangerous innovation representing a major deviation from species-typical and species-appropriate patterns of child care" (Lamb, in press). Exclusive maternal care of infants and young children is a cultural myth of an idealized 1950s, not a reality anywhere in the world either now or in earlier times. Child care has always been shared, usually among female relatives. Until recently, most American children of working parents were cared for by other female relatives, but high rates of female employment have reduced that source of babysitters. What has changed over time and varies cross-nationally is the degree to which child care is bought in the marketplace rather than shared among female relatives.

Today, more American children are cared for by paid providers than by relatives. Relatives have, presumably, some emotional commitment to the health and safety of relatives' offspring; therefore, quality of care was seldom raised as an issue of concern. The predominance of nonrelative care in the last decade has alerted consumers, governments, and the research community to the possibly damaging effects of poor quality care on children's development; the zeitgeist called for critical appraisal of non-maternal care (Scarr, 1985).

In agricultural societies, infants are typically left in the care of siblings, grandmothers, or female neighbors, who are also caring for their own children. In industrialized societies, mothers' employment outside the home has necessitated nonmaternal care of various types. Demand for child care is driven entirely by the economic need for women in the labor force (Lamb, Sternberg, Hwang, & Broberg, 1992), although occasional subgroups, such as upper-class mothers with heavy social schedules, may use extensive nonmaternal child care (Lamb, in press). Tracing historical changes in maternal employment provides a guide to the demand for and use of nonmaternal child care.

Employment Moved Out of the Home and Into the Workplace

Prior to the Industrial Revolution, and in nonindustrial parts of the world today, women are both economically productive workers and primary child caregivers. When employment moved outside the home and into the factory and office, men followed work into new settings, and women generally remained at home, without a direct economic role.

In a correlated development, mothers' roles as knowledgeable caregivers began to be stressed. In the late 19th and early 20th centuries, child rearing was no longer a natural species response but a role that required extensive education and knowledge. Children began to have tender psyches that required maternal attention to develop well. Mothers were given an important emotional role in the home that complemented fathers' economic productivity (Kagan, 1980; Scarr, 1984).

Prior to World War II, few women remained in the labor force after childbearing. The need for industrial workers during the war brought many mothers into factories and offices to replace men away at war. Mothers' employment was culturally sanctioned and supported by the government provision of child-care centers attached to war factories. Mothers, as Rosie the Riveter, took on the many paid work roles that had previously been denied them.

After the war, government and cultural supports for mothers' employment were withdrawn, child-care centers were closed, and mothers were told to go home to make way in the workplace for returning veterans. The birthrate soared and new suburbs were built as federally sponsored highway programs fueled a boom in housing outside of cities. All of this was a direct result of government policy that held as ideal a two-parent family with a working father and a nonworking mother, ensconced in single-family dwelling.

Erroneous predictions about an economic recession after the war, which became instead an economic boom fueled by unfulfilled consumer demand for cars, refrigerators, and housing, left many jobs open to women. Many mothers did not follow official advice to go home, and female employment has grown steadily since. Goods and services that used to be homemade (e.g., clothing, canned goods, and cleaning) came to be increasingly purchased, requiring additional family income. As the divorce rate and single motherhood soared, more mothers needed jobs to support their families. Today most mothers are employed.

In 1995, 62% of mothers with children under six years were employed. This rate was up more than 2% from 1994 and nearly 5% from 1993. Among mothers with children under two years, 58% were working in March 1995, up 4% from 1993 (1996 Green Book, as cited in Hofferth, 1996). The ideal of a nonemployed mother remained strong, however. One legacy for working mothers of the baby-boom generation and beyond is guilt about their employment.

Purposes of Child Care

Three major, often conflicting, purposes for child care create the child-care dilemma we as a society suffer today (Scarr & Weinberg, 1986; Stoney & Greenberg, 1996). First, child care supports maternal employment, which for individual families and for the economy has become a necessity. It is assumed that U.S. working families will pay for their own child-care services. Second, child care serves children's development, which can be enhanced by high-quality early childhood programs, whether or not children's mothers are employed. Again, families are expected to pay for early childhood programs, unless they are poor. Third, child care has been used throughout this century to intervene with economically disadvantaged and ethnic minority children to socialize them to the cultural mainstream. Poor and immigrant children could be fed, immunized, given English language experience, behaviorally trained, given an orderly schedule, and so forth (Scarr & Weinberg, 1986; Stoney & Greenberg, 1996). Taxpayers have paid for these services to the poor.

The roots of child care are in the welfare and reform movements of the 19th century. Day nurseries, which evolved into the child-care centers of today, began in Boston in the 1840s to care for the children of widows and working wives of seamen, two groups of women who had to work outside the home. Reformers, such as Jane Addams, founded day nurseries to care for poor and immigrant children, whose mothers had to work (Scarr & Weinberg, 1986). Preteen school-age children required adult supervision to be safely occupied and kept out of trouble. The primary purpose of day nurseries was to keep children safe and fed while their poor mothers worked. Other benefits, such as early education, were secondary.

By contrast, kindergartens and nursery schools began in the early 20th century to enhance the social development of middle- and upper-class children. For a few hours a week, the children could play with others and experience an enriched learning environment under the tutelage of trained early childhood teachers. Nursery school existed to serve the developmental needs of middle- and upper-class children, whose mothers were not employed (Scarr & Weinberg, 1986).

By the late 1960s, educators and child development researchers recognized the value of nursery schools for poor children, who needed the stimulation and learning opportunities that such early childhood settings afforded children from affluent families. Head Start was designed, in large part, to enhance the learning of poor and minority children—to provide the same kinds of early childhood opportunities that middle-class children had enjoyed for decades. Because many of their mothers were supported by welfare, Head Start could involve mothers in early childhood programs and serve children's developmental needs. As part-day, part-year programs, Head Start did not serve the child-care needs of working mothers.

These three purposes for child care set quite different priorities for the services to be offered and have different assumptions about who will pay for them. Thus, disputes continue about whose goals are to be served by child-care services, who shall pay for them, and what form child care should take. Conflicting advocacy for (a) high-quality, low-cost caregiving, versus (b) high-quality, high-cost, child-centered preschool education, versus (c) intervention and compensation for poor children continues to compete for attention in debates about American child care.

Varieties of Child-Care Arrangements

When the focus is on early childhood education, whether for higher or lower income children, the setting is usually a center or preschool. When the focus is on care while parents work, the setting is often a home. In fact, these distinctions have blurred in recent years, as more and more children move from homes to center-based programs, where they receive both extended care and early education.

Family day care versus center care. Family day-care providers care for children in their own homes. The providers' own children are often included in the mix of children, which can include infants through school-age children who come before and after school. Most family day-care homes accommodate 6 or fewer children and have one caregiver. Some larger homes care for 6 to 20 children and employ aides to assist the family day-care

providers. States generally regulate larger homes. Family day-care homes are for-profit independent providers.

Child-care centers provide group care for children from infancy to school age in age-segregated groups, with smaller ratios of children at younger ages to adults. Facilities vary from church basements to purpose-built centers with specialized spaces and equipment. The most notable differences between homes and centers are educational curricula and staff training, which centers are required to provide and homes are not. Parents prefer center-based care for preschool children and home care for infants and toddlers.

Licensed versus unlicensed care. In all states, child-care centers must be licensed by a state department of social services or its equivalent.[1] Licensure includes regulations on health and safety, ratios of children to adults, group sizes, staff training, and often required play materials. Regular inspections are done semiannually or annually or more frequently if problems have been noted.

Family homes that care for more than six children are usually required to be licensed, although regulations vary considerably from state to state. Most family day-care providers care for fewer than six children and are therefore exempt from any state regulation or inspection. Availability of federal food subsidies to licensed homes, however, has encouraged more family day-care homes to seek licensure or registration. Family day-care homes are rarely visited by state regulators.

Nonprofit versus for-profit centers. In the United States, child-care centers are sponsored by churches, nonprofit community groups, public schools, Head Start, employers, for-profit independent providers, and corporations. Public schools and Head Start serve older preschool children only, whereas other centers usually include younger children as well. Only about half of all centers, however, provide infant care, because the required low ratios of infants to providers make infant care prohibitively expensive.

The mix of public provision and private enterprise in U.S. child care reflects the ambivalence Americans feel about whether child care should be primarily a publicly supported service for children or a business expense for working families (partially offset by tax credits). Should tax dollars be used to supply child care only to poor children, or should all children be eligible for publicly supported child care? Should family day care and privately owned centers profit from the child-care business, or should child care be a nonprofit service (as in Hawaii) like primary education?

Where Are Children Today?

In 1995, there were nearly 21 million children under the age of five years who were not yet enrolled in school. Of these, about 40% were cared for regularly by parents, 21% by other relatives, 31% in child-care centers, 14% in family day-care homes, and 4% by sitters in the child's home. These figures total more than 100% because 9% of children have more than one regular care arrangement, such as enrollment in a part-time preschool program and parental care at home during other hours (Hofferth, 1996). The distribution of center sponsorship is shown in Figure 1.

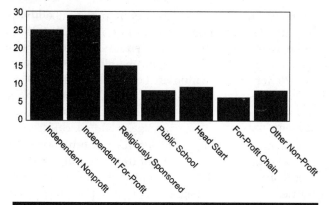

Figure 1
Administrative Auspices of Child-Care Centers (by Percentage) in the United States, 1990 (Willer et al., 1991)

Over the last 30 years, children have been shifted gradually from home to center-based care. In 1965, only 6% of children were cared for in centers; by 1995, 31% were. Use of family day care and care by parents, other relatives, and sitters all declined. Figure 2 shows historical trends in use of different forms of child care. By 1990, in families with employed mothers (three fifths of families with young children), only 37% of infants and 32% of children from one to two years of age were cared for primarily by parents. Of three- to four-year-olds, only 25% were primarily in parental care, and 37% were in child-care centers (Hofferth, 1996).

In surveys by *Working Mother* magazine in 1995 and 1996, readers expressed strong preferences for center-based care over home care, whether by relatives or not. Child safety and parental control over the arrangement were prominent reasons for the preference. Home care is unsupervised and usually unlicensed. Television exposés of abuse and neglect in day-care homes have appeared regularly over the last decade. Relatives do not always abide by parents' child-rearing preferences, such as toilet-training techniques and feeding routines. Paid help is more dependable and controllable. Child-care centers are open even if one caregiver is ill or on vacation (Mason & Kuhlthau, as cited in Mason & Duberstein, 1992).

Relative care is, in general, less costly than other care (Hofferth, 1996). About half of relative care involves payment, but the rates tend to be lower than market rates. Although 23% of parents express a preference for relative care, 77% of mothers prefer another kind of child care (Mason & Kuhlthau, as cited in Mason & Duberstein,

1992). Economic factors play the major role in use of relative care. The more preschool children in the family, the more likely relatives will supply the care, because market discounts for multichild families do not substantially reduce the total cost of child care. The higher the family income, the less likely parents are to choose relative care (Blau & Robbins, 1990).

Older preschool children are more likely than infants and toddlers to be enrolled in center care, but from 1965 to 1995, the use of center care for infants and toddlers grew exponentially, from about 3% in 1965 to 23% in 1993. Parental care of infants and toddlers declined dramatically across that period. School-age care has lagged behind the need for this service and enjoys little public support.

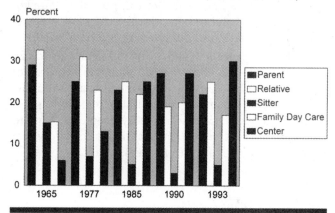

Figure 2
Primary Care for Youngest Preschool Child of Employed Mothers, 1965–1993 (Hofferth, 1996)

Children from more affluent families and those from families on welfare are most likely to be enrolled in centers rather than cared for in homes. Families with an annual income of more than $50,000 can afford center-based programs; those below the poverty line receive subsidies for child care and enroll their children without charge in Head Start. Working families with annual incomes below $25,000 but above the poverty line are the least likely to be able to afford and to use center-based child care.

Nearly 10% of mothers work nonstandard hours; they have fewer choices of child-care arrangements. Only 3% of centers and about 17% of family day-care homes provide evening and weekend care (Hofferth, 1996). In two-parent families, children of evening-shift and weekend workers may be cared for by the other parent or by another relative in the case of single-parent families. Father care is a seldom recognized choice that minimizes costs of child care in a dual-income family.

Presser's data from Detroit suggest that child-care preferences often determine whether mothers work shifts other than 9-to-5. Fully one third of dual-income families have one parent working nonstandard hours to offset child-care costs (Presser, 1992b). When mothers work nights and weekends, and when they have more than one preschool child, fathers are more likely to supply some of the child care. As child-care costs rise, parents are more likely to arrange schedules to provide the care themselves (Mason & Duberstein, 1992).

Much has been said about the shortage of child-care spaces in this country (Hofferth, 1992). With annual increases in the percentage and numbers of working mothers (soon to increase dramatically with welfare reform), the child-care supply is not growing sufficiently to meet the demand for the care of infants and toddlers, of mildly sick children, or of children whose parents work nonstandard hours. Infant and toddler care are scarce nationally; because of low ratio requirements of children to staff, infant and toddler care are very expensive and therefore in particularly short supply. Preschool and after-school care are less costly and more readily available. It is also difficult to find suitable care for disabled children. Even with the Americans With Disabilities Act to encourage nondiscrimination, few facilities can provide competent care for disabled children, particularly those with severe behavior disorders and multiple physical handicaps.

The primary problem is that the market for child care is poorly funded, both by limited parental incomes and by low state subsidies. The price of child care cannot be set high enough in many communities to encourage investment in new facilities or quality programs. Low-income communities have a smaller child-care supply than more affluent ones because of parents' inability to pay for care.

Child-Care Regulations

The 50 states and the District of Columbia display amazing differences in the regulations they have developed to affect cost and quality of child care. Ratios of children to adults in some states (e.g., Maryland, Massachusetts) are less than half of those approved in other states (e.g., Ohio, Texas). Permissible ratios for children under 12 months of age range from 3 to 8 per caregiver. For children ages 12 to 35 months the range among states is from 4 to 13 children per caregiver! Teacher training requirements vary from none (e.g., Georgia, Alabama) to college degrees or advanced credentials (e.g., Illinois, New Jersey). Group sizes permitted for younger children vary from 4 or 6 children, to 20 children, to legally unlimited numbers.

There is a significant cultural and economic gradient from North to South, whereby parents and state regulators in the Northern tier of states demand better quality preschool and child-care programs and are willing to pay more for lower ratios and more highly trained staff. However, in some Northern states with very low ratios and high training requirements, few parents can afford center-based care. Massachusetts, for example, has less than one third the number of child-care center spaces per capita than Texas, a high-ratio, low-training state, has. Low

ratios and teacher training requirements raise the cost of center care to such levels that the vast majority of parents in Massachusetts are forced to use unregulated family day care. By contrast, parents in Texas have the highest provision of center-based programs in the country. The trade-off of quantity and quality in center-based care is a recurring dilemma.

A Labor Force Perspective on Child-Care Research

Despite national ambivalence about maternal employment, the U.S. economy could not function without women employees and entrepreneurs. Today, 48% of workers are women. It is inconceivable that the 80% of these women who are mothers could stay home. Seldom do developmental psychologists consider the economic legitimacy of child care to serve the goal of maternal employment.

There are two major reasons for maternal employment: (a) economic well-being of the family and (b) gender equality (Scarr, 1996). "Child care policies in many countries have been designed at least in part to promote female employment and to equalize potential employment opportunities of men and women" (Lamb, in press).

First and foremost, mothers (and fathers) are employed because their families need or want the income to enhance their standard of living. In today's economy, it is most often a necessity to have two employed parents to support a family with children. Two thirds of mothers are working to keep their families out of poverty (Scarr, Phillips, & McCartney, 1990). With welfare reform, this proportion will increase.

The second reason for maternal employment—to promote economic, social, and political gender equality—is a more complicated issue. The major reason for discrepancies in men's and women's work compensation and career achievements is that family responsibilities fall more heavily on women, especially when there are small children in the home (Scarr, 1996). Most mothers do not maintain full-time employment or have the same commitment to careers that childless women have or that men have, whether they are fathers or not. Unequal child-care responsibilities lead mothers to be less invested in career development and less motivated to maintain continuous, full-time employment. As several commentators have noted, there cannot be gender equality in the workforce until men take more responsibility for child care. According to Supreme Court Justice Ruth Bader Ginsburg, "Women will not be truly liberated until men take equal care of children. If I had an affirmative action plan to design, it would be to give men every incentive to be concerned about the rearing of children" ("Justice Ginsburg Takes on," 1995, p. A4).

Although mothers in the Western industrialized world have increased their economic activity, the gendered division of responsibility and work involved in child-care provision is still the norm in families with young children. When tested for anxiety about leaving their children in child care, fathers expressed more anxiety than mothers, but when asked to rate how their wives felt about leaving children in care, fathers greatly exaggerated their wives' worries about employment and child care (Deater-Deckard, Scarr, McCartney, & Eisenberg, 1994). By inference, fathers think it is the mother's job to worry more about child care, even today. Men's collective choice of nonparticipation in child care helps to maintain men's privileged position in society and in relation to the market and the state (Leira, 1992; Presser, 1992a).

Child Care and Other Family Supports

One often hears liberal policy analysts yearn for the federal government to provide more family-friendly policies that make balancing work and family life less stressful. Corporations vie each year to be on the *Working Mother* magazine list of the top 100 most family-friendly companies. The world's role models of countries with the most family-friendly policies are the Nordic countries.

Family-friendly government policies in the Nordic countries (Sweden, Norway, Finland, Denmark, and Iceland) help mothers to balance work and family life by granting paid, job-guaranteed maternity and parental leaves, child allowances to supplement family income, and part-time work for mothers when their children are young. Although parental leave and part-time employment opportunities can be used by either fathers or mothers, mothers take more than 95% of the leave time and make up virtually all of the part-time workers.

The collective effect of these family-friendly policies is to increase gender inequality to such an extent that Swedish women earn only half of men's wages (in the United States, women earn 77% of men's wages; "Women's Figures," 1997) and hold virtually none of the top jobs in corporations or universities (Cherlin, 1992; Leira, 1992; Scarr, 1996).

Government policies that support maternal absences from the labor force, such as paid parental leaves and child allowances, make balancing work and family life easier for mothers of young children, but they have long-term deleterious consequences for mothers' careers (Scarr, 1996). Although many admire the Swedish system of extensive supports for working parents, including part-time work opportunities when children are young, Cherlin (1992) cited some of the disadvantages:

> Note that you cannot make Partner in a Stockholm law firm working six hours a day. The cost of the system is that its solutions may impede the ability of well-educated mothers to rise up the managerial and professional hierarchies.... That still leaves the problem that women... may lose

experience and continuity in the labor force and the associated promotions and wage increases. (p. 213)

In the United States, where there are few family supports, mothers are more often employed full-time even when their children are infants, thus maintaining more continuous labor force participation, which leads to career advancement, higher incomes, retirement benefits, and other markers of gender equality. Most mothers want to be employed for a variety of reasons. Women's labor force participation is associated with higher family income, greater personal satisfaction, and more social support. However, the double burdens of home and family also lead to role overload and excessive work hours for young mothers in the United States (Scarr, Phillips, & McCartney, 1989). Although working mothers experience greater time stress and role strain (Staines & Pleck, 1983), they express greater satisfaction with their multiple roles than stay-at-home mothers (Scarr, Phillips, & McCartney, 1989).

Significant problems with child-care arrangements and high child-care costs discourage mothers' labor force participation and can lead to depression and marital problems (Ross & Mirowsky, 1988; White & Keith, 1990). If child-care costs were more reasonable, national surveys show that 10–20% more mothers would return to the labor force after giving birth (Mason & Duberstein, 1992). Child-care problems impair women's long-term earning prospects by limiting their participation in the labor force (Cherlin, 1992; Collins & Hofferth, 1996; Mason & Duberstein, 1992; Scarr, 1996).

Income inequalities between men and women are largely explained by the lower labor force participation of mothers in their childbearing years. In 1995, childless women in their 20s and 30s earned 98% of men's wages ("Women's Figures," 1997). In addition, women are less likely than men to be given advanced training opportunities, promotions, and managerial responsibility because they are perceived to have less commitment to careers (Scarr, 1996). Subsidized child care is the one family-friendly government policy that supports gender equality and women's career achievements.

Welfare Reform, or Why Shouldn't Poor Mothers Work Too?

The idea that mothers should be paid to stay at home with children arose during the 1930s, when widows and a few divorcees needed support to rear their children at least to school age. Aid to Families With Dependent Children (AFDC) was the last in a series of programs that was initiated to accomplish this goal. Support levels were generally low, so that a mother and her children could live at the poverty level, but they were provided with medical insurance, food stamps, often housing and clothing allowances, and social services. Gradually, over the past 50 years, welfare (AFDC) recipients came to be identified with never-married minority women and poor White women who had children in their teens and early 20s and were never employed.

As the majority of middle-class mothers entered the labor force in the 1980s, there was a sea-change in thinking about AFDC. By the early 1990s, the majority of middle-class mothers of infants and young children were employed: two thirds when their children were under six years of age and three quarters by the time their children were school age, with most of these mothers working full-time. Married mothers were working at the same rate as single mothers (Scarr, Phillips, & McCartney, 1989). Public empathy for mothers supported by AFDC to stay home with their children evaporated. Why should the taxes of working mothers go to support poor mothers to enjoy the privilege of staying home with their children? Reform of the welfare system rose to the top of the political agenda and was passed in 1996. Welfare will no longer be an open-ended, lifetime entitlement. It will provide time-limited support in emergencies, but mothers of children over three years of age can expect to be employed. Child-care assistance for low-income mothers is the key to welfare reform, because single low-income mothers cannot pay market rates for child care.

"Workfare Means Day Care"

Child care is the essential ingredient in welfare reform and mothers' employment, as indicated by the above heading taken from a recent *Time* magazine article (1996). State by state, policies are being developed to provide child care to permit poor mothers to work. The major intent is to care for children while their mothers are employed, but what quality of care will be afforded by the states? There are no necessary quality assurances, beyond basic health and safety, in the provision of child care that allows mothers to work. Only when one is concerned about the children's development do other qualities of the child-care experience matter.

The Quality/Cost/Affordability Dilemma

Child care is critical to working parents' well-being (Mason & Duberstein, 1992). The availability and affordability of child care of acceptable quality directly affect parents' ability to manage both work and family life. Location, hours of operation, and flexibility (with respect to rules, mildly ill children, and the like) are major factors in the perceived availability of child care. Many parents find their choices quite limited (Galinsky, 1992).

Cost in relation to family income is the major affordability issue (Scarr, 1992b). As in any market-driven service, quality depends on what consumers are willing and able to pay for child care, which economists refer to as the *cost per quality unit of care* (Mason & Duberstein, 1992;

Morris & Helburn, 1996). Consumers who are able to pay a high price will find someone willing to provide the service. Low-income families struggle to find acceptable quality care at a price they can afford, although they pay a higher percentage of their income for child care (23% versus 6% in high-income families). The trade-off of cost and quality of services is a major dilemma in American child care (Morris & Helburn, 1996).

Accessibility and cost of child care per quality unit are overriding issues in evaluating the impact of child care on parents (Prosser & McGroder, 1992). Ease of access, measured in travel time to a child-care center, directly affects how likely a mother is to stay in the labor force (Collins & Hofferth, 1996). Middle- and upper income mothers are much more likely to keep their jobs if they use formal child-care arrangements (day-care centers) than if they have informal or no stable arrangements. Labor force participation among low-income mothers is more sensitive to the availability of relatives to care for children, because they cannot afford to pay market rates for child care (Collins & Hofferth, 1996).

Absenteeism and Productivity Effects

Mothers with secure child care are absent from work and tardy less often and are more productive in the workplace.

> When child care arrangements break down, employed parents are more likely to be absent, to be late, to report being unable to concentrate on the job, to have higher levels of stress and more stress-related health problems, and to report lower parental and marital satisfaction. (Galinsky, 1992, p. 167)

Breakdowns in child-care arrangements are frequent and stressful; in a Portland, Oregon study, 36% of fathers and 46% of mothers who used out-of-home care reported child-care-related stress. Leading causes of child-care breakdown are child illness and a provider who quits (Galinsky, 1992). The greater the number of child-care arrangements, the more likely they are to break and the greater the parental stress. Stable, reliable child care of acceptable quality is clearly related to mothers returning to work and staying in the labor force; this is especially true of middle- and high-income mothers (Collins & Hofferth, 1996; Phillips, 1992).

A Child Development Perspective on Child-Care Research

Three Waves of Research

The ecology of child-care research has undergone some important changes in the past two decades. Three waves of child-care research have been identified (Belsky, 1984; Clarke-Stewart, 1988; McCartney & Marshall, 1989). In the 1970s, the first wave compared maternal care with any kind of nonmaternal care, without assessment of the quality of either setting in which the care took place. The implicit research question was "How much damage is done to infants and young children by working mothers?" There was no consideration of whether variation in child development depended on variation in kind and quality of care, at home or in other child-care settings.

The second wave examined the quality and variety of child-care settings and introduced the idea that children's responses to child care may be individually different. In the 1980s, many child-care studies actually observed child care in process, evaluated quality of care, and assessed children individually.

The third wave of research included not only proximal influences on the child but distal influences as well. Mc-Cartney and Marshall (1989) suggested the inclusion of three systems to describe a true ecological study of the child-care experience: first, variation of child-care quality and type; second, family characteristics; and, third, individual differences among children. Although considerable attention has been devoted to evaluating child-care settings, characteristics of parents and family settings have seldom been integrated into child-care research.

A special note should be made on child-care-as-intervention with children from low-income and disadvantaged families. The best studied interventions, such as the Carolina Abecedarian Project (Ramey, Bryant, Sparling, & Wasik, 1985), used child care to enrich poor children's lives with positive results both concurrently and into primary school. Children with poor learning opportunities at home and without sufficient emotional support are particularly benefited by early childhood programs (Mc-Cartney, Scarr, Phillips, & Grajek, 1985), and the more intensive the intervention, the better the results (Ramey & Ramey, 1992).

Dimensions of Quality

There is an extraordinary international consensus among child-care researchers and practitioners about what quality child care is: It is warm, supportive interactions with adults in a safe, healthy, and stimulating environment, where early education and trusting relationships combine to support individual children's physical, emotional, social, and intellectual development (Bredekamp, 1989).

Although quality of care is a multifaceted concept, the most commonly used measures of center quality are remarkably similar in the dimensions of quality they stress and in their measurement characteristics (Scarr, Eisenberg, & Deater-Deckard, 1994). Determinations of child-care quality are based on a number of criteria, but the most commonly agreed on are health and safety requirements, responsive and warm interaction between staff

and children, developmentally appropriate curricula, limited group size, age-appropriate caregiver: child ratios, adequate indoor and outdoor space, and adequate staff training in either early childhood education or child development (Bredekamp, 1989; Kontos & Fiene, 1987). Caregivers with specific training in child care and child development provide more sensitive and responsive care than do those without such training. In sum, the quality of child care is affected by lower ratios, smaller group sizes, and better qualified teachers (Cost, Quality, and Child Outcomes Study Team, 1995; Scarr, Eisenberg, & Deater-Deckard, 1994; Whitebook, Howes, & Phillips, 1991).

Staff turnover is another common measure of the quality of care. High turnover means that children have fewer opportunities to develop stable, affectionate relationships with caregivers. Stability of care appears to be especially important for infants and toddlers who display more appropriate social behaviors in stable than in unstable care arrangements (Howes & Stewart, 1987; Suwalsky, Zaslow, Klein, & Rabinovich, 1986). Recently, a tri-state study has shown that quality of care is more closely related to teacher wages than to other structural center-care variables (Phillips, Mekos, Scarr, McCartney, & Abbott-Shim, in press; Scarr, Eisenberg, & Deater-Deckard, 1994).

Variations in Quality of Care

Few experienced observers would doubt that center quality in the United States varies from excellent to dreadful and is, on average, mediocre (Cost, Quality, and Child Outcomes Study Team, 1995; Hofferth, Brayfield, Deich, & Holcomb, 1991; National Institute of Child Health and Human Development [NICHD] Early Child Care Research Network, 1996; Scarr, Phillips, McCartney, & Abbott-Shim, 1993). Quality in child-care centers is measured, by observation and interview, in units that are regulated (such as ratios of teachers to children, group sizes, and teacher training) and in dimensions that are process-oriented (such as adult–child interactions and developmentally appropriate activities; Phillips, 1987). In European studies, child-care quality also varies but not as dramatically as in the United States (Lamb, Sternberg, Hwang, & Broberg, 1992).

Family day-care homes have seldom been studied, and those that have been sampled may not be representative of the enormous number of unlicensed, unregulated homes. Studies of family day care have found quality to be highly variable (Galinsky, Howes, Kontos, & Shinn, 1994). In the recent NICHD study (NICHD Early Child Care Research Network, 1996), day-care home quality was, on average, fair to good but again highly variable.

Poor quality child care has been reported to put children's development at risk for poorer language and cognitive scores and lower ratings of social and emotional adjustment (for reviews, see Lamb, in press; Scarr &

Eisenberg, 1993). Studies of center quality and child outcomes, which controlled statistically for family background differences, have found that overall quality has small but reliable effects on language and cognitive development (Goelman & Pence, 1987; McCartney, 1984; Wasik, Ramey, Bryant, & Sparling, 1990), social competence, and social adjustment (McCartney et al., 1997). Parents and caregivers rated children as more considerate, sociable, intelligent, and task-oriented when caregivers engaged in more positive verbal interactions with the children.[2] Other studies have found that children with involved and responsive caregivers display more exploratory behaviors, are more positive (Clarke-Stewart, Gruber, & Fitzgerald, 1994; Holloway & Reichhart-Erickson, 1989), and display better peer relations (Howes, Phillips, & Whitebook, 1992) than children with uninvolved, unresponsive caregivers. The inferences from these findings are not straightforward, however.

Predictably, quality of care selected by parents has been found to be correlated with parents' personal characteristics (Bolger & Scarr, 1995), thereby complicating interpretations of any effects of child care per se. The confound of family and child-care characteristics leads to overestimation of child-care effects that result instead from family differences. For example, children from families with single employed mothers and low incomes were more likely to be found in lower quality care (Howes & Olenick, 1986). Children in high-quality care had parents who were more involved and interested in compliance than parents of children in lower quality care, and behavioral differences were evident in the center. Parents who use more punitive forms of discipline and hold more authoritarian attitudes toward children were found to choose lower quality care for their children (Bolger & Scarr, 1995; Scarr et al., 1993).

In a recent large study, less sensitive mothers who value work more chose poorer quality child care in the infants' first six months, enrolled their infants in centers at earlier ages for more hours per week, and were more likely to have insecurely attached infants (NICHD Early Child Care Research Network, in press). Of course, variations in parents' interactions with their children and in parents' personality, intelligence, and attitudes determine the characteristics that will be transmitted to children genetically as well as environmentally (Scarr, 1992a; 1993). How can these confounds be sorted out?

Many studies statistically covary out measured family characteristics from associations between child care and child outcomes and look at residual associations. When family and child-care qualities are truly confounded, however, it is impossible to covary out all family effects, because one has only a limited set of measures of the families—typically parents' education, income, and occupation, and some personality, cognitive, or attitudinal test scores. Parents who differ on any one of these measures are very likely to differ on many other unmeasured traits that affect associations between child care and child outcomes. Thus, the small, statically reliable associations that have been found between child-care quality and child outcomes are exceedingly difficult to interpret.

Nonmaternal Care

Nonmaternal infant care has been the most controversial issue in the entire child-care research field, but it may soon be laid to rest. Throughout the 1980s and early 1990s, dramatic claims were made about the damaging effects of early entry into "day care" (not defined or measured) on infants' attachments to their mothers (Belsky, 1986, 1988, 1992; Belsky & Rovine, 1988). Reanalyses of data on day care versus "home-reared" infants revealed a slight difference in rates of insecure attachments as measured by the Strange Situation: 37% versus 29% (Clarke-Stewart, 1988, 1989; Lamb, Sternberg, & Prodromidis, 1992). Other measures of attachment showed no relationship to age at entry or amount of infant child care.

Arguments swirled in the public press and developmental literature about whether the results applied only to boys; to infants with insensitive mothers; to infants who experience more than 20, 30, or 35 hours of nonmaternal care a week; or to infants who experience poor quality care (Phillips, McCartney, Scarr, & Howes, 1987). Working mothers were tormented with doubt and guilt (Bowman, 1992). Finally, the NICHD Early Child Care Research Study (NICHD Early Child Care Research Network, in press) of more than 1,000 infants has shown no relationship between age at entry or amount of infant care and attachments as measured by the Strange Situation (for a full review, see Lamb, in press). Naturally, less sensitive, less well-adjusted mothers were much more likely to have insecurely attached infants (NICHD Early Child Care Research Network, in press). Several interaction effects suggested that higher quality care may help to offset poor mothering. Let us hope that is the end of the early child-care controversy.

Lack of Long-Term Effects

Researchers have explored the possible long-term effects of day-care experiences in different qualities of care for children from different kinds of backgrounds. Children from low-income families are definitely benefited by quality child care, which has been used as an intervention strategy (Field, 1991; Ramey et al., 1985; Ramey & Ramey, 1992). Poor children who experience high-quality infant and preschool care show better school achievement and socialized behaviors in later years than similar children without child-care experience or with experience in lower quality care. For poor children, quality child care offers learning opportunities and social and emotional supports that many would not experience at home.

For children from middle- and upper income families, the long-term picture is far less clear. With a few exceptions that can be explained by the confounding of family with child-care characteristics in the United States, research results show that the impact on development from poorer versus better care within a broad range of safe environments is small and temporary. Given the learning opportunities and social and emotional supports that their homes generally offer, child care is not a unique or lasting experience for these children.

Long-term effects of day-care quality were reported in longitudinal studies by Vandell Henderson, and Wilson (1988) and by Howes (1988). The former researchers reported that children who attended better quality day-care centers in the preschool period were better liked by their peers and exhibited more empathy and social competence at age eight than children form poorer quality preschool centers. Howes found that after controlling for the effects of some family characteristics, good school skills and few behavior problems were predicted by high-quality care for both boys and girls. However, age at entry and amount of day care were not related to later academic achievement or to social behaviors, so that one suspects the family effects, confounded with child-care quality (Bolger & Scarr, 1995), accounted for the long-term results.

In contrast to the U.S. findings, the results of two longitudinal studies conducted in Sweden indicated that early age of entry into day care was associated with better school performance and positive teacher ratings from childhood to early adulthood (Andersson, 1989; Hartmann, 1995). Of the many differences in family background that could be only partially controlled, early entrants into child care had better educated mothers who returned to work earlier than less achieving mothers. Again, one suspects that unmeasured family effects account for the long-term positive effects of child care in the Swedish study, as they did for negative effects in the U.S. studies.

A more thorough Swedish study (Broberg, Hwang, & Chace, 1993) reported no long-term effects of differences in child-care environments on children's adjustments or achievement at eight to nine years of age. It should be noted, however, that Sweden's uniformly high-quality child-care centers (Hennessy & Melhuish, 1991) do not really test for the effects of poor child care on later development.

No effects of quality of preschool care on school-age development were also reported in a Dutch retrospective study (Goosens, Ottenhoff, & Koops, 1991). However, there was very little variance in the measure of quality in this study, which may account for that finding.

Four Studies of Long-Term Impact of Varied Child-Care Quality

Study 1. In a large U.S. study of highly varied child-care centers (McCartney et al., 1997; Scarr et al., 1993), 720 young children (ages 12 to 60 months) who were enrolled in 120 child-care centers in three states were evaluated for

social adjustment. Quality of care in the centers and family characteristics were used to predict differences in parents' and teachers' ratings of children's adjustment and observations of social behaviors.

Both structural (e.g., staff to child ratios, teachers' wages, education, training) and process (interactions, programs) measures were used to evaluate quality of care in the centers. Family structural characteristics (e.g., income, educational levels, race, number of children) and processes (e.g., parenting stress, work—family interference, parental attitudes, separation anxieties) represented family effects. Children's own characteristics of age, gender, and child-care history were also used to predict adjustment and social behavior. Thus, center-care quality, family, and child characteristics were jointly used to predict children's social adjustment and social behaviors.

Results showed substantial effects of child and family characteristics on both teachers' and parents' ratings of children's adjustment and social behaviors and very small, but statistically reliable, effects of quality of child care on social adjustment ratings. In a four-year follow-study of 141 children, Deater-Deckard, Pinkerton, and Scarr (1996) reported no longer-term effects of differences in quality of preschool child care on these school-age children's social, emotional, or behavioral adjustment.

Study 2. A study of day-care centers in Bermuda (McCartney, 1984; McCartney et al., 1985; Phillips, McCartney, & Scarr, 1987) emphasized the importance of quality care for infants, toddlers, and preschool children. The major question addressed longitudinally was whether or not the effects of differences in quality of child care in the preschool years continue to be seen at ages five through nine years.

In a follow-up study (Chin-Quee & Scarr, 1994), teacher ratings of social competence and academic achievement were obtained from 127 of the children at ages five, six, seven, and eight years. In hierarchical and simultaneous regressions, family background characteristics, not child-care amounts or qualities, were found to be predictive of social competence and academic achievement in the primary grades. By the school-age years, the effects of infant and preschool child-care experiences were no longer influential in children's development, but family background continued to be important.

Study 3. In another longitudinal study in Bermuda (Scarr, Lande, & McCartney, 1989), the child-care experiences of 117 children, who had been assessed for cognitive and social development at two and four years of age, were examined for long-term effects. At 24 months of age, children in center-based care, where the ratio of infants to caregivers was 8:1, had poorer cognitive and language development than children in family day care or at home with their mothers (who did not differ from each other). These results persisted after controlling for maternal education, IQ, income, and occupational status. However, at 42 to 48 months, no differences were found between children in center care and other children.

Study 4. In Bermuda, an islandwide screening, assessment, and treatment program was implemented to help children with developmental problems (Scarr, McCartney, Miller, Hauenstein, & Ricciuti, 1994). Child-care histories were also ascertained. Two samples were studied: a population sample of 1,100 Bermudian children and a small subsample of children, most of whom were determined to be at risk for developmental problems.

To assess the effects of maternal employment (Scarr & Thompson, 1994), infants with mothers who worked 20 or more hours a week were compared with infants with mothers who worked less than 20 hours a week. To address the effects of entry into nonmaternal care before the age of one, infants who were placed in regular nonmaternal care before the age of one were compared with infants who did not experience regular nonmaternal care before the age of one. Teacher ratings of social competence and academic achievement were obtained for the children at ages five, six, seven, and eight years.

Results revealed that family background variables frequently predicted child social competence and academic achievement measures in both samples. After controlling for family characteristics, no differences in school-age outcomes were found between children whose mothers worked 20 or more hours a week when they were infants and children with mothers who worked less than 20 hours a week in either sample. In addition, age of entry into nonmaternal care before the age of one did not significantly predict any child outcome measures.

Conclusions

In studies in Sweden and Holland, in a large study of child-care centers in the United States, and in three separate studies in Bermuda, differences in child-care experience, both qualitative and quantitative, did not have persistent effects on children's development. In these studies, child-care centers in Bermuda and the United States included both good- and poor-quality care, whereas centers in Sweden and Holland included only good-quality care. Research to date on quality differences does not show a major impact on the development of children from ordinary homes. These results may differ for the children from socioeconomically disadvantaged homes, for whom quality child-care programs may supply missing elements in their lives.

Public Policy and the Quality/Cost Trade-Off

Quality/Cost/Affordability Trade-Off

In general, higher quality child care costs more than lower quality care. Fifty to seventy percent of the cost is in staff salaries, and higher quality centers spend propor-

tionately more on labor (Morris & Helburn, 1996). For example, center-based child care costs twice as much in Massachusetts, which has among the most demanding regulations in the United States, as in Georgia, which has more lenient regulations. In a study of 120 centers in three states, centers in Massachusetts had higher quality care, on average, than those in Georgia, but comparisons of costs of living and incomes showed that families in Massachusetts are economically disadvantaged by the high cost of child care (Hancock, Eisenberg, & Scarr, 1993). Whereas the 1990 media family income for Georgia parents who used center-based care was $50,000, in Massachusetts the median income of families who could afford center care was nearly $80,000. Massachusetts families with an annual income of less than about $60,000 were unable to afford state-regulated quality care.

The more stringent the child-care regulations, the less licensed child care will be available and the more families will be forced to use unregulated care for their children. When regulations become so stringent that most families are priced out of the regulated child-care market, one has to wonder about the wisdom of having such expensive regulations.

Unfortunately, regulations have only tangential effects on the actual quality of care. States cannot legislate warm, sensitive interactions or rich learning opportunities provided by talented teachers. Aside from safety and health considerations, which can be effectively regulated, observed quality of child care is correlated only .30 to .40 with regulated variables, such as ratios and teacher qualifications (Scarr, Eisenberg, & Deater-Deckard, 1994). Therefore, regulations directly produce higher costs but only indirectly improve quality of care.

In addition, parents may not agree that quality defined by professionals is what they want or are willing to pay for in the child care they choose (Cost, Quality, and Child Outcomes Study Team, 1995; Haskins, 1992). Whereas early childhood professionals value discovery learning and hands-on experience, many working class and more traditional parents prefer structured learning and direct instruction for their preschool children. Individual attention to each child requires more staff than a classroom organized for group instruction. Lower ratios equal higher staff costs, which some parents are not willing to support, especially if the program is not what they want anyway.

States should examine the cost:benefit ratio of their regulations and their impact on making child care affordable, available, and of sufficient quality to support good child development without driving most families into the underground market of unregulated care. Surely, we all expect state regulations to protect children and to assure them a supportive environment in child care. That is the minimum government responsibility. Given the wide variation in regulations among the states, however, it should be possible to examine the benefits of greater and lesser costs of child care.

Equity in Child Care

In the United States, a two-tier system is evolving—a higher quality one for both affluent families and the poor, who get public support for child care, and a lower quality one for middle- and lower income working families, who cannot pay for high-quality care (Maynard & McGinnis, 1992; Whitebook et al., 1991). In my opinion and in that of many other child advocates, public support for child care should make quality services available to all children of working families.

To make this dream a reality, we must spend tax moneys efficiently. Government-provided services are the least-cost-effective means to provide quality child care. Compare Head Start expenditures per child with those of a typical child-care center with excellent early educational programs. Head Start spends approximately $5,000 per child annually for part-day (typically three to four hours), part-year (public school calendar) programs.3 For exactly the same amount of money, the government could give poor parents vouchers to purchase quality child care and education in full-day, full-year child-care programs (Cost, Quality, and Child Outcomes Study Team, 1995). Another benefit of vouchers is the reduction in socioeconomic segregation, which results from programs that only poor children may attend. In most nonprofit and for-profit centers, between 5% and 40% of the children are on child-care assistance, whereas in Head Start centers, nearly 100% of the children are on child-care assistance.

Edward Zigler (Zigler & Finn-Stevenson, 1996) has proposed that public schools, well-entrenched institutions in all communities, be used to implement child-care services for preschool children (not infants or toddlers). With varying mixes of federal, state, local, and private funding, including parental fees, Zigler has prompted more than 400 schools to incorporate child care in their educational programs. Public schools can be one mechanism to increase the child-care supply for older children, but critics complain that most schools need to focus exclusively on improving their existing educational programs, which international surveys show to be of poor quality.

States are currently setting child-care reimbursement rates under the new welfare reform legislation. If they are pressured to serve more children, their rates will be too low to give poor parents access to quality care. If they set rates high enough to give poor parents access to quality care, they may not be able to serve all eligible families. Inadequate funding drives states to make Solomonic choices.

Whither Child Care in America?

Repeatedly, international research results have shown only small concurrent effects of child care on children's development and no evidence for long-term effects, un-less the children are seriously disadvantaged. Observation about the small effects on children of differences in quality of care can be enhanced beyond their practical importance by liberal politicians and child advocates, who may demand high-quality child care regardless of cost. Conservatives, however, will ask the logically obvious question: What is the minimal expense for child care that will allow mothers to work and not do permanent damage to children? Conservative politicians will find the research results conveniently permissive of mediocre quality. Mediocre is not the same as deleterious, unsafe, and abusive care, however, and there is some of that in the United States that must be eliminated. Government standards that prevent terrible care are essential for our nation's well-being.

Debates about welfare reform, working mothers, and child care reflect broad societal conflicts about women, families, and children.

- Is child care in America primarily meant to serve the needs of working parents, with little regard for the education of preschoolers, especially disadvantaged children?

- Will nonwelfare working families have to pay for the child care they need, discouraging many women from entering the labor force, or will the public decide that, like primary education, child care is a public service that deserves broad taxpayer support?

- Will regulations on licensed care be made so expensive that most parents will be priced out of the center-care market and forced to use unregulated care in homes? Or, will state regulations be so lax that American child care will be little better than custodial warehousing?

In summary, I hope the United States will decide that child care is both an essential service for working families and an important service to America's children, especially to the poorest among them. Governments have the responsibility to make child care affordable for all working parents and to regulate child care to assure that children are afforded opportunities to develop emotionally, socially, and intellectually. Regardless of who their parents are, children are the next generation for all of us.

NOTES

1. In 11 states, church-sponsored child care is exempt from all but health and safety licensure.
2. Paradoxically, in one study, children's social adjustment was positively related to poorer quality care, but this finding has not been replicated and is probably sample-specific (Phillips, McCartney, & Scarr, 1987).
3. Costs of medical, dental, and social service programs are additional.

REFERENCES

Andersson, B. E. (1989). Effects of public day care—A longitudinal study. *Child Development, 60,* 857–866.

Behrman, R. E. (Ed.). (1996). Financing child care. *The Future of Children, 6*(2).

Belsky, J. (1984). Two waves of day care research: Developmental effects and conditions of quality. In R. C. Ainslie (Ed.), *The child and the day care setting* (pp. 24–42). New York: Praeger.

Belsky, J. (1986). Infant day care: A cause for concern? *Zero to Three. 6,* 1–9.

Belsky, J. (1988). The "effects" of infant day care reconsidered. *Early Childhood Research Quarterly, 3,* 235–272.

Belsky, J. (1992). Consequences of child care for children's development: A deconstructionist view. In A. Booth (Ed.), *Child care in the 1990s: Trends and consequences* (pp. 83–94). Hillsdale, NJ: Erlbaum.

Belsky, J., & Rovine, M. J. (1988). Nonmaternal care in the first year of life and the infant–parent attachment. *Child Development, 59,* 157–167.

Blau, D. M., & Robbins, P. K. (1990, April). *Child care demand and labor supply of young mothers over time.* Paper presented at the annual meeting of the Population Association of America, Toronto. Ontario, Canada.

Bolger, K. E., & Scarr, S. (1995). Not so far from home: How family characteristics predict child care quality. *Early Development and Parenting, 4*(3), 103–112.

Bowman, B. (1992). Child development and its implications for day care. In A. Booth (Ed.), *Child care in the 1990s: Trends and consequences* (pp. 95–100). Hillsdale, NJ: Erlbaum.

Bredekamp, S. (1989, November). *Measuring quality through a national accreditation system for early childhood programs.* Paper presented at the annual meeting of the American Educational Research Association, San Francisco, CA.

Broberg, A. G., Hwang, C. P., & Chace, S. V. (1993, March). *Effects of day care on elementary school performance and adjustment.* Paper presented at the biennial meetings of the Society for Research in Child Development, New Orleans, LA.

Cherlin, A. (1992). Infant care and full-time employment. In A. Booth (Ed.), *Child care in the 1990s: Trends and consequences* (pp. 209–214). Hillsdale, NJ: Erlbaum.

Chin-Quee, D., & Scarr, S. (1994). Lack of longitudinal effects of infant and preschool child care on school-age children's social and intellectual development. *Early Development and Parenting, 3* (2), 103–112.

Clarke-Stewart, A. (1988). The "effects" of infant day care reconsidered: Risks for parents, children, and researchers. *Early Childhood Research Quarterly, 3,* 293–318.

Clarke-Stewart, K. A. (1989). Infant day care: Maligned or malignant? *American Psychologist, 44,* 266–273.

Clarke-Stewart, K. A., Gruber, C. P., & Fitzgerald, L. M. (1994). *Children at home and in day care.* Hillsdale, NJ: Erlbaum.

Collins, N., & Hofferth, S. (1996, May). *Child care and employment turnover.* Paper presented at the annual meeting of the Population Association of America, New Orleans, LA.

Cost, Quality, and Child Outcomes Study Team. (1995). *Cost, quality and child outcomes in child care centers* (Public Report, 2nd ed.) Denver: University of Colorado at Denver, Economics Department.

Deater-Deckard, K., Pinkerton, R., & Scarr, S. (1996). Child care quality and children's behavioral adjustment: A four-year longitudinal study. *Journal of Child Psychology & Psychiatry, 37*(8), 937–948.

Deater-Deckard, K., Scarr, S., McCartney, K., & Eisenberg, M. (1994). Paternal separation anxiety: Relationships with parenting stress, child-rearing attitudes, and maternal anxieties. *Psychological Science, 5*(6), 341–346.

Field, T. (1991). Quality infant day-care and grade school behavior and performance. *Child Development, 62,* 863–870.

Galinsky, E. (1992). The impact of child care on parents. In A. Booth (Ed.), *Child care in the 1990s: Trends and consequences* (pp. 159–171). Hillsdale, NJ: Erlbaum.

Galinsky, E., Howes, C., Kontos, S., & Shinn, M. (1994). *The study of children in family child care and relative care.* New York: Families and Work Institute.

Goelman, H., & Pence, A. R. (1987). Effects of child care, family and individual characteristics on children's language development: The Victoria Day Care Research Project. In D. Phillips (Ed.), *Quality in child care: What does research tell us? Research monographs of the National Association for the Education of Young Children* (pp. 43–56). Washington, DC: National Association for the Education of Young Children.

Goosens, F. A., Ottenhoff, G., & Koops, W. (1991). Day care and social outcomes in middle childhood: A retrospective study. *Journal of Reproductive and Infant Psychology, 9,* 137–150.

Hancock. T., Eisenberg, M., & Scarr, S. (1993, March). *Cost of child care and families' standard of living.* Paper presented at the biennial meetings of the Society for Research in Child Development, New Orleans, LA.

Hartmann, E. (1995). *Long-term effects of day care and maternal teaching on educational competence, independence and autonomy in young adulthood.* Unpublished manuscript, University of Oslo, Oslo, Norway.

Haskins, R. (1992). Is anything more important than day-care quality? In A. Booth (Ed.), *Child care in the 1990s: Trends and consequences* (pp. 101–115). Hillsdale, NJ: Erlbaum.

Hennessy, E., & Melhuish, E. C. (1991). Early day care and the development of school-age children: A review. *Journal of Reproductive and Infant Psychology, 9,* 117–136.

Hofferth, S. (1992). The demand for and supply of child care in the 1990s. In A. Booth (Ed.), *Child care in the 1990s: Trends and consequences* (pp. 3–25). Hillsdale, NJ: Erlbaum.

Hofferth, S. (1996). Child care in the United States today. *The Future of Children: 6*(2), 41–61.

Hofferth, S., Brayfield, A., Deich, S., & Holcomb, P. (1991). *National child care survey 1990.* Washington, DC: The Urban Institute.

Holloway, S. D., & Reichhart-Erickson, M. (1989). Child care quality, family structure, and maternal expectations: Relationship to preschool children's peer relations. *Journal of Applied Developmental Psychology, 4,* 99–107.

Howes, C. (1988). Relations between early child care and schooling. *Developmental Psychology, 24,* 53–57.

Howes, C., & Olenick, M. (1986). Family and child care influences on toddlers' compliance. *Child Development, 57,* 202–216.

Howes, C., Phillips, D. A., & Whitebook, M. (1992). Thresholds of quality: Implications for the social development of children in center-based child care. *Child Development, 63,* 449–460.

Howes, C., & Stewart, P. (1987). Child's play with adults, toys, and peers: An examination of family and child-care influences. *Developmental Psychology, 23,* 423–430.

Justice Ginsburg takes on affirmative action. (1995, April 17). *The Washington Post,* p. A4.

Kagan, J. (1980). Perspectives on continuity. In O. G. Brim & J. Kagan (Eds.), *Constancy and change in human development* (pp. 1–15). Cambridge, MA: Harvard University Press.

Kontos, S., & Fiene, R. (1987). Child care quality, family background, and children's development. *Early Childhood Research Quarterly, 6,* 249–262.

Lamb, M. (in press). Nonparental child care: Context, quality, correlates, and consequences. In W. Damon (Series Ed.) & I. E. Sigel & K. A. Renninger (Vols. Eds.), *Handbook of child psychology: Child psychology in practice* (4th ed.). New York: Wiley.

Lamb, M., Sternberg, K. J., Hwang, P., & Broberg, A. (Eds.). (1992). *Child care in context.* Hillsdale, NJ: Erlbaum.

Lamb, M., Sternberg, K. J., & Prodromidis, M. (1992). The effects of day care on infant–mother attachment: A re-analysis of the data. *Infant Behavior and Development, 15,* 71–83.

Leira, A. (1992). *Welfare states and working mothers.* Cambridge, England: Cambridge University Press.

Mason, K., & Duberstein, L. (1992). Consequences of child care for parents' well-being. In A. Booth (Ed.), *Child care in the 1990s: Trends and consequences* (pp. 127–158). Hillsdale, NJ: Erlbaum.

Maynard, R., & McGinnis, E. (1992). Policies to enhance access to high-quality child care. In A. Booth (Ed.), *Child care in the 1990s: Trends and consequences* (pp. 189–208). Hillsdale, NJ: Erlbaum.

McCartney, K. (1984). The effect of quality of day care environment upon children's language development. *Developmental Psychology, 20,* 244–260.

McCartney, K., & Marshall, N. (1989). The development of child care research. *Newsletter of the Division of Children, Youth, and Family Services, 12*(4), 14–15.

McCartney, K., Scarr, S., Phillips, D., & Grajek, S. (1985). Day care as intervention: Comparisons of varying quality programs. *Journal of Applied Developmental Psychology, 6,* 247–260.

McCartney, K., Scarr, S., Rocheleau, A., Phillips, D., Eisenberg, M., Keefe, N., Rosenthal, S., & Abbott-Shim, M. (1997). Social development in the context of typical center-based child care. *Merrill-Palmer Quarterly, 43*(3), 426–450.

Morris, J., & Helburn, S. (1996, July). How centers spend money on quality. *Child Care Information Exchange,* 75–79.

National Institute of Child Health and Human Development Early Child Care Research Network. (1996). Characteristics of infant child care: Factors contributing to positive caregiving. *Early Childhood Research Quarterly, 11,* 269–306.

National Institute of Child Health and Human Development Early Child Care Research Network. (in press). The effects of infant child care on infant–mother attachment security: Results of the NICHD Study of Early Child Care. *Child Development.*

Phillips, D. (Ed). (1987). *Quality in child care: What does research tell us? Research monographs of the National Association for the Education of Young Children.* Washington, DC: National Association for the Education of Young Children.

Phillips, D. (1992). Child care and parental well-being: Bringing quality of care into the picture. In A. Booth (Ed.), *Child care in the 1990s: Trends and consequences* (pp. 172–179). Hillsdale, NJ: Erlbaum.

Phillips, D., McCartney, K., & Scarr, S. (1987). Child care quality and children's social development. *Developmental Psychology, 23,* 537–543.

Phillips, D., McCartney, K., Scarr, S., & Howes, C. (1987). Selective review of infant day care research: A cause for concern. *Zero to Three, 7,* 18–21.

Phillips, D., Mekos, D., Scarr, S., McCartney, K., & Abbott-Shim, M. (in press). Paths to quality in child care: Structural and contextual influences on classroom environments. *Early Childhood Research Quarterly.*

Presser, H. (1992a). Child care and parental well-being: A needed focus on gender trade-offs. In A. Booth (Ed.), *Child care in the 1990s: Trends and consequences* (pp. 180–185). Hillsdale, NJ: Erlbaum.

Presser, H. (1992b). Child-care supply and demand: What do we really know? In A. Booth (Ed.), *Child care in the 1990s: Trends and consequences* (pp. 26–32). Hillsdale, NJ: Erlbaum.

Prosser, W., & McGroder, S. (1992). The supply and demand for child care: Measurement and analytic issues. In A. Booth (Ed.), *Child care in the 1990s: Trends and consequences* (pp. 42–55). Hillsdale, NJ: Erlbaum.

Ramey, C., Bryant, D., Sparling, J., & Wasik, B. (1985). Project CARE: A comparison of two early intervention strategies to prevent retarded development. *Topics in Early Childhood Special Education, 5* (2), 12–25.

Ramey, C., & Ramey, S. (1992). Early educational intervention with disadvantaged children—to what effect? *Applied and Preventive Psychology, 1,* 131–140.

Ross, C. E., & Mirowsky, J. (1988). Child care and emotional adjustment to wives' employment. *Journal of Health and Social Behavior, 29,* 127–138.

Scarr, S. (1984). Mother care/other care. New York: Basic Books.

Scarr, S. (1985). Constructing psychology: Making facts and fables for our times. *American Psychologist, 40,* 499–512.

Scarr, S. (1992a). Developmental theories for the 1990s: Development and individual differences. *Child Development, 63,* 1–19.

Scarr, S. (1992b). Keep our eyes on the prize: Family and child care policy in the United States, as it should be. In A. Booth (Ed.), *Child care in the 1990s: Trends and consequences* (pp. 215–222). Hillsdale, NJ: Erlbaum.

Scarr, S. (1993). Biological and cultural diversity: The legacy of Darwin for development. *Child Development, 64,* 1333–1353.

Scarr, S. (1996). Family policy dilemmas in contemporary nation-states: Are women benefited by family-friendly governments? In S. Gustavsson & L. Lewin (Eds.), *The future of the nation state: Essays on cultural pluralism and political integration* (pp. 107–129). London: Routledge.

Scarr, S., & Eisenberg, M. (1993). Child care research: Issues, perspectives, and results. *Annual Review of Psychology, 44,* 613–644.

Scarr, S., Eisenberg, M., & Deater-Deckard, K. (1994). Measurement of quality of child care centers. *Early Childhood Research Quarterly, 9,* 131–151.

Scarr, S., Lande, J., & McCartney, K. (1989). Child care and the family: Cooperation and interaction. In J. Lande, S. Scarr, & N. Guzenhauser (Eds.), *Caring for children: Challenge to America* (pp. 21–40). Hillsdale, NJ: Erlbaum.

Scarr, S., McCartney, K., Miller, S., Hauenstein, E., & Ricciuti, A. (1994). Evaluation of an islandwide screening, assessment and treatment program. *Early Development and Parenting, 3*(4), 199–210.

Scarr, S., Phillips, D., & McCartney, K. (19890). Working mothers and their families. *American Psychologist, 44,* 1402–1409.

Scarr, S., Phillips, D., & McCartney, K. (1990). Facts, fantasies, and the future of child care in the United States. *Psychological Science, 1,* 26–35.

Scarr, S., Phillips, D., McCartney, K., & Abbott-Shim, M. (1993). Quality of child care as an aspect of family and child care policy in the United States. *Pediatrics, 91*(1), 182–188.

Scarr, S., & Thompson, W. (1994). Effects of maternal employment and nonmaternal infant care on development at two and four years. Early Development and Parenting, 3(2), 113–123.

Scarr, S., & Weinberg, R. A. (1986). The early childhood enterprise: Care and education of the young. *American Psychologist, 41,* 1140–1146.

Staines, G. L., & Pleck, J. H. (1983). *The impact of work schedules on the family.* Ann Arbor, MI: Institute for Social Research, Survey Research Center.

Stoney, L., & Greenberg, M. H. (1996). The financing of child care: Current and emerging trends. *The Future of Children, 6,* 83–102.

Suwalsky, J., Zaslow, M., Klein, R., & Rabinovich, B. (1986, August). *Continuity of substitute care in relation to infant–mother attachment.* Paper presented at the 94th Annual Convention of the American Psychological Association, Washington, DC.

Vandell, D. L., Henderson, V. K., & Wilson, K. S. (1988). A longitudinal study of children with day-care experiences of varying quality. *Child Development, 59,* 1286–1292.

Wasik, B. H., Ramey, C. T., Bryant, D. M., & Sparling, J. J. (1990). A longitudinal study of two early intervention strategies: Project CARE. *Child Development, 61,* 1682–1696.

White, L., & Keith, B. (1990). The effect of shift work on the quality and stability of marital relations. *Journal of Marriage and the Family, 52,* 453–462.

Whitebook, M., Howes, C., & Phillips, D. (1991). *Who cares? Child care teachers and the quality of care in America.* Final Report of the National Child Care Staffing Study. Oakland, CA: Center on Child Care Staffing.

Willer, B., Hofferth, S., Kisker, E. E., et al. (1991). *The demand and supply of child care in 1990.* Washington, DC: National Association for the Education of Young People.

Women's figures. (1997, January 15). *Wall Street Journal,* p. A15.

Workfare means day care. (1996, December 23). *Time,* 38–40.

Zigler, E. F., & Finn-Stevenson, M. (1996). Funding child care and public education. *The Future of Children, 6,* 104–121.

Sandra Scarr, Department of Psychology, University of Virginia, and KinderCare Learning Centers, Inc., Montgomery, AL.

Correspondence concerning this article should be addressed to Sandra Scarr, 77–6384 Halawai Street, Kailua-Kona, HI 96740. Electronic mail may be sent to sandrascar@aol.com.

From *American Psychologist,* February 1998, pp. 95–108. © 1998 by the American Psychological Association. Reprinted with permission.

Do Working Parents Make The Grade?

Book Excerpt: In the debates over quality time and how to balance work and family, kids are rarely heard. A new 'Ask the Children' study reveals how kids rate their moms and dads—and what children really want.

BY ELLEN GALINSKY

WHENEVER I MENTION THAT I AM STUDYING HOW kids see their working parents, the response is electric. People are fascinated. Parents want to know what I have found, but inevitably they are nervous, too. Sometimes they say, "I wonder what other people's children would say. I'm not sure that I'm ready to hear what mine have to say!"

Why has a comprehensive, in-depth study of this question never been conducted? Because we have been afraid to ask, afraid to know. But now I feel the time is right. The answers of children are illuminating, not frightening. They help us see that our assumptions about children's ideas are often at odds with reality. Ultimately, this information will help us be better parents—and better employees, too. In fact, adding children's voices to our national conversation about work and family life will change the way we think about them forever.

Many of the debates we've been having about work and family miss the mark. For example, we have been locked in a longstanding argument about whether it is "good or bad" for children if their mothers work. Numerous observational studies have found that having a working mother doesn't harm children, yet the debate still rages. Another way to assess this issue is to see whether children of mothers who are not employed and children of working mothers differ in the way they feel they are being parented. In our "Ask the Children" study, we had a representative group of more than 1,000 children in grades three through 12 to evaluate their parents in 12 areas strongly linked to children's healthy development, school readiness and school success. In their responses—rendered in actual letter grades—having a mother who worked was never once predictive of how children assess their mothers' parenting skills. We also found

that while the amount of time children and parents spend together is very important, most children don't want more time with their parents. Instead, they give their mothers and fathers higher grades if the time they do spend together is not rushed but focused and rich in shared activities.

Family Values

56% of parents think their kids want more time together; only 10% of kids want more time with Mom, 15.5% with Dad. Most kids, however, feel they have enough time.

62.5% of parents say they like their work a lot. Only 41% of children say Dad enjoys his job, and 42% say the same about Mom.

44.5% of kids say time with Mom is rushed, 37% say so with Dad. Only 33% of parents think time with their kids is rushed.

23% of kids want their parents to earn more; 14% of parents think kids want this.

It may seem surprising that children whose mothers are at home caring for them full time fail to see them as more supportive. But a mother who is employed can be there for her child or not, just as mothers who are not employed can be. Indeed, children of nonworking fathers see their dads less positively when it comes to making them feel important and loved and to participating in important events in the children's lives. Fathers who work part time are less likely to be seen as encouraging their children's learning. Perhaps fathers who work less than full time or who are unemployed are feeling financial and role strain, which could affect how they interact with their children.

Grading
Dad

He instills good values, but doesn't always know what 'really' goes on

SUBJECT	A	B	C	D	F
Raising me with good values	69%	18%	8%	4%	2%
Appreciating me for who I am	58	21	11	8	2
Encouraging me to enjoy learning	57.5	24	12	4	2
Making me feel important and loved	57	22	13	6	2
Being able to go to important events	55	22	13	5	5.5
Being there for me when I am sick	51.5	20	16	8	4
Spending time talking with me	43	24	19	10	4
Establishing traditions with me	41	26	15	11	7
Being involved in school life	38	24	19	12	7
Being someone to go to when upset	38	22	15	12	13
Controlling his temper	31	27	20	10	12
Knowing what goes on with me	31	30	17	12.5	10

NOTE: GRADES GIVEN BY CHILDREN IN SEVENTH THROUGH 12TH GRADES

That children can appreciate the efforts of working parents is clear. Said one 12-year-old son of working parents: "If parents wish to provide some of the better things in life, both parents need to work and share the home and children responsibilities." A 15-year-old girl whose father works full time and whose mother does not said: "Your children may not like you working now, but it will pay off later on."

The problem isn't that mothers (and fathers) work: it is how we work and how work affects our parenting. For example, we asked the children in this study, "If you were granted one wish to change the way that your mother's or your father's work affects your life, what would that wish be?" We also asked more than 600 parents to guess what their child's response would be. Taken together, 56 percent of parents assume that their children would wish for more time together and less parental time at work. And 50 percent of parents with children up to 18 years old say they feel that they have too little time with their child—fathers (56 percent) even more so than mothers (44 percent).

But only 10 percent of children wish that their mothers would spend more time with them, and 15.5 percent say the same thing about their fathers. And surprisingly, children with employed mothers and those with mothers at home do not differ on whether they feel they have too little time with Mom.

What the largest proportion of children (23 percent) say that they want is for their mothers and their fathers to make more money. I suspect that money is seen as a stress-reducer, given children's other answers. The total number of children who wish that their parents would be less stressed or less tired by work is even larger: 34 percent make this wish for their mothers and 27.5 percent for their fathers. Sympathy for working parents comes through loud and clear: "I would like to thank the parents of America for working so hard to earn money," says

one 15-year-old girl. "I know that a working parent goes through so much for their children."

The study also reveals what children learn from their parents about the world of work. Only about two in five children think their parents like their work a lot, compared with 62.5 percent of parents who say they do. That's probably because many of us have said to our kids, "I have to go to work." Or "I wish I didn't have to leave." We seem to talk around children rather than with them about our jobs. And our reluctance to talk to our children about our work has meant that young people are getting haphazard rather than intentional information, sometimes blaming themselves for distress we pick up on the job, and not fully appreciating the potential of their own future careers.

As a result, many children play detective to figure out what is going on in our jobs that upsets or elates us. They study our moods at the end of the workday. One of our young subjects says you can tell if your parents are in a bad mood "because you get a short and simple answer. If they had a bad day, they won't talk. Or they will just go off by themselves."

What makes a good parent? Through our interviews with parents and children, eight critical parenting skills emerged. We then asked the children in our national survey to grade their own mothers and dads on those criteria. They are:

1. Making the child feel important and loved
2. Responding to the child's cues and clues
3. Accepting the child for who he or she is, but expecting success
4. Promoting strong values
5. Using constructive discipline
6. Providing routines and rituals to make life predictable and create positive neural patterns in developing brains
7. Being involved in the child's education
8. Being there for the child

Grading
Mom

She's there during illness, but sometimes loses her temper

SUBJECT	A	B	C	D	F
Being there for me when I am sick	81%	11%	5%	2%	1%
Raising me with good values	75	15	6	3	2
Making me feel important and loved	64	20	10	5	1
Being able to go to important events	64	20	10	3	3.5
Appreciating me for who I am	64	18	8	6	5
Encouraging me to enjoy learning	59	23	11.5	3	3
Being involved in school life	46	25	14	10	6
Being someone to go to when upset	46	22	14	8	9
Spending time talking with me	43	33	14	6	4
Establishing traditions with me	38	29	17	10	6
Knowing what goes on with me	35	31	15	10	9
Controlling her temper	29	27.5	20.5	12	11

Which of these skills earned parents the highest—and lowest—grades? Among children in the seventh through the 12th grades, mothers are given the highest grades for being there when the child is sick (81 percent gave their mothers an A) and for raising their children with good values (75 percent). They receive the lowest grades for controlling their tempers when their children make them angry (only 29 percent gave their mothers an A) and for knowing what is really going on in their children's lives (35 percent). The age of the child makes a difference. Younger children consistently rate their parents more favorably than older ones, which no doubt reflects the way teenagers separate emotionally from their parents.

Money also matters. In analysis after analysis, the children's perception of their families' economic health is strongly linked to how they rate their moms' and dads' parenting skills. Although the public often views the problems of children as primarily moral in nature, our analyses show that families that do not have to worry about putting bread on the table may have more to give to their children emotionally. They also may be able to raise their children in more positive, cohesive communities.

These findings illustrate why it is so important to ask the children rather than to rely on our own assumptions. The issue of time with children has typically been framed in the public debate as a mothers' issue. But when we ask the children, we see that fathers need to be front and center in this discussion, as well.

Children in the seventh through the 12th grades judge their fathers less favorably than their mothers in some important respects, such as making their child feel important and loved and being someone whom the child can go to if upset. Teenagers are more likely than their younger counterparts to want more time with their fathers. Thirty-nine percent of children 13 through 18 years old feel they have too little time with their fathers, compared with 29 percent of children 8 through 12 years old.

Time spent in shared activities wins parents high marks—but not if it feels hurried or rushed

We found that the quantity of time with mothers and fathers does matter a great deal. Children who spend more time with their mothers and fathers on workdays and nonworkdays see their parents more positively, feel that their parents are more successful at managing work and family responsibilities, and see their parents as putting their families first. "I think that if the parents spend more time with their children, they will become better people in life," says a 12-year-old boy whose father works part time while his mom stays home.

But to move beyond simply cataloging the number of hours children and parents spend together, we looked at what parents and children do while they are together, such as eating a meal, playing a game or sport or exercising, doing homework (together) and watching TV. For all these activities, the same pattern holds: the more frequently parents and children engaged in them together, the more positive the assessment parents got from their children.

But spending time together isn't enough. Many children said their interactions with parents feel rushed and hurried, and they gave their mothers and fathers lower marks as a result. More than two in five (44.5 percent) children feel that their time with their mother is rushed, while 37 percent feel their time with their father is rushed. Some mentioned mornings as particularly hectic times for their families. One 12-year-old girl said of her mother: "She's rushing and telling me to rush…. And my backpack weighs a ton, so if she walks me to school, it's like running down the street. I'm like, 'wait up…'"

Kids who think their families are financially secure feel more positive about Mom and Dad

Predictably, children are more likely to see their parents positively if their time together is calmer. For example: of children 8 through 18 years of age who rate their time with their mothers as very calm, 86 percent give their mothers an A for making them feel important and loved, compared with 63 percent of those who rate their time with their mothers as very rushed. And 80 percent of children who feel their time with their fathers is very calm give them an A for "appreciating me for who I am," compared with only 50.5 percent of those who rate their time with their fathers as very rushed.

The flip side of feeling rushed and distracted with children is concentration and focus. In one-on-one interviews, we asked parents to describe moments when they felt particularly successful at home. Over and over, we heard the word "focus." The mother of a 12-year-old says: "It's the time you spend with your children [when] you are really focused on them that's good; not a distracted time."

Of children in the seventh through 12th grades, 62 percent say that mothers find it "very easy" and 52 percent say that fathers find it very easy to focus on them when they are together.

And children are very attuned to the times when their parents are truly focused on them: "They're not just saying normal things like 'uh huh… uh hmmm.' They seem to be very intent on what I'm saying, they're not just looking away," said a 10-year-old boy. Some children even have "tests" of whether their parent is focusing on them. For example, one 13-year-old boy throws nonsense statements — like "a goldfish on the grass" — into the middle of a sentence to check out whether his parents are really listening to him.

Every analysis we conducted revealed that when children feel that their mothers and fathers can focus on them, they are much more likely to feel that their parents manage their work and family responsibilities more successfully and put their families before their work. And they give their parents much higher marks for all of the parenting skills we examined.

So, is it quantity time or quality time? Clearly, the words we're using to describe time within the family are wrong. To change the debate, we need new words. Since "focus" is the word that parents use to describe the quality of time they treasure most, I suggest we use it. And since parents and children highly value the quantity of time they spend being together, whether sharing a meal or just being around each other in a nonrushed way, we need a phrase for that, too. Children need focused times and hang-around times.

I hope that, as a result of this book, the conversations around work and family will change. When parents and children talk together about these issues, reasonable changes can be made. Children will tell us how some things could be better. Yes, they will still try to push our guilt buttons. Yes, they will still read our moods and plead their case for what they want because kids will be kids. But we are the adults, and we set the tone for our relationships with our children.

I repeat the wisdom of a 12-year-old child: "Listen. Listen to what your kids say, because you know, sometimes it's very important. And sometimes a kid can have a great idea and it could even affect you." So let's ask the children.

From *Newsweek*, August 30, 1999, pp. 52–56. Excerpted from *Ask the Children* by Ellen Galinsky (Morrow, 1999). © 1999 by Ellen Galinsky. Reprinted by permission of William Morrow and Company, Inc.

The Moral Development of Children

*It is not enough for kids to tell right from wrong. They must
develop a commitment to acting on their ideals.
Enlightened parenting can help*

by William Damon

With unsettling regularity, news reports tell us of children wreaking havoc on their schools and communities: attacking teachers and classmates, murdering parents, persecuting others out of viciousness, avarice or spite. We hear about feral gangs of children running drugs or numbers, about teenage date rape, about youthful vandalism, about epidemics of cheating even in academically elite schools. Not long ago a middle-class gang of youths terrorized an affluent California suburb through menacing threats and extortion, proudly awarding themselves points for each antisocial act. Such stories make *Lord of the Flies* seem eerily prophetic.

What many people forget in the face of this grim news is that most children most of the time do follow the rules of their society, act fairly, treat friends kindly, tell the truth and respect their elders. Many youngsters do even more. A large portion of young Americans volunteer in community service—according to one survey, between 22 and 45 percent, depending on the location. Young people have also been leaders in social causes. Harvard University psychiatrist Robert Coles has written about children such as Ruby, an African-American girl who broke the color barrier in her school during the 1960s. Ruby's daily walk into the all-white school demonstrated a brave sense of moral purpose. When taunted by classmates, Ruby prayed for their redemption rather than cursing them. "Ruby," Coles observed, "had a will and used it to make an ethical choice; she demonstrated moral stamina; she possessed honor, courage."

All children are born with a running start on the path to moral development. A number of inborn responses predispose them to act in ethical ways. For example, empathy—the capacity to experience another person's pleasure or pain vicariously—is part of our native endowment as humans. Newborns cry when they hear others cry and show signs of pleasure at happy sounds such as cooing and laughter. By the second year of life, children commonly console peers or parents in distress.

Sometimes, of course, they do not quite know what comfort to provide. Psychologist Martin L. Hoffman of New York University once saw a toddler offering his mother his security blanket when he perceived she was upset. Although the emotional disposition to help is present, the means of helping others effectively must be learned and refined through social experience. Moreover, in many people the capacity for empathy stagnates or even diminishes. People can act cruelly to those they refuse to empathize with. A New York police officer once asked a teenage thug how he could have crippled an 83-year-old woman during a mugging. The boy replied, "What do I care? I'm not her."

A scientific account of moral growth must explain both the good and the bad. Why do most children act in reasonably—sometimes exceptionally—moral ways, even when it flies in the face of their immediate self-interest? Why do some children depart from accepted standards, often to the great harm of themselves and others? How does a child acquire mores and develop a lifelong commitment to moral behavior, or not?

The Six Stages of Moral Judgment

Growing up, children and young adults come to rely less on external discipline and more on deeply held beliefs. They go through as many as six stages (grouped into three levels) of moral reasoning, as first argued by psychologist Lawrence Kohlberg in the late 1950s (*below*). The evidence includes a long-term study of 58 young men interviewed periodically over two decades. Their moral maturity was judged by how they analyzed hypothetical dilemmas, such as whether a husband should steal a drug for his dying wife. Either yes or no was a valid answer; what mattered was how the men justified it. As they grew up, they passed through the stages in succession, albeit at different rates (*bar graph*). The sixth stage remained elusive. Despite the general success of this model for describing intellectual growth, it does not explain people's actual behavior. Two people at the same stage may act differently.   —W.D.

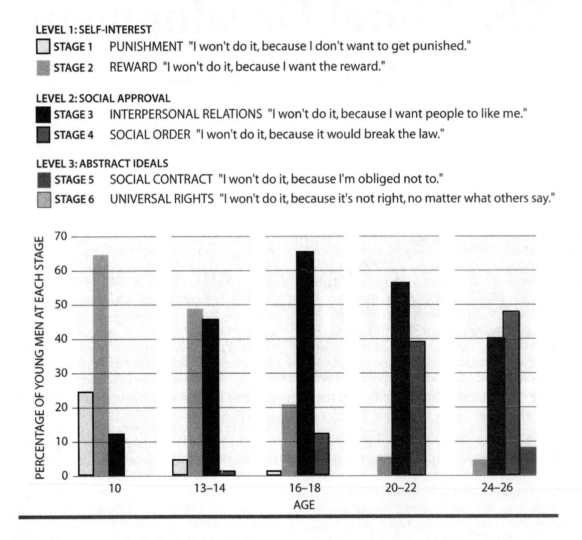

LEVEL 1: SELF-INTEREST
- **STAGE 1**   PUNISHMENT "I won't do it, because I don't want to get punished."
- **STAGE 2**   REWARD "I won't do it, because I want the reward."

LEVEL 2: SOCIAL APPROVAL
- **STAGE 3**   INTERPERSONAL RELATIONS "I won't do it, because I want people to like me."
- **STAGE 4**   SOCIAL ORDER "I won't do it, because it would break the law."

LEVEL 3: ABSTRACT IDEALS
- **STAGE 5**   SOCIAL CONTRACT "I won't do it, because I'm obliged not to."
- **STAGE 6**   UNIVERSAL RIGHTS "I won't do it, because it's not right, no matter what others say."

Edward Bell

Psychologists do not have definitive answers to these questions, and often their studies seem merely to confirm parents' observations and intuition. But parents, like all people, can be led astray by subjective biases, incomplete information and media sensationalism. They may blame a relatively trivial event—say, a music concert—for a deep-seated problem such as drug dependency. They may incorrectly attribute their own problems to a strict upbringing and then try to compensate by raising their children in an overly permissive way. In such a hotly contested area as children's moral values, a systematic, scientific approach is the only way to avoid wild swings of emotional reaction that end up repeating the same mistakes.

The Genealogy of Morals

The study of moral development has become a lively growth industry within the social sciences. Journals are full of new findings and competing models. Some theories focus on natural biological forces; others stress social influence and experience; still others, the judgment that results from children's intellectual development. Although each theory has a different emphasis, all recognize that no single cause can account for either moral or immoral behavior. Watching violent videos or playing shoot-'em-up computer games may push some children over the edge and leave others unaffected. Conventional wisdom dwells on lone silver bullets, but scientific understanding must be built on an appreciation of the complexity and variety of children's lives.

Biologically oriented, or "nativist," theories maintain that human morality springs from emotional dispositions that are hardwired into our species. Hoffman, Colwyn Trevar—then of the University of Edinburgh and Nancy Eisenberg of Arizona State University have established that babies can feel empathy as soon as they recognize the existence of others—sometimes in the first week after birth. Other moral emotions that make an early appearance include shame, guilt and indignation. As Harvard child psychologist Jerome S. Kagan has described, young children can be outraged by the violation of social expectations, such as a breach in the rules of a favorite game or rearranged buttons on a piece of familiar clothing.

Nearly everybody, in every culture, inherits these dispositions. Mary D. Ainsworth of the University of Virginia reported empathy among Ugandan and American infants; Norma Feshbach of the University of California at Los Angeles conducted a similar comparison of newborns in Europe, Israel and the U.S.; Millard C. Madsen of U.C.L.A. studied sharing by preschool children in nine cultures. As far as psychologists know, children everywhere start life with caring feelings toward those close to them and adverse reactions to inhumane or unjust behavior. Differences in how these reactions are triggered and expressed emerge only later, once children have been exposed to the particular value systems of their cultures.

In contrast, the learning theories concentrate on children's acquisition of behavioral norms and values through observation, imitation and reward. Research in this tradition has concluded that moral behavior is context-bound, varying from situation to situation almost independently of stated beliefs. Landmark studies in the 1920s, still frequently cited, include Hugh Hartshorne and Mark May's survey of how children reacted when given the chance to cheat. The children's behavior depended largely on whether they thought they would be caught. It could be predicted neither from their conduct

in previous situations nor from their knowledge of common moral rules, such as the Ten Commandments and the Boy Scout's code.

Later reanalyses of Hartshorne and May's data, performed by Roger Burton of the State University of New York at Buffalo, discovered at least one general trend: younger children were more likely to cheat than adolescents. Perhaps socialization or mental growth can restrain dishonest behavior after all. But the effect was not a large one.

The third basic theory of moral development puts the emphasis on intellectual growth, arguing that virtue and vice are ultimately a matter of conscious choice. The best-known cognitive theories are those of psychologists Jean Piaget and Lawrence Kohlberg. Both described children's early moral beliefs as oriented toward power and authority. For young children, might makes right, literally. Over time they come to understand that social rules are made by people and thus can be renegotiated and that reciprocity in relationships is more fair than unilateral obedience. Kohlberg identified a six-stage sequence in the maturation of moral judgment [see box, "The Six Stages of Moral Judgment"]. Several thousand studies have used it as a measure of how advanced a person's moral reasoning is.

Conscience versus Chocolate

Although the main parts of Kohlberg's sequence have been confirmed, notable exceptions stand out. Few if any people reach the sixth and most advanced stage, in which their moral view is based purely on abstract principles. As for the early stages in the sequence, many studies (including ones from my own laboratory) have found that young children have a far richer sense of positive morality than the model indicates. In other words, they do not act simply out of fear of punishment. When a playmate hogs a plate of cookies or refuses to relinquish a swing, the protest "That's not fair!" is common. At the same time, young children realize that they have an obligation to share with others—even when their parents say not to. Preschool children generally believe in an equal distribution of goods and back up their beliefs with reasons such as empathy ("I want my friend to feel nice"), reciprocity ("She shares her toys with me") and egalitarianism ("We should all get the same"). All this they figure out through confrontation with peers at play. Without fairness, they learn, there will be trouble.

In fact, none of the three traditional theories is sufficient to explain children's moral growth and behavior. None captures the most essential dimensions of moral life: character and commitment. Regardless of how children develop their initial system of values, the key question is: What makes them live up to their ideals or not? This issue is the focus of recent scientific thinking.

Like adults, children struggle with temptation. To see how this tug of war plays itself out in the world of small children, my colleagues and I (then at Clark University)

"Could You Live with Yourself?"

In a distressed neighborhood in Camden, N.J., social psychologist Daniel Hart of Rutgers University interviewed an African-American teenager who was active in community service:

How would you describe yourself?

I am the kind of person who wants to get involved, who believes in getting involved. I just had this complex, I call it, where people think of Camden as being a bad place, which bothered me. Every city has its own bad places, you know. I just want to work with people, work to change that image that people have of Camden. You can't start with adults, because they don't change. But if you can get into the minds of young children, show them what's wrong and let them know that you don't want them to be this way, then it could work, because they're more persuadable.

Is there really one correct solution to moral problems like this one?

Basically, it's like I said before. You're supposed to try to help save a life.

How do you know?

Well, it's just—how could you live with yourself? Say that I could help save this person's life—could I just let that person die? I mean, I couldn't live with myself if that happened. A few years ago my sister was killed, and… the night she was killed I was over at her house, earlier that day. Maybe if I had spent the night at her house that day, maybe this wouldn't have happened.

You said that you're not a bad influence on others. Why is that important?

Well, I try not to be a bad role model. All of us have bad qualities, of course; still, you have to be a role model even if you're a person walking down the street. You know, we have a society today where there are criminals and crooks. There are drug users. Kids look to those people. If they see a drug dealer with a lot of money, they want money, too, and then they're going to do drugs. So it's important that you try not to be a bad influence, because that can go a long way. Even if you say, oh, wow, you tell your little sister or brother to be quiet so Mom and Dad won't wake so you won't have to go to school. And they get in the habit of being quiet [laughs], you're not going to school, things like that. So when you're a bad influence, it always travels very far.

Why don't you want that to happen?

Because in today's society there's just really too much crime, too much violence. I mean everywhere. And I've even experienced violence, because my sister was murdered. You know, we need not to have that in future years, so we need to teach our children otherwise.

devised the following experiment. We brought groups, each of four children, into our lab, gave them string and beads, and asked them to make bracelets and necklaces for us. We then thanked them profusely for their splendid work and rewarded them, as a group, with 10 candy bars. Then the real experiment began: we told each group that it would need to decide the best way to divide up the reward. We left the room and watched through a one-way mirror.

Before the experiment, we had interviewed participants about the concept of fairness. We were curious, of course, to find out whether the prospect of gobbling up real chocolate would overwhelm their abstract sense of right and wrong. To test this thoroughly, we gave one unfortunate control group an almost identical conundrum, using cardboard rectangles rather than real chocolate—a not so subtle way of defusing their self-interest. We observed groups of four-, six-, eight- and 10-year-old children to see whether the relationship between situational and hypothetical morality changed with age.

The children's ideals did make a difference but within limits circumscribed by narrow self-interest. Children given cardboard acted almost three times more generously toward one another than did children given chocolate. Yet moral beliefs still held some sway. For example, children who had earlier expressed a belief in merit-based solutions ("The one who did the best job should get more of the candy") were the ones most likely to advocate for merit in the real situation. But they did so most avidly when they themselves could claim to have done more than their peers. Without such a claim, they were easily persuaded to drop meritocracy for an equal division.

Even so, these children seldom abandoned fairness entirely. They may have switched from one idea of justice to another—say, from merit to equality—but they did not resort to egoistic justifications such as "I should get more because I'm big" or "Boys like candy more than girls, and I'm a boy." Such rationales generally came from children who had declared no belief in either equality or meritocracy. Older children were more likely to believe in fairness and to act accordingly, even when such action favored others. This finding was evidence for the reassuring proposition that ideals can have an increasing influence on conduct as a child matures.

Do the Right Thing

But this process is not automatic. A person must adopt those beliefs as a central part of his or her personal identity. When a person moves from saying "People should be honest" to "I want to be honest," he or she becomes more likely to tell the truth in everyday interactions. A person's use of moral principles to define the self is called the person's moral identity. Moral identity determines not merely what the person considers to be the right course of action but also why he or she would decide: "I myself must take this course." This distinction is crucial to understanding the variety of moral behavior. The same basic ideals are widely shared by even the youngest members of society; the difference is the resolve to act on those ideals.

Most children and adults will express the belief that it is wrong to allow others to suffer, but only a subset of them will conclude that they themselves must do something about, say, ethnic cleansing in Kosovo. Those are the ones who are most likely to donate money or fly to the Balkans to help. Their concerns about human suffering are central to the way they think about themselves and their life goals, and so they feel a responsibility to take action, even at great personal cost.

In a study of moral exemplars—people with long, publicly documented histories of charity and civil-rights work—psychologist Anne Colby of the Carnegie Foundation and I encountered a high level of integration between self-identity and moral concerns. "People who define themselves in terms of their moral goals are likely to see moral problems in everyday events, and they are also likely to see themselves as necessarily implicated in these problems," we wrote. Yet the exemplars showed no signs of more insightful moral reasoning. Their ideals and Kohlberg levels were much the same as everyone else's.

Conversely, many people are equally aware of moral problems, but to them the issues seem remote from their own lives and their senses of self. Kosovo and Rwanda sound far away and insignificant; they are easily put out of mind. Even issues closer to home—say, a maniacal clique of peers who threaten a classmate—may seem like someone else's problem. For people who feel this way, inaction does not strike at their self-conception. Therefore, despite commonplace assumptions to the contrary, their moral knowledge will not be enough to impel moral action.

The development of a moral identity follows a general pattern. It normally takes shape in late childhood, when children acquire the capacity to analyze people—including themselves—in terms of stable character traits. In childhood, self-identifying traits usually consist of action-related skills and interests ("I'm smart" or "I love music"). With age, children start to use moral terms to define themselves. By the onset of puberty, they typically invoke adjectives such as "fairminded," "generous" and "honest."

Some adolescents go so far as to describe themselves primarily in terms of moral goals. They speak of noble purposes, such as caring for others or improving their communities, as missions that give meaning to their lives. Working in Camden, N.J., Daniel Hart and his colleagues at Rutgers University found that a high proportion of so-called care exemplars—teenagers identified by teachers and peers as highly committed to volunteering—had self-identities that were based on moral belief systems. Yet they scored no higher than their peers on the standard psychological tests of moral judgment. The study is noteworthy because it was conducted in an economically deprived urban setting among an adolescent population

often stereotyped as high risk and criminally inclined [see box, "Could You Live with Yourself?"].

At the other end of the moral spectrum, further evidence indicates that moral identity drives behavior. Social psychologists Hazel Markus of Stanford University and Daphne Oyserman of the University of Michigan have observed that delinquent youths have immature senses of self, especially when talking about their future selves (a critical part of adolescent identity). These troubled teenagers do not imagine themselves as doctors, husbands, voting citizens, church members—any social role that embodies a positive value commitment.

How does a young person acquire, or not acquire, a moral identity? It is an incremental process, occurring gradually in thousands of small ways: feedback from others; observations of actions by others that either inspire or appall; reflections on one's own experience; cultural influences such as family, school, religious institutions and the mass media. The relative importance of these factors varies from child to child.

Teach Your Children Well

For most children, parents are the original source of moral guidance. Psychologists such as Diana Baumrind of the University of California at Berkeley have shown that "authoritative" parenting facilitates children's moral growth more surely than either "permissive" or "authoritarian" parenting. The authoritative mode establishes consistent family rules and firm limits but also encourages open discussion and clear communication to explain and, when justified, revise the rules. In contrast, the permissive mode avoids rules entirely; the authoritarian mode irregularly enforces rules at the parent's whim—the "because I said so" approach.

Although permissive and authoritarian parenting seem like opposites, they actually tend to produce similar patterns of poor self-control and low social responsibility in children. Neither mode presents children with the realistic expectations and structured guidance that challenge them to expand their moral horizons. Both can foster habits—such as feeling that mores come from the outside—that could inhibit the development of a moral identity. In this way, moral or immoral conduct during adulthood often has roots in childhood experience.

As children grow, they are increasingly exposed to influences beyond the family. In most families, however, the parent-child relationship remains primary as long as the child lives at home. A parent's comment on a raunchy music lyric or a blood-drenched video usually will stick with a child long after the media experience has faded. In fact, if salacious or violent media programming opens the door to responsible parental feedback, the benefits can far outweigh the harm.

One of the most influential things parents can do is to encourage the right kinds of peer relations. Interactions

How Universal Are Values?

The observed importance of shared values in children's moral development raises some of the most hotly debated questions in philosophy and the social sciences today. Do values vary from place to place, or is there a set of universal values that guides moral development everywhere? Do children growing up in different cultures or at different times acquire fundamentally different mores?

Some light was shed on the cultural issue by Richard A. Shweder of the University of Chicago and his colleagues in a study of Hindu-Brahmin children in India and children from Judeo-Christian backgrounds in the U.S. The study revealed striking contrasts between the two groups. From an early age, the Indian children learned to maintain tradition, to respect defined rules of interpersonal relationships and to help people in need. American children, in comparison, were oriented toward autonomy, liberty and personal rights. The Indian children said that breaches of tradition, such as eating beef or addressing one's father by his first name, were particularly reprehensible. They saw nothing wrong with a man caning his errant son or a husband beating his wife when she went to the movies without his permission. The American children were appalled by all physically punitive behavior but indifferent to infractions such as eating forbidden foods or using improper forms of address.

Moreover, the Indians and Americans moved in opposite directions as they matured. Whereas Indian children restricted value judgments to situations with which they were directly familiar, Indian adults generalized their values to a broad range of social conditions. American children said that moral standards should apply to everyone always; American adults modified values in the face of changing circumstances. In short, the Indians began life as relativists and ended up an universalists, whereas the Americans went precisely the other way.

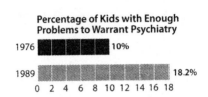

Percentage of Kids with Enough Problems to Warrant Psychiatry

1976 10%

1989 18.2%

0 2 4 6 8 10 12 14 16 18

KIDS THESE DAYS are likier to need mental health services, judging from parents' reports of behavioral and emotional problems

It would be overstating matters, however, to say that children from different cultures adopt completely different moral codes. In Schweder's study, both groups of children thought that deceitful acts (a father breaking a promise to a child) and uncharitable acts (ignoring a beggar with a sick child) were wrong. They also shared a repugnance toward theft, vandalism and harming innocent victims, although there was some disagreement on what constitutes innocence. Among these judgments may be found a universal moral sense, based on common human aversions. It reflects core values—benevolence, fairness, honesty—that may be necessary for sustaining human relationships in all but the most dysfunctional societies.

A parallel line of research has studied gender differences, arguing that girls learn to emphasize caring, whereas boys incline toward rules and justice. Unlike the predictions made by culture theory, however, these gender claims have not held up. The original research that claimed to find gender differences lacked proper control groups. Well-designed studies of American children—for example, those by Lawrence Walker of the University of British Columbia—rarely detect differences between boys' and girls' ideals. Even for adults, when educational or occupational levels are controlled, the differences disappear. Female lawyers have almost the same moral orientations as their male counterparts; the same can be said for male and female nurses, homemakers, scientists, high school dropouts and so on. As cultural theorists point out, there is far more similarity between male and female moral orientations within any given culture than between male and female orientations across cultures.

Generational differences are also of interest, especially to people who bemoan what they see as declining morality. Such complaints, of course, are nothing new [see "Teenage Attitudes," by H. H. Remmers and D. H. Radler; Scientific American, June 1958; and "The Origins of Alienation," by Urie Bronfenbrenner; Scientific American, August 1974]. Nevertheless, there is some evidence that young people today are more likely to engage in antisocial behavior than those a generation ago were. According to a survey by Thomas M. Achenbach and Catherine T. Howell of the University of Vermont, parents and teachers reported more behavioral problems (lying, cheating) and other threats to healthy development (depression, withdrawal) in 1989 than in 1976 (*above*). (The researchers are now updating their survey.) But in the long sweep of human history, 13 years is merely an eye blink. The changes could reflect a passing problem, such as overly permissive fashions in child rearing, rather than a permanent trend.

—*W.D.*

EDWARD BELL; SOURCE; THOMAS M. ACHENBACH AND CATHERINE T. HOWELL with peers can spur moral growth by showing children the conflict between their preconceptions and social reality. During the debates about dividing the chocolate, some of our subjects seemed to pick up new—and more informed—ideas about justice. In a follow-up study, we confirmed that the peer debate had heightened their awareness of the rights of others. Children who participated actively in the debate, both expressing their opinions and listening to the viewpoints of others, were especially likely to benefit.

In adolescence, peer interactions are crucial in forging a self-identity. To be sure, this process often plays out in cliquish social behavior: as a means of defining and shoring up the sense of self, kids will seek out like-minded peers and spurn others who seem foreign. But when kept within reasonable bounds, the in-group clustering generally evolves into a more mature friendship pattern. What can parents do in the meantime to fortify a teenager who is bearing the brunt of isolation or persecution? The most important message they can give is that cruel behavior reveals something about the perpetrator rather than about the victim. If this advice helps the youngster resist taking the treatment personally, the period of persecution will pass without leaving any psychological scars.

Some psychologists, taking a sociological approach, are examining community-level variables, such as whether various moral influences—parents, teachers, mass media and so on—are consistent with one another. In a study of 311 adolescents from 10 American towns and cities, Francis A. J. Ianni of the Columbia University Teachers College noticed high degrees of altruistic behavior and low degrees of antisocial behavior among youngsters from communities where there was consensus in expectations for young people.

Everyone in these places agreed that honesty, for instance, is a fundamental value. Teachers did not tolerate cheating on exams, parents did not let their children lie and get away with it, sports coaches did not encourage teams to bend the rules for the sake of a win, and people of all ages expected openness from their friends. But many communities were divided along such lines. Coaches espoused winning above all else, and parents protested when teachers reprimanded their children for cheating or shoddy schoolwork. Under such circumstances, children learned not to take moral messages seriously.

Ianni named the set of shared standards in harmonious communities a "youth charter." Ethnicity, cultural diversity, socioeconomic status, geographic location and population size had nothing to do with whether a town offered its young people a steady moral compass. The notion of a youth charter is being explored in social interventions that foster communication among children, parents, teachers and other influential adults. Meanwhile

other researchers have sought to understand whether the specific values depend on cultural, gender or generational background [see box, "How Universal Are Values?"].

Unfortunately, the concepts embodied in youth charters seem ever rarer in American society. Even when adults spot trouble, they may fail to step in. Parents are busy and often out of touch with the peer life of their children; they give kids more autonomy than ever before, and kids expect it—indeed, demand it. Teachers, for their part, feel that a child's nonacademic life is none of their business and that they could be censured, even sued, if they intervened in a student's personal or moral problem. And neighbors feel the same way: that they have no business interfering with another family's business, even if they see a child headed for trouble.

Everything that psychologists know from the study of children's moral development indicates that moral identity —the key source of moral commitment throughout life—is fostered by multiple social influences that guide a child in the same general direction. Children must hear the message enough for it to stick. The challenge for pluralistic societies will be to find enough common ground to communicate the shared standards that the young need.

Further Reading

THE MEANING AND MEASUREMENT OF MORAL DEVELOPMENT. Lawrence Kohlberg. Clark University, Heinz Werner Institute, 1981.

THE EMERGENCE OF MORALITY IN YOUNG CHILDREN. Edited by Jerome Kagan and Sharon Lamb. University of Chicago Press, 1987.

THE MORAL CHILD: NURTURING CHILDREN'S NATURAL MORAL GROWTH. William Damon. Free Press, 1990.

ARE AMERICAN CHILDREN'S PROBLEMS GETTING WORSE? A 13-YEAR COMPARISON. Thomas M. Achenbach and Catherine T. Howell in *Journal of the American Academy of Child and Adolescent Psychiatry*, Vol. 32, No. 6, pages 1145–1154; November 1993.

SOME DO CARE: CONTEMPORARY LIVES OF MORAL COMMITMENT. Anne Colby. Free Press, 1994.

THE YOUTH CHARTER: HOW COMMUNITIES CAN WORK TOGETHER TO RAISE STANDARDS FOR ALL OUR CHILDREN. William Damon. Free Press, 1997.

The Author

WILLIAM DAMON remembers being in an eighth-grade clique that tormented an unpopular kid. After describing his acts in the school newspaper, he was told by his English teacher, "I give you an A for the writing, but what you're doing is really shameful." That moral feedback has stayed with him. Damon is now director of the Center on Adolescence at Stanford University, an interdisciplinary program that specializes in what he has called "the least understood, the least trusted, the most feared and most neglected period of development." A developmental psychologist, he has studied intellectual and moral growth, educational methods, and peer and cultural influences on children. He is the author of numerous books and the father of three children, the youngest now in high school.

UNIT 5
Cultural and Societal Influences

Unit Selections

Key Points to Consider

- Alcohol and drug use among adults and teenagers is nothing new. What is new about the research on the outcomes of early use of drugs and alcohol? Did you experiment with or use drugs or alcohol as a teenager or young adult? Why or why not?

- Why do you think American teenagers spend time differently than other similar children outside the United States?

- Who were your role models when you were growing up? Was either of your parents a role model whom you looked up to? Why or why not? Explain why you think the media plays such a large role in influencing whom children admire and look up to.

- Should U.S. public policy be designed to help reduce the enormous number of children living in poverty in our country? Explain.

- Recent research reveals that child abuse results in tragic and enduring damage to children psychologically, emotionally, physically, and neurologically. What do you think we can do to try to prevent such terrible abuses?

- Have you ever had contact with or known anyone with autism? Based on "The Early Origins of Autism," what information or assurances might you give to parents of an autistic child for future prognosis?

 **Links: www.dushkin.com/online/**
These sites are annotated in the World Wide Web pages.

Ask NOAH About: Mental Health
   http://www.noah-health.org/english/illness/mentalhealth/mental.html
Association to Benefit Children (ABC)
   http://www.a-b-c.org
Children Now
   http://www.childrennow.org
Council for Exceptional Children
   http://www.cec.sped.org
National Black Child Development Institute
   http://www.nbcdi.org
Prevent Child Abuse America
   http://www.preventchildabuse.org

Social scientists and developmental psychologists have come to realize that children are influenced by a multitude of social forces that surround them. In this unit we present articles to illuminate how American children and adolescents are influenced by broad factors such as economics, culture, politics, and the media. These influences also affect the family, which is a major context of child development, and many children are now faced with more family challenges than ever. In addition, analysis of exceptional or atypical children gives the reader a more comprehensive account of child development. Thus, articles are presented on special challenges of development, such as poverty, the effects of child abuse, autism, and child soldiers in war.

What will children and life be like in the new millennium? Author Jerry Adler offers a fascinating take on both past history and future possibilities in a wide-ranging article, "Tomorrow's Child." He cites amazing technological and medical advances, economic opportunities, and cultural forces as playing pivotal roles in shaping the child of the future.

With today's hectic pace and multiple demands it comes as no surprise that adults and teenagers face many everyday stresses and challenges. Unfortunately, some young adults turn to abusing alcohol, and the research in "Getting Stupid" documents studies indicating that teenagers who drink are seriously compromising their memory, intellectual, and brain functioning.

Do you think children and adolescents spend their time differently in the United States, as opposed to other countries? Researcher Reed Larson analyzes data from different countries showing significant differences in how American children spend their time as compared to teens in other industrialized societies in "How U.S. Children and Adolescents Spend Time: What It Does (and Doesn't) Tell Us About Their Development." His data show that American teenagers spend significantly less time on schoolwork, have more discretionary time, and spend much more time watching television or interacting with friends than teenagers outside of the U.S. The author asks if U.S. children and adolescents are spending their time in ways that will enhance their development.

Television and media are very popular with children and adolescents. Does the media affect children's choice of heroes? The authors of "Parents or Pop Culture? Children's Heroes and Role Models," find interesting differences in the role models preferred by children who come from different ethnic groups.

Some children all around the world are faced with challenges such as severe poverty, physical abuse, autism, and coping with life-threatening situations such as war. Such children are often

misunderstood and mistreated and pose special challenges. These issues are discussed in "The Effects of Poverty on Children," "Scars That Won't Heal: The Neurobiology of Child Abuse," "Voices of the Children: We Beat and Killed People," and "The Early Origins of Autism." Although these articles are sometimes difficult to read, as future parents, teachers, and caring individuals it is becoming increasingly important for us to learn more about these difficult and tragic situations in order to find ways to improve and ameliorate future problems.

TOMORROW'S CHILD

Amazing medical advances, great economic opportunities, earlier schooling and many new kinds of Barbie dolls are among the wonders in store for the first Americans of a new century.

BY JERRY ADLER

SHE WILL BE CONCEIVED, ALMOST CERTAINLY, sometime in the next six months, and will tumble headfirst into the world nine months later, wholly unconscious of her uniqueness as the first American of the millennium. Escaping by a stroke of the clock the awful burden of the present century, she (or he) will never hear the screams at Dachau or see the sky burst into flames over Hiroshima; the cold war will be as remote as the epic of Gilgamesh. For that matter, even the re-runs of "Barney" will bear the musty reek of the classics. Some things are eternal, though, and present trends indicate that sometime in the next century the average American girl could have more Barbie dolls than she has classmates. Grandchild of baby boomers! The very phrase boggles the mind—although not so much, perhaps, as the fact that of the 8.9 million American children who will be born in the year 2000, at least 70,000 of them are expected to still be alive in 2100.

First, though, they'll survive being dropped on their heads in the delivery room when the Y2K computer bug shuts off the electricity. To each century belongs its own terrors, and also its own pleasures. The child born in the year 2000 may face epidemics of previously unknown tropical diseases, but he also may be able to eat broccoli Jell-O instead of broccoli. And the toy industry may come to the rescue of lonely kids with a doll designed to remind them of their mothers. "We have so many latchkey children in search of a human connection," muses marketing consultant Faith Popcorn. "They'll be able to carry their mother around in doll form!" A lot has been written lately about the future as the venue for abstract breakthroughs in science, technology and medicine, but much less on the concrete questions of how Americans will actually live in it.

Babies born as early as 19 weeks after conception may survive, thanks to a technology enabling them to breathe through a liquid.

The millennium baby will be born into a nation of approximately 275 million, the third largest in the world, and still growing; the midrange estimate of the Census Bureau is that the population will reach 323 million by 2020 and 394 million by midcentury. Where will all those people live? Mostly in California, Texas and Florida, which among them will account for almost three out of 10 Americans by 2025. They will be squeezed onto proportionately less land: the median lot size of a new single-family house will almost certainly continue the slow, steady drop of the last 20 years. Children born in the year 2000 will live, on average, twice as long as those born in 1900. But they will live in bigger houses; the median floor area will reach 2,000 square feet any year now, a 25 percent increase since 1977. "The 800-square-foot Levittown house—that's a big family room now," says Columbia University historian Kenneth T. Jackson.

The cohort born circa 2000 should also benefit from what some economists are calling "the great asset sell-off" of the 21st century—the liquidation of family homes as the baby boomers start retiring in the second and third decades. "Younger Americans will get some great deals" on real estate, says Teresa Ghilarducci, a specialist in economic forecasting at Notre Dame. And, she adds, "it will be a great time to look for and get great jobs." But boomers will also be liquidating their investments, so stock-market values will stagnate. Except in some favored sun-belt locales, families moving out will create what Ghilarducci ominously calls "suburban wastelands." Downtown neighborhoods that haven't gentrified by then will be just out of luck.

The salient economic fact in the child's life may be the growing gap between the haves and have-nots, says Robert Litan, director of economic studies at the Brookings Institution. As disparities of wealth and income continue to widen, he says, "we could find ourselves living in a winner-take-all society. If people don't see economic opportunity, they drop out" of civil society. These trends will play themselves out in an America increasingly populated by minorities. By 2050, the Census Bureau projects an American population that is one-quarter black, Asian or Native

American and one-quarter Hispanic. How the nation fares in the next century will depend on whether those changes widen the socioeconomic gap between races or help close it. And meanwhile, which of the children born in the year 2000 will be chosen for the Harvard class of 2022—bearing in mind that by the time they enroll, the projected cost of a Harvard education will be more than $320,000?

There are a few things we can say with some assurance. Millennium babies will be about the same size as their parents. The long-term trend among Caucasians toward greater size is a factor of better nutrition, but as everyone knows, Americans are already maxed out when it comes to food consumption. Children born in the year 2000 will, however; live longer than ever: 73 years, on average, for a boy, and almost 80 for a girl—approximately double the average life expectancy of a newborn at the turn of the last century. And the figures are expected to rise steadily throughout the first half of the century. Those averages, though, conceal a wide disparity among different races. Whites, interestingly, are about in the middle; the category of Asians and Pacific Islanders will live the longest; blacks the shortest. It is a depressing statistic that a black male born in 2000 will have a life expectancy of 64.6 years—actually *less* than for an older brother born in 1995.

Some of the improvement in life span will come from reducing already low rates of infant death. Dr. James Marks of the Centers for Disease Control estimates that the mortality rate for newborns, around eight per 1,000 live births, could drop to as little as one per 1,000. Premature births account for many newborn deaths, but in the next decade, says bioethicist Arthur Caplan of the University of Pennsylvania, doctors will perform the astonishing feat of keeping alive babies born as early as 19 or 20 weeks after conception, weighing only eight ounces. Preemies younger than about 24 weeks now almost invariably succumb to the failure of their underdeveloped lungs, but techniques are now being developed to allow them to breathe oxygen from a liquid solution until they can sustain themselves in the air.

Even more impressive are advances forecast for in utero surgery. Already doctors can remove fetal tumors and correct conditions such as diaphragmatic hernia— a hole in the diaphragm that can cause serious lung problems. But standard open surgery on a living fetus is a very high-risk procedure. Within the next decade, surgeons will be performing these operations with the help of tiny cameras mounted on needle-like probes, according to Dr. Michael Harrison, head of the Fetal Treatment Center at the University of California, San Francisco. Ultimately, he expects, doctors will be able to do anything on a fetus that can be done after birth. "Heart repairs? We're working on them day and night [in animals]," Harrison says. "It hasn't been done in humans yet, but we will be there in the next century."

A new theory will change our attitudes about child rearing— we don't know what it is yet, but there always is one

---

The road map to the 21st century is being written now in the Human Genome Project, the monumentally ambitious attempt to catalog the entire complement of a normal person's DNA. When it's completed, in about 2003, researchers will be able to identify the genes responsible for many of mankind's most intractable afflictions—such as cystic fibrosis, muscular dystrophy and congenital immune deficiency. As a first step, doctors will be able to diagnose these diseases in utero, and parents will have the chance—and, consequently, the burden—of deciding whether to end the pregnancy. (Some of these tests are already in use.) But by the early years of the next century doctors will perform the equivalent of alchemy, curing disease by directly tinkering with patients' DNA. They will synthesize normal copies of the defective gene, or altered genes that counteract it, and attach them to a "vector" such as a benign virus to carry them into the patient's cells. In combination with Harrison's fetal-surgery techniques, it may be possible to cure congenital conditions even before birth.

For most babies born in the year 2000, smoking and overeating obviously will be a bigger threat to health than birth defects. Childhood obesity "is up dramatically since the '80s," says Marks of the CDC, and is expected to increase among kids who lift a finger only to click a mouse button. But routine genetic screening early in the next century will make a difference there, too, by identifying the health risks specific to each individual. The public-health lesson of this century is that people generally change their lifestyles only under the threat of death, which is why those born in the future will probably not have to sit through so many public-service exhortations about fitness from Arnold Schwarzenegger. Instead, doctors will tell them which particular risks they run, and what they have to do to stay alive—including, for example, the nutritional supplements that will do them the most good. On smoking, diet and exercise the advice is probably going to be pretty much the same as it is now—except that there are always people who will live a long time no matter what they eat. One of the great pleasures of living in the next century may be finding out you're one of them.

In terms of psychological health, a new theory will revolutionize parents' attitudes toward child rearing. No one knows what the new theory will be, but there always is one. The 20th century's succession of mutually contradictory panaceas (more structure; more freedom; it doesn't make a difference) shouldn't obscure the point that until about the 1940s, "most parents didn't give much thought to child development at all," says Jerome Singer, a Yale child psychologist. "From a parenting point of view, children are better off today, and will be better off in the next few decades. Parents realize children need attention and oversight of what's going on in their lives, and those beliefs are penetrating into the lower socioeconomic groups."

And if kids persist in being maladjusted, there will be lots more ways to treat them. Caplan foresees radical new therapies that will rely on virtual-reality simulators (so the patient can practice, say, controlling his aggression in a mock situation) and brain scans that will tell the therapist on the spot whether the patient was learning. With this technique, he says, "you could look for change in real time," a boon to patients and insurance companies alike. There also will be many more problems to treat. The frontier of therapy in the next century will be "sub-syndromal" conditions such as mild depression, social phobias and anxieties. "We'll be treating emotional disabilities that we don't even label today," says Dr. Solomon H. Snyder, who heads the department of neuroscience at Johns Hopkins University. The debates over Prozac and Ritalin, which some authorities suspect are being prescribed indiscriminately, prefigure what will be two of the most important questions in 21st-century medical ethics: How far should we go in "enhancing" people who are essentially normal? And who will pay for it?

The reading wars will continue, with increasing reliance on computers, but kids will still be put to bed with 'Goodnight Moon'

And periodically someone will invent the one and only best method to teach reading, rendering all other techniques hopelessly obsolete. It might well involve computers; there is already a burgeoning market for what's called "lapware," software aimed at children under a year old, who do their computing while sitting on Mommy's lap. "I've seen some that attempt to teach kids to associate letters and sounds with colors," says a very dubious David Elkind, a professor of child development at Tufts University. "That's a skill most children don't have until they're 4 or 5." Whatever the new movement is, it will provoke an equally strong reaction as soon as parents discover that it doesn't automatically turn their toddlers into John Updike. "The reading wars"—basically pitting old-fashioned phonics against everything else—"have been going on for a century and a half, so what chance do we have of ending them by the year 2000?" says Timothy Shanahan, a professor of education at the University of Illinois-Chicago.

The truth, well known to researchers, is that most kids can learn to read with almost any method, and will do it by themselves if left alone with a pile of books. And there will still be books in the next century. As births increased in the 1980s, the number of new children's titles published annually doubled, even as families started buying computers for the first time. Paula Quint, president of the Children's Book Council, expects that as births level off over the next few years the number of new titles will hold steady at about 5,000 a year. A few of these may even turn into classics, but it's safe to say that in the next century and beyond, kids will still be put to bed with "Goodnight Moon."

The change that is likely to make a real difference in the lives of millennium kids is a mundane one: the slow adoption of universal pre-K education. Most of the kids who attend preschool now are from relatively well-off families, even though research shows that the programs most benefit poor children. A few states, in search of a morally unassailable use of gambling proceeds, are dedicating them to providing free programs for 4-year-olds. "In 10 years," predicts Anne Mitchell, a consultant on early-childhood programs, "free preschool will be commonplace."

And in so many other ways, the year 2000 will be a great time to be born. Kids will have terrifically cool ethnic names like Pilar, Selena or Kai—although there may also be a countertrend, fueled by millennial religious fervor, for Biblical names like Isaiah and Elijah. Their mothers are more likely to breast-feed them than has been true for a generation (a quarter of all mothers nursed their children for at least six months last year, up from about 5 percent in 1971). And they will be able, if their parents don't mind, to run around in diapers until they're almost 4. Recognizing a trend toward later toilet training (and bigger kids), Procter & Gamble recently introduced Pampers in size 6, for toddlers 35 pounds and over. Of course, kids who are kept in diapers until the age of 4 can only help drive up the cost of raising them, which, according to U.S. Department of Agriculture statistics, will amount to approximately $250,000 for the first 18 years of a millennium baby's life.

Inevitably, part of that sum will go toward the purchase of Barbie dolls. In the early 1980s, most girls were content with one Barbie; the average collection is now up to 10 and likely to rise in the future as Mattel expands the line into infinity—adding just this year, for example, Chilean, Thai, Polish and Native American Barbies. Last year Mattel added a wheelchair Barbie, and a spokeswoman suggests "there may be more dolls with other disabilities in the future."

Yes, the kid of the future will be, if anything, even more pampered and catered to than the fabled baby boomers themselves, at least in part because there's so much money to be made off them. Leaving the house at 7:30 in the morning for 12-hour days of school, restaurants and shopping, they will require ever-more-elaborate "urban survival clothes," like the currently popular cargo pants in whose capacious pockets one can stow a meatball grinder, a palmtop computer and a jar of The Limited's most exciting new cosmetic product, fruit-scented antibacterial glitter gel. In what marketing guru Popcorn regards as one of the most significant social trends of the next millennium, "cross-aging," kids will be more like adults (and vice versa): "We're going to see health clubs for kids, kids as experts on things like the Internet, and new businesses, like Kinko's for Kids, to provide professional quality project presentations." The travel market of the future will increasingly be geared to kids, and not just at theme parks—24 million business trips included children in 1996, up 160 percent from 1991. So, to anyone who may have wondered whether it was right to bring a child into the uncertain world of the 21st century, it's fair to say, your fears are groundless.

The next millennium is going to be great for kids.

It's the adults who will miss the 1990s.

With PAT WINGERT, KAREN SPRINGEN, ELIZABETH ANGELL *and* MICHAEL MEYER

getting *stupid*

New research indicates that teenagers who drink too much may
lose as much as 10 percent of their brainpower—the difference
between passing and failing in school… and in life

By Bernice Wuethrich

Sarah, a high school senior, drinks in moderation, but many of her friends do not. At one party, a classmate passed out after downing more than 20 shots of hard liquor and had to be rushed to a local emergency room. At another party a friend got sick, so Sarah made her drink water, dressed her in a sweatshirt to keep her warm, and lay her in bed, with a bucket on the floor. Then she brushed the girl's long hair away from her face so that it wouldn't get coated with vomit. "Every weekend, drinking is the only thing people do. Every single party has alcohol," says Sarah. (The names of the teenagers in these stories have been changed to protect their privacy.)

THE MOST RECENT STATISTICS FROM the U.S. Substance Abuse and Mental Health Services Administration's National Household Survey on Drug Abuse indicate that nearly 7 million youths between the ages of 12 and 20 binge-drink at least once a month. And despite the fact that many colleges have cracked down on drinking, Henry Wechsler of the Harvard School of Public Health says that two of every five college students still binge-drink regularly. For a male that means downing five or more drinks

in a row; for a female it means consuming four drinks in one session at least once in a two-week period.

Few teens seem to worry much about what such drinking does to their bodies. Cirrhosis of the liver is unlikely to catch up with them for decades, and heart disease must seem as remote as retirement. But new research suggests that young drinkers are courting danger. Because their brains are still developing well into their twenties, teens who drink excessively may be destroying significant amounts of mental capacity in ways that are more dramatic than in older drinkers.

Scientists have long known that excessive alcohol consumption among adults over long periods of time can create brain damage, ranging from a mild loss of motor skills to psychosis and even the inability to form memories. But less has been known about the impact alcohol has on younger brains. Until recently, scientists assumed that a youthful brain is more resilient than an adult brain and could escape many of the worst ills of alcohol. But some researchers are now beginning to question this assumption. Preliminary results from

several studies indicate that the younger the brain is, the more it may be at risk. "The adolescent brain is a developing nervous system, and the thins you do to it can change it," says Scott Swartzwelder, a neuropsychologist at Duke University and the U.S. Department of Veterans Affairs.

Teen drinkers appear to be most susceptible to damage in the hippocampus, a structure buried deep in the brain that is responsible for many types of learning and memory, and the prefrontal cortex, located behind the forehead, which is the brain's chief decision maker and voice of reason. Both areas, especially the prefrontal cortex, undergo dramatic change in the second decade of life.

Swartzwelder and his team have been studying how alcohol affects the hippocampus, an evolutionarily old part of the brain that is similar in rats and humans. Six years ago, when Swartzwelder published his first paper suggesting that alcohol disrupts the hippocampus more severely in adolescent rats than in adult rats, "people didn't believe it," he says. Since then, his research has shown that the adolescents brain is more easily damaged in the struc-

Jason, 19
DRINKING HISTORY: First drink: age 14, at a party with 18-year-olds. Now drinks three or four times a week.
MOST ALCOHOL EVER CONSUMED: "In school we play beer for beer. I think I got up to 17 beers. One night when I was 15, I had 14 shots of whatever there was, until my friend got really sick and I had to take care of her."
AFTEREFFECTS: "I have been sick from drinking, but I have never blacked out. My social life affects my schoolwork, but drinking does not."

Terry, 19
DRINKING HISTORY: First drink: age 13, stole wine from liquor cabinet. Drinks about two or three times a week.
MOST ALCOHOL EVER CONSUMED: nine shots of liquor.
AFTEREFFECTS: "I have been sick many times, but I always remember what I did. Sometimes if I know I've had too much to drink, it feels better to get it out of my system. If I felt that my drinking was at all hindering my work, I would stop."

Sofia, 18
DRINKING HISTORY: First drink: age 14, "Kahlua in warm milk to help me sleep." Now drinks "once every couple of weeks."
MOST ALCOHOL EVER CONSUMED: "I'm not sure. I drink until I'm buzzed, stop until my buzz wears off, then maybe have more. I've never had enough to be out of control or even be hungover."
AFTEREFFECTS: "I'm a pretty conscientious student, and I don't drink enough to let it affect my schoolwork."

Stanley, 19
DRINKING HISTORY: First drink: age 14, at a friend's house. Now drinks every weekend.
MOST ALCOHOL EVER CONSUMED: two 40 oz. beers and three shots of liquor.
AFTEREFFECTS: "I've been sick and blacked out. After a night of drinking I don't get out of bed until 12:00 or 1:00 p.m. So I'm unable to do all my schoolwork."

Cindy, 18
DRINKING HISTORY: First drink: age 14, at a party. "In high school I drank every weekend."
MOST ALCOHOL EVER CONSUMED: three shots vodka, four shots rum, two screwdrivers, one strawberry daiquiri, and one beer.
AFTEREFFECTS: "In high school I had all B 's and A – 's. I don't drink that much in college, and I have a B/B – average. Go figure. I put more effort into my college work though because I'm not rushing out at 6 o'clock to get a good six hours in of drinking."

Joe, 19
DRINKING HISTORY: First drink: age 4, sipped father's beer and didn't like it. Now drinks once every week or two.
MOST ALCOHOL EVER CONSUMED: 10 mixed drinks.
AFTEREFFECTS: "I've vomited on three occasions because of alcohol. That's it though. Drinking has not affected my schoolwork."

tures that regulate the acquisition and storage of memories.

Learning depends on communication between nerve cells, or neurons, within the hippocampus. To communicate, a neuron fires an electrical signal down its axon, a single fiber extending away from the cell's center. In response, the axon releases chemical messengers, called neurotransmitters, which bind to receptors on the receiving branches of neighboring cells. Depending on the types of neurotransmitters released, the receiving cell may be jolted into action or settle more deeply into rest.

But the formation of memories requires more than a simple firing or inhibition of nerve cells. There must be some physical change in the hippocampal neurons that represents the encoding of new information. Scientists believe that this change occurs in the synapses, the tiny gaps between neurons that neurotransmitters traverse. Repeated use of synapses seems to increase their ability to fire up connecting cells. Laboratory experiments on brain tissue can induce this process, called long-term potentiation. Researchers assume that something similar takes places in the intact living brain, although it is impossible to observe directly. Essentially, if the repetitive neural reverberations are strong enough, they burn in new patterns of synaptic circuitry to encode memory, just as the more often a child recites his ABCs, the better he knows them.

Swartzwelder's first clue that alcohol powerfully disrupts memory in the adolescent brain came from studying rat hippocampi. He found that alcohol blocks long-term potentiation in adolescent brain tissue much more than in adult tissue.

Next, Swartzwelder identified a likely explanation. Long-term potentiation—and thus memory formation—relies in large part on the action of a neurotransmitter known as glutamate, the brain's chemical kingpin of neural excitation. Glutamate strengthens a cell's electrical stimulation when it binds to a docking port called the NMDA receptor. If the receptor is blocked, so is long-term potentiation, and thus memory formation. Swartzwelder found that exposure to the equivalent of just two beers inhibits the NMDA receptors in the hippocampal cells of adolescent rats, while more than twice as much is required to produce the same effect in adult rats. These findings led him to suspect that alcohol consumption might have a dramatic impact on the ability of adolescents to learn. So he set up a series of behavioral tests.

The younger the brain, the *more it may be at risk*

First, Swartzwelder's team dosed adolescent and adult rats with alcohol and ran them through maze-learning tests. Compared with the adult rats, the adolescents failed miserably. To see whether similar results held true for humans, Swartzwelder recruited a group of volunteers aged 21 to 29 years old. He couldn't use younger subjects because of laws that forbid drinking before age 21. He chose to split the volunteers into two groups: 21 to 24 years old and 25 to 29 years old. "While I couldn't argue that these younger folks are adolescents, even in their early twenties their brains are still developing," Swartzwelder says. After three drinks, with a blood-alcohol level slightly below the National Highway Traffic Safety Administration's recommended limit—.08 percent—the younger group's learning was impaired 25 percent more than the older group's.

Intrigued by these results, Swartzwelder's colleague Aaron White, a biological psychologist at Duke, set out to discover how vulnerable the adolescent brain is to long-term damage. He gave adolescent and adult rats large doses of alcohol every other day for 20 days—the equivalent of a 150-pound human chugging 24 drinks in a row. Twenty days after the last binge, when the adolescent rats had reached adulthood, White trained them in a maze-memory task roughly akin to that performed by a human when remembering the location of his car in a parking garage.

Both the younger and older rats performed equally well when sober. But when intoxicated, those who had binged as adolescents performed much worse. "Binge alcohol exposure in adolescence appears to produce long-lasting changes in brain function," White says. He suspects that early damage caused by alcohol

could surface whenever the brain is taxed. He also suspects that the NMDA receptor is involved, because just as alcohol in the system inhibits the receptor, the drug's withdrawal overstimulates it—which can kill the cell outright.

During the fall semester last year, at least 11 college students died from alcohol-related causes—at California State University at Chico, Colgate University in New York, Old Dominion University in Virginia, the University of Michigan, Vincennes University in Kentucky, Washington and Lee University in Virginia, and Washington State University. No one knows how many other students were rushed to emergency rooms for alcohol poisoning, but at Duke, 11 students had visited local ERs in just the first three weeks of school, and in only one night of partying, three students from the University of Tennessee were hospitalized.

STUDENTS WHO DRINK HEAVILY sometimes joke that they are killing a few brain cells. New research suggests that this is not funny. Some of the evidence is anatomical; Michael De Bellis at the University of Pittsburgh Medical Center used magnetic resonance imaging to compare the hippocampi of subjects 14 to 21 years old who abused alcohol to the hippocampi of those who did not. He found that the longer and the more a young person had been drinking, the smaller his hippocampus. The average size difference between healthy teens and alcohol abusers was roughly 10 percent. That is a lot of brain cells.

De Bellis speculates that the shrinkage may be due to cell damage and death that occurs during withdrawal from alcohol. Withdrawal is the brain's way of trying to get back to normal after prolonged or heavy drinking. It can leave the hands jittery, set off the classic headache, generate intense anxiety, and even provoke seizures, as neurons that had adjusted to the presence of alcohol try to adjust to its absence. Because alcohol slows down the

transmission of nerve signals—in part by stopping glutamate from activating its NMDA receptors—nerve cells under the influence react by increasing the number and sensitivity of these receptors. When drinking stops, the brain is suddenly struck with too many hyperactive receptors.

Hyperactive receptors *can cause cell death*

Mark Prendergast, a neuroscientist at the University of Kentucky, recently revealed one way these hyperactive receptors kill brain cells. First, he exposed rat hippocampal slices to alcohol for 10 days, then removed the alcohol. Following withdrawal, he stained the tissue with a fluorescent dye that lit up dead and dying cells. When exposed to an alcohol concentration of about .08 percent, cell death increased some 25 percent above the baseline. When concentrations were two or three times higher, he wrote in a recent issue of *Alcoholism: Clinical and Experimental Research*, the number of dead cells shot up to 100 percent above baseline.

Prendergast says that the younger brain tissue was far more sensitive. Preadolescent tissue suffered four to five time more cell death than did adult tissue. In all cases, most of the death occurred in hippocampal cells that were packed with NMDA receptors. To home in on the cause, he treated another batch of brain slices with the drug MK-801, which blocks NMDA receptors. He reasoned that if overexcitability during alcohol withdrawal was causing cell death, blocking the receptors, should minimize the carnage. It did, by about 75 percent.

Now Prendergast is examining what makes the receptors so lethal. By tracking radioactive calcium, he found that the overexcited receptors open floodgates that allow calcium to swamp the cell. Too much calcium can turn on suicide genes that cause the neuron to break down its own membrane. Indeed, that is exactly what Prendergast observed during alcohol withdrawal: Overactive receptors opened wide, and the influx of calcium became a raging flood.

Prendergast says that four or five drinks may cause a mild withdrawal. And, according to Harvard's Wechsler, 44 percent of college students binge in this manner. More alarming, 23 percent of them consume 72 percent of all the alcohol that college students drink.

Chuck was 15 the first time he binged— on warm beers chugged with friends late at night in a vacant house. Six years later, celebrating his 21st birthday, he rapidly downed four shots of vodka in his dorm room. Then he and his friends drove through the snowy night to a sorority party at a bar, where he consumed another 16 drinks. Chuck's friends later told him how the rest of the night unfolded. He danced in a cage. He spun on the floor. He careened around the parking lot with a friend on his back. Halfway home, he stumbled out of the car and threw up. A friend half carried him home down frozen roads at 2 a.m. "I don't remember any of this," Chuck says. But he does remember the hangover he lived with for two days, as his brain and body withdrew from booze.

RECENT HUMAN STUDIES SUPPORT a conclusion Prendergast drew from his molecular experiments: The greatest brain damage from alcohol occurs during withdrawal. At the University of California at San Diego and the VA San Diego Health Care System, Sandra Brown, Susan Taper, and Gregory Brown have been following alcohol-dependent adolescents for eight years. Repeated testing shows that problem drinkers perform more poorly on tests of cognition and learning than do nondrinkers. Furthermore, "the single best predictor of neuropsychological deficits for adolescents is withdrawal symptoms," says principal investigator Sandra Brown.

The psychologists recruited a group of 33 teenagers aged 15 and 16, all heavy drinkers. On average, each teen had used alcohol more than 750 times—the equivalent of drinking every day for two and a half years. Bingeing was common: The teens downed an average of eight drinks at each sitting. The researchers matched drinkers with nondrinkers of the same gender and similar age, IQ, socioeconomic background, and family history of alcohol use. Then, three weeks after the drinkers had their last drink, all the teens took a two-hour battery of tests.

The teens with alcohol problems had a harder time recalling information, both verbal and nonverbal, that they had learned 20 minutes earlier. Words such as *apple* and *football* escaped them. The performance difference was about 10 percent. "It's not serious brain damage, but it's the difference of a grade, a pass or a fail," Tapert says. Other tests evaluated skills needed for map learning, geometry, or science. Again, there was a 10 percent difference in performance.

"The study shows that just several years of heavy alcohol use by youth can adversely affect their brain functions in ways that are critical to learning," Sandra Brown says. She is following the group of teenagers until they reach age 30, and some have already passed 21. "Those who continue to use alcohol heavily are developing attentional deficits in addition to the memory and problem-solving deficits that showed up early on," Brown says. "In the past we thought of alcohol as a more benign drug. It's not included in the war on drugs. This study clearly demonstrates that the most popular drug is also an incredibly dangerous drug."

Brown's research team is also using functional magnetic resonance imaging to compare the brain function of alcohol abusers and nondrinkers. Initial results show that brains of young adults with a history of alcohol dependence are less active

than the brains of nondrinkers during tasks that require spatial working memory (comparable to the maze task that White conducted on rats). In addition, the adolescent drinkers seem to exhibit greater levels of brain activity when they are exposed to alcohol-related stimuli. For instance, when the drinkers read words such as *wasted* or *tequila* on a screen, the nucleus accumbens—a small section of the brain associated with craving—lights up.

The nucleus accumbens is integral to the brain's so-called pleasure circuit, which scientists now believe undergoes major remodeling during adolescence. Underlying the pleasure circuit is the neurotransmitter dopamine. Sex, food, and many drugs, including alcohol, can all induce the release of dopamine, which creates feelings of pleasure and in turn encourages repetition of the original behavior. During adolescence, the balance of dopamine activity temporarily shifts away from the nucleus accumbens, the brain's key pleasure and reward center, to the prefrontal cortex. Linda Spear, a developmental psychobiologist at Binghamton University in New York, speculates that as a result of this shift in balance, teenagers may find drugs less rewarding than earlier or later in life. And if the drugs produce less of a kick, more will be needed for the same effect. "In the case of alcohol, this may lead to binge drinking," she says.

When Lynn was a freshman in high school, she liked to hang out at her friend John's apartment. More often than not, his father would be drinking beer. "He was like, 'Help yourself,'" Lynn says. Friends would come over and play drinking games until four or five in the morning. The longer the games continued, the tougher the rules became, doubling and tripling the number of drinks consumed. One night, Lynn came home drunk. Her mother talked her through her options, sharing stories of relatives who had ruined their lives drinking. Lynn struggled with her choices. A year later she still drinks, but she's kept a pact with her girlfriends to stop bingeing.

DURING ADOLESCENCE, THE PREFRONTAL cortex changes more than any other part of the brain. At around age 11 or 12, its neurons branch out like crazy, only to be seriously pruned back in the years that follow. All this tumult is to good purpose. In the adult brain, the prefrontal cortex executes the thought processes adolescents struggle to master: the ability to plan ahead, think abstractly, and integrate information to make sound decisions.

Now there is evidence that the prefrontal cortex and associated areas are among those most damaged in the brains of bingeing adolescents. Fulton Crews, director of the Center for Alcohol Studies at the University of North Carolina at Chapel Hill, has studied the patterns of cell death in the brains of adolescent and adult rats after four-day drinking bouts. While both groups showed damage in the back areas of the brain and in the frontally located olfactory bulb, used for smell, only the adolescents suffered brain damage in other frontal areas.

That youthful damage was severe. It extended from the rat's olfactory bulk to the interconnected parts of the brain that process sensory information and memories to make associations, such as "This smell and the sight of that wall tell me I'm in a place where I previously faced down an enemy." The regions of cell death

in the rat experiment corresponded to the human prefrontal cortex and to parts of the limbic system.

The limbic system, which includes the hippocampus, changes throughout adolescence, according to recent work by Jay Giedd at the National Institute of Mental Health in Bethesda, Maryland. The limbic system not only encodes memory but is also mobilized when a person is hungry or frightened or angry; it helps the brain process survival impulses. The limbic system and the prefrontal cortex must work in concert for a person to make sound decisions.

Damage to the prefrontal cortex and the limbic system is especially worrisome because they play an important role in the formation of an adult personality. "Binge drinking could be making permanent long-term changes in the final neural physiology, which is expressed as personality and behavior in the individual," Crews says. But he readily acknowledges that such conclusions are hypothetical. "It's very hard to prove this stuff. You can't do an experiment in which you change people's brains."

Nonetheless, evidence of the vulnerability of young people to alcohol is mounting. A study by Bridget Grant of the National Institute on Alcohol Abuse and Alcoholism shows that the younger someone is when he begins to regularly drink alcohol, the more likely that individual will eventually become an alcoholic.

Grant found that 40 percent of the drinkers who got started before age 15 were classified later in life as alcohol dependent, compared with only 10 percent of those who began drinking at age 21 or 22. Overall, beginning at age 15, the risk of future alcohol dependence decreased by 14 percent with each passing year of abstention.

The study leaves unanswered whether early regular drinking is merely a marker of later abuse or whether it results in long-term changes in the brain that increase the later propensity for abuse. "It's got to be both," Crews says. For one thing, he points out that studies of rats and people have shown that repeated alcohol use makes it harder for a person—or a rat—to learn new ways of doing things, rather than repeating the same actions over and over again. In short, the way alcohol changes the brain makes it increasingly difficult over time to stop reaching for beer after beer after beer.

Ultimately, the collateral damage caused by having so many American adolescents reach for one drink after another may be incalculable. "People in their late teens have been drinking heavily for generations. We're not a society of idiots, but we're not a society of Einsteins either," says Swartzwelder. "What if you've compromised your function by 7 percent or 10 percent and never known the difference?"

How U.S. Children and Adolescents Spend Time: What It Does (and Doesn't) Tell Us About Their Development

Reed W. Larson[1]
Department of Human and Community Development,
University of Illinois, Urbana, Illinois

Abstract
Young people develop as "the sum of past experiences," and data on their time use are one means of quantifying those experiences. U.S. children and adolescents spend dramatically less time than in the agrarian past in household and income-generating labor. Because such labor is usually repetitive and unchallenging, this reduction has probably not deprived youths of crucial developmental experience. The schoolwork replacing this time has a clearer relationship to developmental outcomes. American teens, however, spend less time on schoolwork than teens in other industrialized countries. American teenagers have more discretionary time, much spent watching television or interacting with friends; spending large amounts of time in these activities is related to negative developmental outcomes. Increasing amounts of young people's discretionary time, however, appear to be spent in structured voluntary activities, like arts, sports, and organizations, which may foster initiative, identity, and other positive developmental outcomes.

Keywords
time use; developmental experiences

Children's and adolescents' use of time, a topic of public debate since the 1920s, has reemerged as an issue of national concern. Alarm is voiced that American youths do too little homework, spend too little time with their parents, and spend too much time watching television and, now, playing computer games or surfing the Internet. The after-school hours have been identified as a time of risk, when unsupervised children are endangered and teenagers use drugs, commit crimes, and have sex. The underlying question is whether young people are spending their time in ways that are healthy and prepare them for adulthood in the competitive, global world of the 21st century. Another, related question is whether young people are being overscheduled and denied the creative, exploratory freedom of youth.

Time, as economists tell us, is a resource—one that can be used productively or squandered. For developmental psychologists, study of children's and adolescents' use of this resource offers a means to examine their portfolio of daily socialization experiences. Data on their time spent in different activities provide estimates of how much they are engaged with the information, social systems, developmental opportunities, and developmental liabilities associated with each context. Of course, information on time spent in specific activities is only a rough proxy for actual socialization experiences. The impact of watching TV for 2 hr depends on whom a child is with, what the child watches, and how the child interprets it. Even two siblings eating supper with their parents each night may have much different experiences of this time. Nonetheless, assessment of time spent in different activities provides a useful starting point for evaluating a population's set of developmental experiences.

Table 1. *Average daily time use of adolescents in 45 studies*

Activity	Nonindustrial, unschooled populations	Postindustrial, schooled populations		
		United States	Europe	East Asia
Household labor	5–9 hr	20–40 min	20–40 min	10–20 min
Paid labor	0.5–8 hr	40–60 min	10–20 min	0–10 min
Schoolwork	—	3.0–4.5 hr	4.0–5.5 hr	5.5–7.5 hr
Total work time	6–9 hr	4–6 hr	4.5–6.5 hr	6–8 hr
TV viewing	*insufficient data*	1.5–2.5 hr	1.5–2.5 hr	1.5–2.5 hr
Talking	*insufficient data*	2–3 hr	*insufficient data*	45–60 min
Sports	*insufficient data*	30–60 min	20–80 min	0–20 min
Structured voluntary activities	*insufficient data*	10–20 min	1.0–20 min	0–10 min
Total free time	4–7 hr	6.5–8.0 hr	5.5–7.5 hr	4.0–5.5 hr

Note: The estimates in the table are averaged across a 7-day week, including weekdays and weekends. Time spent in maintenance activities like eating, personal care, and sleeping is not included. The data for nonindustrial, unschooled populations come primarily from rural peasant populations in developing countries. Adapted from Larson and Verma (1999).

A LIFTED BURDEN OF REPETITIVE DRUDGERY

If we look back over the past 200 years, the most striking historic change in young people's use of time is that youths spend much less time on labor activities today than they did in America's agrarian past. In current nonindustrialized agrarian settings, household and income-generating labor fills 6 hr a day by middle childhood and reaches full adult levels of 8 or more hours per day by the early teens. By comparison, in the contemporary United States, time spent on household chores averages 15 to 30 min per day in childhood and 20 to 40 min in adolescence; income-generating activities account for little or no time, except among employed older teenagers (Larson & Verma, 1999).

Has this dramatic reduction in labor taken away valuable developmental experiences? In a comprehensive review, Goodnow (1988) found remarkably little evidence that household chores foster development. Children gain activity-specific skills (e.g., cooking skills), and care of younger children, if well-supervised, may bring positive outcomes. But evidence for broader developmental gains is thin. In reality, much time spent on chores in traditional agrarian settings involved highly repetitive activities, like carrying water and weeding fields; likewise, in contemporary America, most chores are mundane, with little challenge or developmental content. Evidence on the developmental benefits of U.S. adolescents' employment is more positive but also mixed. Definitive longitudinal studies indicate that employment during adolescence increases likelihood of employment and wages in early adulthood; however, teen employment over 20 hr per week is associated with greater delinquency, school misconduct, and substance use (Mortimer, Harley, & Aronson, 1999). Except in atypical circumstances in which youths have intellectually challenging jobs, it is hard to argue that more than 15 to 20 hr of employment per week brings additional developmental gains. Certainly, spending some time in chores and, especially, employment may provide useful learning experiences, but the dramatic reduction in youths' time in these repetitive labor activities appears to be a developmental plus.

Historically, this large burden of labor has been replaced by schooling, and schooling has clearer benefits. Young people often feel bored and unmotivated while doing schoolwork, as they do during chores and employment, and many experience schoolwork, too, as drudgery. But unlike labor activities, schoolwork brings experiences of high challenge and concentration. Amount of time spent in education correlates with youths' knowledge, intelligence, and subsequent adult earnings (Ceci & Williams, 1997), and is related to growth of a society's economy. Thus, economically and in other ways, the displacement of labor by schoolwork is a positive change in young people's time use.

American youths, however, spend less time on schoolwork than youths in most industrialized nations. As with other activities, the largest cross-national differences occur in adolescence (Table 1). U.S. teens spend approximately three fifths the amount of time on schoolwork that East Asian teens do and four fifths the time that European teens do. These differences are mostly attributable to American teens doing less homework, estimated at 20 to 40 min per day, as compared with 2.0 to 4.0 hr in East Asia and 1.0 to 2.5 hr in Europe. These figures do not take into account national differences in length of the school year (it is shortest in the United States) and overlook differences between individual students and school districts—some U.S. schools and state legislatures have recently taken action to increase homework. These figures also over-look possible differences in quality of instruction: An hour of school-work may yield more learning in one country than in another. Nonethe-less, they provide on explanation for American students' lower test scores and raise questions about whether American youths are being disad-vantaged in the new competitive global marketplace.

THE EXPANSE OF FREE TIME

What American youths, especially adolescents, have in greater quanti-ties than young people in other in-dustrialized nations is discretionary time. Studies carried out since the 1920s have found that 40 to 50% of U.S. teenagers' waking time (not counting summer vacations) is spent in discretionary activities. Current es-timates are 25 to 35% in East Asia and 35 to 45% in Europe. Whether this time is a liability or gives American youths an advantage depends largely on what they do with it.

Media Use

American teens spend much of their free time using media, particu-larly watching television. Studies in-dicate that TV viewing is American youths' primary activity for 1.5 to 2.5 hr per day on average. Curiously, the averages in other nations are quite similar. Within the United States, rates of viewing are found to be highest in late childhood and among boys, youths of low socioeco-nomic status (SES), and African Americans across income levels.

Current theories emphasize that viewers are active, not passive—they "use" media. Research indicates, however, that TV is rarely used for positive developmental experiences and that viewing is associated with developmental liabilities. A high amount of time watching entertain-ment TV—which constitutes most of youth's viewing—is associated with obesity and changed perceptions of sexual norms. Watching more than 3

to 4 hr per day is associated with lower school grades. Controlled lon-gitudinal studies show that rates of viewing violence predict subsequent aggression (Strasburger, 1995). TV watching may sometimes be used for relaxation: Much viewing occurs in the late evening, when young peo-ple wind down before bed. But, on balance, TV time is developmentally unconstructive.

The new kid on the block, of course, is computer and Internet use, and we know little about develop-mental impacts of these new media. Rates of use in the United States are still small, but are increasing steadily. A recent national survey found recreational computer use to account for an average of 30 min per day for youths over age 8, with greater use among higher-SES youngsters (Roberts, Foehr, Rideout, & Brodie, 1999). Children spend more time playing computer games, whereas adolescents devote more time to e-mail and other Internet ac-tivities. As with television, there are important concerns; about effects of violent and pornographic content, commercial exploitation, participa-tion in deviant Internet groups, and social isolation among frequent us-ers. At the same time, computers and the Internet permit more active indi-vidualized use than television and thus have more developmental promise. Young people can use these media to obtain information, de-velop relationships with people dif-ferent from themselves, learn job skills, and even start companies, irre-spective of their age, gender, ethnic-ity, and physical appearance. The question of developmental benefits versus liabilities for this use of time is not likely to have a singular con-clusion; answers are likely to differ across uses and users.

Unstructured Leisure

The largest amount of U.S. youths' free time is spent playing, talking, hanging out, and participat-ing in other unstructured leisure ac-tivities, often with friends. Play is

more frequent in childhood than in adolescence, accounting for 1.5 to 3.0 hr per day in the elementary years. It is gradually displaced by talking, primarily with peers. U.S. first grad-ers appear to spend about as much time playing as first graders in Japan and Taiwan, but play falls off more quickly with age in East Asia (Stevenson & Lee, 1990).

Abundant theory and research suggest that play promotes positive development. Piaget viewed play as an arena for experimentation and adaptation of mental schemas (in-cluding concepts and strategies) to experience. Research substantiates that play has relationships to chil-dren's cognitive, linguistic, social, and emotional development (Fisher, 1992). McHale, Crouter, and Tucker (2000), however, found that among 10-year-olds, more time spent in out-door play was associated with lower school grades and more conduct problems. Thus, more time playing does not necessarily facilitate more development.

Adolescents' talking, it can be ar-gued, is play at a symbolic level. So-cial interaction is an arena for exploration and development of emotional, interpersonal, and moral schemas. Therefore, we might expect time spent interacting with peers to be associated with developmental gains similar to those for time spent playing. Little research has directly addressed this question, but longitu-dinal research shows that spending more time interacting with friends in unstructured contexts predicts higher rates of problem behavior (Osgood, Wilson, O'Malley, Bachman & Johnston, 1996). This relationship is undoubtedly complex, depending on the content of interaction, indi-vidual dispositions, and numerous other factors. But these findings cer-tainly contradict the argument that youths need large amounts of un-structured, free time.

Structured Leisure Activities

U.S. adolescents stand out from East Asian youths in time spent in voluntary structured activities, like sports, arts, music, hobbies, and organizations. (Insufficient comparative data exist for younger children.) Even so, the current media image of "overscheduled kids" is misleading. Among American teens, the average amount of time spent in these activities per day is measured in minutes, not hours (Table 1), although there is mixed evidence suggesting this time is increasing (Fishman, 1999; Zill, Nord, & Loomis, 1995).

What are the developmental benefits and costs of spending time in these activities? When participating, young people report experiencing high challenge, concentration, and motivation. This combination, which rarely occurs elsewhere in youths' lives, suggests they are engaged and invested in ways that provide unique opportunities for growth. Theory and a partial body of research suggest that these activities are associated with development of identity and initiative, reduced delinquency, and positive adult outcomes (Larson, 2000; Mahoney, 2000), although some studies have found sports participation increases alcohol use. More research is needed, but there is good reason to hypothesize that, under the right conditions, structured activities provide unique developmental experiences.

CONCLUSIONS

Are U.S. children and adolescents spending their time in ways consistent with optimal development? This question, I confess, makes me cringe. Taken to its logical conclusion, it suggests submitting every moment of youth to utilitarian "time and motion study." We know too well from current trends in education that when things can be measured—for example, by test scores—policy discussions focus on measures as ends in themselves, irrespective of more important harder-to-measure variables. Given our limited state of knowledge and the loose relationship between how time is spent and what youths actually experience, overemphasis on time allocation is certain to mislead. It

also overlooks individual and cultural differences in learning processes and developmental goals. Human development is not a board game that can be won by having one's pieces spend the most time on selected squares. Developmental science needs models that conceptualize time as one among many variables affecting growth.

With these cautions firmly in mind, it seems important to consider quantities of time as part of the package when appraising young people's portfolio of developmental experiences. Should U.S. teenagers' schoolwork time be lengthened to match that of East Asian teens? In fact, East Asian societies are engaged in intense public debates about the stress and developmental costs associated with their adolescents' exclusionary focus on school achievement. Recent U.S. efforts to require more homework for all young people are probably justified, and there are empirical rationales for experiments with lengthening the school year and redistributing summer vacation throughout the calendar. But I think the most pressing issue for U.S. youths is not further increasing schoolwork time, but ensuring consistent quality in what happens during this time. My research shows that adolescents, including honor students, are frequently bored during schoolwork (this is also true in East Asia). It may be less important to pack more studying into the day than for researchers and practitioners to find ways to increase the quality of engagement for all students.

Are Americans' large quantities of discretionary time—40 to 50% of waking hours—a developmental asset or liability? A romantic view sees large blocks of unstructured time giving youths opportunities to explore, create structure on their own, learn to think outside the box, and perhaps "find themselves" in the existential ground zero of free choice. The underlying reality is that, left to themselves, children and adolescents often choose to spend time in

unchallenging activities, like hanging out with friends and watching TV. Although some social interaction and time for relaxation are undoubtedly useful, it seems unlikely that spending many hours in unchallenging contexts fosters development. The hypothesis that youths need and benefit from unstructured free time, nonetheless, remains worthy of creative research, especially if the time they spend on schoolwork increases.

The small but possibly growing amount of time children and adolescents spend in structured voluntary activities provides more developmentally promising use for some of these discretionary hours. In these activities, youths often experience challenge and exercise initiative. When adult leaders give responsibility to youths, they may provide better contexts for learning to create structure and think outside the box than can be found in free play or social interaction (Heath, 1999). In the absence of better knowledge, however, the current rush to create activities for after-school hours is unwise. Research is needed to determine the features of these activities associated with positive outcomes and how to fit participation to individuals' developmental readiness. A fundamental question is how to create activities with enough structure to contain and channel behavior without compromising youths' sense of agency.

Ultimately, development is probably best served by combinations of complementary activities, including those that shape good habits, teach literacy, build interpersonal relationships, foster initiative, and provide relaxation. The task of future research is to illuminate how quantities and qualities of experiences in different activities act in combination to affect development. Certainly, development is much more than an additive "sum of past experiences." We need to consider how individuals interpret, synthesize, and grow from experiences. Evaluation of time allocation is a useful entry point for examining links between experience and development, but only one small piece of a much more complex inquiry.

Recommended Reading

Larson, R., & Verma, S. (1999). (See References)

Robinson, J., & Bianchi, S. (1997). The children's hours. *American Demographics, 19* (12), 20–24.

Stevenson, H. W., & Stigler, J. W. (1992). *The learning gap.* New York: Simon & Schuster.

Wartella, E., & Mazzarella, S. (1990). A historical comparison of children's use of leisure time. In R. Butsch (Ed.), *For fun and profit: The transformation of leisure into consumption* (pp. 173–194). Philadelphia: Temple University Press.

Note

1. Address correspondence to Reed W. Larson, Department of Human and Community Development, University of Illinois, 1105 W. Nevada St., Urbana, IL 61801; e-mail: larsonr@uiuc.edu.

References

Ceci, S. J., & Williams, W. M. (1997). Schooling, intelligence, and income. *American Psychologist, 52,* 1051–1058.

Fisher, E. P. (1992). The impact of play on development: A meta-analysis. *Play & Culture, 5,* 159–181.

Fishman, C. (1999). The smorgasbord generation. *American Demographics, 21* (5), 55–60.

Goodnow, J. J. (1988). Children's household work: Its nature and functions. *Psychological Bulletin, 103,* 5–26.

Heath, S. B. (1999). Dimensions of language development: Lessons from older children. In A. S. Masten (Ed.), *The Minnesota Symposium on Child Psychology: Vol. 29. Cultural processes in child development* (pp. 59–75). Mahwah, NJ: Erlbaum.

Larson, R. (2000). Towards a psychology of positive youth development. *American Psychologist, 55,* 170–183.

Larson, R., & Verma, S. (1999). How children and adolescents spend time across cultural settings of the world: Work, play and developmental opportunities. *Psychological Bulletin, 125,* 701–736.

Mahoney, J. L. (2000). School extracurricular activity participation as a moderator in the development of antisocial patterns. *Child Development, 71,* 502–516.

McHale, S. M., Crouter, A. C., & Tucker, C. J. (2000, March). *Free time activities in middle childhood: Links with adjustment in early adolescence.* Paper presented at the biannual meeting of the Society for Research on Adolescence, Chicago.

Mortimer, J. T., Harley, C., & Aronson, P. (1999). How do prior experiences in the workplace set the stage for transitions to adulthood? In A. Booth, A. C. Crouter, & M. J. Shanahan (Eds.), *Transitions to adulthood in a changing economy: No work, no family, no future?* (pp. 131–159). Westport, CT: Praeger.

Osgood, D. W., Wilson, J. K., O'Malley, P. M., Bachman, J. G., & Johnston, L. D. (1996). Routine activities and individual deviant behavior. *American Sociological Review, 61,* 635–655.

Roberts, D. F., Foehr, U. G., Rideout, V. J., & Brodie, M. (1999). *Kids & media @ the new millennium.* Menlo Park, CA: Kaiser Family Foundation.

Stevenson, H. W., & Lee, S. (1990). Context of achievement. *Monographs of the Society for Research in Child Development, 55*(1–2).

Strasburger, V. C. (1995). *Adolescents and the media.* Thousand Oaks, CA: Sage.

Zill, N., Nord, C. W., & Loomis, L. S. (1995). *Adolescent time use, risky behavior, and outcomes: An analysis of national data.* Rockville, MD: Westat.

Parents or Pop Culture?
Children's Heroes and Role Models

What kind of heroes a culture promotes reveals a great
deal about that culture's values and desires.

Kristin J. Anderson and Donna Cavallaro

One of the most important features of childhood and
adolescence is the development of an identity. As children shape their behavior and values, they may look to
heroes and role models for guidance. They may identify
the role models they wish to emulate based on possession
of certain skills or attributes. While the child may not
want to be exactly like the person, he or she may see *possibilities* in that person. For instance, while Supreme Court
Justice Ruth Bader Ginsberg may not necessarily directly
influence girls and young women to become lawyers, her
presence on the Supreme Court may alter beliefs about
who is capable of being a lawyer or judge (Gibson & Cordova, 1999).

Parents and other family members are important role
models for children, particularly early on. Other influences may be institutional, such as schools, or cultural,
such as the mass media. What kind of heroes a culture
promotes reveals a great deal about the culture's values
and desires. Educators not only can model important behaviors themselves, but also can teach about values,
events, and people that a culture holds dear.

Television, movies, computer games, and other forms
of media expose children to an endless variety of cultural
messages. Which ones do children heed the most? Whom
do children want to be like? Do their role models vary according to children's ethnicity and gender? Finally, what
role can educators play in teaching children about role
models they may never have considered?

This article examines the impact of the mass media on
children's choices of heroes and role models. The authors
address the questions posed above in light of results from

a survey and focus groups conducted with children ages
8 to 13.

THE MENU OF POP CULTURE CHOICES

Television and Film for Children

Male characters—cartoon or otherwise—continue to be
more prevalent in children's television and film than female characters. Gender-stereotyped behaviors continue
to be the norm. For instance, male characters are more
commonly portrayed as independent, assertive, athletic,
important, attractive, technical, and responsible than female characters. They show more ingenuity, anger, leadership, bravery, and aggression, and they brag, interrupt,
make threats, and even laugh more than female characters do. In fact, since male characters appear so much
more frequently than female characters, they do more of
almost *everything* than female characters. Also, while the
behavior of female characters is somewhat less stereotypical than it was 20 years ago, in some ways male characters behave *more* stereotypically than 20 years ago (for
instance, males are now in more leadership roles, are
more bossy, and are more intelligent) (Thompson &
Zerbinos, 1995). These gender-stereotyped images, and
the inflexibility of male characters' roles, make for a restricted range of role models.

Parents, educators, and policymakers are also concerned about the aggressive and violent content in children's programs. Gerbner (1993) studied the violent content of children's programs and observed that "despite all the mayhem, only 3.2% of Saturday morning characters suffer any injury"; thus, children do not learn about the likely consequences of aggressive action. In children's shows, bad characters are punished 59 percent of the time. Even more telling, good characters who engage in violence are punished only 18 percent of the time. The characters that might be the most appealing to kids— the heroes and protagonists—rarely feel remorse, nor are they reprimanded or impeded when they engage in violence (National Television Violence Study, 1998). The authors found that 77 percent of the children surveyed watch television every day. Thus, many children may be learning to use violence as a problem-solving tool.

Characters in animated films also tend to follow stereotypes. While some positive changes in the portrayal of ethnic minority and female characters can be noted, both groups often remain narrowly defined in children's animated films. In his discussion of Disney films, Henry Giroux (1997) notes how the villains in the film *Aladdin* are racially stereotyped. The main character, Aladdin, the hero of the film, is drawn with very light skin, European features, and no accent. Yet the villains in the story appear as Middle Eastern caricatures: they have beards, large noses, sinister eyes, heavy accents, and swords. *Pocahontas*, who in real life was a young Native American girl, was portrayed by Disney as a brown-skinned, Barbie-like supermodel with an hourglass figure (Giroux, 1997). Consequently, animated characters, even those based on historical record, are either stereotyped or stripped of any meaningful sign of ethnicity. Fortunately, educators have the power to counter such unrealistic images with more accurate representations of historical characters.

Real-Life Television Characters

While some progress can be seen in the representation of ethnic minorities on television, the late 1990s actually brought a decrease in the number of people of color on prime time programming. In 1998, only 19 percent of Screen Actors Guild roles went to people of color. Roles for African American, Latinos, and Native Americans decreased from 1997 to 1998 (Screen Actors Guild [SAG], 1999). Women make up fewer than 40 percent of the characters in prime time. Female characters tend to be younger than male characters, conveying the message to viewers that women's youthfulness is more highly valued than other qualities. In terms of work roles, however, female characters' occupations are now less stereotyped, while male characters' occupations continue to be stereotyped (Signorielli & Bacue, 1999). This research suggests that girls' potential role models are somewhat less gender-stereotyped than before, while boy's potential role models are as narrowly defined as ever.

From Comic Book to Playground

Superheroes are the larger-than-life symbols of American values and "maleness." Perhaps the medium in which superheroes are most classically represented is comic books, which date back to the 1930s. The role of the hero is central to the traditional comic book. While female superheroes can be found in comics today (e.g., Marvel Girl, Phoenix, Shadow Cat, Psylocke), they represent only a small proportion—about 24 percent of Marvel Universe superhero trading cards (Young, 1993). Moreover, women and people of color do not fare well in superhero comics. To the extent that female characters exist, they often appear as victims and nuisances. People of color are marginalized as well. African American and Native American characters are more likely to be portrayed as villains, victims, or simply incompetent than as powerful and intelligent (Pecora, 1992).

One indirect way to gauge the impact of role models on children is to examine the nature of superhero play. Superhero play involving imitation of media characters with superhuman powers is more prevalent among boys than girls (Bell & Crosbie, 1996). This might be a function of the mostly male presence of superhero characters in comics and on television, or it may be due to girls receiving more sanctions from parents and teachers against playing aggressively. Children's imitations of superheroes in play concerns many classroom teachers, because it usually involves chasing, wrestling, kicking, and mock battles. Some researchers argue that superhero play may serve an important developmental function by offering children a sense of power in a world dominated by adults, thus giving children a means of coping with their frustrations. Superhero play also may allow children to grapple with ideas of good and evil and encourage them to work through their own anxieties about safety. Such play also may help children safely express anger and aggression (Boyd, 1997).

Other researchers and educators express concern that superhero play may legitimize aggression, endanger participants, and encourage stereotypical male dominance (Bell & Crosbie, 1996). One researcher observed children's superhero play in a school setting and found that boys created more superhero stories than girls did, and that girls often were excluded from such play. When girls were included they were given stereotypical parts, such as helpers or victims waiting to be saved. Even powerful female X-Men characters were made powerless in the boys' adaptations (Dyson, 1994). Thus, without teacher intervention or an abundance of female superheroes, superhero play may only serve to reinforce gender stereotypes.

One way to gauge popular culture's influence on superhero play is to compare the kind of play children engaged in before and after the arrival of television. In one retrospective study (French & Pena, 1991), adults between the ages of 17 and 83 provided information about their favorite childhood play themes, their heroes, and the qualities of those heroes. While certain methodological pitfalls common to retrospective studies were unavoidable, the findings are nevertheless intriguing. People who grew up before television reported engaging in less fantasy hero play and playing more realistically than kids who grew up with television. While media was the main source of heroes for kids who grew up with television, the previous generations found their heroes not only from the media, but also from direct experience, friends/siblings, and parents' occupations (French & Pena, 1991).

Recent Media Forms: Music Television and Video Games

Video games and music television videos are relatively recent forms of media. In a recent poll, girls and boys from various ethnic backgrounds reported that television and music were their favorite forms of media (Children Now, 1999). What messages about race/ethnicity and gender emerge from music videos—the seemingly perfect merger of children's favorite two media? Seidman (1999) found that the majority of characters were white (63 percent) and a majority were male (63 percent). When people of color, especially women of color, appeared in a video, their characters were much less likely to hold white collar jobs. In fact, their occupations were more gender-stereotyped than in real life. Gender role behavior overall was stereotypical. Thus, music television is yet another domain that perpetuates racial and gender stereotypes.

In the survey described below, the authors found that nearly half (48 percent) of the children surveyed played video and computer games every day or almost every day. Boys, however, were much more likely than girls to play these games. Of those who play computer/video games every day or almost every day, 76 percent are boys and only 24 percent are girls. Consequently, girls and boys might be differentially influenced by the images represented in video and computer games.

What *are* the images presented in video and computer games? Dietz's (1998) content analysis of popular video and computer games found that 79 percent of the games included aggression or violence. Only 15 percent of the games showed women as heroes or action characters. Indeed, girls and women generally were *not* portrayed—30 percent of the videos did not include girls or women at all. When female characters were included, 21 percent of the time they were the damsel in distress. Other female characters were portrayed as evil or as obstacles. This research points to at least two implications of these games. First, girls may not be interested in playing these video and computer games, because the implicit message is that girls are not welcome as players, and that girls and

women can only hope to be saved, destroyed, or pushed aside (see also Signorielli, 2001). Second, these images of girls and women found in video and computer games may influence boys' perceptions of gender.

In the past few years, a growing number of computer and video games geared toward girls have been made available by companies such as Purple Moon and Girl Games. These games have adventurous content without the violence typical of games geared toward boys. Two of the best-selling computer games for girls, however, have been *Cosmopolitan Virtual Makeover* and *Barbie Fashion Designer*. While these games may encourage creativity, ultimately their focus is on beauty. One columnist addresses the dilemma of creating games that will appeal to girls while fostering creativity and ingenuity:

> A girl given a doll is being told, "Girls play with dolls just like mommies take care of babies." A boy given a computer game is being told, "Boys play with computers just like daddies use them for work." A girl given *Barbie Fashion Designer* is being told, "Girls play with computers just like girls play with dolls." A lucky few might get the message that, as some girls exchange dolls for real babies, others might progress from *Barbie Fashion Designer* to real-life fashion designer, or engineering systems designer, or software designer. But there's a good chance that many will not. (Ivinski, 1997, p. 28)

As more and more educators begin using the Internet, CD-ROMS, and videos as teaching tools (Risko, 1999), they will be faced with the challenge of finding materials that fairly represent a wide range of characters, people, and behavior. Paradoxically, the use of "new" technology, such as CD-ROMs and computer games, implies that a student is going to enjoy a progressive, cutting-edge experience. However, educators must be vigilant about the content, as they should be with any textbook or film. The cutting-edge format of these new technologies does not guarantee nonstereotyped material.

A SURVEY OF CHILDREN'S ROLE MODELS AND HEROES

Whom do children actually choose as role models, and why? The authors surveyed children about their heroes and role models, both people they know and famous people or imaginary characters. Survey questions also addressed children's interaction with television, film, computer/video games, books, and comic books. The children talked about their answers in small groups. One hundred and seventy-nine children, ages 8 to 13, were surveyed from five day camp sites in central and southern California. The ethnic breakdown of the survey sample was as follows: 24 African Americans, 31 Asian

Americans, 74 Latinos, 1 Middle Eastern American, 2 Native Americans, 45 whites, and 2 "other." Ninety-five girls and 84 boys participated. The samples of ethnic and gender categories were then weighted so that each of these demographic groups, when analyzed, reflects their actual contribution to the total population of children in the United States.

Do Children Admire People They Know or Famous People?

The survey began with the following: "We would like to know whom you look up to and admire. These might be people you know, or they might be famous people or characters. You may want to be like them or you might just think they are cool." More respondents described a person they knew (65 percent) rather than a person they did not know, such as a person or character in the media (35 percent). When asked in focus groups why they picked people they knew instead of famous people, one 10-year-old white girl said, "I didn't put down people I don't know because when nobody's paying attention, they do something bad." Another student said, "Some [media figures] are just not nice. Some famous people act good on TV but they're really horrible." Thus, some children employed a level of skepticism when judging the worthiness of a role model.

Figure 1 represents the percentages of role models the children knew versus media heroes they identified. Similar to the overall sample, 70 percent of the African American and 64 percent of the White children chose people they knew as heroes. In contrast, only 35 percent of the Asian American kids and 49 percent of the Latino kids named people they knew. This latter finding seems paradoxical; Asian American and Latino children would seem more likely to choose people they know as role models because their ethnic groups are represented less frequently in mass media than are African Americans and whites. Perhaps Asian American and Latino children have internalized a message that they should not look up to fellow Asian Americans or Latinos as role models, or it may be a byproduct of assimilation. Obviously, further work in this area is needed.

On average, responses from girls and boys differed. While both girls and boys named people they knew as their heroes, 67 percent of the girls did so as compared with only 58 percent of the boys. Since boys and men are seen more frequently as sports stars, actors, and musicians, girls may have a smaller pool of potential role models from which to choose. Another factor might be that the girls in this study reported watching less television than the boys did, and so they may have known fewer characters. Sixty-seven percent of the girls reported watching television one hour a day or more, while 87 percent of the boys reported watching television this amount.

Do Children Choose Role Models Who Are Similar to Themselves?

One feature of role modeling is that children tend to choose role models whom they find relevant and with whom they can compare themselves (Lockwood & Kunda, 2000). Children who do not "see themselves" in the media may have fewer opportunities to select realistic role models. Two ways to assess similarity is to consider the ethnicity and gender of children's chosen role models. Do children tend to select heroes who are of their same ethnic background? Because data was not available on the ethnic background of the reported role models whom the children knew personally, the authors examined only the heroes from the media, whose backgrounds were known, to explore this question (see Figure 2). African American and white children were more likely to have media heroes of their same ethnicity (67 percent for each). In contrast, Asian American and Latino children chose more white media heroes than other categories (40 percent and 56 percent, respectively). Only 35 percent of the Asian Americans respondents, and 28 percent of the Latino respondents, chose media heroes of their own ethnicity.

How can we explain the fact that African American and white children are more likely to have media heroes of their same ethnicity, compared to Asian American and Latino children? There is no shortage of white characters for white children to identify with in television and film, and African Americans now make up about 14 percent of television and theatrical characters (SAG, 2000). While African American characters are represented less frequently than white characters, their representation on television, film, and music television is much higher than for Asian American and Latino characters (e.g., Asians represent 2.2 percent, and Latinos represent 4.4 percent, of television and film characters) (SAG, 2000). Also, fewer famous athletes are Asian American or Latino, compared to African American or white.

Also of interest was whether children choose role models of the same, or other, gender. Overall, children in this study more often chose a same-gender person as someone they look up to and admire. This pattern is consistent across all four ethnic groups, and stronger for boys than girls. Only 6 percent of the boys chose a girl or woman, while 24 percent of the girls named a boy or man. Asian American boys actually picked male heroes exclusively. Asian American girls chose the fewest female role models (55 percent) compared to the other girls (see Figure 3). These findings associated with Asian American children present a particular challenge for educators. Asian Americans, and particularly Asian American women, are seldom presented as heroes in textbooks. This is all the more reason for schools to provide a broader and more diverse range of potential role models.

184

Figure 1

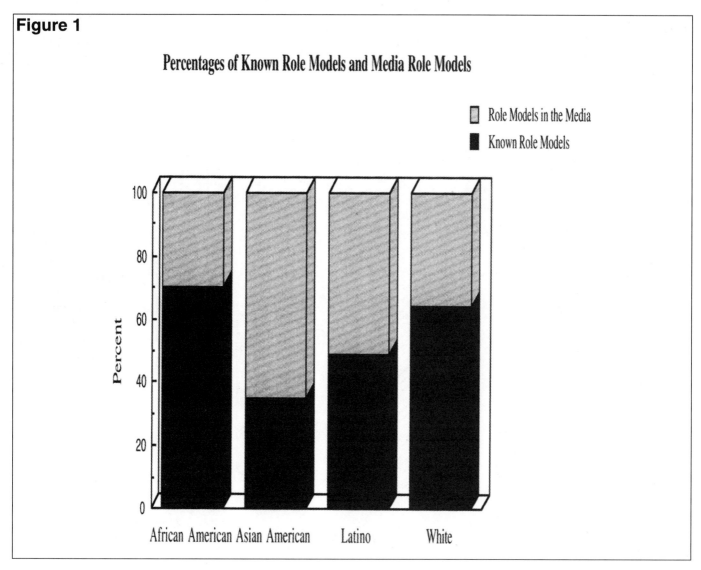

Percentages of Known Role Models and Media Role Models

☐ Role Models in the Media
■ Known Role Models

At the same time, it has been reported that boys will tend to imitate those who are powerful (Gibson & Cordova, 1999). Thus, while boys tend to emulate same-gender models more than girls do, boys may emulate a woman if she is high in social power. Therefore, boys may be especially likely to have boys and men as role models because they are more likely to be portrayed in positions of power. It also has been noted that college-age women select men *and* women role models with the same frequency, whereas college-age men still tend to avoid women role models. The fact that young women choose both genders as role models might be a result of the relative scarcity of women in powerful positions to serve as role models (Gibson & Cordova, 1999).

Who Are Children's Role Models and Heroes?

Overall, children most frequently (34 percent) named their parents as role models and heroes. The next highest category (20 percent) was entertainers; in descending or-

der, the other categories were friends (14 percent), professional athletes (11 percent), and acquaintances (8 percent). Authors and historical figures were each chosen by only 1 percent of the children.

Patterns were somewhat different when ethnicity was taken into account. African American and white children chose a parent more frequently (30 percent and 33 percent, respectively). In contrast, Asian Americans and Latinos chose entertainers (musicians, actors, and television personalities) most frequently (39 percent for Asian Americans and 47 percent for Latinos), with parents coming in second place. When gender was taken into account, both girls and boys most frequently mentioned a parent (girls 29 percent, boys 34 percent), while entertainers came in second place. Figure 4 illustrates these patterns.

When taking both ethnicity and gender into account, the researchers found that Asian American and Latina girls most frequently picked entertainers (50 percent of the Asian American girls and 41 percent of the Latinas), while African American and white girls chose parents (33 percent and 29 percent, respectively). Asian American boys most frequently named a professional athlete (36

Figure 2

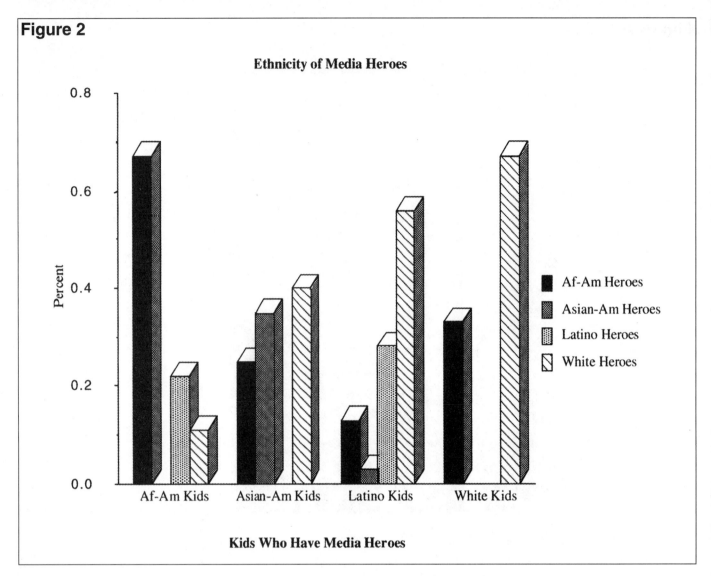

percent), African American boys most frequently picked a parent (30 percent), Latino boys most frequently chose entertainers (54 percent), and white boys picked parents (38 percent).

What Qualities About Their Role Models and Heroes Do Children Admire?

When asked why they admired their heroes and role models, the children most commonly replied that the person was nice, helpful, and understanding (38 percent). Parents were appreciated for their generosity, their understanding, and for "being there." For instance, an 11-year-old African American girl who named her mother as her hero told us, "I like that she helps people when they're in a time of need." Parents were also praised for the lessons they teach their kids. A 9-year-old Asian American boy told us, "I like my dad because he is always nice and he teaches me."

The second most admired feature of kids' role models was skill (27 percent). The skills of athletes and entertain-

ers were most often mentioned. One 12-year-old white boy said he admires Kobe Bryant because "he's a good basketball player and because he makes a good amount of money." A 10-year-old Asian American girl chose Tara Lipinski because "she has a lot of courage and is a great skater." A 9-year-old Latino boy picked Captain America and said, "What I like about Captain America is his cool shield and how he fights the evil red skull." The third most frequently mentioned characteristic was a sense of humor (9 percent), which was most often attributed to entertainers. For instance, a 10-year-old Latino boy picked Will Smith "because he's funny. He makes jokes and he dances funny."

These findings held true for children in all four ethnic groups and across the genders, with two exceptions: boys were more likely than girls to name athletes for their skill, and entertainers for their humor. Given the media attention to the U.S. women's soccer team victory in the World Cup in 1999, and the success of the WNBA (the women's professional basketball league), the researchers expected girls to name women professional athletes as their heroes. However, only four girls in the study did so. Despite recent

Figure 3

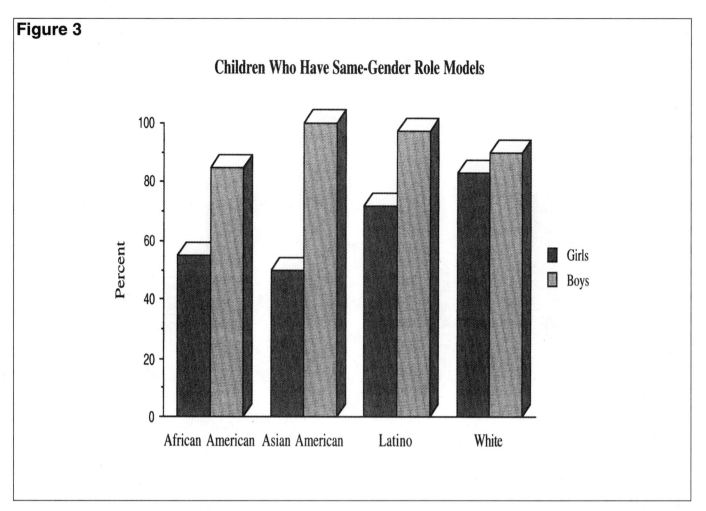

Children Who Have Same-Gender Role Models

strides in the visibility of women's sports, the media continue to construct men's sports as the norm and women's sports as marginal (e.g., references to men's athletics as "sports" and women's athletics as "women's sports").

When children's heroes were media characters, African American and white children were more likely to name media heroes of their same ethnicity. In contrast, Asian American and Latino children tended to name media heroes who were not of their same ethnicity.

Summary and Implications

Whether the children in this study had heroes they knew in real life, or whether they chose famous people or fictional characters, depended, to some extent, on the respondents' ethnicity and gender. Overall, however, the most frequently named role model for kids was a parent. This is good news for parents, who must wonder, given

the omnipresence of the media, whether they have any impact at all on their children. Popular culture was a significant source of heroes for children as well. Entertainers were the second most frequently named role models for the children, and the number increases significantly if you add professional athletes to that category. The attributes that children valued depended on whom they chose. For instance, children who named parents named them because they are helpful and understanding. Media characters were chosen because of their skills. When children's heroes were media characters, African American and white children were more likely to name media heroes of their same ethnicity. In contrast, Asian American and Latino children tended to name media heroes who were not of their same ethnicity. Children kept to their own gender when choosing a hero; boys were especially reluctant to choose girls and women as their heroes.

The frequency with which boys in this study named athletes as their role models is noteworthy. Only four girls in the study did the same. The implications of this gender difference are important, because many studies find that girls' participation in sports is associated with a number of positive attributes, such as high self-esteem and self-efficacy (Richman & Shaffer, 2000). Therefore, school and community support of girls' athletic programs and recognition of professional women athletes would go

Figure 4

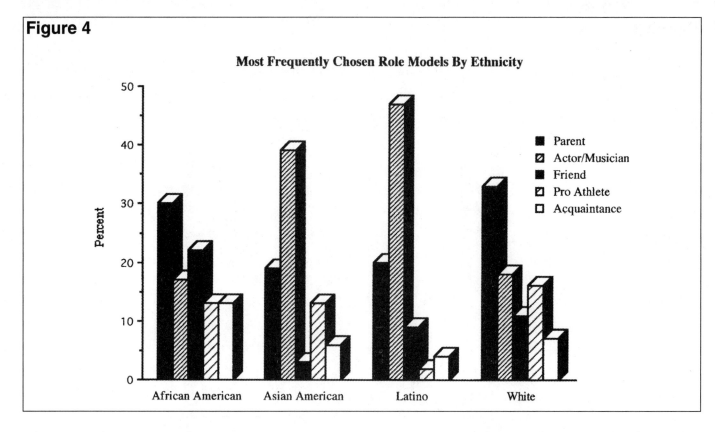

Most Frequently Chosen Role Models By Ethnicity

Legend:
- Parent
- Actor/Musician
- Friend
- Pro Athlete
- Acquaintance

a long way to encourage girls' participation in sports, as well as boys' appreciation of women athletes as potential role models.

The mass media are hindered by a narrow view of gender, and by limited, stereotyped representations of ethnic minorities. Parents and educators must take pains to expose children to a wider variety of potential role models than popular culture does. Historical figures and authors constituted a tiny minority of heroes named by the children surveyed. Educators can play a significant role by exposing students to a wide range of such historical heroes, including people from various professions, people of color, and women of all races.

Finally, educators could capitalize on children's need for guidance to expose them to a greater variety of role models. Doing so affirms for the children that their race and gender are worthy of representation. A variety of potential heroes and role models allows children to appreciate themselves and the diversity in others.

References

Bell, R., & Crosbie, C. (1996, November 13). Superhero play of 3-5-year-old children. Available: http://labyrinth.net.au/~cccav/sept97/superhero.html.

Boyd, B. J. (1997). Teacher response to superhero play: To ban or not to ban. *Childhood Education, 74*, 23–28.

Children Now. (1999, September). *Boys to men: Messages about masculinity.* Oakland, CA: Author.

Dietz, T. L. (1998). An examination of violence and gender role portrayals in video games: Implications for gender socialization. *Sex Roles, 38*, 425–433.

Dyson, A. H. (1994). The ninjas, the X-men, and the ladies: Playing with power and identity in an urban primary school. *Teachers College Record, 96*, 219–239.

French, J., & Pena, S. (1991). Children's hero play of the 20th century: Changes resulting from television's influence. *Child Study Journal, 21*, 79–94.

Gerbner, G. (1993). *Women and minorities on television: A study in casting and fate.* A report to the Screen Actors Guild and the American Federation of Radio and Television Artists, Philadelphia: The Annenberg School of Communication, University of Pennsylvania.

Gibson, D. E., & Cordova, D. I. (1999). Women's and men's role models: The importance of exemplars. In A. J. Murrell, F. J. Crosby, & R. J. Ely (Eds.), *Mentoring dilemmas: Developmental relationships within multicultural organizations* (pp. 121–141). Mahwah, NJ: Lawrence Erlbaum Associates.

Giroux, H. A. (1997). Are Disney movies good for your kids? In S. R. Steinberg & J. L. Kincheloe (Eds.), *Kinderculture: The corporate construction of childhood* (pp. 53–67). Boulder, CO: Westview Press.

Ivinski, P. (1997). Game girls: Girl market in computer games and educational software. *Print, 51*, 24–29.

Lockwood, P., & Kunda, Z. (2000). Outstanding role models: Do they inspire or demoralize us? In A. Tesser, R. B. Felson, et al. (Eds.), *Psychological perspectives on self and identity* (pp. 147–171). Washington, DC: American Psychological Association.

National Television Violence Study. Vol. 3. (1998). Thousand Oaks, CA: Sage.

Pecora, N. (1992). Superman/superboys/supermen: The comic book hero as socializing agent. In S. Craig (Ed.), *Men, masculinity, and the media* (pp. 61–77). Newbury Park, CA: Sage.

Richman, E. L., & Shaffer, D. R. (2000). "If you let me play sports": How might sport participation influence the self-esteem of adolescent females? *Psychology of Women Quarterly, 24*, 189–199.

Risko, V. J. (1999). The power and possibilities of video technology and intermediality. In L. Semali & A. Watts Pailliotet (Eds.), *Intermediality: The teachers' handbook of critical media literacy* (pp. 129–140). Boulder, CO: Westview Press.

Screen Actors Guild. (1999, May 3). *New Screen Actors Guild employment figures reveal a decline in roles for Latinos, African American and Native American Indian performers.* Press Release. Available: www.sag.org

Screen Actors Guild. (2000, December 20). *Screen Actors Guild employment statistics reveal percentage increases in available roles for African Americans and Latinos, but total number of roles to minorities decrease in 1999.* Press Release. Available: www.sag.org.

Seidman, S. A. (1999). Revisiting sex-role stereotyping in MTV videos. *International Journal of Instructional Media, 26,* 11.

Signorielli, N. (2001). Television's gender role images and contribution to stereotyping: Past, present, future. In D. G. Singer & J. L. Singer (Eds.), *Handbook of children and the media* (pp. 341–358). Thousand Oaks, CA: Sage.

Signorielli, N., & Bacue, A. (1999). Recognition and respect: A content analysis of prime-time television characters across three decades. *Sex Roles, 40,* 527–544.

Thompson, T. L., & Zerbinos, E. (1995). Gender roles in animated cartoons: Has the picture changed in 20 years? *Sex Roles, 32,* 651–673.

Young, T. J. (1993). Women as comic book superheroes: The "weaker sex" in the Marvel universe. *Psychology: A Journal of Human Behavior, 30,* 49–50.

Authors' Notes:

This project was conducted in conjunction with Mediascope, a not-for-profit media education organization. The terms "hero" and "role model" tend to be used interchangeably in the literature. When a distinction between the terms is made, role models are defined as known persons (e.g., parents, teachers) and heroes are defined as figures who may be less attainable, or larger than life. Both kinds of persons and figures are of interest here; therefore, the terms are used interchangeably, and we specify whether known people or famous figures are being discussed.

Kristin J. Anderson is Assistant Professor, Psychology and Women's Studies, Antioch College, Yellow Springs, Ohio. Donna Cavallaro is graduate student, counseling psychology, Santa Clara University, Santa Clara, California.

The Effects of Poverty on Children

Abstract

Although hundreds of studies have documented the association between family poverty and children's health, achievement, and behavior, few measure the effects of the timing, depth, and duration of poverty on children, and many fail to adjust for other family characteristics (for example, female headship, mother's age, and schooling) that may account for much of the observed correlation between poverty and child outcomes. This article focuses on a recent set of studies that explore the relationship between poverty and child outcomes in depth. By and large, this research supports the conclusion that family income has selective but, in some instances, quite substantial effects on child and adolescent well-being. Family income appears to be more strongly related to children's ability and achievement than to their emotional outcomes. Children who live in extreme poverty and who live below the poverty line for multiple years appear, all other things being equal, to suffer the worst outcomes. The timing of poverty also seems to be important for certain child outcomes. Children who experience poverty during their preschool and early school years have lower rates of school completion than children and adolescents who experience poverty only in later years. Although more research is needed on the significance of the timing of poverty on child outcomes, findings to date suggest that interventions during early childhood may be most important in reducing poverty's impact on children.

Jeanne Brooks-Gunn
Greg J. Duncan

In recent years, about one in five American children—some 12 to 14 million—have lived in families in which cash income failed to exceed official poverty thresholds. Another one-fifth lived in families whose incomes were no more than twice the poverty threshold.[1,2] For a small minority of children—4.8% of all children and 15% of children who ever became poor—childhood poverty lasted 10 years or more.[3]

Income poverty is the condition of not having enough income to meet basic needs for food, clothing, and shelter. Because children are dependent on others, they enter or avoid poverty by virtue of their family's economic circumstances. Children cannot alter family conditions by themselves, at least until they approach adulthood. Government programs, such as those described by Devaney, Ellwood, and Love in this journal issue, have been developed to increase the likelihood that poor children are provided basic

necessities. But even with these programs, poor children do not fare as well as those whose families are not poor.[4]

What does poverty mean for children? How does the relative lack of income influence children's day-to-day lives? Is it through inadequate nutrition; fewer learning experiences; instability of residence; lower quality of schools; exposure to environmental toxins, family violence, and homelessness; dangerous streets; or less access to friends, services, and, for adolescents, jobs? This article reviews recent research that used longitudinal data to examine the relationship between low-income poverty and child outcomes in several domains.

Hundreds of studies, books, and reports have examined the detrimental effects of poverty on the well-being of children. Many have been summarized in recent reports such as *Wasting America's Future* from the Children's Defense Fund and *Alive and Well?* from the National Center for

Children in Poverty.[5] However, while the literature on the effects of poverty on children is large, many studies lack the precision necessary to allow researchers to disentangle the effects on children of the array of factors associated with poverty. Understanding of these relationships is key to designing effective policies to ameliorate these problems for children.

This article examines these relationships and the consequences for children of growing up poor. It begins with a long, but by no means exhaustive, list of child outcomes (see Table 1) that have been found to be associated with poverty in several large, nationally representative, cross-sectional surveys. This list makes clear the broad range of effects poverty can have on children. It does little, however, to inform the discussion of the causal effects of income poverty on children because the studies from which this list is derived did not control for other variables associated with poverty. For example, poor families are more likely to be headed by a parent who is single, has low educational attainment, is unemployed, has low earning potential and is young. These parental attributes, separately or in combination, might account for some of the observed negative consequences of poverty on children. Nor do the relationships identified in the table capture the critical factors of the timing, depth, and duration of childhood poverty on children.[6,7]

This article focuses on studies that used national longitudinal data sets to estimate the effects of family income on children's lives, independent of other family conditions that might be related to growing up in a low-income household. These studies attempt to isolate the effect of family income by taking into account, statistically, the effects of maternal age at the child's birth, maternal education, marital status, ethnicity, and other factors on child outcomes.[2,8] Many used data on family income over several years and at different stages of development to estimate the differential effects of the timing and duration of poverty on child outcomes. The data sets analyzed include the Panel Study of Income Dynamics (PSID), the National Longitudinal Survey of Youth (NLSY), Children of the NLSY (the follow-up of the children born to the women in the original NLSY cohort), the National Survey of Families and Households (NSFH), the National Health and Nutrition Examination Survey (NHANES), and the Infant Health and Development Program (IHDP). These rich data sets include multiple measures of child outcomes and family and child characteristics.

This article is divided into four sections. The first focuses on the consequences of poverty across five child outcomes. If income does, in fact, affect child outcomes, then it is important not only to identify these outcomes but also to describe the pathways through which income operates. Accordingly, in the second section, five pathways through which poverty might operate are described. The third section focuses on whether the links between poverty and outcomes can reasonably be attributed to income rather than

other family characteristics. The concluding section considers policy implications of the research reviewed.

Effects of Income on Child Outcomes

Measures of Child Well-Being

As illustrated in Table 1, poor children suffer higher incidences of adverse health, developmental, and other outcomes than non-poor children. The specific dimensions of the well-being of children and youths considered in some detail in this article include (1) physical health (low birth weight, growth stunting, and lead poisoning), (2) cognitive ability (intelligence, verbal ability, and achievement test scores), (3) school achievement (years of schooling, high school completion), (4) emotional and behavioral outcomes, and (5) teenage out-of-wedlock childbearing. Other outcomes are not addressed owing to a scarcity of available research, a lack of space, and because they overlap with included outcomes.

While this review is organized around specific outcomes, it could also have been organized around the various ages of childhood.[9-11] Five age groups are often distinguished—prenatal to 2 years, early childhood (ages 3 to 6), late childhood (ages 7 to 10), early adolescence (ages 11 to 15), and late adolescence (ages 16 to 19). Each age group covers one or two major transitions in a child's life, such as school entrances or exits, biological maturation, possible cognitive changes, role changes, or some combination of these. These periods are characterized by relatively universal developmental challenges that require new modes of adaptation to biological, psychological, or social changes.[10]

Somewhat different indicators of child and youth well-being are associated with each period. For example, grade retention is more salient in the late childhood years than in adolescence (since most schools do not hold students back once they reach eighth grade[12]). Furthermore, low income might influence each indicator differently. As an illustration, income has stronger effects on cognitive and verbal ability test scores than it has on indices of emotional health in the childhood years.

Physical Health

Compared with nonpoor children, poor children in the United States experience diminished physical health as measured by a number of indicators of health status and outcomes (see Table 1). In the 1988 National Health Interview Survey; parents reported that poor children were only two-thirds as likely to be in excellent health and almost twice as likely to be in fair or poor health as nonpoor children. These large differences in health status between poor and nonpoor children do not reflect adjustment for potentially confounding factors (factors, other than income, that may be associated with living in poverty) nor do they distinguish between long- or short-term poverty or the timing of poverty. This sec-

Table 1

Selected Population-Based Indicators of Well-Being for Poor and Nonpoor Children in the United States

Indicator	Percentage of Poor Children (unless noted)	Percentage of Nonpoor Children (unless noted)	Ratio of Poor to Nonpoor Children
Physical Health Outcomes (for children between 0 and 17 years unless noted)			
Reported to be in excellent health[a]	37.4	55.2	0.7
Reported to be in fair to poor health[a]	11.7	<+>6.5	1.8
Experienced an accident, poisoning, or injury in the past year that required medical attention[a]	11.8	14.7	0.8
Chronic asthma[a]	4.4	4.3	1.0
Low birth weight (less than 2,500 grams)[b]	1.0	>0.6	1.7
Lead poisoning (blood lead levels 10 u/dl or greater)[c]	16.3	4.7	3.5
Infant mortality[b]	1.4 deaths per 100 live births	0.8 death per 100 live births	1.7
Deaths During Childhood (0 to 14 years)[d]	1.2	0.8	1.5
Stunting (being in the fifth percentile for height for age for 2 to 17 years)[e]	10.0	5.0	2.0
Number of days spent in bed in past year[a]	5.3 days	3.8 days	1.4
Number of short-stay hospital episodes in past year per 1,000 children[a]	81.3 stays	41.2 stays	2.0
Cognitive Outcomes			
Developmental delay (includes both limited and long-term developmental deficits) (0 to 17 years)[a]	5.0	3.8	1.3
Learning disability (defined as having exceptional difficulty in learning to read, write, and do arithmetic) (3 to 17 years)[a]	8.3	6.1	1.4
School Achievement Outcomes (5 to 17 years)			
Grade repetition (reported to have ever repeated a grade)[a]	28.8	14.1	2.0
Ever expelled or suspended[a]	11.9	6.1	2.0
High school dropout (percentage 16- to 24-year olds who were not in school or did not finish high school in 1994)[f]	21.0	9.6	2.2
Emotional or Behavioral Outcomes (3 to 17 years unless noted)			
Parent reports child has ever had an emotional or behavioral problem that lasted three months or more[g]	16.4	12.7	1.3
Parent reports child ever being treated for an emotional problem or behavioral problem[a]	2.5	4.5	0.6
Parent reports child has experienced one or more of a list of typical child behavioral problems in the last three months[h] (5 to 17 years)	57.4	57.3	1.0
Other			
Female teens who had an out-of-wedlock birth[i]	11.0	3.6	3.1
Economically inactive at age 24 (not employed or in school)[j]	15.9	8.3	1.9
Experienced hunger (food insufficiency) at least once in past year[k]	15.9	1.6	9.9
Reported cases of child abuse and neglect[l]	5.4	0.8	6.8
Violent crimes (experienced by poor families and nonpoor families)[m]	5.4	2.6	2.1
Afraid to go out (percentage of family heads in poor and nonpoor families who report they are afraid to go out in their neighborhood)[n]	19.5	8.7	2.2

Note: This list of child outcomes reflects findings from large nationally representative surveys that collect data on child outcomes and family income. While most data comes from the 1988 National Health Interview Survey Child Health Supplement, data from other nationally representative surveys are included. The rates presented are from simple cross-tabulations. In most cases, the data do not reflect factors that might be important to child outcomes other than poverty status at the time of data collection. The ratios reflect rounding. *(Notes continued on next page.)*

(Notes continued from previous page)

[a] Data from the 1988 National Health Interview Survey Child Health Supplement (NHS-CHS),a nationwide household interview survey. Children's health status was reported by the adult household member who knew the most about the sample child's health,usually the child's mother. Figures calculated from Dawson,D.A. Family structure and children's health: United States,1988. Vital Health and Statistics,Series 10,no. 178. Hyattsville,MD: U.S. Department of Health and Human Services,Public Health Service,June 1991; and Coiro,M.J.,Zill,n.,and Bloom,B. Health of our nation's children. Vital Health and Statistics,Series 10,no. 191. Hyattsville,MD: U.S. Department of Health and Human Services,Public Health Service,December 1994.

[b] Data from the National Maternal and Infant Health Survey,data collected in 1989 and 1990,with 1988 as the reference period. Percentages were calculated from the number of deaths and number of low birth weight births per 1,000 live births as reported in Federman,M.,Garner,T.,Short,K.,et al. What does it mean to be poor in America? Monthly Labor Review (May 1996) 119,5:10.

[c] Data from the NHANES III,1988-1991. Poor children who lived in families with incomes less than 130% of the poverty threshold are classified as poor. All other children are classified as nonpoor.

[d] Percentages include only black and white youths. Percentages calculated from Table 7 in Rogot,E. A mortality study of 1.3 million persons by demographic,social and economic factors: 1979-1985 follow-up. Rockville,MD: National Institutes of Health,July 1992.

[e] Data from NHANES II,1976-1980. For more discussion,see the Child Indicators article in this journal issue.

[f] National Center for Education Statistics. Dropout rates in the United States: 1994. Table 7,Status dropout rate,ages 16-24,by income and race ethnicity: October 1994. Available online at: http://www.ed.gov/NCES/pubs/r941007.html.

[g] Data from the NHIS-CHS. The question was meant to identify children with common psychological disorders such as attention deficit disorder or depression,as well as more severe problems such as autism.

[h] Data from the NHIS-CHS. Parents responded "sometimes true," "often true," or "not true" to a list of 32 statements typical of children's behaviors. Each statement corresponded to one of six individual behavior problems--antisocial behavior,anxiety,peer conflict/social withdrawal,dependency,hyperactivity,and headstrong behavior. Statements included behaviors such as cheating or lying,being disobedient in the home,being secretive,and demanding a lot of attention. For a more complete description,see Section P-11 of the NHIS-CHS questionnaire.

[i] Data from the Panel Study of Income Dynamics (PSID). Based on 1,705 children ages 0 to 6 in 1968; outcomes measured at ages 21 to 27. Haveman,R.,and Wolfe,B. Succeeding generations: On the effect of investments in children. New York: Russell Sage Foundation,1994,p. 108,Table 4,10c.

[j] Data from the PSID. Based on 1,705 children ages 0 to 6 in 1968; outcomes measured at ages 21 to 27. In Succeeding generations: On the effect of investments in children. Haveman,R.,and Wolfe,B. New York: Russell Sage Foundation,1994,p. 108,Table 4,10d. Economically inactive is defined as not being a full-time student,working 1,000 hours or more per year; attending school part time and working 500 hours; a mother of an infant or mother of two or more children less than five years old; a part-time student and the mother of a child less than five years old.

[k] Data from NHANES III,1988-1991. Figures reflect food insufficiency,the term used in government hunger-related survey questions. For a more in-depth discussion,see Lewit,E.M.,and Kerrebrock,N. Child indicators: Childhood hunger. The Future of Children (Spring 1997) 7,1:128-37.

[l] Data from Study of National Incidence and Prevalence of Child Abuse and Neglect: 1988. In Wasting America's future. Children's Defense Fund. Boston: Beacon Press,1994,pp. 5-29,87,Tables 5-6. Poor families are those with annual incomes below $15,000.

[m] Data from the National Crime Victimization Interview Survey. Results are for households or persons living in households. Data were collected between January 1992 and June 1993 with 1992 as the reference period. Percentages are calculated from number of violent crimes per 1,000 people per year. Reported in Federman,M.,Garner,T.,Short,K.,et al. What does it mean to be poor in America? Monthly Labor Review (May 1996) 119,5:9.

[n] Data from the Survey of Income and Program Participation. Participation data collection and reference periods are September through December 1992. Reported in Federman,M.,Garner,T.,Short,K.,et al. What does it mean to be poor in America?<%2> Monthly Labor Review (May 1996) 119,5:9.

---

tion reviews research on the relationship of poverty to several key measures of child health, low birth weight and infant mortality, growth stunting, and lead poisoning. For the most part, the focus is on research that attempts to adjust for important confounding factors and/or to address the effect of the duration of poverty on child health outcomes.

Birth Outcomes

Low birth weight (2,500 grams or less) and infant mortality are important indicators of child health. Low birth weight is associated with an increased likelihood of subsequent physical health and cognitive and emotional problems that can persist through childhood and adolescence. Serious physical disabilities, grade repetition, and learning disabilities are more prevalent among children who were low birth weight as infants, as are lower levels of intelligence and of math and reading achievement. Low birth weight is also the key risk factor for infant mortality (especially death within the first 28 days of life), which is a widely accepted indicator of the health and well-being of children.[13]

> Poverty status had a statistically significant effect on both low birth weight and the neonatal mortality rate for whites but not for blacks

Estimating the effects of poverty alone on birth outcomes is complicated by the fact that adverse birth outcomes are more prevalent for unmarried women, those with low levels of education, and black mothers—all groups with high poverty rates. One study that used data from the NLSY to examine the relationship between family income and low birth weight did find, however, that among whites, women with family income below the federal poverty level in the year of birth were 80% more likely to have a low birth weight baby as compared with women whose family incomes were above the poverty level (this study statistically controlled for mothers' age, education, marital status, and smoking status). Further analysis also showed that the duration of poverty had an important effect; if a white woman was poor both at the time when she entered the longitudinal NLSY sample and at the time of her pregnancy (5 to 10 years later), she was more than three times more likely to deliver a low birth weight infant than a white woman who was not poor at both times. For black women in this sample, although the odds of having a low birth weight baby were twice the odds for white mothers, the probability of having a low birth weight baby was not related to family poverty status.[14]

Other studies that used county level data to examine the effects of income or poverty status and a number of pregnancy-related health services on birth outcomes for white and black women also found that income or poverty status had a statistically significant effect on both low birth weight and the neonatal mortality rate for whites but not for blacks.[15,16]

Growth Stunting

Although overt malnutrition and starvation are rare among poor children in the United States, deficits in children's nutritional status are associated with poverty. As described more fully in the Child Indicators article in this journal issue, stunting (low height for age), a measure of nutritional status, is more prevalent among poor than nonpoor children. Studies using data from the NLSY show that differentials in height for age between poor and nonpoor children are greater when long-term rather than single-year measures of poverty are used in models to predict stunting. These differentials by poverty status are large even in models that statistically control for many other family and child characteristics associated with poverty.[17]

Lead Poisoning

Harmful effects of lead have been documented even at low levels of exposure. Health problems vary with length of exposure, intensity of lead in the environment, and the developmental stage of the child—with risks beginning prior to birth. At very young ages, lead exposure is linked to stunted growth,[18] hearing loss,[19] vitamin D metabolism damage, impaired blood production, and toxic effects on the kidneys.[20] Additionally, even a small increase in blood lead above the Centers for Disease Control and Prevention (CDC) current intervention threshold (10 μg/dL) is associated with a decrease in intelligence quotient (IQ).[21]

Today, deteriorating lead-based house paint remains the primary source of lead for young children. Infants and toddlers in old housing eat the sweet-tasting paint chips and breathe the lead dust from deteriorating paint. Four to five million children reside in homes with lead levels exceeding the accepted threshold for safety,[22] and more than 1.5 million children under six years of age have elevated blood lead levels.[23]

Using data from NHANES III (1988–1991), one study found that children's blood lead levels declined as family income increased.[23] All other things being equal, mean blood lead levels were 9% lower for one- to five-year-olds in families with incomes twice the poverty level than for those who were poor. Overall blood levels were highest among one- to five-year-olds who were non-Hispanic blacks from low-income families in large central cities. The mean blood lead level for this group, 9.7 μg/dL, was just under the CDC's threshold for intervention and almost three times the mean for all one- to five-year-olds.

Cognitive Abilities

As reported in Table 1, children living below the poverty threshold are 1.3 times as likely as nonpoor children to experience learning disabilities and developmental delays. Reliable measures of cognitive ability and school achievement for young children in the Children of the NLSY and IHDP data sets have been used in a number of studies to examine the relationship between cognitive ability and poverty in detail.[6,24–26] This article reports on several studies that control for a number of potentially important family characteristics and attempts to distinguish between the effects of long- and short-term poverty.

The effects of long-term poverty on measures of children's cognitive ability were significantly greater than the effects of short-term poverty.

A recent study using data from the Children of the NLSY and the IHDP compared children in families with incomes less than half of the poverty threshold to children in families with incomes between 1.5 and twice the poverty threshold. The poorer children scored between 6 and 13 points lower on various standardized tests of IQ, verbal ability, and achievement.[25] These differences are very large from an educational perspective and were present even after controlling for maternal age, marital status, education, and ethnicity. A 6- to 13-point difference might mean, for example, the difference between being placed in a special education class or not. Children in families with incomes closer to, but still below, the poverty line also did worse than children in higher-income families, but the differences were smaller. The smallest differences appeared for the earliest (age two) measure of cognitive ability; however, the sizes of the effects were similar for children from three to eight. These findings suggest that the effects of poverty on children's cognitive development occur early.

The study also found that duration of poverty was an important factor in the lower scores of poor children on measures of cognitive ability. Children who lived in persistently poor families (defined in this study as poor over a four-year span) had scores on the various assessments six to nine points lower than children who were never poor.[25] Another analysis of the NLSY that controlled for a number of important maternal and child health characteristics showed that the effects of long-term poverty (based on family income averaged over 13 years prior to testing of the child) on measures of children's cognitive ability were significantly greater than the effects of short-term poverty (measured by income in the year of observation).[26]

A few studies link long-term family income to cognitive ability and achievement measured during the school years. Research on children's test scores at ages seven and eight found that the effects of income on these scores were similar in size to those reported for three-year-olds.[25] But research relating family income measured during adolescence on cognitive ability finds relatively smaller effects.[27] As summarized in the next section, these modest effects of income on cognitive ability are consistent with literature showing modest effects of income on schooling attainment, but both sets of studies may be biased by the fact that their measurement of parental income is restricted to the child's adoles-

cent years. It is not yet possible to make conclusive statements regarding the size of the effects of poverty on children's long-term cognitive development.

School Achievement Outcomes

Educational attainment is well recognized as a powerful predictor of experiences in later life. A comprehensive review of the relationship between parental income and school attainment, published in 1994, concluded that poverty limited school achievement but that the effect of income on the number of school years completed was small.[28] In general, the studies suggested that a 10% increase in family income is associated with a 0.2% to 2% increase in the number of school years completed.[28]

Several more recent studies using different longitudinal data sets (the PSID, the NLSY and Children of the NLSY) also find that poverty status has a small negative impact on high school graduation and years of schooling obtained. Much of the observed relationship between income and schooling appears to be related to a number of confounding factors such as parental education, family structure, and neighborhood characteristics.[28–30] Some of these studies suggest that the components of income (for example, AFDC) and the way income is measured (number of years in poverty versus annual family income or the ratio of income to the poverty threshold) may lead to somewhat different conclusions. But all the studies suggest that, after controlling for many appropriate confounding variables, the effects of poverty per se on school achievement are likely to be statistically significant, yet small. Based on the results of one study, the authors estimated that, if poverty were eliminated for all children, mean years of schooling for all children would increase by only 0.3% (less than half a month).[30]

For low-income children, a $10,000 increase in mean family income between birth and age 5 was associated with nearly a full-year increase in completed schooling.

Why do not the apparently strong effects of parental income on cognitive abilities and school achievement in the early childhood years translate into larger effects on completed schooling? One possible reason is that extrafamilial environments (for example, schools and neighborhoods) begin to matter as much or more for children than family conditions once children reach school age. A second possible reason is that school-related achievement depends on both ability and behavior. As is discussed in the Emotional and Behavioral Outcomes section, children's behavioral problems, measured either before or after the transition into school, are not very sensitive to parental income differences.

A third, and potentially crucial, reason concerns the timing of economic deprivation. Few studies measure income from early childhood to adolescence, so there is no way to know whether poverty early in childhood has noteworthy effects on later outcomes such as school completion. Because family income varies over time,[31] income measured during adolescence, or even middle childhood, may not reflect income in early childhood. A recent study that attempted to evaluate how the timing of income might affect completed schooling found that family income averaged from birth to age 5 had a much more powerful effect on the number of school years a child completes than does family income measured either between ages 5 and 10 or between ages 11 and 15.[7] For low-income children, a $10,000 increase in mean family income between birth and age 5 was associated with nearly a full-year increase in completed schooling. Similar increments to family income later in childhood had no significant impact, suggesting that income may indeed be an important determinant of completed schooling but that only income during the early childhood years matters.

Emotional and Behavioral Outcomes

Poor children suffer from emotional and behavioral problems more frequently than do nonpoor children (see Table 1). Emotional outcomes are often grouped along two dimensions: externalizing behaviors including aggression, fighting, and acting out, and internalizing behaviors such as anxiety, social withdrawal, and depression. Data regarding emotional outcomes are based on parental and teacher reports. This section reviews studies that distinguish between the effects of long- and short-term poverty on emotional outcomes of children at different ages.

One study of low birth weight five-year-olds using the IHDP data set found that children in persistently poor families had more internalizing and externalizing behavior problems than children who had never been poor. The analysis controlled for maternal education and family structure and defined long-term poverty as income below the poverty threshold for each of four consecutive years. Short-term poverty (defined as poor in at least one of four years) was also associated with more behavioral problems, though the effects were not as large as those for persistent poverty.[6]

Two different studies using the NLSY report findings consistent with those of the IHDP study. Both found persistent poverty to be a significant predictor of some behavioral problems.[26,32] One study used data from the 1986 NLSY and found that for four- to eight-year-olds persistent poverty (defined as a specific percentage of years of life during which the child lived below the poverty level) was positively related to the presence of internalizing symptoms (such as dependence, anxiety, and unhappiness) even after controlling for current poverty status, mother's age, educa-

tion, and marital status. In contrast, current poverty (defined by current family income below the poverty line) but not persistent poverty was associated with more externalizing problems (such as hyperactivity, peer conflict, and headstrong behavior).[32]

> ## Problematic emotional outcomes are associated with family poverty; however, the effects of poverty on emotional outcomes are not as large as its effects on cognitive outcomes.

The second study used NLSY data from 1978–1991 and analyzed children ages 3 to 11. On average children living in long-term poverty (defined by the ratio of family income to the poverty level averaged over 13 years) ranked three to seven percentile points higher (indicating more problems) on a behavior problem index than children with incomes above the poverty line. After controlling for a range of factors including mother's characteristics, nutrition, and infant health behaviors, the difference remained though it dropped in magnitude. This study also found that children who experienced one year of poverty had more behavioral problems than children who had lived in long-term poverty.[26]

The above studies demonstrate that problematic emotional outcomes are associated with family poverty. However, it is important to note that the effects of poverty on emotional outcomes are not as large as those found in cognitive outcomes. Also these studies do not show that children in long-term poverty experience emotional problems with greater frequency or of the same type as children who experience only short-term poverty. These studies analyzed data for young children. Few studies have examined the link between emotional outcomes and poverty for adolescents. One small study of 7th- to 10th-graders in the rural Midwest did not find a statistically significant relationship between poverty and emotional problems, either internalizing or externalizing.[33] Self-reporting by the adolescents rather than maternal reporting, as used in the data sets on younger children, may account for the differences found in the effects of income on emotional outcomes in this study as compared with the previously reviewed research. It may also be that younger children are more affected by poverty than older children.

These findings point to the need for further research to improve understanding of the link between income and children's emotional outcomes.

Teenage Out-of-Wedlock Childbearing

The negative consequences for both mothers and children associated with births to unwed teen mothers make it a source of policy concern.[34] Although the rate of out-of-wedlock births among poor teens is almost three times as high as the rate among those from nonpoor families (see Table 1), the literature on linkages between family income and out-of-wedlock childbearing is not conclusive. A recent review of the evidence put it this way: "[P]arental income is negative and usually, but not always, significant.... The few reports of the quantitative effects of simulated changes in variables suggest that decreases in parental income... will lead to small increases in the probability that teen girls will experience a nonmarital birth."[28]

> A child's home environment accounts for a substantial portion of the effects of family income on cognitive outcomes in young children.

A recent study, which used data from the PSID to investigate factors in teen out-of-wedlock births, found that variations in income around the poverty threshold were not predictive of a teenage birth but that the probability of a teenager's having an out-of-wedlock birth declined significantly at family income levels above twice the poverty threshold.[35] The duration and timing of poverty had no effect on the probability of a teen out-of-wedlock birth. These findings are somewhat different from those reported for cognitive outcomes and school achievement. In the case of

cognitive outcomes for young children, the variation in income mattered most to children at very low levels of income; for school achievement, the timing and duration of poverty seemed to have important differential effects on outcomes.

Why should poverty status matter more for schooling than for childbearing? This difference is consistent with the more general result that parental income appears more strongly linked with ability and achievement than with behavior. The factors influencing teenage out-of-wedlock childbearing are less well understood than the factors influencing schooling completion: interventions have generally been much less successful in altering teen birthrates than in keeping teens in school.[36,37]

Pathways Through Which Poverty Operates

The research reviewed thus far suggests that living in poverty exacts a heavy toll on children. However, it does not shed light on the pathways or mechanisms by which low income exerts its effects on children. As the term is used in this discussion, a "pathway" is a mechanism through which poverty or income can influence a child outcome. By implication, this definition implies that a pathway should be causally related to both income and at least one child outcome. Exploration of these pathways is important for a more complete understanding of the effects of poverty on children; moreover, exploration of pathways can lead to the identification of leverage points that may be amenable to policy intervention and remediation in the absence of a change in family income.

©Steven Rubin

Research on the size and strength of the pathways through which income might influence child health and development is still scanty. In this section, five potential pathways are discussed: (1) health and nutrition, (2) the home environment, (3) parental interactions with children, (4) parental mental health, and (5) neighborhood conditions. Space limitations preclude a discussion of other potential pathways such as access to and use of prenatal care, access to pediatric care, exposure to environmental toxins, household stability, provision of learning experiences outside the home, quality of school attended, and peer groups. Further, few studies have tested pathway models using these variables.

Health and Nutrition

Although health is itself an outcome, it can also be viewed as a pathway by which poverty influences other child outcomes, such as cognitive ability and school achievement. As discussed previously poor children experience increased rates of low birth weight and elevated blood lead levels when compared with nonpoor children. These conditions have, in turn, been associated with reduced IQ and other measures of cognitive functioning in young children and, in the case of low birth weight, with increased rates of learning disabilities, grade retention, and school dropout in older children and youths.

A 1990 analysis indicated that the poverty-related health factors such as low birth weight, elevated blood lead levels, anemia,[38] and recurrent ear infections and hearing loss contributed to the differential in IQ scores between poor and nonpoor four-year-olds.[39] The findings suggest that the cumulative health disadvantage experienced by poor children on these four health measures may have accounted for as much as 13% to 20% of the difference in IQ between the poor and nonpoor four-year-olds during the 1970s and 1980s.[39]

As discussed in the Child Indicators article in this journal issue, malnutrition in childhood (as measured by anthropometric indicators) is associated with lower scores on tests of cognitive development. Deficits in these anthropometric measures are associated with poverty among children in the United States, and the effects can be substantial. One recent study found that the effect of stunting on short-term memory was equivalent to the difference in short-term memory between children in families that had experienced poverty for 13 years and children in families with incomes at least three times the poverty level.[26]

Home Environment

A number of studies have found that a child's home environment—opportunities for learning, warmth of mother-child interactions, and the physical condition of the home—accounts for a substantial portion of the effects of family income on cognitive outcomes in young children. Some large longitudinal data sets use the HOME scale as a measure of the home environment. The HOME scale is made up of items that measure household resources, such as reading materials and toys, and parental practices, such as discipline methods. The HOME scale has been shown to be correlated with family income and poverty, with higher levels of income associated with improved home environments as measured by the scale.[7,40]

Parents who are poor are likely to be less healthy, both emotionally and physically, than those who are not poor.

Several studies have found that differences in the home environment of higher- and lower-income children, as measured by the HOME scale, account for a substantial portion of the effect of income on the cognitive development of preschool children and on the achievement scores of elementary school children.[6,26,37] In one study, differences in the home environment also seemed to account for some of the effects of poverty status on behavioral problems. In addition, the provisions of learning experiences in the home (measured by specific subscales of the HOME scale) have been shown to account for up to half of the effect of poverty status on the IQ scores of five-year-olds.[37,41]

Parental Interactions with Children

A number of studies have attempted to go beyond documentation of activities and materials in the home to capture the effects of parent-child interactions on child outcomes. Much of the work is based on small and/or community-based samples. That work suggests that child adjustment and achievement are facilitated by certain parental practices. There is also some evidence that poverty is linked to lower-quality parent-child interaction and to increased use of harsh punishment. This research suggests that parental practices may be an important pathway between economic resources and child outcomes.

Evidence of such a parental-practice pathway from research using large national data sets of the kind reviewed in this article is less consistent. One NLSY-based study found that currently poor mothers spanked their children more often than nonpoor mothers and that this harsh behavior was an important component of the effect of poverty on children's mental health.[32] Mothers' parenting behavior was not, however, found to be an important pathway by which persistent poverty affected children's mental health. A more recent study using the National Survey of Families and Households found that the level of household income was only weakly related to effective parenting and that differences in parent practices did not account for much of the association between poverty and child well-being.[42]

Among adolescents, family economic pressure may lead to conflict with parents, resulting in lower school grades, reduced emotional health, and impaired social relationships.[33,43] Other work suggests that it may be income loss or economic uncertainty due to unemployment, underemployment, and unstable work conditions, rather than poverty or low income per se, that is a source for conflict between parents and teens leading to emotional and school problems.[33,44]

Parental Mental Health

Parents who are poor are likely to be less healthy, both emotionally and physically, than those who are not poor.[45] And parental irritability and depressive symptoms are associated with more conflicted interactions with adolescents, leading to less satisfactory emotional, social, and cognitive development.[43,46,47] Some studies have established that parental mental health accounts for some of the effect of economic circumstances on child health and behavior. Additionally, poor parental mental health is associated with impaired parent-child interactions and less provision of learning experiences in the home.[33,41,48]

> Low income may lead to residence in extremely poor neighborhoods characterized by social disorganization and few resources for child development.

Neighborhood Conditions

Another possible pathway through which family income operates has to do with the neighborhoods in which poor families reside. Poor parents are constrained in their choice of neighborhoods and schools. Low income may lead to residence in extremely poor neighborhoods characterized by social disorganization (crime, many unemployed adults, neighbors not monitoring the behavior of adolescents) and few resources for child development (playgrounds, child care, health care facilities, parks, after-school programs).[49,50] The affluence of neighborhoods is associated with child and adolescent outcomes (intelligence test scores at ages 3 and 5 and high school graduation rates by age 20) over and above family poverty.[37,51] Neighborhood residence also seems to be associated with parenting practices, over and above family income and education.[52] Neighborhood effects on intelligence scores are in part mediated by the learning environment in the home.[52,53] Living in neighborhoods with high concentrations of poor people is associated with less provision of learning experiences in the homes of preschoolers, over and above the links seen between family income and learning experiences.

A key issue that has not been fully explored is the extent to which neighborhood effects may be overestimated because neighborhood characteristics also reflect the choices

of neighborhood residents. One study that examined the effects of peer groups (as measured by the socioeconomic status of students in a respondent's school) on teenage pregnancy and school dropout behavior found that while student body socioeconomic status seemed to be an important predictor of both dropout and teen pregnancy rates, it did not appear to be related to those outcomes in statistical models that treated this peer characteristic as a matter of family choice.[54]

How Much Does Income Cause Child Outcomes?

It may seem odd to raise this question after summarizing evidence indicating that family income does matter—across the childhood and adolescent years and for a number of indicators of well-being. However, these associations have been demonstrated when a relatively small set of family characteristics are controlled through statistical analyses. It is possible, therefore, that other important family characteristics have not been controlled for and that, as a result of this omission, the effects of income are estimated incorrectly.... Distinguishing between the effects on children of poverty and its related events and conditions is crucial for public policy formulation. Programs that alter family income may not have intended benefits for children if the importance of family income has been mismeasured.

Despite the evidence reviewed in this article and elsewhere, there is an important segment of the population who believes that income per se may not appreciably affect child outcomes. This viewpoint sees parental income mainly as a proxy for other characteristics such as character (a strong work ethic) or genetic endowment that influence both children and parents. A recent book by Susan Mayer, *What Money Can't Buy: The Effect of Parental Income on Children's Outcomes*,[55] presents a series of tests to examine explicitly the effects of income on a set of child outcomes. In one test, measures of income *after* the occurrence of an outcome are added to statistical models of the effects of income and other characteristics on a child outcome. The idea behind this test is that unanticipated future income can capture unmeasured parental characteristics but cannot have caused the child outcome. The inclusion of future income frequently produced a large reduction in the estimated impact of prior parent income. Mayer also tries to estimate the effects on children of components of income (for example, asset income) that are independent of the actions of the family. Although these tests provide some support for the hypothesis that family income may not matter much for child outcomes, even Mayer admits that these statistical procedures are not without their problems. For example, prior income and future income are highly correlated, and if parents take reasonable expectations of future income into consideration in making decisions regarding the well-being of children, then the assumption that child outcomes are independent of future income, which underlies the first test, is violated.

A second approach to the problem that omitted variables may bias the estimation of the effects of income and poverty on children looks at siblings within families. Siblings reared in the same family share many of the same unmeasured family characteristics. Thus, comparing children at the same age within families makes it possible to look at the income of the family at different time points (for example, if a firstborn was five years of age in 1985 and the second child was five years of age in 1988, it is possible to look at their achievement levels at this age and the average family income between 1980 and 1985 for the firstborn and between 1983 and 1988 for the second child). One study that used this approach found that sibling differences in income were associated with sibling differences in completed schooling, which gave support to the notion that family income matters.[7]

Perhaps the most convincing demonstration of the effects of income is to provide poor families with income in the context of a randomized trial. In four Income Maintenance/Negative Income Tax Experiments in the 1960s and 1970s, experimental treatment families received a guaranteed minimum income. (These experiments are discussed in more detail in the article by Janet Currie in this journal issue.) Substantial benefits resulting from increased income effects were found for child nutrition, early school achievement, and high school completion in some sites but not in others. These results might be viewed as inconclusive; however, since the site with the largest effects for younger children (North Carolina) was also the poorest, one interpretation of the results is that income effects are most important for the very poorest families.[56,57]

Conclusion

The evidence reviewed in this article supports the conclusion that family income can substantially influence child and adolescent well-being. However, the associations between income and child outcomes are more complex and varied than suggested by the simple associations presented in Table 1. Family income seems to be more strongly related to children's ability and achievement-related outcomes than to emotional outcomes. In addition, the effects are particularly pronounced for children who live below the poverty line for multiple years and for children who live in extreme poverty (that is, 50% or less of the poverty threshold). These income effects are probably not due to some unmeasured characteristics of low-income families: family income, in and of itself, does appear to matter.

The timing of poverty is also important, although this conclusion is based on only a small number of studies. Low income during the preschool and early school years exhibits the strongest correlation with low rates of high school completion, as compared with low income during the childhood and adolescent years.[7,58] Poor-quality schooling, which is correlated with high neighborhood poverty, may exacerbate this effect.[59] These findings suggest that early childhood interventions may be critical in reducing the impact of low income on children's lives.

The pathways through which low income influences children also suggest some general recommendations. Nutrition programs, especially if they target the most undernourished poor, may have beneficial effects on both physical and cognitive outcomes. Lead abatement and parental education programs may improve cognitive outcomes in poor children residing in inner-city neighborhoods where lead is still an important hazard.

Because about one-half of the effect of family income on cognitive ability is mediated by the home environment, including learning experiences in the home, interventions might profitably focus on working with parents. An example is the Learningames curriculum in which parents are provided instruction, materials, and role playing in learning experiences.[60] Other effective learning-oriented programs might also be pursued.[61–63]

Finally, income policies (as discussed by Robert Plotnick in this journal issue) and in-kind support programs (as discussed by Devaney, Ellwood, and Love in this journal issue) can have immediate impact on the number or children living in poverty and on the circumstances in which they live. Most important, based on this review, would be efforts to eliminate deep and persistent poverty especially during a child's early years. Support to families with older children may be desirable on other grounds, but the available research suggests that it will probably not have the same impact on child outcomes as programs focused on younger children.

The authors would like to thank the National Institute of Child Health and Human Development Research Network on Child and Family Well-being for supporting the writing of this article. The Russell Sage Foundation's contribution is also appreciated as is that of the William T. Grant Foundation, and the Canadian Institute for Advanced Research. The authors are also grateful for the feedback provided by Linda Baker, Pamela K. Klebanov, and Judith Smith and would like to thank Phyllis Gyamfi for her editorial assistance.

Notes

1. Hernandez, D.J. *America's children: Resources from family government and the economy.* New York: Russell Sage Foundation, 1993.
2. Duncan, G.J., and Brooks-Gunn, J., eds. *Consequences of growing up poor.* New York: Russell Sage Foundation, 1997.
3. Duncan, G.J., and Rodgers, W.L. Longitudinal aspects of childhood poverty. *Journal of Marriage and the Family* (November 1988) 50,4:1007–21.
4. Chase-Lansdale, P.L., and Brooks-Gunn, J., eds. *Escape from poverty: What makes a difference for children?* New York: Cambridge University Press, 1995.
5. Children's Defense Fund. *Wasting America's future.* Boston: Beacon Press, 1994; Klerman, L. *Alive and well?* New York: National Center for Children in Poverty, Columbia University, 1991.

6. Duncan, G.J., Brooks-Gunn, J., and Klebanov, P.K. Economic deprivation and early-childhood development. *Child Development* (1994) 65,2:296–318.

7. Duncan, G.J., Yeung, W., Brooks-Gunn, J., and Smith, J.R. How much does childhood poverty affect the life chances of children? *American Sociological Review,* in press.

8. Hauser, R., Brown, B., and Prosser W. *Indicators of children's well-being.* New York: Russell Sage Foundation, in press.

9. Brooks-Gunn, J., Guo, G., and Furstenberg, F.F., Jr. Who drops out of and who continues beyond high school?: A 20-year study of black youth. *Journal of Research in Adolescence* (1993) 37,3:271–94.

10. Graber, J.A., and Brooks-Gunn, J. Transitions and turning points: Navigating the passage from childhood through adolescence. *Developmental Psychology* (1996) 32,4:768–76.

11. Rutter, M. Beyond longitudinal data: Causes, consequences, changes and continuity. *Journal of Counseling and Clinical Psychology* (1994) 62,5:928–90.

12. Guo, G., Brooks-Gunn, J., and Harris, K.M. Parents' labor-force attachment and grade retention among urban black children. *Sociology of Education* (1996) 69,3:217–36.

13. For a review of the causes and consequences of low birth weight in the United States, see Shiono, P., ed. Low Birth Weight. *The Future of Children* (Spring 1995) 5,1:4–231.

14. Starfield, B., Shapiro, S., Weiss, J., et al. Race, family income, and low birth weight. *American Journal of Epidemiology* (1991) 134,10:1167–74.

15. Corman, H., and Grossman, M. Determinants of neonatal mortality rates in the U.S.: A reduced form model. *Journal of Health Economics* (1985) 4,3:213–36.

16. Frank, R., Strobino, D., Salkever, D., and Jackson, C. Updated estimates of the impact of prenatal care on birthweight outcomes by race. *Journal of Human Resources* (1992) 27,4:629–42.

17. Miller, J., and Korenman, S. Poverty and children's nutritional status in the United States. *American Journal of Epidemiology* (1994) 140,3:233–43.

18. Schwartz, J., Angle, C., and Pitcher, H. Relationship between childhood blood lead levels and stature. *Pediatrics* (1986) 77,3:281–88.

19. Schwartz, J., and Otto, D. Lead and minor hearing impairment. *Archives of Environmental Health* (1991) 46,5:300–05.

20. Agency for Toxic Substances and Disease Registry. *The nature and extent of lead poisoning in the US.: A report to Congress.* Washington, DC: U.S. Department of Health and Human Services, 1988, Section II, p. 7.

21. Schwartz, J. Low level lead exposure and children's IQ: A meta-analysis and search for threshold. *Environmental Research* (1994) 65,1:42–55.

22. Ronald Morony, Deputy Director, U.S. Department of Housing and Urban Development, Office of Lead Based Paint Abatement and Poisoning Prevention, Washington, DC. Personal communication, November 20, 1996.

23. Brody, D.J., Pirkle, L., Kramer, R., et al. Blood lead levels in the U.S. population. *Journal of the American Medical Association* (1994) 272,4:277–81.

24. Brooks-Gunn, J., McCarton, C.M., Casey, P.H., et al. Early intervention in low birth weight premature infants: Results through age 5 years from the Infant Health and Development Program. *Journal of the American Medical Association* (1994) 272,16: 1257–62.

25. Smith, J.R., Brooks-Gunn, J., and Klebanov, P. The consequences of living in poverty for young children's cognitive and verbal ability and early school achievement. In *Consequences of growing up poor.* G.J. Duncan and J. Brooks-Gunn, eds. New York: Russell Sage Foundation, 1997.

26. Korenman, S., Miller, J.E., and Sjaastad, J.E. Long-term poverty and child development in the United States: Results from

the National Longitudinal Survey of Youth. *Children and Youth Services Review* (1995)17,1/2:127–51.

27. Peters. E., and Mullis, N. The role of the family and source of income in adolescent achievement. In *Consequences of growing up poor:* G. Duncan and J. Brooks-Gunn, eds. New York: Russell Sage Foundation, 1997.

28. Haveman, R., and Wolfe, B. The determinants of children's attainments: A review of methods and findings. *Journal of Economic Literature* (1995) 33,3:1829–78.

29. Teachman, J., Paasch, K.M., Day, R., and Carver, K.P. Poverty during adolescence and subsequent educational attainment. In *Consequences of growing up poor:* G. Duncan and J. Brooks-Gunn, eds. New York: Russell Sage Foundation, 1997.

30. Haveman, R., and Wolfe, B. *Succeeding generations: On the effect of investments in children.* New York: Russell Sage Foundation, 1994.

31. Duncan, G.J. Volatility of family income over the life course. In *Life-span development and behavior.* Vol. 9. P. Baltes, D. Featherman, and R.M. Lerner, eds. Hillsdale, NJ: Erlbaum, 1988, pp. 317–58.

32. McLeod, J.D., and Shanahan, M.J. Poverty, parenting and children's mental health. *American Sociological Review* (June 1993) 58,3:351–66.

33. Conger, R.D., Conger, K.J., and Elder, G.H. Family economic hardship and adolescent adjustment: Mediating and moderating processes. In *Consequences of growing up poor:* G. Duncan and J. Brooks-Gunn, eds. New York: Russell Sage Foundation, 1997.

34. Hotz, V.J., McElroy, S.W., and Sanders, S.G. Costs and consequences of teenage childbearing. *Chicago Policy Review.* Internet: http://www.spc.uchicago.edu/cpr/Teenage_Child.htm.

35. Haveman, R., Wolfe, B., and Wilson, K. Childhood poverty and adolescent schooling and fertility outcomes: Reduced form and structural estimates. In *Consequences of growing up poor.* G.J. Duncan and J. Brooks-Gunn, eds. New York: Russell Sage Foundation, 1997.

36. U.S. Department of Health and Human Services. *Report to Congress on out-of-wedlock childbearing.* PHS-95–1257. Hyattsville, MD: DHHS, September 1995.

37. Brooks-Gunn, J., Duncan, G.J., Klebanov, P.K., and Sealand, N. Do neighborhoods influence child and adolescent behavior? *American Journal of Sociology* (1993) 99,2:335–95.

38. Iron-deficiency anemia is an important health problem that was traditionally identified with child poverty. Iron-deficiency anemia has been associated with impaired exercise capacity, increased susceptibility to lead absorption, and developmental and behavioral problems; see Oski, F. Iron deficiency in infancy and childhood. *The New England Journal of Medicine.* (July 15, 1993) 329,3:190–93. The importance of iron-deficiency anemia and its sequelae among poor children in the United States today is unclear. Increased use of iron-fortified foods and infant formulas along with their provision through public nutrition programs such as the Special Supplemental Food Program for Women, Infants, and Children (see the article by Devaney, Ellwood, and Love in this journal issue) have contributed to a dramatic decline in anemia; see Yip, R., Binkin, N.J., Fleshood, L., and Trowbridge, F.L. Declining prevalence of anemia among low-income children in the U.S. *Journal of American Medical Association* (1987) 258,12:1623. Between 1980 and 1991, the prevalence of anemia among infants and children through age five declined from 7% to 3%. Still, low-income children participating in public health programs have a higher-than-average prevalence of anemia; see Yip, R., Parvanta, I., Scanlon, K., et al. Pediatric Nutrition Surveillance System—United States,

1980–1991. *Morbidity and Mortality Weekly Report* (November 1992) 41,SS-7:1–24. In part, this is because risk of anemia is a criterion for enrollment in these programs and also because these low-income children have low iron levels.

39. Goldstein, N. *Explaining socioeconomic differences in children's cognitive test scores.* Working Paper No. H-90-1. Cambridge, MA: Malcolm Wiener Center for Social Policy, John F. Kennedy School of Government, Harvard University, 1990.

40. Garrett, P., Ng'andu, N., and Ferron, J. Poverty experience of young children and the quality of their home environments. *Child Development* (1994) 65,2:331–45.

41. Bradley, R.H. Home environment and parenting. In *Handbook of parenting:* M. Bornstein, ed. Hillsdale, NJ: Erlbaum, 1995.

42. Hanson, T., McLanahan, S., and Thomson, E. Economic resources, parental practices, and child well-being. In *Consequences of growing up poor:* G.J. Duncan and J. Brooks-Gunn, eds. New York: Russell Sage Foundation, 1997.

43. Conger, R.D., Ge, S., Elder, G.H., Jr., et al. Economic stress, coercive family process and developmental problems of adolescents. *Child Development* (1994) 65,2:541–61.

44. McLoyd, V.C. The impact of economic hardship on black families and children: Psychological distress, parenting, and socioemotional development. *Child Development* (1990) 61,2:311–46.

45. Adler, N.E., Boyce, T., Chesney, M.A., et al. Socioeconomic inequalities in health: No easy solution. *Journal of the American Medical Association* (1993) 269:3140–45.

46. Liaw, F.R., and Brooks-Gunn, J. Cumulative familial risks and low birth weight children's cognitive and behavioral development. *Journal of Clinical Child Psychology* (1995) 23,4:360–72.

47. McLoyd, V.C., Jayaratne, T.E., Ceballo, R., and Borquez, J. Unemployment and work interruption among African American single mothers. Effects on parenting and adolescent socioemotional functioning. *Child Development* (1994) 65,2:562–89.

48. Brooks-Gunn, J., Klebanov, P.K., and Liaw, F. The learning, physical, and emotional environment of the home in the context of poverty: The Infant Health and Development Program. *Children and Youth Services Review* (1995)17,1/2.251–76.

49. Wilson, W.J. *The truly disadvantaged. The inner city, the underclass, and public policy.* Chicago: University of Chicago Press, 1987.

50. Sampson, R., and Morenoff, J. Ecological perspectives on the neighborhood context of urban poverty: Past and present. In *Neighborhood poverty: Conceptual, methodological, and policy approaches to studying neighborhoods.* Vol. 2. J. Brooks-Gunn, G. Duncan, and J.L. Aber, eds. New York: Russell Sage Foundation, in press.

51. Brooks-Gunn, J., Duncan, G.J., and Aber, J.L., eds. *Neighborhood poverty: Context and consequences for children.* Vol. 1. New York: Russell Sage Foundation, in press.

52. Klebanov, P.K., Brooks-Gunn, J., and Duncan, G.J. Does neighborhood and family poverty affect mother's parenting, mental health and social support? *Journal of Marriage and Family* (1994) 56,2:441–55.

53. Klebanov, P.K., Brooks-Gunn, J., Chase-Lansdale, L., and Gordon, R. The intersection of the neighborhood and home environment and its influence on young children. In *Neighborhood poverty: Context and consequences for children.* Vol. 1. J. Brooks-Gunn, G.J. Duncan, and J.L. Aber, eds. New York: Russell Sage Foundation, in press.

54. Evans, W.N., Oates, W.E., and Schwab, R.M. Measuring peer group effects: A study of teenage behavior. *Journal of Practical Economy* (1992) 100,5:966–91.

55. Mayer S.E. *What money can't buy: The effect of parental income on children's outcomes.* Cambridge, MA: Harvard University Press, 1997.

56. Kershwa, D., and Fair, J. *The New Jersey income maintenance experiment.* Vol. I. New York: Academic Press, 1976.

57. Salkind, N.J., and Haskins, R. Negative income tax: The impact on children from low-income families. *Journal of Family Issues* (1982) 3,2:165–80.

58. Baydar, N., Brooks-Gunn, J., and Furstenberg, E.F., Jr. Early warning signs of functional illiteracy: Predictors in childhood and adolescence. *Child Development* (1993) 64,3:815–29.

59. Alexander, K.L., and Entwisle, D.R. Achievement in the first 2 years of school: Patterns and processes. *Monographs of the Society for Research in Child Development* (1988) 53,2:1–153.

60. Sparling, J.J., and Lewis, J. *Partner for learning.* Lewisville, NC: Kaplan, 1984.

61. Olds, D.L., and Kitzman, H. Review of research on home visiting for pregnant women and parents of young children. *The Future of Children* (Winter 1993) 3,3:53–92.

62. Brooks-Gunn, J., Denner, J., and Klebanov, P.K. Families and neighborhoods as contexts for education. In *Changing populations, changing schools: Ninety-fourth yearbook of the National Society for the Study of Education, Part II.* E. Flaxman and A. H. Passow, eds. Chicago, IL: National Society for the Study of Education, 1995, pp. 233–52.

63. Brooks-Gunn, J. Strategies for altering the outcomes of poor children and their families. In *Escape from poverty: What makes a difference for children?* P.L. Chase-Lansdale and J. Brooks-Gunn, eds. New York: Cambridge University Press, 1996.

Jeanne Brooks-Gunn, Ph.D., is Virginia and Leonard Marx professor of child development and education, and is director of the Center for Young Children and Families at Teachers College, Columbia University.

Greg J. Duncan, Ph.D., is a professor of education and social policy, and is a faculty associate at the Institute for Policy Research, Northwestern University.

From *The Future of Children*, Summer/Fall 1997, pp. 55–71. © 1997 by the Center for the Future of Children of the David and Lucile Packard Foundation. Reprinted by permission. *The Future of Children* journals and executive summaries are available free of charge by faxing mailing information to: Circulation Department (650) 948-6498.

SCARS THAT WON'T HEAL: The Neurobiology of Child Abuse

Maltreatment at an early age can have enduring negative effects on a child's brain development and function

By Martin H. Teicher

In 1994 Boston police were shocked to discover a malnourished four-year-old locked away in a filthy Roxbury apartment, where he lived in dreadfully squalid conditions. Worse, the boy's tiny hands were found to have been horrendously burned. It emerged that his drug-abusing mother had held the child's hands under a steaming-hot faucet to punish him for eating her boyfriend's food, despite her instructions not to do so. The ailing youngster had been given no medical care at all. The disturbing story quickly made national headlines. Later placed in foster care, the boy received skin grafts to help his scarred hands regain their function. But even though the victim's physical wounds were treated, recent research findings indicate that any injuries inflicted to his developing mind may never truly heal.

Though an extreme example, the notorious case is unfortunately not all that uncommon. Every year child welfare agencies in the U.S. receive more than three million allegations of childhood abuse and neglect and collect sufficient evidence to substantiate more than a million instances.

It is hardly surprising to us that research reveals a strong link between physical, sexual and emotional mistreatment of children and the development of psychiatric problems. But in the early 1990s mental health professionals believed that emotional and social difficulties occurred mainly through psychological means. Childhood maltreatment was understood either to foster the development of intrapsychic defense mechanisms that proved to be self-defeating in adulthood or to arrest psychosocial development, leaving a "wounded child" within. Re-

searchers thought of the damage as basically a software problem amenable to reprogramming via therapy or simply erasable through the exhortation "Get over it."

New investigations into the consequences of early maltreatment, including work my colleagues and I have done at McLean Hospital in Belmont, Mass., and at Harvard Medical School, appear to tell a different story. Because childhood abuse occurs during the critical formative time when the brain is being physically sculpted by experience, the impact of severe stress can leave an indelible imprint on its structure and function. Such abuse, it seems, induces a cascade of molecular and neurobiological effects that irreversibly alter neural development.

Extreme Personalities

THE AFTERMATH of childhood abuse can manifest itself at any age in a variety of ways. Internally it can appear as depression, anxiety, suicidal thoughts or posttraumatic stress; it can also be expressed outwardly as aggression, impulsiveness, delinquency, hyperactivity or substance abuse. One of the more perplexing psychiatric conditions that is strongly associated with early ill-treatment is borderline personality disorder. Someone with this dysfunction characteristically sees others in black-and-white terms, often first putting a person on a pedestal, then vilifying the same person after some perceived slight or betrayal. Those afflicted are also prone to volcanic outbursts of anger and transient episodes of paranoia or psychosis. They typically have a history of intense, unstable relationships, feel empty or unsure of their identity, commonly try to escape through substance abuse, and experience self-destructive or suicidal impulses.

More than THREE MILLION allegations of childhood ABUSE and NEGLECT are received every year.

While treating three patients with borderline personality disorder in 1984, I began to suspect that their early exposure to various forms of maltreatment had altered the development of their limbic systems, The limbic system is a collection of interconnected brain nuclei (neural centers) that play a pivotal role in the regulation of emotion and memory. Two critically important limbic regions are the hippocampus and the amygdala, which lie below the cortex in the temporal lobe. The hippocampus is thought to be important in the formation and retrieval of both verbal and emotional memories, whereas the amygdala is concerned with creating the emotional content of memory—for example, feelings relating to fear conditioning and aggressive responses.

Overview/*Insight into Child Abuse*

- Until recently, psychologists believed that mistreatment during childhood led to arrested psychosocial development and self-defeating psychic defense mechanisms in adults. New brain imaging surveys and other experiments have shown that child abuse can cause permanent damage to the neural structure and function of the developing brain itself.
- This grim result suggests that much more effort must be made to prevent childhood abuse and neglect before it does irrevocable harm to millions of young victims. New approaches to therapy may also be indicated.

My McLean colleagues Yutaka Ito and Carol A. Glod and I wondered whether childhood abuse might disrupt the healthy maturation of these brain regions. Could early maltreatment stimulate the amygdala into a state of heightened electrical irritability or damage the developing hippocampus through excessive exposure to stress hormones? We reasoned further that hippocampal harm or amygdaloid overexcitation could produce symptoms similar to those experienced by patients with temporal lobe epilepsy (TLE), which sporadically disrupts the function of these brain nuclei. During TLE seizures, patients remain conscious while experiencing a range of psychomotor symptoms brought on by electrical storms within these regions. Associated effects include the abrupt onset of tingling, numbness or vertigo; motor-related manifestations such as uncontrollable

staring or twitching; and autonomic symptoms such as flushing, nausea or the "pit in your stomach" feeling one gets in a fast-rising elevator. TLE can also cause hallucinations or illusions in any of the five senses. It is not unusual, for instance, for one afflicted with this condition to experience Alice-in-Wonderland-like distortions of the sizes or shapes of objects. Disconnected feelings of déjà vu and mind-body dissociation are also common.

Abuse-Driven Brain Changes

TO EXPLORE the relation between early abuse and dysfunction of the limbic system, in 1984 I devised a checklist of questions that assess the frequency with which patients experience TLE-related symptoms. In 1993 my co-workers and I reported results from 253 adults who came to an outpatient mental health clinic for psychiatric evaluation. Slightly more than half reported having been abused physically or sexually, or both, as children. Compared with patients who reported no ill-treatment, average checklist scores were 38 percent greater in the patients with physical (but not sexual) abuse and 49 percent higher in the patients with sexual (but not other physical) mistreatment. Patients who acknowledged both physical and sexual abuse had average scores 113 percent higher than patients reporting none. Maltreatment before age 18 had more impact than later abuse, and males and females were similarly affected.

In 1994 our McLean research team sought to ascertain whether childhood physical, sexual or psychological abuse was associated with brain-wave abnormalities in electroencephalograms (EEGs), which provide a more direct measure of limbic irritability than our checklist. We reviewed the records of 115 consecutive admissions to a child and adolescent psychiatric hospital to search for a link. We found clinically significant brain-wave abnormalities in 54 percent of patients with a history of early trauma but in only 27 percent of nonabused patients. We observed EEG anomalies in 72 percent of those who had documented histories of serious physical and sexual abuse. The irregularities arose in frontal and temporal brain regions and, to our surprise, specifically involved the left hemisphere rather than both sides, as one would expect.

Our findings dovetailed with a 1978 EEG study of adults who were victims of incest. The study's author, Robert W. Davies of the Yale University School of Medicine, and his team had found that 77 percent exhibited EEG abnormalities and 27 percent experienced seizures.

Subsequent work by other investigators using magnetic resonance imaging (MRI) technology has confirmed an association between early maltreatment and reductions in the size of the adult hippocampus. The amygdala may be smaller as well. In 1997 J. Douglas Bremner, then at the Yale University School of Medicine, and his colleagues compared MRI scans of 17 adult survivors of childhood physical or sexual abuse, all of whom had posttraumatic stress disorder (PTSD), with 17 healthy subjects matched for age, sex, race, handedness, years of education, and years of alcohol abuse. The left hippocampus of abused patients with PTSD was, on average, 12 percent

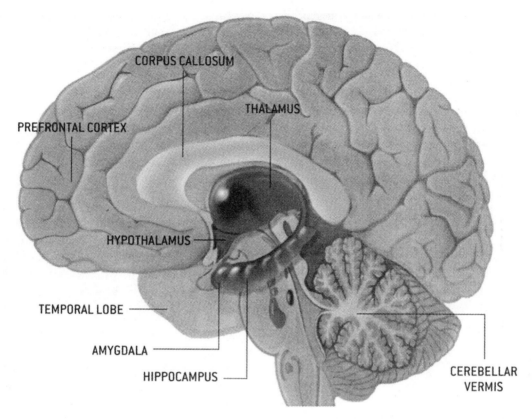

Carol Donner

ANTISOCIAL BEHAVIOR resulting from abuse appears to be caused by overexcitation of the limbic system, the primitive midbrain region that regulates memory and emotion. Two relatively small, deep-lying brain structures—the hippocampus and amygdala—are thought to play prominent roles in generating this kind of interpersonal dysfunction. The hippocampus is important in determining what incoming information will be stored in long-term memory. The principal task of the amygdala is to filter and interpret incoming sensory information in the context of the individual's survival and emotional needs and then to help initiate appropriate responses.

smaller than the hippocampus of the healthy control subjects, but the right hippocampus was of normal size. Not surprisingly, given the important role of the hippocampus in memory function, these patients also scored lower on verbal memory tests than the nonabused group.

In 1997 Murray B. Stein of the University of California at San Diego also found left hippocampal abnormalities in 21 adult women who had been sexually abused as children and who had PTSD or dissociative identity disorder (also called multiple personality disorder, a condition thought by some researchers to be common in abused females). Stein determined that in these women the volume of the left hippocampus was significantly reduced but that the right hippocampus was relatively unaffected. In addition, he found a clear correspondence between the degree of reduction in hippocampus size and the severity of the patients' dissociative symptoms. In 2001 Martin Driessen of Gilead Hospital in Bielefeld, Germany, and his colleagues reported a 16 percent reduction in hippocampus size and an 8 percent reduction in amygdala size in adult women with borderline personality disorder and a history of childhood maltreatment.

On the other hand, when Michael D. De Bellis and his colleagues at the University of Pittsburgh School of Medicine carefully measured MRI images of the hippocampus in 44

maltreated children with PTSD and 61 healthy control subjects in 1999, they failed to observe a significant difference in volume.

My McLean colleagues Susan Andersen and Ann Polcari and I obtained similar results in our recently completed volumetric analysis of the hippocampus in 18 young adults (18 to 22 years of age) with a history of repeated forced sexual abuse accompanied by fear or terror, who were compared with 19 healthy age-matched controls. Unlike in previous studies, the control subjects were not patients but were recruited from the general public and had fewer mental health problems. We observed no differences in hippocampal volume. Like Driessen's group, however, we did find a 9.8 percent average reduction in the size of the left amygdala, which correlated with feelings of depression and irritability or hostility. We asked ourselves why the hippocampus was smaller in abused subjects in studies from Bremner's, Stein's and Dreissen's groups but normal in De Bellis's and in our own investigations. Of the several possible answers, the most likely is that stress exerts a very gradual influence on the hippocampus, so adverse effects may not be discernible at a gross anatomical level until people get older.

Moreover, animal studies by Bruce S. McEwen of the Rockefeller University and Robert M. Sapolsky of Stanford University had previously demonstrated the marked vulnerability of the hippocampus to the ravages of stress. Not only is the hippocampus particularly susceptible because it develops slowly, it also is one of the few brain regions that continues to grow new neurons after birth. Further, it has a higher density of receptors for the stress hormone cortisol than almost any other area of the brain. Exposure to stress hormones can significantly change the shape of the largest neurons in the hippocampus and can even kill them. Stress also suppresses production of the new granule cells (small neurons), which normally continue to develop after birth.

Experiments with rats by Christian Caldji, Michael J. Meaney of McGill University and Paul M. Plotsky of Emory University have shown that early stress reconfigures the molecular organization of these regions. One major result is the alteration of the protein subunit structure of GABA receptors in the amygdala. These receptors respond to gamma aminobutyric acid, the brain's primary inhibitory neurotransmitter, and GABA attenuates the electrical excitability of neurons. Reduced function of this neurotransmitter produces excessive electrical activity and can trigger seizures. This discovery provides an elegant molecular explanation for our findings of EEG abnormalities and limbic irritability in patients with childhood abuse.

Left-Side Problems

THE EFFECT on the limbic system was only the most expected consequence of childhood trauma. We were intrigued, however, by our earlier observation that ill-treatment was associated with EEG abnormalities in the left hemisphere. This inspired us to examine the effect of early abuse on the development of the left and right hemispheres. We chose to use EEG coherence, a sophisticated quantitative analysis method that provides evidence about the brain's microstructure—its wiring and circuitry. Conventional EEG, in contrast, reveals brain function. The EEG coherence technique accomplishes its task by generating a mathematical measure of the degree of cross-correlation among the elaborate neuronal interconnections in the cortex that process and modify the brain's electrical signals. In general, abnormally high levels of EEG coherence are evidence of diminished development among these neuron interchanges.

Researchers thought of the damage as a SOFTWARE PROBLEM amenable to reprogramming via therapy.

Our research team used this technique in 1997 to compare 15 healthy volunteers with 15 child and adolescent psychiatric patients who had a confirmed history of intense physical or sexual abuse. Coherence measures showed that the left cortices of the healthy control subjects were more developed than the right cortices, a result that is consistent with what is known about dominant hemisphere anatomy—that is, right-handed people tend to be left-cortex dominant. The maltreated patients, however, were notably more developed in the right cortex than the left, even though all were right-handed and hence left-dominant. The right hemispheres of abused patients had developed as much as the right hemispheres of the control subjects, but their left hemispheres lagged substantially behind. This anomalous result showed up regardless of the patient's primary diagnosis. And although the effect extended throughout the entire left hemisphere, the temporal regions were most affected, which supported our original hypothesis.

The left hemisphere is specialized for perceiving and expressing language, whereas the right hemisphere specializes in processing spatial information and in processing and expressing emotions—particularly negative emotions. We had wondered whether mistreated children might store their disturbing memories in the right hemisphere and whether recollecting these memories might preferentially activate the right hemisphere.

To test this hypothesis, Fred Schiffer worked in my laboratory at McLean in 1995 to measure hemispheric activity in adults during recall of a neutral memory and then during recall of an upsetting early memory. Those with a history of abuse appeared to use predominantly their left hemispheres when thinking about neutral memories and their right when recalling an early disturbing memory. Subjects in the control group used both hemispheres to a comparable degree for either task, suggesting that their responses were more integrated between the two hemispheres.

Because Schiffer's research indicated that childhood trauma was associated with diminished right-left hemisphere integration, we decided to look for some deficiency in the primary pathway for information exchange between the two hemispheres, the corpus callosum. In 1997 Andersen and I collaborated with Jay Giedd of the National Institute of Mental Health to search for the posited effect. Together we found that in boys who had been abused or neglected, the middle parts of the corpus callosum were significantly smaller than in the control groups. Furthermore, in boys, neglect exerted a far greater effect than any other kind of maltreatment. In girls, however, sexual abuse was a more powerful factor, associated with a major reduction in size of the middle parts of the corpus callosum. These results were replicated and extended in 1999 by De Bellis. Likewise, the effects of early experience on the development of the corpus callosum have been confirmed by research in primates by Mara M. Sanchez of Emory.

Our latest finding had its roots in the seminal studies of Harry F. Harlow of the University of Wisconsin-Madison. In the 1950s Harlow compared monkeys raised by their mothers with monkeys reared by wire or terrycloth surrogate mothers. Monkeys raised with the surrogates became socially deviant and highly aggressive adults. Working with Harlow, W. A. Mason of the Delta Primate Center in Louisiana discovered that these consequences were less severe if the surrogate mother was swung from side to side. J. W. Prescott of the National Institute of Child Health and Human Development hypothesized that this movement would be conveyed to the cerebellum, particularly the middle part, called the cerebellar vermis, located at the back of the brain just above the brain stem. Among other functions, the vermis modulates the brain-stem nuclei that control

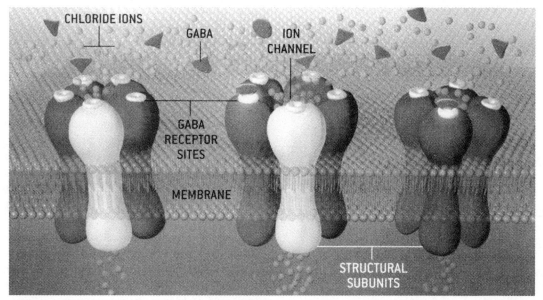

Carol Donner

FEWER INHIBITIONS: Stress causes changes to normal postsynaptic receptors (*left*) for gamma aminobutyric acid (GABA), the major inhibitory neurotransmitter in the central nervous system. It may lead to overstimulation of neurons, resulting in limbic system irritability. The presence of GABA lowers the electrical excitability of neurons by allowing greater flow of chloride ions (*center*). Loss of one of the GABA receptor's key structural subunits impairs its ability to moderate neural activity (*right*).

the production and release of the neurotransmitters norepinephrine and dopamine. Like the hippocampus, this part of the brain develops gradually and continues to create neurons after birth. It has an even higher density of receptors for stress hormones than the hippocampus, so exposure to such hormones can strongly affect its development.

Abnormalities in the cerebellar vermis have recently been reported to be associated with various psychiatric disorders, including manic-depressive illness, schizophrenia, autism and attention-deficit/hyperactivity disorder. These maladies emerge from genetic and prenatal factors, not childhood mistreatment, but the fact that vermal anomalies seem to sit at the core of so many psychiatric conditions suggests that this region plays a critical role in mental health.

Dysregulation of the vermis-controlled neurotransmitters norepinephrine and dopamine can produce symptoms of depression, psychosis and hyperactivity as well as impair attention. Activation of the dopamine system has been associated with a shift to a more left hemisphere–biased (verbal) attentional state, whereas activation of the norepinephrine system shifts attention to a more right hemisphere–biased (emotional) state. Perhaps most curiously, the vermis also helps to regulate electrical activity in the limbic system, and vermal stimulation can suppress seizure activity in the hippocampus and amydala.

R. G. Heath, working at Tulane University in the 1950s, found that Harlow's monkeys had seizure foci in their fastigial nuclei and hippocampus. In later work with humans, he found that electrical stimulation of the vermis reduced the frequency of seizures and improved the mental health in a small number of patients with intractable neuropsychiatric disorders. This result led my colleagues and me to speculate whether childhood abuse could produce abnormalities in the cerebellar vermis that con-

tributed to psychiatric symptoms, limbic irritability and gradual hippocampal degeneration.

To begin to test this hypothesis, Carl M. Anderson recently worked in tandem with me and with Perry Renshaw at the Brain Imaging Center at McLean. Anderson used T2-relaxometry methods, a new MRI-based functional imaging technique we developed. For the first time, we can monitor regional cerebral blood flow at rest without the use of radioactive tracers or contrast dyes.

When the brain is resting, the neuronal activity of a region closely matches the amount of blood that area receives to sustain this activity. Anderson found a striking correlation between the activity in the cerebellar vermis and the degree of limbic irritability indicated by my TLE-related question checklist in both healthy young adult controls and young adults with a history of repeated sexual abuse.

At any level of limbic symptomatology, however, the amount of blood flow in the vermis was markedly decreased in the individuals with a history of trauma. Low blood flow points to a functional impairment in the activity of the cerebellar vermis. On average, abused patients had higher checklist scores presumably because their vermis could not activate sufficiently to quell higher levels of limbic irritability.

Together these findings suggest an intriguing model that explains one way in which borderline personality disorder can emerge. Reduced integration between the right and left hemispheres and a smaller corpus callosum may predispose these patients to shift abruptly from left- to right-dominated states with very different emotional perceptions and memories. Such polarized hemispheric dominance could cause a person to see friends, family and co-workers in an overly positive way in one state and in a resoundingly negative way in another—which is

207

the hallmark of this disorder. Moreover, limbic electrical irritability can produce symptoms of aggression, exasperation and anxiety. Abnormal EEG activity in the temporal lobe is also often seen in people with a greatly increased risk for suicide and self-destructive behavior.

Adaptive Detriment

OUR TEAM INITIATED this research with the hypothesis that early stress was a toxic agent that interfered with the normal, smoothly orchestrated progression of brain development, leading to enduring psychiatric problems. Frank W. Putnam of Children's Hospital Medical Center of Cincinnati and Bruce D. Perry of the Alberta Mental Health Board in Canada have now articulated the same hypothesis. I have come to question and re-evaluate our starting premise, however. Human brains evolved to be molded by experience, and early difficulties were routine during our ancestral development. Is it plausible that the developing brain never evolved to cope with exposure to maltreatment and so is damaged in a nonadaptive manner? This seems most unlikely. The logical alternative is that exposure to early stress generates molecular and neurobiological effects that alter neural development in an adaptive way that prepares the adult brain to survive and reproduce in a dangerous world.

What traits or capacities might be beneficial for survival in the harsh conditions of earlier times? Some of the more obvious are the potential to mobilize an intense fight-or-flight response, to react aggressively to challenge without undue hesitation, to be at heightened alert for danger and to produce robust stress responses that facilitate recovery from injury. In this sense, we can reframe the brain changes we observed as adaptations to an adverse environment.

STRESS sculpts the brain to exhibit various ANTISOCIAL, though adaptive, behaviors.

Although this adaptive state helps to take the affected individual safely through the reproductive years (and is even likely to enhance sexual promiscuity), which are critical for evolu-

tionary success, it comes at a high price. McEwen has recently theorized that overactivation of stress response systems, a reaction that may be necessary for short-term survival, increases the risk for obesity, type II diabetes and hypertension; leads to a host of psychiatric problems, including a heightened risk of suicide; and accelerates the aging and degeneration of brain structures, including the hippocampus.

We hypothesize that adequate nurturing and the absence of intense early stress permits our brains to develop in a manner that is less aggressive and more emotionally stable, social, empathic and hemispherically integrated. We believe that this process enhances the ability of social animals to build more complex interpersonal structures and enables humans to better realize their creative potential.

Society reaps what it sows in the way it nurtures its children. Stress sculpts the brain to exhibit various antisocial, though adaptive, behaviors. Whether it comes in the form of physical, emotional or sexual trauma or through exposure to warfare, famine or pestilence, stress can set off a ripple of hormonal changes that permanently wire a child's brain to cope with a malevolent world. Through this chain of events, violence and abuse pass from generation to generation as well as from one society to the next. Our stark conclusion is that we see the need to do much more to ensure that child abuse does not happen in the first place, because once these key brain alterations occur, there may be no going back.

MORE TO EXPLORE

Developmental Traumatology, Part 2: Brain Development. M. D. De Bellis, M. S. Keshavan, D. B. Clark, B. J. Casey, J. N. Giedd, A. M. Boring, K. Frustaci and N. D. Ryan in *Biological Psychiatry*, Vol. 45, No. 10, pages 1271–1284; May 15, 1999.
Wounds That Time Won't Heal: The Neurobiology of Child Abuse. Martin H. Teicher in *Cerebrum* (Dana Press), Vol. 2, No. 4, pages 50–67; Fall 2000.
McLean Hospital: **www.mcleanhospital.org/**

MARTIN H. TEICHER is an associate professor of psychiatry at Harvard Medical School, director of the Developmental Biopsychiatry Research Program at McLean Hospital in Belmont, Mass., and chief of the Developmental Psychopharmacology Laboratory at the Mailman Research Center at McLean.

The Early Origins of Autism

*New research into the causes of this baffling disorder is focusing
on genes that control the development of the brain*

by Patricia M. Rodier

Autism has been mystifying scientists for more than half a century. The complex behavioral disorder encompasses a wide variety of symptoms, most of which usually appear before a child turns three. Children with autism are unable to interpret the emotional states of others, failing to recognize anger, sorrow or manipulative intent. Their language skills are often limited, and they find it difficult to initiate or sustain conversations. They also frequently exhibit an intense preoccupation with a single subject, activity or gesture.

These behaviors can be incredibly debilitating. How can you be included in a typical classroom if you can't be dissuaded from banging your head on your desk? How can you make friends if your overriding interest is in calendars? When children with autism also suffer from mental retardation—as most of them do—the prognosis is even worse. Intensive behavioral therapy improves the outcome for many patients, but their symptoms can make it impossible for them to live independently, even if they have normal IQs.

I became involved in the search for autism's causes relatively recently—and almost by accident. As an embryologist, I previously focused on various birth defects of the brain. In 1994 I attended a remarkable presentation at a scientific conference on research into birth defects. Two pediatric ophthalmologists, Marilyn T. Miller of the University of Illinois at Chicago and Kerstin Strömland of Goteborg University in Sweden, described a surprising outcome from a study investigating eye motility prob-

lems in victims of thalidomide, the morning-sickness drug that caused an epidemic of birth defects in the 1960s. The study's subjects were adults who had been exposed to the drug while still in the womb. After examining these people, Miller and Strömland made an observation that had somehow eluded previous researchers: about five percent of the thalidomide victims had autism, which is about 30 times higher than the rate among the general population.

When I heard these results, I felt a shock of recognition, a feeling so powerful that I actually became dizzy and began to hyperventilate. In the effort to identify autism's causes, researchers had long sought to pinpoint exactly when the disorder begins. Previous speculation had focused on late gestation or early postnatal life as the time of origin, but there was no evidence to back up either hypothesis. The connection with thalidomide suddenly threw a brilliant new light on the subject. It suggested that autism originates in the early weeks of pregnancy, when the embryo's brain and the rest of its nervous system are just beginning to develop. Indeed, Miller and Strömland's work convinced me that the mystery of autism could soon be solved.

Genetic Factors

At least 16 of every 10,000 babies are born with autism or one of its related disorders [*see "The Spectrum of Autism Disorders"*]. Since autism was first identified in 1943, scientists have made great strides in describing its symptoms. The biologi-

cal basis for autism, however, has been elusive - an unfortunate circumstance, because such an understanding could enable researchers to identify the leading risk factors for autism and possibly to design new treatments for the condition.

At least 16 of every 10,000 babies are born with autism or one of its related disorders

By examining the inheritance of the disorder, researchers have shown that autism runs in families, though not in a clear-cut way. Siblings of people with autism have a 3 to 8 percent chance of being diagnosed with the same disorder. This is much greater than the 0.16 percent risk in the general population but much less than the 50 percent chance that would characterize a genetic disease caused by a single dominant mutation (in which one faulty gene inherited from one parent is sufficient to cause the disorder) or the 25 percent chance that would characterize a single recessive mutation (in which a copy of the faulty gene must be inherited from each parent). The results fit best with models in which variants of several genes contribute to the outcome. To complicate matters further, relatives of people with autism may fail to meet all the criteria for the disorder but still have some of its symptoms. Although these relatives may have some of the gene variants linked to autism—whatever they may be—for some reason the

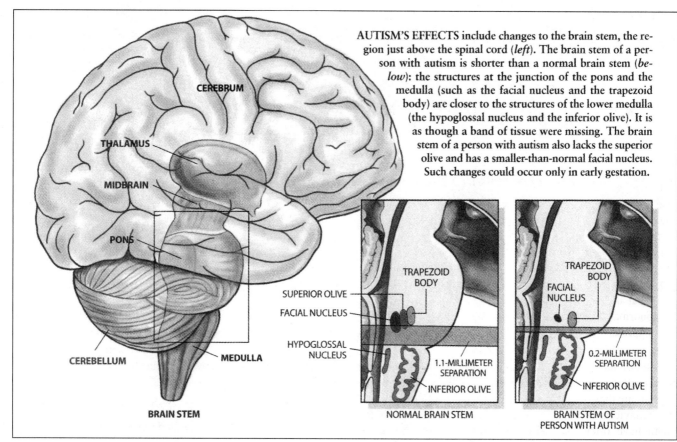

AUTISM'S EFFECTS include changes to the brain stem, the region just above the spinal cord (*left*). The brain stem of a person with autism is shorter than a normal brain stem (*below*): the structures at the junction of the pons and the medulla (such as the facial nucleus and the trapezoid body) are closer to the structures of the lower medulla (the hypoglossal nucleus and the inferior olive). It is as though a band of tissue were missing. The brain stem of a person with autism also lacks the superior olive and has a smaller-than-normal facial nucleus. Such changes could occur only in early gestation.

NORMAL BRAIN STEM

BRAIN STEM OF PERSON WITH AUTISM

TERESE WINSLOW

genetic factors are not fully expressed in these individuals.

Studies of twins in the U.K. confirm that autism has a heritable component but suggest that environmental influences play a role as well. For example, if genetic factors alone were involved, monozygotic (identical) twins, who share the same genes, should have a 100 percent chance of sharing the same diagnosis. Instead, when one twin has autism, the second twin has only a 60 percent chance of being diagnosed with the same disorder. That twin also has an 86 percent chance of having some of autism's symptoms. These figures indicate that other factors must modify the genetic predisposition to the disorder.

The Embryology of Autism

Several environmental risk factors are already known. In utero exposure to rubella (German measles) or to birth defect-causing substances such as ethanol and valproic acid increases the chances that autism will develop. People with certain genetic diseases, such as phenylketonuria and tuberous sclerosis,

also have a greater chance of developing autism. None of these factors, however, is present frequently enough to be responsible for many cases. Furthermore, most exposures to diseases or hazardous substances would be likely to affect both members of a pair of twins rather than just one. Some of the environmental influences must be more subtle than those identified so far. Researchers do not know how the multiple factors combine to make some people display symptoms while allowing others to escape them. This variation makes the search for autism's causes especially difficult.

In their 1994 study Miller and Strömland added another environmental contributor to autism: thalidomide exposure in utero. All their subjects—Swedish adults born in the late 1950s and early 1960s– exhibited some of the malformations for which thalidomide is infamous: stunted arms and legs, misshapen or missing ears and thumbs, and neurological dysfunctions of the eye and facial muscles. Because scientists know which organs of the embryo are developing at each stage of pregnancy, they can pin-

point the exact days when a malformation can be induced: the thumb is affected as early as day 22 after conception, the ears from days 20 to 33, and the arms and legs from days 25 to 35. What made the new study so exciting for me was Miller and Strömland's discovery that most of the thalidomide victims with autism had anomalies in the external part of their ears but no malformations of the arms or legs. This pattern indicated that the subjects had been injured very early in gestation—20 to 24 days after conception—before many women even know they are pregnant.

For embryologists, nothing tells us so much about *what* happened to an embryo as knowing *when* it happened. In the case of thalidomide-induced autism, the critical period is much earlier than many investigators would have guessed. Very few neurons form as early as the fourth week of gestation, and most are motor neurons of the cranial nerves, the ones that operate the muscles of the eyes, ears, face, jaw, throat and tongue. The cell bodies of these neurons are located in the brain stem, the region between the spinal

Thalidomide Timeline

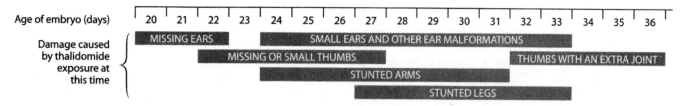

BIRTH DEFECTS caused by thalidomide vary depending on when the mother was exposed to the drug.

cord and the rest of the brain. Because these motor neurons develop at the same time as the external ears, one might predict that the thalidomide victims with autism would also suffer from dysfunctions of the cranial nerves. Miller and Strömland confirmed this prediction—they found that all the subjects with autism had abnormalities of eye movement or facial expression, or both.

The next logical question was, "Are the cases of autism after thalidomide exposure similar to cases of unknown cause, or are they different?" Aside from their behavioral symptoms, people with autism have often been described not only as normal in appearance but as unusually attractive. They are certainly normal in stature, with normal-to-large heads. The few studies that have tested nonbehavioral features of people with autism, however, have concluded that there are indeed minor physical and neurological anomalies in many cases, and they are the same ones noted in thalidomide-induced autism. For example, minor malformations of the external ears—notably posterior rotation, in which the top of the ear is tilted backward more than 15 degrees–are more common in children with autism than in typically developing children, children with mental retardation or siblings of children with autism. Dysfunctions of eye movement had been associated with autism before the thalidomide study, and lack of facial expression is one of the behaviors used to diagnose the condition.

The Neurobiology of Autism

I s it possible that all the symptoms of autism arise from changes in the function of the cranial nerves? Probably not. It is more likely that the nerve dysfunctions in people with autism reflect an early brain in-

jury that not only affects the cranial nerves but also has secondary effects on later brain development. That is, the injury to the brain stem might somehow interfere with the proper development or wiring of other brain regions, including those involved in higher-level functions such as speech, resulting in the behavioral symptoms of autism. Or perhaps the ear malformations and cranial nerve dysfunctions are only side effects of an injury that we don't understand. Whatever the true situation may be, the anomalies in patients with autism of unknown cause were much the same as the anomalies in the thalidomide victims with autism. The conclusion was clear: many cases of autism, if not all, are initiated very early in gestation.

The region of the brain implicated by the thalidomide study—the brain stem—is one that has rarely been considered in studies of autism or in studies of other kinds of congenital brain damage, for that matter. On a simplistic level, neurobiologists associate the brain stem with the most basic functions: breathing, eating, balance, motor coordination and so forth. Many of the behaviors disturbed in autism, such as language, planning and interpretation of social cues, are believed to be controlled by higher-level regions of the brain, such as the cerebral cortex and the hippocampus in the forebrain.

Yet some symptoms common in autism—lack of facial expression, hypersensitivity to touch and sound, and sleep disturbances—do sound like ones more likely to originate in the brain regions associated with basic functions. Furthermore, the most consistently observed abnormality in the brains of people with autism is not a change in the forebrain but a reduction in the number of neurons in the cerebellum, a large processing center of the hindbrain that has long been known to have critical functions in the control of muscle movement.

One reason for scientists' confusion about the brain regions involved in autism may be that our assumptions about where functions are controlled are shaky. For example, the laboratory group led by Eric Courchesne of the University of California at San Diego has shown that parts of the cerebellum are activated during certain tasks requiring high-level cognitive processing. Another difficulty is that the symptoms of autism are so complex. If simpler behavioral abnormalities could be shown to be diagnostic of the disorder, researchers might have a better chance of identifying their source in the nervous system [see "A Simpler Symptom of Autism"].

Many cases of autism, if not all, are initiated very early in gestation.

In 1995 our research team had the opportunity to follow up on the thalidomide study by examining the brain stem of a person with autism. The tissue samples came from the autopsy of a young woman who had suffered from autism of unknown cause; she had died in the 1970s, but fortunately the samples of her brain tissue had been preserved. When we examined the woman's brain stem, we were struck by the near absence of two structures: the facial nucleus, which controls the muscles of facial expression, and the superior olive, which is a relay station for auditory information. Both structures arise from the same segment of the embryo's neural tube, the organ that develops into the central nervous system. Counts of the facial neurons in the woman's brain showed only about 400 cells, whereas counts of facial neurons in a control brain showed 9,000.

Overall, the woman's brain was normal in size; in fact, it was slightly heavier than the average brain. I hypothesized

The Spectrum of Autism Disorders

A diagnosis of autism requires that the patient exhibit abnormal behaviors in three categories [see "Diagnostic Categories"] and have especially notable deficits in the category of social interaction. In addition, clinicians have identified several related disorders that share some of the behavioral features of autism but have different emphases or additional symptoms. For example, Pervasive Development Disorder, Not Otherwise Specified (PDD-NOS) denotes patients who miss fulfilling the autism creiteria in one of the three categories. As is true of autism, PDD-NOS includes patients with the whole range of IQs. Asperger syndrome is used to describe patients with normal IQs and no evidence of language delay. Two much rarer diagnoses are Childhood Disintegrative Disorder, in which normal early development is followed by regression to severe disability, and Rett syndrome, a progressive neurological disorder that occurs only in females.

Although many scientists have long known that autism is an inherited disease, recently family studies by Peter Szatmari's group at McMaster University in Ontario suggest that it is the spectrum of symptoms that runs in families, rather than a single diagnosis. For example, a child with autism may have a brother with asperger syndrome, or a woman with

autism may have a nephew with PDD-NOS. These family studies strongly suggest that at least three of the diagnoses—autism, PDD-NOS, and Asperger sundrome—arise from some of the same inherited factors.   —P.M.R.

Diagnostic Categories

Impairment of Social Interaction: Failure to use eye contact, facial expression or gestures to regulate social interaction; failure to seek comfort; failure to develop relationships with peers.

Impairment of Communication: Failure to use spoken language, without compensating by gesture; deficit in initiating or sustaining a converstation, despite adequate speech; aberrant language (for example, repeating a question instead of replying).

Restricted and Repetitive Interests and Behaviors: Abnormally intense preoccupation with one subject or activity; distress over change; insistence on routines or rituals with no purpose; repetitive movements, such as hand flapping.

---

that the brain stem was lacking only the specific neurons already identified—those in the facial nucleus and the superior olive—and to test that idea I decided to measure the distances between a number of neuroanatomical landmarks. I was surprised to discover that my hypothesis was absolutely wrong. Although the side-to-side measures were indeed normal, the front-to-back measures were astonishingly reduced in the brain stem of the woman with autism. It was as though a band of tissue had been cut out of the brain stem, and the two remaining pieces had been knit back together with no seam where the tissue was missing.

For the second time in my life, I felt a powerful shock of recognition. I heard a roaring in my ears, my vision dimmed, and I felt as though my head might explode. The shock was not generated by the unexpected result but by the realization that! had seen this pattern of shortening before, in a paper that showed pictures of abnormal mouse brains. When I retrieved the article from the stacks of papers on my office floor, I found that the correspondence between the brain I had been studying and the mouse brains de-

scribed in the article was even more striking than I had remembered. Both cases exhibited shortening of the brain stem, a smaller-than-normal facial nucleus and the absence of a superior olive. Additional features of the mice were clearly related to other anomalies associated with autism: they had ear malformations and lacked one of the brain structures controlling eye movement.

What had altered the brains of these mice? It was not exposure to thalidomide or any of the other environmental factors associated with autism but the elimination of the function of a gene. These were transgenic "knockout" mice, engineered to lack the expression of the gene known as *Hoxa1* so that researchers could study the gene's role in early development. The obvious question was, "Could this be one of the genes involved in autism?"

The literature supported the idea that *Hoxa1* was an excellent candidate for autism research. The studies of knockout mice showed that *Hoxa1* plays a central role in development of the brain stem. Groups in Salt Lake City and London had studied different knockout strains with similar results. They found that the

gene is active in the brain stem when the first neurons are forming—the same period that Miller and Strömland had identified as the time when thalidomide caused autism. *Hoxa1* produces a type of protein called a transcription factor, which modulates the activity of other genes. What is more, *Hoxa1* is not active in any tissue after early embryogenesis. If a gene is active throughout life, as many are, altered function of that gene usually leads to problems that increase with age. A gene active only during development is a better candidate to explain a congenital disability like autism, which seems to be stable after childhood.

Hoxa1 is what geneticists call a "highly conserved" gene, meaning that the sequence of nucleotides that make up its DNA has changed little over the course of evolution. We assume that this is a characteristic of genes that are critical to survival: they suffer mutations as other genes do, but most changes are likely to be fatal, so they are rarely passed on to subsequent generations. Although many other genes appear in several forms—for example, the genes that encode eye color or blood type—highly conserved genes are not commonly

A Simpler Symptom of Autism

Scientists at York University and the Hospital for Sick Children in Toronto have recently identified an autism-related behavior that is much simpler than the array of behaviors that have traditionally been used to diagnose the condition. Susan Bryson and her doctoral student Reginald Landry have found that children with autism respond abnormally to a task involving their reactions to visual stimuli. Because this mental activity is probably mediated by a primitive part of the brain—most likely the brain stem or the cerebellum, or both—the discovery has important implications for the neurobiology of autism. Bryson and Landry's work could also help clinicians develop a simpler way to test children for the disorder.

In their study Bryson and Landry observed the reactions of two groups of children, those with autism and those without it, as they watched lights flashing on video screens. The children ranged in age from four to seven. In the first test, each child was placed in front of a three-screen panel, and a flashing light appeared on the middle screen. This stimulus prompted the children to focus their eyes on the flashes. Then the middle screen went blank, and a flashing light appeared on the far-right or the far-left screen of the panel. Both groups of children shifted their eyes to that screen. In the second test, however, the lights on the middle screen kept flashing while the lights appeared on the other screen. The children without autism shifted focus on the new stimulus, but the children with autism remained "stuck" on the first stimulus and failed to turn their eyes to the new one. The two tests were repeated many times for each child.

Bryson and Landry found that children with other kinds of brain damage are perfectly normal in their ability to disengage from one stimulus and focus on another. Children with autism, however, repeatedly fail to disengage from the first stimulus, even if they are highly intelligent. Researchers suspect that this ability is a low-level brain function because it typically appears in infants—as early as three to four months after birth—and in children with low IQs. Animals also orient themselves toward new stimuli, so scientists could conceivably use a similar test in animal studies to verify whether genetic manipulations or toxicologic exposures have produced this symptom of autism.

—P.M.R.

found in multiple versions (also known as polymorphic alleles, or allelic variants). The fact that no one had ever discovered a variant of *Hoxa1* in any mammalian species suggested that my colleagues and I might have trouble finding one in cases of autism. On the other hand, it seemed likely that if a variant allele could be found, it might well be one of the triggers for the development of the disorder.

Zeroing in on *HOXA1*

The human version of the gene, labeled as *HOXA1*, resides on chromosome 7 and is relatively small. It contains just two protein-coding regions, or exons, along with regions that regulate the level of protein production or do nothing at all. Deviations from the normal sequence in any part of a gene can affect its performance, but the vast majority of disease-causing variations are in the protein-coding regions. Thus, we began the search for variant alleles by focusing on the exons of *HOXA1*. Using blood samples from people with autism and from subjects in a control group, we extracted the DNA and looked for deviations from the normal sequence of nucleotides.

The good news is that we have identified two variant alleles of *HOXA1*. One has a minor deviation in the sequence of one of the gene's exons, meaning that the protein encoded by the variant gene is slightly different from the protein encoded by the normal gene. We have studied this newly discovered allele in detail, measuring its prevalence among various groups of people to determine if it plays a role in causing autism. (The other variant allele is more difficult to investigate because it involves a change in the physical structure of the gene's DNA.) We found that the rate of the variant allele among people with autism was significantly higher than the rate among their family members who do not have the disorder and the rate among unrelated individuals without the disorder. The differences were much greater than would be expected by chance.

The bad news is that, just as the family studies had predicted, *HOXA1* is only one of many genes involved in the spectrum of autism disorders. Furthermore, the allele that we have studied in detail is variably expressed—its presence does not guarantee that autism will arise. Preliminary data indicate that the variant allele occurs in about 20 percent of the people who do not have autism and in about 40 percent of those who do. The allele approximately doubles the risk of developing the condition. But in about 60 percent of people with autism, the allele is not present, meaning that other genetic factors must be contributing to the disorder.

To pin down those factors, we must continue searching for other variants in *HOXA1*, because most genetic disorders result from many different deviant alleles of the same gene. Variations in other genes involved in early development may also predispose their carriers to autism. We have already discovered a variant allele of *HOXB1*, a gene on chromosome 17 that is derived from the same ancestral source as *HOXA1* and has similar functions in the development of the brain stem, but its effect in autism appears to be minor. Other investigators are scrutinizing candidate regions on chromosome 15 and on another part of chromosome 7. Although researchers are focusing on alleles that increase the risk of autism, other alleles may decrease the risk. These could help explain the variable expression of the spectrum of autism- related disorders.

Even a minimal understanding of the genetic basis of autism would be of great value. For example, researchers could transfer the alleles associated with autism from humans to mice, engineering them to be genetically susceptible to the disorder. By exposing these mice to substances suspected of increasing the risk of autism, we would be able to study the interaction of environmental factors with genetic background and perhaps compile an expanded list of substances that women need to avoid during early pregnancy. What is more, by examining the development of these genetically engineered mice, we could learn more about the brain damage that underlies autism. If researchers can determine exactly what is wrong with the brains of people with autism, they may be able to suggest drug therapies or other treatments that could ameliorate the effects of the damage.

Devising a genetic test for autism—similar to the current tests for cystic fibrosis, sickle cell anemia and other diseases—would be a much more difficult task. Because so many genes appear to be involved in the disorder, one cannot accurately predict the odds of having a child with autism by simply testing for one or two variant alleles in the parents. Tests might be developed, however, for the siblings of people with autism, who often fear that their own children will inherit the disorder. Clinicians could look for a set of well- established genetic risk factors in both the family member with autism and the unaffected sibling. If the person with autism has several high-risk alleles, whereas the sibling does not, the sibling would at least be reassured that his or her offspring would not be subject to the known risks within his or her family.

Nothing will make the search for autism's causes simple. But every risk factor that we are able to identify takes away some of the mystery. More important, new data spawn new hypotheses. Just as the thalidomide results drew attention to the brain stem and to the *HOXA1* gene, new data from developmental genetics, behavioral studies, brain imaging and many other sources can be expected to produce more welcome shocks of recognition for investigators of autism. In time, their work may help alleviate the terrible suffering caused by the disorder.

Further Information

AUTISM IN THALIDOMIDE EMBRYOPATHY: A POPULATION STUDY. K. Strömland, V. Nordin, M. Miller, B. Åkerström and C. Gillberg in *Developmental Medicine and Child Neurology*, Vol. 36, No. 4, pages 351–356; April 1994.

EMBRYOLOGICAL ORIGIN FOR AUTISM: DEVELOPMENTAL ANOMALIES OF THE CRANIAL NERVE MOTOR NUCLEI. P. M. Rodier, J. L. Ingram, B. Tisdale, S. Nelson and J. Romano in *Journal of Comparative Neurology*, Vol. 370, No. 2, pages 247–261; June 24, 1996.

THINKING IN PICTURES: AND OTHER REPORTS FROM MY LIFE WITH AUTISM. Temple Grandin. Vintage Books, 1996.

More information on autism is available at the Web page of the National Alliance for Autism Research at www.naar.org

PATRICIA M. RODIER is professor of obstetrics and gynecology at the University of Rochester. She has studied injuries to the developing nervous system since she was a postdoctoral fellow in embryology at the University of Virginia, but she began to investigate autism only after hearing the results of the thalidomide study. Rodier has assembled a group of scientists from many disciplines at six institutions to study the genetic and environmental causes of the disorder and says that working with experts from other fields is rejuvenating.

VOICES OF THE CHILDREN:

We beat and killed people...

Leaders gather at the U.N. this week to discuss the world's kids, including child soldiers. NEWSWEEK went to Sierra Leone to talk in depth with four real experts.

BY TOM MASLAND

THE FOUR BOYS AT ST. FRANCIS PRIMARY School don't stand out much. They're just a bit bigger than other fourth and fifth graders crowded onto rough benches in the otherwise bare classrooms. And teachers at St. Francis say the four are doing well—eager to learn, more disciplined than their younger classmates. But look closely, and you see that the four are different from their fellow students in other ways. Their knees are battered from crawling through the West African bush, and they have ugly welts from incisions once stuffed with heroin and cocaine. The letters RUF—for Revolutionary United Front—are carved across the chest of one boy. And the external marks only hint at the scars within—at the horrors the boys suffered, and perpetrated, as forced conscripts in an unimaginably brutal civil war.

The four boys from Makeni, Sierra Leone, won't be among child delegates join-

ing more than 60 heads of state at United Nations headquarters in New York this week. They've barely thought about one of the main issues involved in the U.N. Special Session on Children—how the international community can roll back the growing exploitation of children in war. Experts say soldiers under the age of 15 have fought in more than half of the world's 55 ongoing or just-ended wars. Children are easy to recruit, low cost and malleable. From the "little bees" of Colombia to the "baby brigades" of Sri Lanka, they have become the cannon fodder of choice.

In a world absorbed with the "war on terror," with headlines blaring about terrified Americans and terrorized Israelis or Palestinians, the atrocities committed against some of these children almost demand a new language to encompass a further extreme of horror. The kids of the

Mideast get more attention, either as disciples of terror or as victims of occupation. But nobody has been more exploited than the kids of Sierra Leone. They may not come from a strategically important country, or a place that, for now anyway, represents a danger to the world's rich nations. But the growing use of children has changed the dynamics of warfare, and must be treated as a new security threat. The question before the United Nations this week will be how to muster the will to enforce longstanding international conventions and three new resolutions on children and armed conflict. The latest protocols on children's rights took force in February, and condemned the use of child soldiers and their sexual exploitation.

Some may dismiss teenage ex-combatants as war criminals who don't have much to contribute to a debate on human rights. Indeed, these boys say they can now look only to God for forgiveness. Yet they are, in a very intimate way, the world's leading experts on child warfare. And their eyewitness accounts—shocking as they are—convey the unthinkable inhumanity of those who coerced them into combat. To that end, NEWSWEEK recently spent three days debriefing these four young veterans, selected from among 25 ex-combatants who attend the 1,023-student primary school in Makeni, a rundown market town 90 miles northeast of the capital, Freetown. All lost close relatives in the war; two stammer uncontrollably. Abdul Rahman Kamera, 15, still lives with the rebel commander who nicknamed him "Go Easy"; he can find no living relative. Zakaria Turay, 14, whose war name was "Ranger," and Abbas Fofanah, 16, who went by "G-Pox," live with aunts. Only Alieu Bangura, 14, called "Major" by his fellow warriors, has been reunited with his mother. All are destitute, barely getting enough to eat. Their stories:

"They brought a grown-up man, put his hand on a stump and amputated it. They gave me a gun and I refused it. They fired between my feet. I took the gun."

Before the War

ABDUL RAHMAN: I remember that my grandmother used to prepare cooked food to sell. Early in the morning she used to take food to where she was selling it. I would go and collect the dishes. After school I would go to the house, get drinking water, wash my uniform and go to my companions to play football. I liked to play defense. In the house, we played a board game with seeds, called Tin Tan Ton. When the moon was full we used to take our mats outside and tell stories and then sing. We would swim in a stream. The older ones would dunk us. My favorite time was when I came home from school and my grandmother was still selling. I would go and eat, and she would put in a lot of extra meat for me.

ABBAS: In the morning my mother would ask me to sweep and clean. My father drove a big truck. When the moon was full I would play with my companions. We would bounce a ball and play hide-and-seek in the moonlight. We lived in

Bo, near where the Makeni vehicles used to park. My grandmother sent word from Burkina Faso that she had no child to play with. I was sent to Burkina. I used to sell for my grandmother. She gave me palm oil and onions to go and sell.

"Before a battle, they would make a shallow cut [on the temple] and put powder in. Afterward, I didn't see any human being having value."

ALIEU: In the morning I would sweep under our mango tree, then wash my face and go to school. At night we used to tell stories in the moonlight. My father was the superintendent of our district [in Makeni]. On weekends I would go with my father to his farm. I carried water for him.

Forced Into Service

ALIEU: I was abducted during Operation Pay Yourself, in 1998. I was 9 years old. Six rebels came through our yard. They went to loot for food. It's called *jaja*—"get food." They said, "We want to bring a small boy like you—we like you." My mother didn't comment; she just cried. My father objected. They threatened to kill him. They argued with him at the back of the house. I heard a gunshot. One of them told me, "Let's go, they've killed your father." A woman rebel grabbed my hand roughly and took me along. I saw my father lying dead as we passed.

ABDUL RAHMAN: I was in class, second grade. I was 8 years old. They threatened to kill us. In front of us, they brought a grown-up man, going gray. They put his hand on a stump and amputated it. They gave me a gun and I refused it. They fired between my feet. I took the gun.

ABBAS: I was on my way to the market when a rebel demanded I come with him. The commander said to move ahead with him. My grandmother argued with him. He shot her twice. I said he should kill me, too. They tied my elbows behind my back. At the base, they locked me in the toilet for two days. When they let me out, they carved the letters RUF across my chest. They tied me so I wouldn't rub it until it was healed.

ZAKARIA: I was captured in Freetown on May 25, 1997. I was carrying pans in the street. A rebel told me, "Put your pans down and come carry our load." We walked all the way to Makeni.

The Drug Factor

ALIEU: We smoked *jambaa* [marijuana] all the time. They told us it would ward off disease in the bush. Before a battle, they would make a shallow cut here [on the temple, beside his right eye] and put powder in, and cover it with a plaster. Afterward I did not see anything having any value. I didn't see any human being having value. I felt light.

ZAKARIA: My missions included diamond mining near Kono, drug purchasing, collecting ammunition in Liberia, looting villages and capturing civilians. I used to buy drugs at the Liberian border from a man called Papi. They forced us to take them. This is where they would cut and put the "brown-brown" [heroin]. [He shows a raised welt on his left pectoral.] We would then inhale cocaine. During operations, I sometimes would take it two or three times a day. I felt strong and powerful. I felt no fear. When I was demobilized I felt weak and cold and had no appetite for three weeks.

ABBAS: They gave me injections in the leg [shows track marks] and cut the back of my head to put in cocaine [shows scar]. The smaller ones are the ones who stand in front, the elder ones behind. So they give the boys the injections. It happened any time we were going on the attack—more than 25 times.

"When villagers refused to clear out of an area we would strip them naked and burn them. Sometimes we used plastic and sometimes a tire."

Atrocities Up Close

ALIEU: The first time I killed anybody was during my first battle, at Lunsar. We captured 10 civilians. The CO [commanding officer] was asking them where the government soldiers were, and they refused to say. The CO told me to kill one of them, or he would shoot me. I shot [the civilian] in the chest…

216

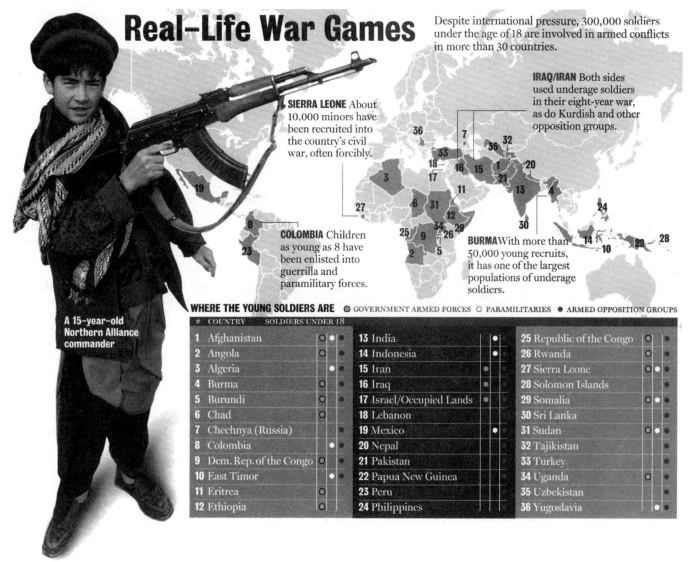

Real-Life War Games

Despite international pressure, 300,000 soldiers under the age of 18 are involved in armed conflicts in more than 30 countries.

SIERRA LEONE About 10,000 minors have been recruited into the country's civil war, often forcibly.

IRAQ/IRAN Both sides used underage soldiers in their eight-year war, as do Kurdish and other opposition groups.

COLOMBIA Children as young as 8 have been enlisted into guerrilla and paramilitary forces.

BURMA With more than 50,000 young recruits, it has one of the largest populations of underage soldiers.

A 15-year-old Northern Alliance commander

WHERE THE YOUNG SOLDIERS ARE ● GOVERNMENT ARMED FORCES ○ PARAMILITARIES ● ARMED OPPOSITION GROUPS

#	COUNTRY	Govt	Para	Opp
1	Afghanistan	○	●	●
2	Angola	●		●
3	Algeria			●
4	Burma	●		●
5	Burundi	●		●
6	Chad	●		
7	Chechnya (Russia)			●
8	Colombia		●	●
9	Dem. Rep. of the Congo	○		●
10	East Timor		●	●
11	Eritrea	●		
12	Ethiopia	●		
13	India	●		●
14	Indonesia	●		●
15	Iran			●
16	Iraq	●		
17	Israel/Occupied Lands	●		
18	Lebanon			●
19	Mexico		●	●
20	Nepal			●
21	Pakistan			●
22	Papua New Guinea			●
23	Peru			●
24	Philippines			●
25	Republic of the Congo	○		●
26	Rwanda	○		●
27	Sierra Leone	○	●	●
28	Solomon Islands			●
29	Somalia	○	●	●
30	Sri Lanka			●
31	Sudan	○	●	●
32	Tajikistan			●
33	Turkey			●
34	Uganda	○		●
35	Uzbekistan			●
36	Yugoslavia		●	●

SOURCE: THE COALITION TO STOP THE USE OF CHILD SOLDIERS; RESEARCH BY JOSH ULICK, GRAPHIC BY STANFORD KAY—NEWSWEEK

After Lunsar, I was a small-boy commander. I commanded 10 boys, aged 10 to 16.

ABBAS: When we caught *kamajors* [progovernment militiamen] we would mutilate them by parts and display them in the streets. When villagers refused to clear out of an area we would strip them naked and burn them to death. Sometimes we used plastic and sometimes a tire. Sometimes they would partially sever a person's neck, then leave him on the road to die slowly. I saw a pregnant woman split open to see what the baby's sex was. We had met her on the streets of Kabala. Two officers, "O5" and "Savage," argued over it and made a bet. Savage's boys opened the woman. It was a girl. The baby lived.

In Kabala I was forced to do amputations. We had a cutlass, an ax and a big log. We called the villagers out and let them stand in line. You ask [the victims] whether they want a long hand or a short hand [the amputation at the wrist or elbow]. The long hand you put in a different bag from the short hand. If you have a large number of amputated hands in the bag, the promotion will be automatic, to various ranks.

We gang-raped women, sometimes six people at a time. I didn't feel much because I was drugged and I was just there for sex. One of my friends was having sex with a girl when she complained she was tired. He took out his pistol and shot into her vagina. But usually we would let them stagger and go.

I remember one tough operation. We were dressed all in black, we were the ones they called the cobras. We killed people, we cooked them, we ate them and then we broke their pots.

ZAKARIA: I remember when I was manning the heavy machine gun. No one dared stand in front of me. I killed when I said, "You! If you leave I will kill you!" We were the men who amputated hands and used the same cut hand to slap the victim. We beat and killed people, not even afraid of the consequences. We were ready to commit any crimes. We were the rough ones.

ABDUL RAHMAN: My schoolmates and I met our old teacher, and we knocked him down. We killed the teacher and we took his books and burned them, and then we took some of the papers to the toilet to wipe ourselves.

ZAKARIA: They [older rebels] would [impale people] when the drugs had taken hold and they wanted to play wicked games. They want to see blood. Some of them drink blood. Especially on the war fronts, where there's no food, no water, when we killed civilians we would cut a hole on the top of the arm, above the wrist, and press on the arm, and drink.

"I am praying for forgiveness so that more fruitful things can come our way, praying that God will help us to become good people."

And Now, the Aftershocks

ABBAS: Sometimes I feel dizzy, and I feel like doing bad things. I go in the house and lie down... Three months ago a friend insulted me, called me a rebel who killed so many people and destroyed the whole world. I said, "You won't make remarks like that again." I met a woman slicing potato leaves. I snatched the knife from her and stabbed him. I ripped his skin... When I see a pretty woman passing I think of the times in the bush when we were raping women, when I could just call her and say, "Come here, let's go."

ALIEU: If someone offends me, I think back: if I had been in the bush, how I would have dealt with him. I feel ashamed of myself... I dream about what happened. Sometimes I feel scared, because I've killed, I've drunk blood, I've smoked jambaa—I worry that these things will take over, that they'll lead me to do bad things again. The drugs we took made me feel very light. I worry that I'm not as intelligent as I was before.

ZAKARIA: Most times I dream, I have a gun, I'm firing, I'm killing, cutting, amputating. I feel afraid, thinking perhaps that these things will happen to me again. Sometimes I cry... When I see a woman I'm afraid of her. I've been bad with women; now I fear that if I go near one she'll hit me. Perhaps she will kill me.

Facing the Future

ABDUL RAHMAN: The only thing I'm thinking about is to go further with my schooling, and let me reap the benefits. That's all I pray for. We're all human beings, and you [foreigners] sat and watched this country being destroyed. You have the money and you will not help.

ABBAS: Right now I want to be a doctor or teacher. I want to go to America to learn a very powerful job. Let me be able to do something for my people.

ALIEU: After I have finished my university I want to be a doctor or a teacher. Father God, I have a future plan for this country that will make this country develop. I thank God that I have survived, they did not kill me in the bush. They used to punish me, do all kinds of bad things to me, but they did not kill me... Please support us. Right now we don't have books, we don't have pens, we don't even have uniforms. Let them send some things for us.

ZAKARIA: I am praying for forgiveness so that more fruitful things can come our way, praying that God will help us to become good people.

Protecting Others

ABBAS: We need a leader who would take good care of this country. The rebellion started because of bad leadership. God must forgive boys like us. It was not our fault. It was the fault of the elders. Those who committed the highest crimes should be punished.

ALIEU: The guilty can be prosecuted. They should be taken to court, and let them explain what happened. Thinking about the part I've played, I'm thinking I may be liable to appear in court.

ZAKARIA: Right now, the war is over, but what happened to us should not repeat itself with our children. With only small things to compensate us for what we've been through, we will be able to pick ourselves up.

THE TASK OF PROSECUTING THOSE WHO exploited such children is monumental. In West Africa, Liberia's Charles Taylor pioneered the use of "small-boy units" during his drive for power in the 1990s. Security analysts estimate that he and others used 15,000 children as combatants in that war, and now Taylor is Liberia's president— and fending off a new rebellion. Neighboring Sierra Leone's war was an extension of Liberia's brutal conflict. The RUF gained control of the country's rich diamond fields, selling through Liberia. Sierra Leonean commanders who had served under Taylor took an estimated 10,000 children as combatants during the decadelong conflict, which the United Nations officially declared finished only this year.

At least the world will try to punish the boys' bosses. Last month U.N. Secretary-General Kofi Annan appointed a U.S. Defense Department lawyer as chief prosecutor for the U.N.'s Sierra Leone War Crimes Tribunal. David Crane will head prosecutions at a court charged with trying violations of Sierra Leonean and international humanitarian law since Nov. 30, 1996—the date when rebels signed a peace accord that later collapsed. RUF rebel leader Foday Sankoh will be among the first to go to trial. He has been jailed since May 2000.

But many of the big fish may wriggle free. The rebels didn't keep good records. Unlike the Balkans, where war-crimes cases are succeeding, none of Sierra Leone's neighbors supports prosecutions; these countries are all implicated. The biggest fish of all is Taylor, who has no interest in cooperating. If the West hopes to extract pledges of support from other countries in the region, it will have to condition aid on their compliance. Finally, the victimized societies need to look inward, to ask themselves hard questions about what they have done to encourage the treatment of people as commodities. A nation like Sierra Leone will cheat itself if it expects foreigners alone to deliver a cure. Child warriors everywhere need elders to look up to.

Index

Index

Test Your Knowledge Form

We encourage you to photocopy and use this page as a tool to assess how the articles in *Annual Editions* expand on the information in your textbook. By reflecting on the articles you will gain enhanced text information. You can also access this useful form on a product's book support Web site at *http://www.dushkin.com/online/*.

NAME: _____   DATE: _____

TITLE AND NUMBER OF ARTICLE: _____

BRIEFLY STATE THE MAIN IDEA OF THIS ARTICLE: _____

_____

LIST THREE IMPORTANT FACTS THAT THE AUTHOR USES TO SUPPORT THE MAIN IDEA:

_____

WHAT INFORMATION OR IDEAS DISCUSSED IN THIS ARTICLE ARE ALSO DISCUSSED IN YOUR TEXTBOOK OR OTHER READINGS THAT YOU HAVE DONE? LIST THE TEXTBOOK CHAPTERS AND PAGE NUMBERS:

_____

LIST ANY EXAMPLES OF BIAS OR FAULTY REASONING THAT YOU FOUND IN THE ARTICLE:

_____

LIST ANY NEW TERMS/CONCEPTS THAT WERE DISCUSSED IN THE ARTICLE, AND WRITE A SHORT DEFINITION:

We Want Your Advice

ANNUAL EDITIONS revisions depend on two major opinion sources: one is our Advisory Board, listed in the front of this volume, which works with us in scanning the thousands of articles published in the public press each year; the other is you—the person actually using the book. Please help us and the users of the next edition by completing the prepaid article rating form on this page and returning it to us. Thank you for your help!

ANNUAL EDITIONS: Child Growth and Development 03/04

ARTICLE RATING FORM

Here is an opportunity for you to have direct input into the next revision of this volume.
We would like you to rate each of the articles listed below, using the following scale:

1. **Excellent: should definitely be retained**
2. **Above average: should probably be retained**
3. **Below average: should probably be deleted**
4. **Poor: should definitely be deleted**

Your ratings will play a vital part in the next revision.
Please mail this prepaid form to us as soon as possible.
Thanks for your help!

RATING	ARTICLE	RATING	ARTICLE
_____	1. The End of Nature Versus Nurture	_____	29. Scars That Won't Heal: The Neurobiology of Child Abuse
_____	2. Making Time for a Baby	_____	30. The Early Origins of Autism
_____	3. The Mystery of Fetal Life: Secrets of the Womb	_____	31. Voices of the Children: We Beat and Killed People
_____	4. The Quest for a Super Kid		
_____	5. Long-Term Recall Memory: Behavioral and Neuro-Developmental Changes in the First 2 Years of Life		
_____	6. Evolution and Developmental Sex Differences		
_____	7. Categories in Young Children's Thinking		
_____	8. Do Young Children Understand What Others Feel, Want, and Know?		
_____	9. Giftedness: Current Theory and Research		
_____	10. The First Seven … and the Eighth: A Conversation With Howard Gardner		
_____	11. How Should Reading Be Taught?		
_____	12. Where the Boys Are		
_____	13. Emotional Intelligence: What the Research Says		
_____	14. What Ever Happened to Play?		
_____	15. Gender and Group Process: A Developmental Perspective		
_____	16. Girls Just Want to Be Mean		
_____	17. Bullying Among Children		
_____	18. Contemporary Research on Parenting: The Case for Nature $BBand$BE Nurture		
_____	19. What Matters? What Does Not? Five Perspectives on the Association Between Marital Transitions and Children's Adjustm		
_____	20. Who's in Charge Here?		
_____	21. American Child Care Today		
_____	22. Do Working Parents Make the Grade?		
_____	23. The Moral Development of Children		
_____	24. Tomorrow's Child		
_____	25. Getting Stupid		
_____	26. How U.S. Children and Adolescents Spend Time: What It Does (and Doesn't) Tell Us About Their Development		
_____	27. Parents or Pop Culture? Children's Heroes and Role Models		
_____	28. The Effects of Poverty on Children		

(Continued on next page)

ANNUAL EDITIONS: CHILD GROWTH AND DEVELOPMENT 03/04

BUSINESS REPLY MAIL
FIRST-CLASS MAIL PERMIT NO. 84 GUILFORD CT

POSTAGE WILL BE PAID BY ADDRESSEE

McGraw-Hill/Dushkin
530 Old Whitfield Street
Guilford, Ct 06437-9989

Ill....ll...l...l...ll.l...ll.l.l.l...l.l.l.l.l...l.l.l

ABOUT YOU

Name _____   Date _____

Are you a teacher? ☐   A student? ☐
Your school's name _____

Department _____

Address _____ City _____ State ___ Zip ___

School telephone # _____

YOUR COMMENTS ARE IMPORTANT TO US!

Please fill in the following information:
For which course did you use this book?
_____

Did you use a text with this ANNUAL EDITION? ☐ yes ☐ no
What was the title of the text?
_____

What are your general reactions to the *Annual Editions* concept?
_____

Have you read any pertinent articles recently that you think should be included in the next edition? Explain.
_____

Are there any articles that you feel should be replaced in the next edition? Why?
_____

Are there any World Wide Web sites that you feel should be included in the next edition? Please annotate.
_____

May we contact you for editorial input? ☐ yes ☐ no
May we quote your comments? ☐ yes ☐ no